The Ontario Historical Studies Series

The Ontario Historical Studies Series was instituted by Order-in-Council (Ontario) on April 14, 1971 under the supervision of a Board of Trustees of professional historians and knowledgeable laymen, with the object of promoting "scholarly research into the history of Ontario, and particularly into the life and times of those who have taken roles of leadership in this Province . . ."

As planned, the Series comprises some fifty volumes concerning major aspects of the life of the province from its establishment in 1791 as Upper Canada to the present time. Among these are an extensive bibliography, biographies of the principal premiers, a historical atlas, a variety of works on political, economic, social and cultural topics, and as the culmination of the Series a definitive history of Ontario incorporating the findings of the biographies and theme studies. An additional project is the recording on tape of interviews with a wide selection of significant men and women in the life of the Province, which beyond their immediate use to writers in the Series will prove a highly valuable resource for future students in the field of historical research.

The hope is that the publications of the Series as they appear year by year over the next decade will be widely welcomed and will enable general readers and scholars alike to appreciate more fully the distinctive features of Ontario as one of the principal regions of Canada.

At present the members of the Board of Trustees are:

Financial support for the Series is provided by the Government of Ontario through the Ministry of Culture and Recreation.

Joseph Schull

ONTARIO SINCE 1867

Ontario Historical Studies Series

McClelland and Stewart

The Canadian Publishers
McClelland and Stewart Limited,
25 Hollinger Road,
Toronto, Ontario.
M4B 3G2

Printed and bound in Canada

Photo Credits: Photograph of the last cabinet of
the Frost regime, from the Ontario Department
of Travel and Publicity, courtesy Allan Grossman.
Photographs of the Cobalt Mining Company, and
of laying track for the National Transcontinental
Railway in the Cochrane District, from the
Rev. W. L. L. Lawrence Collection, Cochrane
Railway and Pioneer Museum. Photograph of the
Acton recruiting office and posters, from the
Acton Free Press – A. T. Brown Collection,
Archives of Ontario. All other photographs
reproduced courtesy of the Archives of Ontario.

Canadian Cataloguing in Publication Data

Schull, Joseph, 1910-
  Ontario since 1867

(Ontario historical studies series   ISSN 0380-9188)

Bibliography: p.
Includes index.
ISBN 0-7710-7990-7

1. Ontario—History—1867-   I. Title.
II. Series.

FC3075.S34   971.3'03   C78-001325-5
F1058.S34

Contents

For Hélène,
Christiane,
Joey and
Michael.

Editors' Statement

Those familiar with the history of Ontario will know that in recent years no general history of the province has been written and that the research on which a comprehensive history might be based has not been done. The purpose of the Ontario Historical Studies Series is to remedy this situation. At this time, however, there is a genuine need for a narrative account of the development of the province based upon the available secondary sources. Hence, some years ago, the Board of Trustees commissioned Mr. Joseph Schull to write a history of Ontario from 1867 to 1961, in which he would endeavour to set out the principal themes in the development of the province.

The Board and the Editors are very grateful to Mr. Schull for undertaking this task. He has brought to it the perspective and the sense of detachment of one whose roots are in Western Canada and whose residence is outside the province. He has responded generously to our editorial advice. We hope that his description of the foundations and the characteristic features of modern Ontario will be useful and stimulating to all those who have an interest in our history and our present condition.

Goldwin French,
Editor-in-Chief.

Toronto
May 30, 1978.

Peter Oliver,
Associate Editor.

Preface

This book is an attempt to sketch the history of Ontario from the time of Confederation to the beginning of the 1960s. It was undertaken as one volume in the Ontario Historical Studies Series in order that the student and general reader could have a general outline of Ontario's growth and development. To achieve this I have had to omit much and to deal summarily with many matters. An adequate treatment of many aspects of provincial life must await the publication over the next ten years of the other volumes in the Series.

As are all surveys, this work is concerned with salient themes and outstanding public figures who dominated the provincial landscape. In consulting the general literature and other studies I have had to select from the available information and in so doing I have sought to write a balanced account. To the extent that this has been achieved, the volume may serve as an introduction to the student. For the general reader, it is hoped, it will have some elements of discovery. It has been said sometimes of Ontario that it is so much taken for granted, so much a prisoner of its stereotypes, that it is actually little known. The province, like the famous elephant to the blind men of Hindustan, is only recognized by the part that each man knows. The purpose of this book is to convey at least an outline and some of the qualities and character of the whole animal. If the reader is led to duplicate my experience, he will have some surprises in store for him and meet some interesting people.

Dr. Goldwin S. French, the Editor of the Ontario Historical Studies Series, has been a patient supervisor. Professor Peter Oliver of York University, the Associate Editor, has been guide, critic, research director and always-helpful friend. I am indebted to him for compiling a bibliography from an untidy list of books and authorities consulted, for a week alone in his home during which I was free to ramble at will through the library he has compiled on Ontario subjects, and for good humour and patience through the trials of two years.

Prefacing it at once with the statement that they are responsible for none of the faults, errors and omissions in the work, I should like to offer my thanks to Professors Carl Berger, Maurice Careless, J.J. Talman, Peter George, Eleanor Cook and Germaine Warkentin for reading the draft manuscript and making suggestions which, I hope, led to an improvement. For help in research I have to thank Marion Beyea, Gary Fagan and the late Kathleen Shaw. My thanks go as always to the Ontario Archives, the Public Archives of Canada and to the Rare Book Section of the Library of the University of Toronto, as well as to the Library itself. I have warm memories of the helpfulness of Carol Pratap and Linda Fudge in the secretarial department.

My sister, Helen Schull, was an invaluable secretary, compiler, and keeper of voluminous notes; and I have a larger debt than I can acknowledge to Hélène, my wife.

Rosemère, Quebec.   Joseph Schull
30 May, 1978.

Chapter One

First Challenges

1.

In 1791, when "His Majesty's Province of Quebec" was divided into two parts, a failure of government was accepted and a new experiment begun. The thirty years since the conquest, and more particularly the eight years since the end of the American Revolution, had convinced the authorities of British North America that their English-speaking subjects would not live easily with the French. It was not so true of the English commercial classes, who were prosperous and well established. For those who were still to come, however, or had not yet made their way, it seemed obvious that the best and most promising arrangement was a separation of governments. The thousands of new arrivals, most of them Loyalists driven from the Thirteen Colonies, would be better in a province of their own.

That province was to be known as Upper Canada, separated by the Ottawa River from the province of Lower Canada. Its first Lieutenant-Governor, the leader of the pioneers, was to be John Graves Simcoe. He was a vigorous man of forty, with a stocky body and a pair of hard blue eyes. A graduate of Eton and Oxford, he had distinguished himself as an officer in the Revolutionary War. He had gone home with the defeat, sat for a term as a member of the House of Commons, and had fairly leaped at his new appointment in Canada. To his mind the success of the American rebels and the breaking-away from Britain had been a work of fools and blunderers that a better man could repair. Allegiance might be restored and the empire reunited by the force of a great example. Upper Canada, freed of the entangling French and settled by loyal British, would show the world and the Americans what good government could be and what good government could do. It would provide in the new province, as the British Constitution provided in the homeland, "as

11

much freedom and happiness as it is possible to be enjoyed under the subordination necessary to civilized society."[1]

Simcoe himself was of the line of British colonial emissaries who would dress for dinner in the jungle. His whole political faith was based on the principle of leadership by an aristocracy. His distaste for, and his various dicta about, the colonials who were not gentlemen and who dined with their own servants have echoed down through many pages of history. What is equally to be remembered, however, is his attitude to the work in hand. He saw himself not only as governor of a colony and commander of a garrison outpost but as the potential healer of a great historic wound. For George Washington and the other rulers of rebels he had only an embittered contempt. In a new war, he was sure, there would be a reversal of revolution, yet his constant concern was to postpone war and dilute the opposing force.

Simcoe detested Yankee ways and Yankee talk, and he had no doubt that "wild and phrenetic democracy"[2] was a virulent danger to Canada. Yet for the American people themselves, as the hands and stuff of nation-building, he had the cool respect of the administrator and the soldier. Thousands of Americans were Loyalists and had left their homes to prove it; they would be the very core of growth. Thousands of others were only British astray, sheep to be recalled to the fold. They would be as welcome in Simcoe's province as the British from the old homeland, and the more who came the better. They would enjoy the virtues of the British Constitution and they would be bound in faith by an established Church of England. They would be ruled by enlightened men of lands and status who might one day form the nucleus of a colonial peerage. Here in this northern wilderness, a new Britain in America would be the magnetic force to rejoin a sundered people.

With all this at the base of his work and thinking, the governor faced his province. It ran west and south from the line of the Ottawa River, following the St. Lawrence lowlands and the shore of Lake Ontario and continuing round Lake Erie to the confluence of the Detroit River, some 500 miles away. Between Lake Ontario and Lake Erie, already known to the explorers and the soldiers of old wars, was the jut of the Niagara peninsula, the rise of the great escarpment and the tumbling rush of the falls. Beyond that, following the escarpment northward, dividing Lake Huron from Erie and capped by the Bruce peninsula, was the wedge of the greater west. It thrust down from the head of Georgian Bay, narrowing to a blunt protuberance that glared across at Detroit, washed by water, embraced by American territory and still part of a threatened and disputed wilderness. To the north, where maps were meaningless, the bateaux of the Nor'west fur traders bound for the *pays d'en haut*, traced out on their long passage the line of the effective boundary. They went up the Ottawa River to its meeting point with the Mattawa, some 300 miles northwest of Montreal. From there they ran the Mattawa to the portage into Lake Nipissing and followed the French River from the lake to Georgian Bay. Above that line were the folds of the height of land, the northward flowing rivers and the delta of Hudson Bay. To the south was Upper Canada, seamed with its half-known waters and with many still unknown, a sprawled, irregular ribbon of continuous virgin forest.

Beneath the forest was the soil, and beneath too much of that was the rock of the Canadian Shield, the governing factor of all future development. Uncounted millions of years, unknown eruptions of earth, the shifting of mighty waters and ages of moving ice had shaped this land to imperatives that still remained to be discovered. From the Arctic south along the line of the Great Lakes the harsh Precambrian sub-face ran down in a huge V to the very junction of the St. Lawrence with Lake Ontario. It was narrowed in, far to the north and west, by the coast of marsh and scrubland that sloped toward Hudson Bay. It gave back from its point along the shores of the lakes themselves and again along the line of the St. Lawrence lowlands, but that was the last retreat. From there to the north and eastward it underlay the continent.

The millennia that shaped and folded the Shield had been followed by glaciers spreading a mantle of drift. It was a rolling blanket of clay, sand and stones, shifted and worn by other millions of years and by the claws of receding ice. By the time of man there was soil, and forest growing from the soil, over much of the bald rock face. But it was for the most part thin and treacherous, inhospitable to any growth, and often eroded again to the bare rock. Much of its river drainage, unable to cut through rock, lay widened out in areas of swampy muskeg. Only the toughest scrub or the hardiest of northern trees could win here in the bitter fight for life. Spruce, fir and balsam covered millions of acres to the very rim of the Arctic, and there were vast stands of pine in the southern region. But the deeper-rooted hardwoods, and the land that farmers looked for, lay below the margins of the Shield. Fortunately the water highway lay there too. For the men who came in Simcoe's day, or were there ahead of him, there seemed to be land enough.

The frame of population that awaited the soldier-governor had been building for ten years, and in the western tip of the province for even longer than that. Essex County, named by Simcoe in 1792, lay across the river from Detroit. French voyageurs and later French farmers had settled there in the days before the conquest to supply the needs of the fur trade. They were to remain now, as French-speaking British subjects with others who crossed to join them when Detroit became American territory.

Farther east at Niagara, during the American Revolution, the war itself had induced a flow of people. For five years, between 1778 and 1783, the peninsula had served as a wintering place for Butler's corps of Rangers. British and German Loyalists, supported by many Indians, they had been recruited and had done their fighting in the Mohawk valley. Little by little, as the war turned against them, they had settled in by the Niagara and become more farmers than soldiers. They had been joined by other Loyalists as the war came to an end. British and Germans, Quakers and French Huguenots had arrived like most of Butler's men from Pennsylvania and New York. By 1784, with over two hundred families clearing land in the peninsula, the waterways and the wagon trails were bringing new arrivals. Many of the wagons passed on to the west, rounding Lake Ontario to the place where Hamilton would grow, or farther west by denser trails along the north shore of Lake Erie. To the valley of the Grand River that emptied into Lake Erie came the Iroquois of the Six Nations, the Loyalists of Joseph Brant. They had deserved well of the British and been adequately repaid in land, though in later years they would lose much of it to white men.

To the east of Lake Ontario the St. Lawrence River divided Canada from New York. It was the last of many waters to be crossed by other fugitives expelled from the rebel states. From the Thousand Islands to the narrowing where Cornwall now stands they emerged from the woods and bush trails and crossed to British territory. As they spread on the north shore, clustered in the Bay of Quinte and began to fringe the margin of Lake Ontario, the greater movement of Loyalists flowed in from the south and east. It was the first wave of planned and orderly settlement, with surveyors moving ahead of it to trace out township lines. Here for their grants of land, supplied with their tools and rations, were merchants, traders, artisans and men of every profession, with the troops from disbanded regiments and barking half-pay officers to give them spine and strength.

Whatever their former trades had been, the first tool here was the axe, and it was put to use along the lake and the river. By 1792, when Simcoe arrived at Kingston to assume his official duties, there was a strip of civilization between the great forest and the water. The farms of the little settlements were still bestrewn with stumps, but they were already yielding wheat. Grist mills ground the wheat, sawmills cut the timber, and small craft carried produce in the first beginnings of trade. Among the clusterings of log houses there was occasionally a church to be found, and even rarely a school. Fervent British loyalty was part of the pervading air, and more than that was a sense of sure beginnings. It was the work of soldiers who still had soldierly ways and of gentlemen-officers still insistent on status. It was the work above all of tough and stubborn civilians who had made and lost a homeland and were prepared to begin another. They had brought their skills with their tools, some of them had brought their books, and all of them had brought their urge for getting on. The sharp one-time Yankees who had chosen to remain British had relinquished none of their Yankee business sense. Many were middle-aged, some had been well-to-do, but hardly any had been men of large estate. The greater number had been farmers, tradesmen or labourers, but they were all farmers here. Scarred but not beaten by the vicissitudes of the war, they had turned to face the wilderness with a government at their backs. They would get all they could and demand more than they got from the servants of that government, but they would never be idle men and they were not frightened men. Remembering every sacrifice and tedious in self-esteem, they were nevertheless the resilient stuff of a nation.

In 1792 Simcoe established his capital at the mouth of the Niagara River. The place was to be called Newark, and it was to be the home of parliament and government. From "Navy Hall," the log hut by the wharf that provided a "Council Room," the Legislature of Upper Canada was summoned to its first session.[3] The date set was September 17, and the needs of the farms took precedence over the call to official duties. Of the seven gentlemen appointed to the Legislative Council five remained away, and of the sixteen commoners of the Assembly only five appeared. Nevertheless, in full dress gold and scarlet, wearing his cocked hat and flanked by his aides and secretaries, the governor opened proceedings and read his proclamation. The British Constitution, as adapted for colonial use, had come to Upper Canada.

From the eastern states of the Union and along the southern shores of the lakes the American rush to the west had already begun. The lakes themselves and the bulk of Upper Canada were mere obstacles in its path. On any map, to any view of the future, that wedge of British territory thrusting deep southwest into the heart of the American advance seemed certain to be engulfed. The republic was

15

still hostile, there was to be war with the French in Europe, the empire was threatened everywhere, and Upper Canada was a weak and vulnerable outpost. It was soon impressed on Simcoe that his capital was particularly vulnerable. Newark would not do; it was too near to the Americans, and the same was true of Kingston. He set out west from the Niagara country, following the Erie shore, and turned off to the wilderness along the course of the Thames River. It ran through rich country, moving back from the boundary, and divided well inland at a place of wide-branched forks. He liked that western country and he liked the site for a capital. He conceived of a London built around those forks, and a London there would be. But there was still more to be considered.

If war came with the Americans it would be governed by broad waters, and Lake Ontario was the key. Linked to the east with the indefensible St. Lawrence, it would still command and threaten the western lakes. Its northern shore could be held, its water would carry warships, and along its frontage of wilderness was the gap of a potential harbour. Toronto Bay, close to the mouth of the Humber toward the western end of the lake, seemed little more than a stretch of weedy shoreline. But it was half-enclosed by the scraggy neck of a peninsula that could be made to bristle with guns, and it had known guns before. The remains of old trading posts and the ruins of old forts told of its former use. Rivers, lakes and a series of easy portages, running from Toronto northward, gave onto Georgian Bay and opened from there on Lake Huron and the route to the far west. The bay on Lake Ontario could be a centre of trade in peace and a commanding base in war. It was ugly and uninspiring as the site of a new capital, but for present needs it was also indispensable. Still hoping for better, and not yet quite prepared to abandon Newark, Simcoe yielded himself to the thrust of history. The place on Toronto Bay, now to be named York, was to be "the permanent Naval Arsenal of Ontario, and in some respects of Upper Canada."[4]

Communications by land were also necessary, for war, trade and growth. The governor used his soldiers to hack out trails through the forest and begin his famous "streets." Dundas Street was to run from the tip of the west country and become the link with Kingston. It ran in Simcoe's day, an abomination of ruts, swamp and sinkholes, from the forks of the Thames to the head of Lake Ontario and from there on to York. Yonge Street, following the portage and water route that led to Georgian Bay, was to be a northward arm from York. During his four years in Canada, Simcoe drove it only to the lake that bears his name. He had all too much to do and all too little time to complete many of his beginnings.

Always fearing and preparing for a new war with the Americans, he still held out a welcome to those of them who came in peace. As the Loyalist flow slackened new thousands followed it prepared to exchange their allegiance for good Canadian land. Some were Yankee speculators, grabbing at free grants and prepared to leave when they had sold out at a profit. Far more, however, were hungry to put down roots. Few gave thought to the border as a dividing line of peoples and fewer still gave promise of a great reknitting of the empire or the healing of rebellion's wound. They were a fringe of the westward movement that went on below the border, and only a casual fringe. Yet they were the flesh and blood of nationhood and most of them came to stay.

Out of the stream of passage that flowed below the lakes, from New York and Pennsylvania through Ohio and Indiana and on to Illinois, the rivulets trickled aside to British territory. They welled up through the west country and along the northern Erie shore, began to fill and overfill the rich lands by the Niagara and reached on in a loop round Lake Ontario. At the same time to the east, behind the St. Lawrence river frontage claimed by the first Loyalists, settlement began to fill the back concessions.

From the British Isles at this time there was little immigration. The mother country was thousands of miles away, absorbed in her wars with the French and needing her own men. Except in the province's eastern tip where the Ottawa joined the St. Lawrence, the French of Lower Canada seemed a people equally remote. The newcomers were Americans, not yet products of the melting-pot, sons of the varied nations. There was a strong Germanic tinge, for Germans had served in the armies and settled much of the territory of an empire under Hanoverian rulers. There was a strong religious tinge, often German as well, and the men of this type who came were usually men of peace. Quakers and German Mennonites arrived in sober groups, purposeful and well prepared. They had strong horses and stout wagons, with the floors of the boxes caulked to swim a river. They brought their furniture and tools, with well-fed livestock trailing along behind them, and they brought their faith and bibles. They were here for godly homes and they had come with means to build them. There were other groups of Huguenots, also men who disliked turbulence and rebellion and men who knew good land. Moving with them and apart from them, mainly out to the west country where Simcoe saw most promise, were the men of the other peoples and of all faiths and none, the muscle and gristle of Yankeedom transplanted to British soil.

Simcoe watched and nourished it all, building on his own beliefs. The men he gathered round him, the developing corps of officialdom, were men of his mind and heart. From his little parliament at

Newark the laws and decrees went out, shaping the frame of a society. It was to be ordered, stable, British, subordinate in due degree, with a propertied aristocracy for the guidance of free men. It was to be fortified against democracy by the rule of English law, and it was to support the Church of England as the keeper of Christian faith. All this was accepted, all this was acknowledged as part of the massive movement that was filling the vacant lands. Yet it was dismissed as breath and paper by the actual facts of growth. The new men, hacking, girdling and burning away the forest, were as remote from the ideals of government as they were set in their own ways. They had brought their faiths and preachers, and their views of parliaments and politics and of rulers' place in the scheme. Growth came of itself, made its own rules, sprawled and spread under edicts, defeating them at every turn.

Already the first-come Loyalists were sounding a new complaint. The province was becoming "a compleat American colony."[5] Men of the disbanded regiments and others who had been driven from homes in the Thirteen Colonies were discovering American grant-holders "whom they had encountered under the banners of the rebellion."[6] Yet at the same time the older settlers were prospering, with the clearing of farms behind them. They were exchanging goods with each other, and some were exchanging books. "I send you in a box the first six volumes of Gibbon's Roman History . . . I also send you Hume's History of England."[7] Here too was the precariously established church, already troubled by dissenters and occasionally by its own eccentrics.

> Mr. Langhorne, (wrote the Reverend John Stuart of Kingston complaining to his bishop of one rebellious cleric,) is obstinate, refractory and self-willed ... However he is regular and industrious and is rather gaining ground. For people are so accustomed to his oddities that he might walk naked through his parish without any particular notice being taken of it.[8]

To the west of Lake Ontario and above the Niagara peninsula was country filling with newer immigration. There were Loyalists here too and there were the stolid, quiet, always growing settlements of the German farmers. But the stir of growth was predominantly a Yankee stir, unorganized, undirected, hacking its own way.

> When an American comes over to Canada to take out a location-ticket, (wrote one observer of the region,) he immediately sets to work in the fall of the year and slashes and burns the wood on perhaps eight acres of land; then, walking through his new field among the stumps with a bag of Indian corn seed about his neck

and his axe in his hand, he makes a hole in the ground with it and dropping two or three seeds into it he closes the hole with his foot, and he thus disposes of his whole seed. He then, perhaps, returns to the States, or hires himself out to work till the time of harvest comes around, when he returns to his field and reaps it. He may now think of building a log-house: he prepares the timber, the neighbours collect in 'a bee' and assist him to erect his dwelling; he roofs and floors it with bark, the doors and windows are cut out, the hinges are of wood as are sometimes the locks, the light is admitted through oiled paper, the table is a rough board and the stools cuts of round logs. He brings his wife and a barrel or two of pork; more land is cleared; pigs, poultry and cattle are seen to increase; the log house is converted into a stable, and a frame house is substituted.[9]

Over all this growth and all this turbulent contrast the soldier-governor presided for the four years of his term. He left like many others, frustrated by work half-done, recalled to other duties in the sprawling empire. The raw new province went on its way without him, changing its shape and essence, oblivious of most of his hopes. Yet somehow his name remained and some of the hopes endured. That thrust of a British purpose, that sense of a British destiny was not to leave with Simcoe. It was to underlie the future and all the changes of the future, another Canadian Shield.

Notes

1. Quoted in Fred Landon, *Western Ontario and the American Frontier* (Toronto: McClelland and Stewart Limited, 1967), p. 3.
2. *Ibid.*, p. 4.
3. Alexander Fraser, *A History of Ontario*, 2 Vols. (Toronto: The Canada History Company, 1907), Vol. 1, p. 206.
4. Richard A. Preston, *Kingston Before the War of 1812* (Toronto: The Champlain Society, 1959), p. 236.
5. Gerald M. Craig, *Upper Canada, The Formative Years, 1784-1841* (Toronto: McClelland and Stewart Limited, 1967), p. 87.
6. Landon, *Western Ontario and The American Frontier*, p. 16.
7. Preston, *Kingston Before the War of 1812*, p. 318.
8. *Ibid.*, p. 291
9. Landon, *Western Ontario and the American Frontier*, p. 248, quoting J. E. Alexander, *Transatlantic Sketches*.

Chapter Two

A Province Grown

1.

A child born on the day that Simcoe assumed the governorship of Upper Canada would have been five months short of his seventy-sixth birthday when the province became Ontario. In the space of a full lifetime the wilderness settlements made by the pioneers had linked themselves in a broadly based community. It was still raw in much, it was churning in complex growth, but it had established character and direction.

There had been a period of major decision during the War of 1812. When the war began, of some 100,000 people in Upper Canada, about four-fifths had come from the United States. They had not returned to the United States at its close, nor forsaken their new allegiance. There had been much questionable loyalty, battles had been indecisive, and military power had not decided the issue. The decisive factor was a kind of aggressive content, a faith in the work begun and in the terms that governed the work. The faith was a matter of the heart for old Loyalists, but it commanded at least the assent of newer men. They had set their hands to the plough, and many had been given the plough under British dispensation. Throughout the war and after it they held on in the furrow.

They were soon joined, and soon to be far outnumbered, by immigrants from the British Isles. With the end of the Napoleonic Wars and the demobilization of armies, the motherland's surplus manpower was directed to both the Canadas. Soldiers and their officers came to the upper province as they had done in Loyalist days; there was a broad sprinkling of ambitious and adventurous gentry, and a welcome access of tradesmen. With them were Scottish crofters, families of Irish peasants, and some of the gaunt thousands who had haunted British slums. They arrived in orderly waves through the decade of the 1820s, filling the St. Lawrence back country, taking land on the Ottawa, opening Toronto's hinterland and moving on to the west.

With the 1830s and 1840s, through the tumult of change in Europe, the first waves rose at times to a brutal flood. Machines were displacing workmen in British cities, landlords were driving peasants from Scottish and Irish farmlands, and miserable and famished thousands were in search of new homes. They came, all too many of them, in stinking hulks of immigrant ships that were nurseries of death and plague. They arrived in tattered thousands in Upper and Lower Canada, dumped by distraught officialdom on a people who could not support them and bringing the cholera years.

Yet the dead were buried, the living found their way, and scarred by its tragedies and cruelties the movement still went on. The British flow slackened but an American trickle resumed, while great colonization companies dealing in millions of acres fostered and imposed a more intensive settlement. Privateers of development, they acquired fortunes and founded future dynasties, but they also established homes for lesser men. The lesser men themselves, fighting their way through hard and lonely lives, created a pattern of ordered civilization.

2.

By the middle 1860s, as Confederation approached, some 1,500,000 people were distributed across the province. The St. Lawrence lowlands were filled. Cornwall, Prescott, Brockville and Gananoque were all growing ports, and Kingston was a city of 13,000 people. Bereft of its earlier hope to be the permanent capital of the province, it was mellow with history and sober with disappointment. Its well-proportioned buildings, all sedate and English-seeming and all made of the local bluish-tinged limestone, gave one traveller the impression "that the inhabitants have put their city into half mourning."[1] The impression was soon dispelled, however, by docks, wharves and warehouses and the coming and going of steamers, rafts and barges. Always the great trans-shipment point between Lake Ontario and the St. Lawrence, Kingston grew on traffic from the east, the west and the north.

Along the Lake Ontario shoreline the band of settled country went back for sixty miles. York had become Toronto in 1834, and its growing hinterland extended to Georgian Bay. Farms and orchards covered the Niagara peninsula by the 1860s, and in the great wedge of the west country below the Bruce peninsula most of the forest was gone. The cleared land, some of it overworked now, had become the major granary of the province. Wheat and barley were the great crops but all grains were grown, and livestock breeding and dairying were bringing diversification. It was a change brought on for the most part by the demand for Ontario products from the eastern United States. In some areas, however, diversification was forced, for long years of "wheat mining" had exhausted much of the soil. Bad methods and bad luck had produced their quota of failure, life for the average farmer was still hard and rough, but successful men were thriving. Their log cabins had been replaced by frame houses or houses of brick and stone. There had been time for a lawn or garden or a neat, white picket fence. Often shade trees, planted by the farmer himself, replaced the older forest he had hacked down in his youth. The house looked out on a road that was seldom more than a rutted country trail, but it led to a nearby town.

Usually the town had grown up on water around a sawmill and a grist mill. It smelt of wood and horse-droppings and in the autumn of ground grain, but it had changed like the farms themselves. Along with the shacks and hitching-posts and the knocked-up shops and taverns the town of the 1860s had often a shady square, a mellowing old courthouse and other public buildings that had been raised in brick or stone. Handsome churches built of the same materials had frequently as sombre background the hulk of a brick jail. The blacksmith, carpenter and harness maker, everywhere indispensable, were becoming the older mainstays of a growing cluster of tradesmen. Bricklayers, coopers, wagon-makers, painters, printers, furniture-makers and stone masons, with mechanics and other craftsmen gathered in small factories, were part of a developing industry supported by local needs.

Hardly a town of consequence was without its local newspaper, and there was much in print to supplement them. By 1857 the English readers of the province were served by some 150 weekly, semi-weekly or monthly publications, of which seventeen were religious and four were trade journals. Five weeklies were published in the German language. World news and broader regional coverage were supplied by the city dailies, and Toronto's *Globe*, published by George Brown, was province-wide in its influence. It had one rival in Toronto and eight in the other cities. Hamilton and London each had two dailies, and Kingston boasted four.[2] In all weeklies and dailies a lively, continuing debate on public issues was supported by extensive advertising.

On the farms in the prosperous regions, responsive to this advertising, the home trades were passing. Soap and candles, shoes, clothes and dressgoods that had once been made at home were now bought at the store. The Massey factory at Newcastle and the Harris

22

factory at Beamsville supplied the farmer's implements. New mechanical stumpers pulled the stumps in the fields; the days of chain and oxen were gone with the wooden plough. The iron plough opened the furrows, the seed drill planted the seed, and mowers, binders, hay-balers, threshing machines and separators were beginning to come into use. Many could not buy them, particularly on the tired land, where diversification and crop rotation had not yet won acceptance. Thousands were struggling on poor farms with old methods and implements they could not afford to replace, and there were desolate, weed-grown areas where broken men had left. There had been good years and bad years even for the luckiest farmer, and there had been midgeflies, rust and drought. But agricultural societies had provided good leadership, and fall fairs and conventions had encouraged the progressive man. The Red Fife wheat from Peterborough county had come to subdue rust, and the insect plagues and other threats were being reduced too.

In the east and north of the province, as settlement filled the south, immigrants had followed lumbermen to the forests of the lower Shield. They had become lumbermen themselves, clearing their own land grants and selling the pine and spruce. That done, however, they had discovered the thin soil, the remoteness from permanent markets and the early frosts that killed their ripening grain. In most cases, even when the farmer produced a crop it was only to supply a lumber camp where he was also a part-time worker. There had been much sweat and heartbreak along the upper reaches of the Ottawa and in the stretch of the "Huron-Ottawa Tract" between the river and Georgian Bay. It had been the same in the Bruce peninsula where deep earth thinned to rock. But the lands that would not give wheat seemed inexhaustible in wood, and northern lumbering was a primary staple trade.

French Canadians and Irishmen made up most of the workers. Housed in the shanty camps, they fought by their bunks at night, and sweated through days with the broadaxe bringing the great trunks down. Teams of horses and steam engines hauled the timber out. It was cut by steam sawmills into planks or "deals" for export that were three or four inches thick. Assorted lumber of every size went out to the building trade. Whole trunks of pine, sometimes as much as 200 feet in length, were simply "squared" with the axe and forwarded as great baulks, usually bound for England. For over half a century, as the spring break-up came and the ice gave way and the timber slides were opened, the province's pine and hardwood had been travelling Canadian rivers. Now it was mainly pine. The cribs rode down by a network of lesser streams toward the Ottawa and the St. Lawrence or southwest toward Lake Huron. On the greater waters, lashed into huge rafts with cabins and crews aboard them, the timber went on to market driven by sweeps and sail.

Along the Ottawa lumbering had built up Bytown, south of the Chaudière Falls, at the point where the Gatineau and Rideau met the parent river. The place had become a centre for the great barons of the industry, and a roaring, welcoming shantytown for thirsty men from the woods. Then it had changed its nature through the drives of national growth. Bytown had become Ottawa in 1855. By 1867 the great Gothic bulk of the new parliament buildings stood "nobly on a magnificent river, with high, overhanging rock and a natural grandeur of position," overlooking a sprawling city of 15,000 people. A hundred miles from the river's junction with the St. Lawrence and safer than other cities from the fear of American invasion, it was to be the new Dominion's capital.

3.

Canals and railways had served developing industries and shaped the pattern of growth. Lake Ontario and Lake Erie were joined by the Welland Canal. Kingston was joined with Ottawa and the Ottawa River system by way of the Rideau Canal. Designed as a passage free of the American threat, it crossed the east of the province well back from the St. Lawrence. Yet in both Canadas the race with the Americans for trade compelled use of the St. Lawrence, and it had been dredged, channelled and deepened as a projected "master" route. The master routes, however, were to be imposed by railway builders, who by 1867 were well started on their work.

The Grand Trunk, the supplanter of Simcoe's Dundas Street, traversed the breadth of the province west and east. The Northern ran from Toronto to the foot of Georgian Bay, opening the Yonge Street country and making Collingwood a port. The Great Western and the Buffalo, Brantford and Goderich, crossing the Niagara fruitlands and the fat southwestern wheatlands, were pulling up towns and cities and uncovering new resources. Cobourg and Port Hope, both of them on Lake Ontario and within twenty miles of each other, had separate railways probing north toward Peterborough. An Ottawa-Brockville line and an Ottawa-Prescott line were feeding timber down to the St. Lawrence ports. From Lake Huron east to the Niagara country, from Toronto to the lower Shield, from the Upper Ottawa to the St. Lawrence and along the line of the basin there were railways now and sometimes competing railways. Laid down in the 1850s through a decade of tumultuous growth, they were more than the province needed and more than it could afford. But they had been built with an eye to the future by aggressive, ambitious men.

The routes chosen by the railways decided the fate of towns. Bypassed centres declined while new towns sprang up and local industries expanded wherever the rails came. Toronto could command railways and it was still served by waterways, developing and growing too. Luxurious passenger steamers and larger and larger freighters plied the lakes and the St. Lawrence and came to dock at Toronto. Along the front each autumn, as the harvest moved toward the seaboard, "canal boats by the hundred – by the thousand – railway cars in countless multitudes, are groaning day and night with the precious burden from the overflowing granaries of the fertile west."[3] There was as large a flow from the east, for the city of 50,000 dominated provincial industry and controlled provincial commerce. Fire insurance and life insurance, the banking business and the businesses of trust and loan companies were all predominantly in Toronto, with little left outside. Its stock exchange was a barometer of provincial business and its produce exchange the greatest provincial market. The Northern came down from Collingwood to its station by City Hall. The trains of the Grand Trunk and the trains of the Great Western rumbled along the front. The smoke of an expanding industry was thickening beside the lake, and flour mills, breweries, distilleries, rolling mills, foundries, stove and furniture factories were surrounded by many rivals. Clothing, dressgoods and boot and shoe makers, food processors and packers, and makers of a range of products from steel safes to candles and from lace and yarn to cigars and pipe tobacco supplied the medley demanded by civilization.

The city, as the capital of the province, was its intellectual and political centre and a home of established wealth. Its built-up area extended back from the lakefront to a little above Bloor Street, and a mile and a half of rooftops stretched between the Humber and the Don. Banking, business and commercial life centred mainly on Bay Street, with Church and York competing. Yonge Street pierced the city like an arrow bound for the north; and wide, paved King Street was the place for the best shops and for carriages and promenades. Toronto did not boast of its old legislative building, but Osgoode Hall on Queen Street was a stately home for the law. With Upper Canada College there were Knox, Trinity and St. Michael's, and a Normal School for the training of provincial teachers. Of seventy churches serving the various religions, St. James' stood out as the cathedral of the Church of England, rivalled by St. Michael's, the Roman Catholic cathedral, said to contain in its spire a fragment of the True Cross. Overlooking King Street was the red brick clocktower surmounting St. Lawrence Hall. Great political debates and business meetings resulting in public projects had been held in

25

the hall for nearly a quarter-century, and Torontonians set their watches by its clock. The *Globe* building, proclaiming the success of George Brown's newspaper, was said to be one of the finest in North America. The Grand Opera House, four storeys high, was on Adelaide near Yonge, and all too near on Queen Street, close by Trinity College, was the yellow brick bulk of the provincial Lunatic Asylum. Dressed with cut stone, it had slits of windows fitted with iron sashes "constructed to rise and fall about five inches – sufficient for the admission of fresh air, but not wide enough for a patient to pass through."[4]

The drill shed and the garrison quarters maintained for British troops still looked out from the front. Amid the ten acres of the Horticultural Gardens stood the glass and brick Pavilion, a North American version of the Crystal Palace. Centred in Queen's Park, the University of Toronto dominated its green knoll. It rose in rough-cut stone, a high Norman tower, throwing out wide wings that enclosed lawns and walks. The ravine fell off in front of it, sloping toward Taddle Creek and the whole park, fittingly enough, seemed a setting for the massive building.

There was an Englishness about Toronto that would have appealed to Simcoe. Its fine houses on Jarvis Street and the fringes of Queen's Park were set in ample grounds. Carriages rolled from their driveways, glittering and well-kept. The scions of the oldest families were usually attached to the militia, conscientiously loyal and wearing a soldierly air. They took their sport at a yacht club, a hunt club and a jockey club, and frequently played whist. Sleighing and skating parties, concerts, balls and the theatre enlivened the winter season. Entertainment was governed by a stiff Victorian ritual, and at long formal dinners the protocol was exact. Equally characteristic of a sober-sided elite was the renowned Toronto Sunday and the family march to church. Beneath all that, however, was a vigorous rush of business and a clash of lively minds. Churchmen, lawyers, educators and the leaders of other professions all gathered in Toronto and made their presence felt. The great merchants and industrialists were often their near neighbours. The promoter and the entrepreneur, assembling capital in Toronto, were among the central forces that quickened growth in the province. Also part of the city and of life on its lower levels was an exploited, ill-paid working class and a maze of dingy slums. There were hospitals, jails and workhouses for the sick, derelict and destitute, but for the "lower orders" generally there was not much thought or care. Toronto the Good gave leadership and encouraged and fostered growth, but it left the church and the philanthropist to cope with social problems.

Apart from Toronto, in the west country London grew on the

Thames, drawing from the rich wheatlands. Hamilton around the lake, on its fine harbour overlooked by the escarpment, was Toronto's strong competitor for the flow of grain and trade. In iron founding and metal work it was already moving ahead. Most of its coal and ore came from the United States, but there were high hopes in the city that it had discovered native resources. "Bog iron" mined in Madoc and Marmora to the north of the Bay of Quinte, was being shipped to Hamilton and used. The first of the heavy industries was a glint along the horizon.

There was also another industry that was now ten years old, with its scope still to be discovered. At the heart of Lambton county, a little in from Lake Huron, there were swamps of evil gumbo that could be cut much like peat. It would burn better than peat, as Indians had shown the white men, and it could be used to grease an axle. It was "rock oil," a welling of ancient crude, and it could be boiled down to asphalt or refined to kerosene. There was no great demand for it but the peat had been dug away and the product sold as a lubricant or for use in oil lamps. The first wells had gone down, drilled under the swamps, and the first gushers had come. Two towns, Oil Springs and Petrolia, had grown up round the swamps and were now served by a railway. From fifteen wells in the region some 800 barrels a day were coming up, still to serve as a lubricant or as asphalt or kerosene. The other uses of the product awaited a later day, but it was generally agreed that rock oil had a future.

4.

By 1861, when the third census was taken, the pattern of population had been well established. It did not change essentially with the growth of the next six years. What it showed, first of all, was the passing of the early comers. More than half the people, some 63 per cent, were now native born and mainly of British stock. Another 20 per cent had been born in the British Isles, more of them Scots than English and more Irish than Scots. Some 3 per cent were of French origin, 2 per cent of German origin, and less than 4 per cent were American born. Upper Canada was British, overwhelmingly British, but it was seamed with many of the fissures that divide faiths and men.

The Church of England was not the established church; that hope was gone. There were more Methodists than Anglicans in Upper Canada, and almost as many of the Presbyterian persuasions. Eighteen per cent of the people were Roman Catholic, 4 per cent were Baptist, and 2 per cent were Lutheran. There were Quakers, Tunkers, Mennonites and a dozen scatterings of other faiths as well as of unbelievers.[5] The priest, the itinerant preacher and the dissenting minister had been free to roam the province from its first beginnings. Whatever the views of officialdom, and whatever the cost in controversy, there had never been persecution.

There were the same grainings and cross-grainings among the various national origins, with the same resulting strains. Scot differed from Scot, American differed from American and English opinion ranged the breadth of the spectrum. Among the 200,000 Irish there were Orangemen of the Protestant north and Roman Catholics of the south, still vociferously pursuing their ancient quarrel. As politics came with development and development shaped politics, all these differences perplexed the emerging parties. Yet much had been done together or was at least accepted by all.

There was to be no aristocracy in this province of stubborn levellers who had broken the Family Compact. The breath of the great republic had blown through Upper Canada and had not made it American. But it had transformed Britishness, clipped the wings of officialdom and curtailed the power of a wealthy ruling clique. Even before Simcoe the earliest of the town meetings had discussed common concerns and imposed common decisions. Through his time and beyond, as part of the genius of the province, the tradition of local government, and of self-government in all fields, established itself and grew. By 1849, with the passing of the Municipal Corporations Act, the basic level had been given form and structure. A municipality was "a locality the inhabitants of which are incorporated," whether it was a county, township, city, town or village. Municipal government, individual but integrated, extended across the province, with elected councils headed by mayors or reeves imposing local taxes, promoting local improvements and administering local affairs. It was the first and nearest authority over the citizen, the base of superior government and the training ground for rising provincial leaders.

Government embraced schooling, schooling touched on religion, and religious faith was often involved with language. The desire for "separate" schools, whether of faith or language, was opposed to the general Protestant wish for common "national" schools. It divided Upper Canada, with its majority of the Protestant faith, from the French in Lower Canada, which was mainly Roman Catholic. Yet some Irish, Scots and English in Upper Canada who were also Roman Catholics, and even a scattering of Protestants, desired separate schools. Maintained privately, they were beyond most men's means, yet state support of any school demanded a broad consensus. Egerton Ryerson, Methodist preacher, teacher and journalist, was a statesman who was seeking to cope with the enduring problems of education. By 1867, as Superintendent of Schools, he had fought through twenty years for a fixed idea. "Education is a public good, ignorance is a public evil . . . every child should receive an education . . . if the parent or guardian cannot provide him with such an education the State is bound to do so."[6]

As the state took up its burden it had followed Ryerson's plan, though not to the extent he wished. A system of common schools was established throughout the province, open to all children, officially non-sectarian and under Ryerson's direction. Within that frame, moreover, as a concession to Roman Catholics, room was made for separate schools.

It was a hard-wrung and still disputed concession, exacted by slow degrees through many years. Repugnant to most Protestants, it was regrettable to Ryerson himself, since his final goal was one unified system. Yet the child in the Catholic school, among teachers of his own faith, would be free from the risk of "insult." He would be taught, like students in common schools, from a centrally-set curriculum and be subject to provincial standards. Separateness remained a flaw but it had been minimized and was at present unavoidable, in more cases than that of Roman Catholics. Ryerson, who had taught Indians, arranged for the teaching of Indians in their own language. He provided schools for Negroes in white communities that were not prepared to teach them. With wide-minded pragmatism, where children spoke no English, he provided schools in German, French and Gaelic. They were, in his view, humane and temporary expedients for conditions that would change later. He was equally optimistic about the larger question of religion. Sectarianism, he thought, would be reduced in time through the work of enlightened men, and a new harmony arrive with "enlarged views of Christian relations between different classes in the community."[7]

Above the level of the common schools were the Grammar Schools, or high schools, all non-sectarian and partially supported by the state. The concession to Catholic or any faith did not apply here; there were no separate secondary schools except for a few maintained by various churches. On the university level there were five major colleges: Trinity College at Toronto for the Church of England, Victoria College at Cobourg for the Methodists, Queen's College at Kingston for Presbyterians of the Established Church of Scotland, Knox College at Toronto for Presbyterians of the Free Church of Scotland and St. Michael's College at Toronto for Roman Catholics. Yet none of these was directly supported by the state. Forty years earlier the Anglican Bishop John Strachan had established King's College as an arm of the Church of England to be maintained with public funds. He had been opposed almost immediately by the

29

other rival religions, and long years of wrestling had ensued between the "established" church and dissenters, between Protestants and Roman Catholics and between high Anglicans and low. The result had been the secular state and the emergence of the principle of "voluntaryism" as a part of public policy. Churches and their institutions should depend on the voluntary support of their own members,[8] and the state should favour none. It should be the "collective parent" in higher education, secular, non-sectarian and following its own course.

In 1849, despite the efforts of Strachan to maintain Anglican control, King's College had been secularized and subsequently Trinity College had replaced it as an Anglican institution. Four years later with the creation of University College, the University became an examining body. By 1859, with its noble home complete, University College was open in Queen's Park. The "Godless university" to many religious men, it still stood as an expression of the general mind of the province.

5.

Rebellions in the two Canadas in 1837 had led to a reunion of the provinces in 1841. Through a later quarter-century the colliding ambitions of growth and implacable problems of government had brought political deadlock. That was coming to an end with the approach of Confederation. In the new Dominion of Canada and in the relations of its four provinces great questions remained unanswered and enormous problems remained unsolved. For most people, however, in the province that was to become Ontario it was a time of relief and hope.

John A. Macdonald, the Conservative lawyer from Kingston, and George Brown, proprietor of the Toronto *Globe*, stood as party leaders who had realized an old dream. They had been bitter enemies before and were enemies again, but for a little while they had been statesmen united in a common work. Sinking their own differences and hammering those of their followers into the frame of the one purpose, they had created the coalition that had made Confederation. Yet they could have done little without George Etienne Cartier, the leader in Lower Canada, and the other leaders in the two maritime provinces. Nor could they have done much without the forces in their own province that prodded and pulled them on.

The conservatism that bred Macdonald had flowed in with the Loyalists, driven from American homes. An enduring love of empire and an equally strong antipathy to American republicanism was rooted in the St. Lawrence valley, in the old Niagara country and in the first and largest settlements that grew to be towns and cities. Enriched by Simcoe's coming and stamped with his own Britishness, they acquired a new dimension during the rise of the French republic. Revolution in America, followed within thirteen years by revolution in France, had been followed in turn by Napoleon and the wars that wracked Europe. Simcoe came as those wars were beginning and brought with him from the mother country the outrage felt at the French. A new ingredient of conservatism, its suspicion of all Frenchness, was joined to anti-Americanism, a fear of revolution and a native love of order.

As the first comers and the first builders and governors, Loyalists and the official class banded together. Quite naturally there were large grants of land and privileges of trade and commerce for loyal and aggressive men. It was also quite natural that friends, relatives and friends of friends of officialdom should be given the posts of trust. A broad, fraternal network, spreading as the province grew, included men of the professions and men of the favoured churches. Government, business and the professions, all hand in hand, inclined to stability in religion and authority in politics. The Upper Canadian Tory, as he began to become recognizable, was usually a member of the Church of England or Scotland, and occasionally a Roman Catholic.

Development of the province in the shadow of the United States was infused not only with fear but with growing rivalry for trade. The ambitions of private men were at one with the needs of the state, for all growth was in part a measure of defence. The Welland Canal and the first canals on the St. Lawrence made William Hamilton Merritt rich and powerful. Yet quite naturally and pragmatically they had involved the help of government, for there was no capital in the country to promote the work without it. There was the same pragmatic partnership in other "national" works, and without that much would have gone undone. Yet the entrepreneur and the legislator were often one and the same, and the result of the long process was a powerful and wealthy clique. The maligned Family Compact grew up on the work of the first comers and the ablest men of the country and could claim much for its achievements. By the 1830s, however, its weight and grip had become unendurable and the reform movements began.

William Lyon Mackenzie brought the brief explosion of rebellion, and after him the political climate began to change dramatically. The great western peninsula, to which most of the Americans had come, was the restless home of change and democratization. It was the nursery of the Clear Grits, those Calvinists of reform, who claimed to be "pure sand, without a particle of dirt."[9] Parochial and largely rural, they detested the privilege and patronage which usually bypassed them. They spoke for small communities with grievances against the cities. They were born to a watchful distrust of all centralized rule and of all appointed rulers. They pressed for a wider franchise, for cheaper and simpler processes in the administration of the law, for easier treatment of the mortgaged farm debtor and for rigid control of all government spending. Many Grits were Presbyterians, yet they also included Baptists and other Evangelical sects. They came to include George Brown, though he was a businessman of Toronto and as wide and imperial in his ambitions as any man of the Compact. It was his accession to their leadership that changed and tamed the Grits, leading them out of their parochialism to a wider view of the province and teaching them to reach for power.

During the same period the Conservative party changed. The Family Compact crumbled and old tradition and ambition, still powerful but always a little more malleable, evolved in newer forms. There was more room in the Conservative party for men of liberal views, for dissenting Protestant sects, and even for Tory reformers. Geography lost its hold and religious boundaries became weaker until there was no firm distinction between the currents of clashing thought. There were Clear Grits in Loyalist country and stout Conservatives in the west, while the growing cities had men of all convictions.

It was a Reform party grown from the older Grits and a Liberal-Conservative party much broadened in its outlook that came together to form the Confederation coalition. An impelling force was the American Civil War, with the old fear of invasion heightened by the vast conflict, and justified in the aftermath by some ugly border raids. Yet the first and basic force was the province's own dynamic, locked in and frustrated by imposed political union.

Since the middle 1850s businessmen in Toronto had been looking to the far west. The Northwestern Steamboat Company, with communications from Collingwood to the head of the Great Lakes, had become the Northwestern Navigation and Transportation Company with plans to cross the continent by the waterways and by roads. Adventurous Upper Canadians, well ahead of the plans, were already passing the lakehead and settling on the Red River, opening a prospect there. The great, mysterious, still unopened north lay even nearer home. The St. Lawrence basin and the Ottawa were equally imperious concerns as routes for future trade. But they were all shared, and they were all obstructed in part, by an ever-watchful and jealous Lower Canada.

To the English merchants there the rivalry was economic, but the root cause was religion and nationalities. For long years the very will to survive, to remain Catholic and French, had seemed to the British Protestant to be a denial of natural forces. Through the same years, to the French, it had been the be-all and the end-all of most political action. The harsh early stridencies had been a little abated by time, a little submerged by progress, but the essential conflict remained. The union's joint parliament, speaking its two languages and legislating for both sections, was caught in the dilemma of peoples. There was no expansion of Britishness that did not somehow threaten the place of the French. There was no assertion of Frenchness that did not manage to rub the English raw. The two disparate families, joined as a single household, were only achieving stalemate.

That was now to be broken. On March 29, 1867, the British North America Act received royal assent, and on July 1, it came into effect. Upper and Lower Canada, achieving a partial parting, were to be relieved of many strains. The links of a federal union promised to sit more lightly, with the weight shared by New Brunswick and Nova Scotia. Each province would be autonomous in the moulding of its own people and in the use of natural resources, yet the binding thread of a common national purpose was to give coherence to all.

It was a large work, and it was a work forced by Ontario. She was to acquire a provincial legislature to decide her own concerns. She was to be dominant in the Confederation, and the ambitions of the Confederation were as wide as the continent itself. Representation according to population – the "Rep by Pop" that had been a battle-cry of Brown – would give her the directing power she had lacked in the older union. In a House of Commons with 181 members she would have eighty-two seats. Of the thirteen members who were to make up the federal cabinet, five were Ontario men. The Prime Minister was Macdonald, the man from Kingston, and the Dominion capital was Ottawa. The St. Lawrence route, freed of obstructing tariffs, was to be developed in common with Quebec. An inter-colonial railway, demanded by the maritime provinces, would provide the central provinces with another route to the sea. Ontario itself, separate from a Lower Canada that had dreaded English expansion, could open the westward road to the Red River. And beyond that, quickened by the thought of railways, the hopes of province and nation-builders reached on to the Pacific.

Notes

1. Quoted by Frederick H. Armstrong and Neil C. Hultin in "The *Anglo-American Magazine* Looks at Urban Upper Canada on the Eve of the Railway Era" in *Profiles of a Province* (Toronto: Ontario Historical Society, 1967), p. 49.
2. See "The Newspaper Press of Canada West, 1850-60" by J. J. Talman, Transactions of the Royal Society of Canada, 3rd Series, Section II, Vol. XXXIII, 1939.
3. Quoted by P. B. Waite in *The Life and Times of Confederation* (Toronto: University of Toronto Press, 1962), p. 117.
4. *York-Toronto 1793-1884*, Memorial Volume (Toronto: Hunter-Rose, 1884), p. 242.
5. See John S. Moir, *Church and State in Canada West* (Toronto: University of Toronto Press, 1959); also 1861 census.
6. J. Donald Wilson, Robert M. Stamp, Louis-Philippe Audet, *Canadian Education, A History* (Toronto: Prentice-Hall of Canada, 1970), p. 231.
7. *Ibid.*, p. 233.
8. Moir, *Church and State in Canada West*, p. xi.
9. Dale C. Thomson, *Alexander Mackenzie, Clear Grit* (Toronto: Macmillan of Canada, 1960), p. 123.

Chapter Three

The First Administrations

1.

On Friday, December 27, 1867, in the old red brick home of former colonial assemblies, the first legislature of Ontario began its work. Its eighty-two members were elected from the same constituencies that elected federal members; and, since the principle of "dual representation" prevailed, some of the Ontario legislators were also members of the Dominion House of Commons. All had won their seats at the first general election, which had pitted George Brown at the head of dissident Reformers against the Conservatives and coalitionists of John A. Macdonald. John Sandfield Macdonald, as principal Ontario architect of his great namesake's victory, was now Premier of the province, with a cabinet of five members. It was a small group, but it was considered large enough. According to the common view, the functions of a provincial legislature would be little more than those of a "glorified county council."

The preparations for the opening day appear to have been economical. The government was accused in some unfriendly quarters of having ransacked the second-hand stores of Toronto for much of its new furniture. According to the *Globe*, the legislative chamber itself had been refurbished extensively. But there had been

> no attempt at lavish ornamentation (and) elsewhere in the building chaos reigns supreme. The departmental offices wear a demoralized appearance as yet, while committee rooms and most of the various anterooms are in a state which would apparently tax the powers of a conjurer to reduce to one of order, and are besides . . . thick with dust.[1]

By 3.00 in the afternoon of December 27, troops, bands and a guard of honour were deployed before the low range of buildings facing on

Front Street, "surrounded by considerable open space which gives full effect to the insignificance of their appearance."[2] Arriving in a four-horse carriage accompanied by a mounted escort, Lieutenant-Governor Sir Henry William Stisted was ushered into the House. There was a difference in one respect from proceedings at the capital in Ottawa and at the provincial capital in Quebec. Ontario, at Brown's insistence, had a unicameral legislature; there was no Senate as in the Dominion parliament and no Legislative Council as in the case of the lower province. There was therefore none of the ritual of summoning members of the Commons to the bar of "the other place."

The Lieutenant-Governor, entering the legislative chamber, assumed the chair and awaited the coming of the mace. When it was set on the table he announced through the clerk of the House that he did not see fit to declare the cause of the summoning of this parliament until the members had chosen a Speaker. With that word he withdrew. The next day he returned, to find an elected Speaker and read the Speech from the Throne.

It was a sober, businesslike document without major pretensions, but it gave a hint of the pressures building behind it. Much was to be done to complete the structure of government. There was a need for local works and social improvement, and even more for expansion and immigration. Roads must be pushed north from the older, settled regions to explore the potential of the Shield. Muskoka and Haliburton figured largely in the plans, but as far north as Lake Nipissing and as far east as the region of the upper Ottawa there were great hopes for agricultural development. They were to be fostered by homestead grants and by every encouragement and assistance, particularly to British immigrants. The growth of the lumber industry and the hope of locating mineral ores both called for the building of more railways. The Speech set out, in all, a large program of work for a glorified county council.

John Sandfield Macdonald, the man who had written the Speech, was a Roman Catholic and a Scot, born among the highlanders of Glengarry county fifty-five years earlier. A wealthy barrister, well-established in Cornwall, he was plagued by ill-health and wore the scars of a long political career. Yet it had been an energetic career and at least in youth he had had a lively personal life. During the troubles of the 1830s he had served as an officer of the militia and occasionally as a military courier. Detailed by the Upper Canadian government to carry despatches to Washington, he had met a girl on the way. She was a Louisiana Creole holidaying in Saratoga, and was much attracted to the dashing Scots Canadian. The result was a later visit to her home in Louisiana and a stern rebuff from the father. That, in turn, was followed by a swift elopement and thirty subsequent years of happy married life.

In Sandfield Macdonald's Ivy Hall at Cornwall hospitality was prodigal and French and English were spoken interchangeably. For every other reason, in this eastern neck of the province so near to Lower Canada, the French interest had been strong in Sandfield's thinking. He was a Reformer, an Upper Canadian and a politician and businessman devoted to his own province, but he had different views and shadings from most of the western Grits. He accepted harmony with the French as a first political essential and he looked to the St. Lawrence basin, first, last and always, as the major centre of economic development.

He was pawky, difficult, erratic and stubborn in his own views. Enemies he made freely and he had been engaged in furious battles through the ups and downs of the years. Yet it seemed difficult to dislike Sandfield permanently. Tall, lean, cadaverous, always troubled with a cough, he had a way of dropping in on current adversaries and opening his heart profanely about mutually shared trials. He had been a party leader and a Premier of the old province of Canada, and he had promoted various schemes for a better union. Yet he had opposed Confederation as a plan too big for its time. His views had divided him from Brown, confirmed his lifelong hostility to John A. Macdonald, and left him temporarily as a man without a party. In another way, however, he had become the man that the times called for.

John A. Macdonald, as Prime Minister of the Dominion that had been made by a coalition, required a coalitionist as Premier of the new Ontario. He should be able to ignore the old divisions of parties and proceed from a clean slate. Sandfield Macdonald was a pragmatist and could be made to accept the fact of Confederation. He was at least as opposed to Brown as he was to his Tory namesake, and the other Macdonald had notable arts of persuasion. There was a burying of old hatchets, Sandfield Macdonald was won, and the two went out to the hustings for the first general election.

It had been both federally and provincially a confused battle. To John A. Macdonald, the only respectable issue was the issue of Confederation. To be against Coalition, therefore, although increasingly it was dominated by Conservative interests, was to be against the Dominion itself. The men who had made the nation should be given the chance to govern it. New issues would rise and party quarrels would come, but they should be left to evolve with time. The only work for the present was to set a national course.

On the other side was the new party of Reform, banded together and reorganized under the leadership of George Brown. With Confederation accomplished, the aversion of Brown for Macdonald and for Macdonald's political methods had fragmented the coalition. To Grits departing with their leader it had become the vehicle of Toryism, returning to its old sins. They had a loud answer to the cry for political harmony and to the other claim that they were a factious opposition. The Prime Minister was corrupt, the men about him were corrupt, and the work of guiding the Dominion should be given to other hands.

The result of a hot summer and the protracted war of the polls had been personal disaster for Brown. Defeated in his own riding, he was never to take a seat in the House of Commons. For the Reform party, in the face of general defeat, there was a complete reversal of prospects. They were not to be the dominant voice in the new Dominion, interpreting that "constitution" that was still so vaguely known. The work would be in other, possibly hostile hands, with less concern for Ontario's vital interests. Their own provincial parliament, that small custodian of purely local powers, began at once to assume a new importance. Yet even here they were not yet to be masters, for they had lost on both fronts.

It was, provincially at least, a somewhat equivocal loss, likely to be redeemed by enduring Grit strength. John Sandfield Macdonald, though he was now Premier of Ontario, had won his place by appealing to all parties. His junior coalition or "Patent Combination," as the newspapers dubbed his cabinet, was not distinguished by much internal harmony. He was compelled to ride herd on Conservatives with long memories and on old and new Reformers who were still of a liberal bent. He had also to deal with an inexperienced Assembly. Of its eighty-two members sixty-nine had never sat in a legislature, and some supporters of the Premier were as difficult as the men who faced them. Across the aisle, moreover, was a vigorous opposition, as diverse as Sandfield's following but in no way quelled by defeat.

The opposition was dominated though not yet led by the sombre, spectacled presence of the rising Edward Blake. Thirty-four years old and a prosperous Toronto barrister, Blake like the Premier himself was a member of the federal parliament as well as the provincial House. He was new to both scenes but a man with a future, in his own and other eyes. In the first session at Ottawa, preceding the meeting of the first provincial assembly, Blake had sat with Sandfield to the left of Mr. Speaker. Whatever they were in Toronto, both men in Ottawa were still nominally Reformers and opposed to the Conservative government. On the day parliament opened Sandfield had actually found himself, through various casual accidents, in the seat reserved for the leader of the opposition.

Tall, cold, assured and wearing the air of the law courts, Blake had risen to excoriate his official colleague. Why had he travelled the province as the other Macdonald's shadow, "tall and thin as a shadow ought to be, which followed his every footstep, re-echoed his every word, applauded his every sentiment?"[3] No principles had been involved; it had been done to win an election, and now the Premier of Ontario was a subservient federal agent. As a first resentful sounding of the theme of subordination, it was to emerge through other battles as a prevailing theme with Blake. For the Patent Combination he had only a high contempt. In his eyes it was merely a Tory ministry dominated from Ottawa, with neither wish nor freedom to consult the interests of the province. Yet always watchful and dangerous and always harping on principle, Blake was faced with the dilemma that confronted the two Macdonalds. There was actually no party possessed of a settled policy, and there were few clear lines of division between federal and provincial powers. These remained to be defined in the building of province and nation, and for all the claims of the leaders they were groping their way together.

2.

Sandfield Macdonald's government was to have four years in office. It projected in its first budget a revenue for the year of some $1,800,000.00, with no direct taxation. Over half the amount expected was to come from Dominion subsidies, about a quarter from Crown lands, and the balance from fees, licences and other casual income. Expenditures were estimated at slightly less than $1,300,000.00, which would leave a comfortable surplus. Both in that year and following years optimism was borne out and some of the surplus spent, with criticism from the opposition but also with co-operation. Not only the men in government but the men across the aisle were aware of provincial needs, some of which were in the field of social policy.

The Ontario of the pioneers had been as hard as most new countries on its sick, its criminal and its helpless. Law-breakers went to jail, the handicapped, insane and indigent were often deposited with them, and orphans went to apprenticeships that closely resembled slavery. Private charity redeemed many of the evils, but the bleak public picture reflected the public mind. Those who could not compete for any reason, were to be swept aside or caged. Even by the 1830s, as the workhouse came on the scene, it was criminal to be poor and helpless. The House of Industry, in the wording of the Act creating it, was for the indigent, the dissolute, the vagrant and "all such as spend their time and property in public houses to the neglect of their lawful calling."[4]

By the middle 1840s there were "outdoor" measures of relief, and with the stirring of public conscience the conditions in jails improved. Reformatories were established, separating the young offender from the hardened older criminal, and separate prisons were established for men and women. At the same time, and from the same concern, came the first asylums for the insane. Hospitals there had always been, treating what ills they could, often excellently administered and serving large communities. But they were private institutions, frequently assisted by government but neither inspected nor controlled, and always woefully deficient in facilities for special care. Beyond the sick and the insane, the criminal and the assisted poor, were the deaf and blind who were forgotten and the young who lived in a void. As late as 1866, government inspectors were reporting on Toronto's "City Arabs," destitute, unapprenticed and below the rim of society, "for whom our admirable and costly common schools are perfectly useless."[5] Across the whole social spectrum, when Ontario became a province, there was a lack of co-ordination and there were blank areas of neglect.

Many remained empty when the government of Sandfield Macdonald completed its four years. It was still very much a creature of its own times. Yet some requirements were recognized and a little was done to meet them. By 1871 an institution for the deaf was established in Belleville and a home and school for the blind were being built in Brantford. A new asylum for the insane was opened in London and not only the asylum in Toronto but its branches at Orillia and Malden were considerably improved and enlarged. Reformatories were provided with workshops and with other accommodations that removed them from the class of jails, while attempts were made to persuade counties to improve the jails themselves. The inspection system remained woefully inadequate, but promise came in the person of a new Inspector. John Woodburn Langmuir, appointed to the post in 1868, was to be a powerful force for reform through years to come. The appropriation of $150,000.00 for a new central prison to be built in Toronto was a proof that crime still flourished. Yet it also pointed the way to some advance. Much of the size of the prison and much of the money spent on it would be accounted for by the provision of machines and workshops. The prisoner was to be given work that would point the way to a trade. The idea had been accepted that the criminal might be changed, that he was more than human waste.

In education the dominant figure was still Egerton Ryerson, and in 1871 came the crown of the old man's work. The system of common schools, confirmed and strengthened by the full acceptance of compulsory local assessment, was extended to the secondary field. The

"Grammar Schools," had been schools for the well-to-do. Government grants provided the salaries of teachers, but fees were required of students. The vast majority of parents refused or were unable to pay them. The schools, moreover, were poorly and casually supervised, frequently very bad, and rigidly locked in old classical curricula. They were at best preparatory schools on an antiquated English model. The Ontario student left them half-prepared or unprepared for life in his own province.

By 1853 the discontent with the schools had caused some changes. Common schools and Grammar Schools could unite for continuity under closer government control. Yet the system was still permissive and the loose arrangement had not brought much advance. The schools were still for the few, nor were they satisfactory or relevant even for the privileged class. The poor remained outside them and the rich often avoided them, sending their children to private institutions. What Ryerson proposed was sweeping and effective change. The principle of compulsory local taxation should be extended to support the secondary level of schools. Schools of both kinds should be harmonized and co-ordinated under the Council of Public Instruction. They should be not only free but compulsory for all school-age children. There should be significant changes in nomenclature, a general raising of standards both in teaching and supervision, and a new advance in practical flexibility. Common schools were to be "public" schools, and Grammar Schools divided into two classes. The high school, in which technical training would be given a major emphasis, was to train the student bound for business or trade. The Collegiate Institute, retaining some of the old classical curriculum, would fit him more specifically for the university and the professions.

Not all of it was attained, and none without political storms. The Council of Public Instruction, totally controlled by Ryerson, was an expanding separate power within the province. It administered government grants, established its own policies, set curricula, selected and supplied textbooks, controlled teaching methods and the quality of teacher training. In the eyes of the opposition, and particularly of Edward Blake, Ryerson controlled too much and some of his plans were bad. He was demanding an increase in teaching staff that was beyond present means. The emphasis on technical training would direct students away from the university, and the training itself was bound to be second-rate. To farmers, to city tradesmen and also to Roman Catholics, compulsion in education would be unacceptable.

When the Act was passed by the legislature in 1871, Ryerson's hopes fell short in two basic particulars. Completely free schooling, at least on the secondary level, was to be delayed for forty years. Compulsory attendance was left to arrive by stages. It applied as first enacted to only four months of the year, and then only to children between the ages of seven and twelve. Yet the Normal School, an earlier creation of Ryerson, was first enlarged and then supplemented by a second. A technical college was established and would be flourishing a century later as the Ryerson Institute of Technology. Public schools, high schools and collegiates, co-ordinated as Ryerson planned, were directed and administered by him through the Council of Public Instruction. They would only be so briefly; there would be a Department of Education within a matter of five years and it would develop without Ryerson. Yet it would still wear his stamp and conform to much of his thought, perhaps for rather too long. The broad features of the system and most of its internal workings remained intact into the twentieth century.

3.

The same year that saw the passing of the school act brought legislation for an agricultural college. It would not be established at Guelph for another three years, but the need was becoming recognized. At the same time commerce along with agriculture was entering a new era. Hamilton and London, as trade, transport and industrial centres, were reaching out through the west. Toronto with its large banks and widening financial tentacles was competing with Montreal. It was changing within itself in its ways of retail trade, for Timothy Eaton had come. Sales for cash only and at one inflexible price were beginning to replace the days of dragged-out credit. Robert Simpson arrived in Toronto in 1871, and prosperity with modern merchandising went forward hand in hand. Money, work and widening opportunities were all present in old southern Ontario. But the future had to be thought of, and the future lay with the north.

Lumbering, as it extended from the Ottawa, had crossed the lower Shield country to the head of Georgian Bay and was moving west from there. The complex of camps in the woods and ports at the mouths of rivers was approaching Lake Superior. The magnificent pine of Canada, that was now the property of Ontario, had an inexhaustible market in the American midwest. It still flowed to the St. Lawrence by all the well-worn routes. It came down through Georgian Bay to Collingwood and Penetanguishene, and much went to Lake Huron ports on passage through to Michigan. Even Thunder Bay, the mysterious western hinterland at the head of the Great Lakes, was a terminal for ships from Collingwood on regular summer sailings.

In that region, moreover, as the stands of pine went down, the wild, rocky country was beginning to promise ore. Along the Lake Superior shoreline copper, iron, lead, zinc and gold deposits had been known for many years. Silver had been discovered, and Silver Islet, a dot in Lake Superior, was then returning to its developers some million dollars a year. As a mine it was short-lived, but it drew men to the country, created supporting growth and was a factor moving the government to a fateful change of policy. For years past the Crown had exacted royalties on all minerals and ore. By the Mining Act of 1869, not only were royalties abolished, but Crown and private lands were opened to the licensed prospector. He could stake and register a claim and for an annual rent of $1.00 per acre have full rights to the minerals and ore discovered. The result was a surge of prospecting, an increase of capital for the industry and eventually some huge finds. But for long years, till the act was changed again, the great resource so regally handed over would return nothing to the province.

The government's first concern, however, was still the peopling of the country, and lumbering was the impelling force. The trade was building steamer lines, accenting the demand for railways, and creating sawmill towns. Parry Sound and Midland on inlets of Georgian Bay, Orillia above Lake Simcoe, Fenelon Falls, Bobcaygeon, Madoc and Tweed were all important settlements. They were loosely linked, moreover, by a pattern of wretched roads, to a settled south that pursued a fixed idea. Lumbering was still to be the prelude to a great advance in agriculture. It was a firm tenet of statesmanship that the land of the nearer north, particularly the Muskoka and Haliburton regions, with their great forests and infinite maze of waterways, would some day yield to the plough. Out of this hope came encouragement of immigration and larger measures to attract the northern settler.

In 1868 the Free Grant and Homestead Act was adapted from the American system that was opening the midwest. In the Muskoka-Parry Sound region, between Georgian Bay and the upper Ottawa River, Crown land formerly held for sale was offered as free grants in lots of a hundred acres. The homesteader, after five years of residence, and provided he had built shelter and cleared a portion of his land, would have clear title to the farm. For half a dollar an acre he could buy a second lot. What he could not do was encroach on the rights of lumbermen where tracts were reserved for timber. He could use pine as he needed it to put up his own buildings but he could offer none for sale. The farmer went to the wilderness to subsist only on his land.

The government did much to help him, hoping to recoup its

money from the sale of reserved timber. "Colonization roads," branching off from the southern roads and inferior even to them, were pushed north toward the Shield. Grants for implements and livestock supplemented earlier provisions, and the grant of a hundred acres was increased to 200. Colonization railways, added to other plans, brought on a rash of building later to be regretted. Wooden rails and narrow gauge were both expedients considered in the haste to reach the north. In a few cases narrow gauge was adopted, creating problems of connection with the broad gauge southern lines. South and north, however, and wide-spaced or narrow-spaced, a multitude of rails went down. By 1871 the Kingston-Pembroke railway, the Toronto-Nipissing and the Toronto-Grey-Bruce were all under construction. The Canada-Atlantic of J. R. Booth, the lumberman, and the southern Credit Valley to join St. Thomas with Toronto had each acquired their charters. Some 570 miles, much of it pointing northward, was being added to the railway system through the work of private builders and the help of government subsidies.

Still more was projected. A government measure of 1871 established a Railway Aid Fund of $1,500,000.00 for use on approved projects. It encouraged a building fever that was sweeping the municipalities, and was attacked by the opposition as a sop to political friends. The private builder, if he could obtain a municipal subsidy, would also receive a provincial subsidy of between $2,000.00 and $4,000.00 per mile. Since the cabinet could administer the fund without recourse to the legislature, it seemed obvious that loyal municipalities and the private supporters of the government would come in for most of the grants. The fear was not borne out in the time remaining to the Premier, and the fund and the zest for building still remained. Waterways as well as railways opened the Muskoka region where tourists of a later day would discover a wilderness paradise. In May of 1870, an official tourist himself, Sandfield visited Muskoka with an impressed and impressive party. He went by rail to Lake Simcoe, on by water to Washago, and from there by stage and waterways to the outpost northern settlements. He saw magnificent scenery, a wealth of timber and lumber camps, but the promising farm was rare.

Everywhere throughout the north country there were areas of good land, but much of it lay in valleys and was practically inaccessible to the newly arriving settler. He could move only by roads, or trails that passed for roads, most of which followed the high rims of the valleys. Even there they were bad, constantly used by lumbermen, and cut to pieces by the wheels of heavy wagons. Corduroy sank in swamps or was washed away by floods. Bridges, supports

44

and cribbing, for roads and railways alike, were destroyed by great forest fires and the terrible summer storms. Settlers burning brushwood often started the fires, and so did locomotives with sparks from their belching stacks. Whatever man attempted seemed viciously beaten back; the environment remained hostile.

> Oh the horrors of that journey! (wrote one English gentlewoman of a memorable passage north.) The road was most dreadful – our first acquaintance with 'corduroy' roads. The forest gradually closed in on us, on fire on both sides, burnt trees crashing down in all directions, here and there one right across the road, which had to be dragged out of the way before we could go on.[6]

There were welcomes of as little promise for many another family. And beyond that the bleak years stretched ahead. A settler came too often totally inexperienced, to a grant of rocky bush or a stump-strewn timber clearing in the midst of towering woods. If there was pine growing on his land he was not allowed to sell it; he could only cut for his house and barn and fences. The pine belonged to the lumberman; the farmer here was an intruder on a great industry and at war with the country itself. There were the thin soil, the early frosts, the swarms of flies and mosquitoes and the savage winter cold. Neighbours and markets alike were always difficult, and at times quite impossible, to reach. Some men fought it through, more fortunate in land and skills, and lived to see good farms. Others withered with their hopes in trapped and desolate communities that survived as backwoods slums. Many of the bold and younger set out for the far west, redeeming failure in the east. Yet failure it still was in terms of government policy, though it would be years yet before the fact was recognized. The pattern developed in old southern Ontario, with its broad wheatfields and rich and varied agriculture, would not be repeated in the north. Neither railways, roads nor money could change the nature of the Shield.

4.

On December 19, 1871, in the first session of the second Ontario legislature, Sandfield Macdonald's government met defeat. The ailing Premier resigned, to be succeeded by Edward Blake. He left political bitterness and a host of unsolved problems, but he also left a substantial record of achievement. He had been a careful, practical manager; his government was well run. Provincial revenues were buoyant, there was a good surplus in the treasury and administration had been honest.

Nor had the Premier feared reform, though he was less the reformer than Blake. He had lessened the crude abuses disfiguring

45

most elections, excluded members of the legislature from paid public appointments and widened the electoral franchise. The right to a vote was still based on land, but the required amount of real property had been scaled down to values of $400.00 in the cities, $300.00 in towns and $200.00 in incorporated villages and townships. They were low enough for Sandfield. He had resisted further reductions and he refused to concede that a salaried man, not possessed of property, might be entitled to the right to vote. He would not accept the idea of the secret ballot, and he recoiled angrily from radicals who were for complete manhood suffrage. He had put an end, however, to the old, leisurely elections, dragging on for weeks. In all general elections, from Sandfield's time onward, polling was to be simultaneous and confined to a single day.

He had differed stubbornly from Blake on dual representation, the practice allowing a provincial member to hold a federal seat. Blake, almost from the beginning, had fought to change the law. The Ontario member, he thought, sitting in the senior as well as the junior House, was exposed to the constant threat of federal influence. Sandfield, with equal firmness, upheld the dual principle. It made use of the best men in both the greater and lesser fields, it promoted national harmony. Yet more than ever now, both to Blake and George Brown, the Macdonald taste for "harmony" was becoming a major evil.

The federal and provincial governments, as they sorted out their powers, had proceeded not only with caution but with co-operation from Blake. He had advised Sandfield on bills before the legislature, and his advice had often been accepted. John A. Macdonald, as provincial acts reached him and he studied their operation, had occasionally consulted Blake. In spite of basic differences and the occasional sharp dispute, there had been a real effort to determine and define functions.

Yet the developing nation, no less than the evolving parties, had inevitably opened fields of future conflict. Blake stood up for Ontario, as the Dominion's major taxpayer, when better terms were granted to Nova Scotia. The subsidy of $2,000,000.00 was a sop to buy peace, and it was not prescribed by the Act of Confederation. In Blake's eyes it violated the constitution and established the greatest province, which would be paying at least half, as subordinate to the other three. Their votes, combined in the federal parliament, were taking away her money for a use she did not support. Few politicians of that time could be brought to support Blake, yet he had raised a ripple of concern. For the first time Ontario's dominance of the new and sprawling union was revealed as insecure.

A larger question was lifting over the horizon. In the far west and to the north the territories of the Hudson's Bay Company enclosed much of Ontario. By 1869 they were to be taken over by the Dominion, and the question of boundaries rose. The Company's charter, as given in 1670, had granted a region vast and vague enough. It had been infringed since by wars and treaties with the French and by later treaties with the Americans, but it was roughly defined by what was known of geography and of the continent's lakes and rivers. From west of Lake Superior, north of the height of land, water flowed toward the Bay and trade followed the water. The east and south, as the drainage basin of the St. Lawrence, was reserved for future settlement. The north and west, however, as far as the Rocky Mountains, was the property of the Hudson's Bay Company and seen as the land of fur.

The enormous claim, ignored by Indian tribes and nibbled away by settlement, had been threatened for a hundred years. In 1850 the old province of Canada, concluding a treaty with the Ojibwas, extended its sphere of interest to Lake Superior. In 1858 it established the District of Algoma, with its southern and eastern boundaries along Lake Huron, its western on Lake Superior, and its northern undefined but extending to James Bay. Canada was invading the region of northward flowing water, and a year later it turned its eyes to the west. In 1859, as an official agent of the government on the Lake Superior shoreline, Simon J. Dawson was planning a boat and wagon route and dreaming beyond that.

> A continuous railroad – 195 miles in length – might be made between Lake Superior and Rainy Lake, and another, of 91½ miles, between Lac Plat and Fort Garry. If this were done, and two locks constructed at Fort Frances, the Red River Settlement would be within less than two days journey of Lake Superior . . . This would bring Fort Garry within five day's journey of Toronto.[7]

There was no such railway by the time of Confederation, but there was Dawson's boat and wagon route as far as the Red River. There was a steady trickle of westward-moving settlement, and a standing quarrel with the tenacious Hudson's Bay Company. That quarrel was settled in 1869 when the Dominion government, by purchasing the North-West Territories, became the new proprietor. In the same year, however, the grounds of an internal quarrel began to be staked out. On November 3, 1869, at the opening of the third session of the first Ontario legislature, Lieutenant-Governor W.P. Howland, who had replaced General Stisted, delivered the Speech from the Throne. It was expedient, he proposed, that since the North-West Territories were to become a part of Canada, the boundary line should be determined between them and the province of Ontario.

47

By 1870 the Territories had been taken over, and by 1871 a commission of two members had been established to fix the boundaries. It had not reported when Sandfield Macdonald left office, but already there were ominous signs. In the view of William McDougall, the provincially-appointed commissioner, the Ontario boundary should extend indefinitely northward beyond the height of land and far enough to the westward to enclose Lake of the Woods. The federal commissioner, however, presumably more responsive to the views of the Dominion government, was inclined to another finding. It shocked Ontario, and with reason, for it seemed to transform her future. Locked off from the north by the line of the height of land, she was to be locked in to the east. The line favoured by the Dominion, on the basis of old treaties, was to run due north from the junction point of the Ohio and the Mississippi, the boundary of French Canada at the time of the English conquest. Projected from that point, it would intersect Lake Superior about 300 miles to the east of Lake of the Woods. Prince Arthur's Landing and Fort William, with much of the lakehead territory and a huge area to the west, would be shorn away from Ontario and become the property of the Dominion.

It loomed only as a threat when Blake took over the province, and he instantly rejected the prospect of such a finding. Yet it remained heavy in the air, and the air between province and Dominion was already heavy enough. In 1870 the first Riel uprising and the troubles on the Red River had resulted in the creation of the province of Manitoba. It was the "postage stamp" province where Métis opposed Ontarians, blocking the path of progress on the fringe of the new west. The province was embittered by the "murder" of Thomas Scott, the young Ontario Orangeman who had been put to death by Riel's provisional government. Riel himself was at large, assisted to leave the country by John A. Macdonald for the sake of Quebec support. The young men of Canada First had emerged, as outraged intellectuals, disgusted with all politics, promoting a superior Englishness and a new "national sentiment." It was not a sentiment that left much room for the French, and it had increased strains with Quebec. Catholic and Protestant differences, revived at the Red River, were enhanced by an Orange faction that would never forget Scott. Separate schools and religion, those basic issues of conflict, were awaking from a brief sleep.

All this had weakened Sandfield Macdonald, the Catholic Premier allied with the federal government. His Railway Aid Fund, attacked by the opposition as an enormous political slush fund, had hurt him more than it had yet helped the railways. It was failing health, however, and the effect of his own attitudes that eventually brought him down. If he did not quite view the legislature as an expanded county council, he did show a considerable contempt of its powers. He was sometimes accused of carrying policy in his pocket and revealing it as he saw fit. The choice of sites for the location of public buildings, the revaluing of Crown lands, and even decisions on railways had often been made in cabinet and only reported to the House. The result when it came to election time was a fatal reduction of strength and eventual resignation. By December of 1871 the Grit reformers of Ontario, with their watchful care of money and their insistent thirst for democracy, were firmly set in the saddle.

Problems and opportunities and the weight of responsibility had changed the functions of Ontario's provincial government. Or rather, they had revealed the functions. It was not, after all, an enlarged municipal council; it was a body ruling a state within a state. It had become that for all Grit Ontarians, the more so through the disputes with federal power. John A. Macdonald, the always determined centralizer, had ignited a flame of provincial independence. Its guardian was the provincial legislature, the disdained "local authority," and the Grit Premier would have no intrusion on his field. Blake made it explicit on his second day in office. Sandfield Macdonald's ministry, he told the House, "was formed upon the principle and understanding that it and the Government of the Dominion should work together – play into each other's hands." There was to be none of that in future. "As citizens of the Province of Ontario we are called upon to frame our own policy ... we deprecate, nay more, we protest most strongly against any interference on the part of any government with our perfect freedom of action."[8]

5.

In a single session as Premier, his last in the Ontario House, Blake abolished dual representation. That link was broken between the federal and provincial parliaments. For all the clash with Ryerson over educational reform, nothing basic was changed. Blake was as strong as his predecessor in support of the railway building and he was prepared to spend more money. Under his regime, however, grants from the Railway Aid Fund required the approval of the legislature.

In the single year of the Blake administration 5,031 square miles of timber berths were sold at public auction. The sales, as always, were actually only leases, conveying the right to cut and sell the timber. Nevertheless, as a huge disposal of resources not to be equalled again in twenty years, they came in for a spate of criticism. Ontario had

49

begun to realize that its forests were not endless and to think of the longer future. Yet the present had its claims too. Sawmills, new employment and increased trade and traffic would all come from that pine. The land would be there, and still the property of Ontario, when the trees were cleared away. It was better to clear them now and transform them into wealth than to leave the stands to be eaten away by fire. Or so Blake thought, and his critics were soon silenced.

He was a great figure and he was to do much for Ontario, but not as Premier of the province. On October 21, 1872, after less than a year in office, he walked round to a quiet house on Simcoe Street in the shadow of Osgoode Hall. George Brown went with him and they were later joined by Alexander Mackenzie, the federal leader of the Reformers and Blake's Provincial Treasurer. The three men had converged on Oliver Mowat, the Vice-Chancellor of Ontario. Blake was thinking, as he often was, of retiring from public life, and if he went on at all it would be only in the federal field. The provincial office was open, Mowat was urged to take it, and at the end of a long discussion he was persuaded to acquiesce.

It must have been a daunting prospect for a man of fifty-two. The mutton-chop fringing his cheeks and the hair combed tidily back from an ample forehead were already tinged with grey. Mowat was small and chunky, spectacled and soft-voiced, an unimpressive figure who had never sought to impress. There was often a glint of humour in the eyes behind the spectacles, and at other times the cool steel of authority. His great forte, however, was sedate and thoughtful care. He spoke hesitantly, listened patiently and delayed every decision till it had ripened in his own mind. Yet no one then or ever doubted the quality of the mind, or the canny political generalship to be revealed in the years ahead.

He had been born in Kingston of a Presbyterian family, Conservative in political leanings like most of its Kingston neighbours. He had been first indentured as a law clerk to the young Kingston barrister, John A. Macdonald. From Kingston he had gone to Toronto to establish his own practice, and he was thirty-seven before he entered politics. By that time his political views had changed. He was first elected to the assembly of old Canada as a member of the Reform party and a protégé of George Brown. Through the next seventeen years he had served in three ministries, always supporting Brown and increasingly becoming an irritant to the Macdonald who had taught him law. He had gone with Brown to the Quebec Conference for the framing of Confederation and he had been more interested than Brown, and rather more insistent, on the question of "local authorities." It was Mowat's resolution that had defined provincial powers. In the same year, with the Quebec Conference concluded, he seemed to have considered his political work done. On the invitation of John A. Macdonald he had accepted the Vice-Chancellorship and moved to the Ontario bench.

He had been respected and admired as a judge and his home reflected the man, with its fine Victorian library, its closely-knit relationships and its constant flow of friends. Most of the best of Toronto's good society was to be seen at the Mowat table, where the abstaining host's wineglass would be filled with cold tea. Life, as remembered afterward, was good there for the children and for the children's children when they came. "It all stemmed," said one of them, "from Grandpapa who sat at God's right hand."[9]

It would be a hard change from that to the brawls of the political arena. Mowat knew them well, and was aware of what to expect. He would be attacked for years afterward as a judge who had left the bench, rejoined a political party and "degraded" the judicial office. He would have to cope, in place of the retiring Blake, with half-initiated programs and newly-arising problems accompanying relentless growth. The province had scarcely found itself either within its own lands or within the fabric of the Dominion. It wrestled with the federal government and was troubled by inner faction as creeds and schools again loomed as an issue. There was the North-West to be thought of, Riel was unforgotten and muted racial conflict was assuming a sharper tone. Yet beyond that and embracing it all was the development of people and province, with its challenge and fascination. The politician, controlling nothing, might only hope to guide it, yet caution, balance and compromise might steer it along in peace. That work, for the next quarter-century, was to be in the hands of the careful man.

Notes

1. Toronto *Globe*, December 27, 1867.
2. *York-Toronto 1793-1884*, p. 288.
3. Debates, House of Commons, November 11, 1867, pp. 23-26.
4. Richard B. Splane, *Social Welfare in Ontario, 1791-1893* (Toronto: University of Toronto Press, 1965), p. 71.
5. *Ibid.*, p. 229.
6. Mrs. King, letter. Quoted in *Muskoka and Haliburton, 1615-1875*, edited by Florence B. Murray, (Toronto: Champlain Society, Ontario Series), 1963, p. 197.
7. S. J. Dawson's Report on the *Routes Between Lake Superior and Red River, 1859*, in *Thunder Bay District, 1821-1892*, edited by Elizabeth Arthur, (Toronto: Champlain Society, Ontario Series, 1973), p. 94.
8. Toronto *Globe*, December 23, 1871.
9. Quoted by A. Margaret Evans in *Oliver Mowat and Ontario, 1872-1896: A Study in Political Success*, Ph. D. Thesis, University of Toronto, 1967.

Chapter Four

Land and Growth

1.

Oliver Mowat as "the Christian statesman" and equally as the "little tyrant" has left an image of sedate, sustained authority. As a political athlete, however, he had the essential qualities of the star.

> He was a Mameluke when roused, (said George William Ross, one of the colleagues who later succeeded him as Premier.) Naturally conservative, when the psychological moment arrived he would cast his idols to the moles and bats and lead a procession of the most advanced radicals with all the enthusiasm of a new convert. He rarely left his seat during the longest sittings, and I have on several occasions walked home with him as the street lights were being extinguished, without hearing him even complain of being tired.[1]

With all that went a responsible view of power. Change, in Mowat's view, must arise from felt needs, be stimulated by a consensus and advance at the people's pace. The leader's work was to know the mind of his constituency, to interpret the major thrust of public opinion and finally to give it shape.

On November 22, 1872, he was elected by acclamation to the riding of North Oxford in the provincial legislature. He was to hold that seat through his political life in the province, and as Attorney-General and Premier he was to lead his party in six general elections. That he won them all could be attributed to good politics, to an ample use of patronage and a knowledge of the public mood. Yet he left for the federal field with his prestige and power unshaken and he was welcomed back to the province as Lieutenant-Governor. He was more than a political success story; he was the expression of the Ontario of his times.

He had fine ministers about him during the course of twenty-four years, including two future premiers, Arthur Sturgis Hardy and

George William Ross. He chose carefully, changed reluctantly, supported his men loyally and received loyalty in return. For almost eight years, before the advent of Ross, the frail, scholarly Adam Crooks was in charge of education. T.B. Pardee, later succeeded by Hardy, had sixteen years in the Ministry of Crown Lands. He was devoted, able, rugged as some of the harsh lands he administered, and he must have been a man of charm. "When the Creator makes such men," said John Willison of the *Globe*, "he must feel very pleasantly toward his creatures."[2] C.F. Fraser, a Scottish Catholic from a Protestant constituency in Grenville county, had twenty years in control of public works. A strong defender of his faith, he was in turn defended by Mowat. J.M. Gibson, though he was not a member of the cabinet until 1889, was a great figure at the dawn of the mining age, and John Dryden was a powerful force in agriculture. S.C. Wood, A.M. Ross and Richard Harcourt were others of a strong group. "My colleagues and myself have always been a band of brothers,"[3] said the Premier in later years, speaking of his whole ministry. There was never a doubt, however, as to who controlled the band. Final responsibility and the grip of ultimate authority lay with Mowat.

2.

As Mowat's regime began, Ontario's rural life was being changed by the pull of cities. New factories and industries were attracting farmers' sons. The United States was another competitor for manpower, and so was Manitoba. By the middle 1880s, with the building of the CPR, the further west had become a new attraction. Thousands of immigrants merely passed through the province, bound for the open prairies. Native Ontarians followed, either to the west or the United States. Between 1870 and 1900 Ontario's net loss in native-born people amounted to some 110,000 while of a half million immigrants who had chosen to remain in the province most were settled in the urban sector. As the nineteenth century ended, the proportion of rural to urban population which had been 80.6 per cent in 1871, had shrunk to 57.12 per cent. Among Ontario's total of 2,183,000 people the farming sector was a dwindling or static asset, but only in terms of numbers. In influence, tradition and outlook it remained the spine of the province.

For much of that it could thank its own leaders and its farmers' organizations. The "Grange" movement, imported from the United States, was to be deeply entrenched in Ontario for more than a generation. As a force outside politics and a pool of farmers' views, it was to be influential in its time and seminal for the long future. There would be no farmers' movement and hardly a social movement touching on rural life that was not indebted to the Grange.

The Grangers, or National Grange of the Patrons of Husbandry, had been founded in Washington, D.C., in 1867 by seven American farmers. Organized as a secret society with the usual ritual trappings, its "pleasing, beautiful and appropriate" ceremonies were designed "not only to charm the fancy but to cultivate and enlarge the mind and purify the heart, having at the same time strict adaptation to rural pursuits."[4] Exclusively devoted to agriculture, the Grange was non-sectarian and non-political, and accepted women members as well as men. The core of its organization was the individual Grange, and in each of these local lodges the "Laborer," the "Harvester" and the "Husbandman" worked side by side with the "Maid," "Shepherdess" and "Gleaner." With the rhetoric and titles, however, went a sharp awareness of the practical and a devotion to farmers' needs.

The movement crossed to Quebec in the early 1870s, and established a Grange in Prescott county, Ontario, in 1874. By that time, on the American side, distributed through forty-one states, there were 22,000 similar local Granges. Amid the strains of reconstruction after the Civil War, with the land-grabbing, railway building and the growth of great monopolies, the Grange leaders had been effective champions of the farmer. Government control of freight rates, the reduction of interest charges and the breaking-up of monopolies were all part of their program. Grange co-operatives were established for the purchase of farm implements and the marketing of farm products, and a chain of co-operative retail stores was the first in the United States. In the age of the great tycoon, whose lesser Canadian counterparts were soon to become familiar, the Grange fought for the farmer and taught the farmer to fight. With the land as his first stronghold he must develop, improve, diversify, and he must mobilize to impress his needs on government. Broad, clear-visioned and alert to new conditions, it was a program ripe for Ontario and came to a ready welcome.

By September of 1874 Quebec and Ontario Granges were holding a convention in Toronto. By 1879, with the movement approaching its peak, there were 650 Granges in the province with a membership of about 26,000. Various Granger journals proved to be short-lived, and some aims of the movement were ahead of Canadian times. Attacks on the credit and mortgage systems and on monopolies and railway gouging had only limited success. In Ontario, agrarian anger did not focus, as it did in the United States, on the exactions of the railway but rather on the middleman who, it was alleged, was robbing the farmer of the fruits of his toil. Grange purchasing and marketing ventures and Grange co-operative stores were part of the Ontario landscape for a matter of thirty years. In Bruce county the

Grange operated a salt mine, opposing the salt monopoly, and through most of the 1880s it offered its members fire and life insurance. More permanent than all of this, however, and the very heart of its work, was the improvement of the farmers' status and the maintenance of farm morale.

What the Grange lacked was the thrust and edge of a political party, but that was soon to come. The Patrons of Industry were another fraternal order, again of American origin but with more aggressive views. The farmer, in their eyes, was a patron of all industry and entitled to share the fruits. The first Ontario lodge was established in Lambton county in 1887, crossing over from Michigan. Within two years the order had become indigenous and was developing a class consciousness in support of farmers' views. In 1891 representatives of 300 lodges of the Patrons of Industry met in London to approve a political program previously drafted by a committee. The result was in harmony with the Grange and a familiar echo to Mowat. Patrons of Industry, like other reformers before them, demanded improved electoral machinery and greater protection of agriculture against monopolies and combinations. A resurrection of Grittism in new and impatient strength was confronting the age of industrialism and voicing the cry of the farms. In Mowat's last election of 1894 he was opposed not only by Conservatives but by a new party of Patrons who captured seventeen seats. That he was able to return without them was proof of his own strength, but it was even more significant that he was able to govern with them. Basic to all his policies, whatever the problems dealt with and whatever the delays imposed, were respect for the farmers' political power and awareness of farm needs.

From his first session onward, beginning slowly as usual, there was a long series of measures for the reclamation of land. Government funds and loans, available to municipalities and to individual farmers, enabled them to drain swamp lands and lower-lying areas. The "fever and ague" patches gradually disappeared. Tile drains and larger outlet ditches, sometimes crossing the face of a whole township, created pastures and grainfields where there had been sludgy scrub before. In the course of twenty years, for the expenditure of $1,000,000.00, some 300,000 acres came to be recovered, often doubling their value. "I killed deer in that section thirty years ago when the water was knee-deep," said one farmer, standing among the peach orchards and strawberry fields of Essex county. "Now it is good, splendid dry land."[5]

An agricultural commission, reporting in 1881, opened some eyes with regard to diversification. Barley and flax were coming to replace wheat, and there were more feed grains grown for the dairying and livestock industries. But there was still much apathy toward the recovery of exhausted land, and far too many farms without fences, shade or wind-breaks. Little new growth was replacing the vanished forests. The methods of cheese and butter making were often careless and dirty and the handling of home-killed meat was sometimes worse.

> The hogs, (reported one meat packer to the commission,) are frozen and taken to the country stores, piled up like cordwood and gnawed by hogs, dogs, cats and rats. They are covered with dust and dirt, pitched about with no more care than cordwood, kept in a country warehouse for two or three weeks, sometimes months . . . and by the time they reach us they are more like carrion than human food.[6]

The answer to all that was a flow of legislation, gradually fostering improvement. In 1882 a Department of Agriculture was established, with Charles A. Drury as its first minister. In the same year, as a division of that department, the Ontario Bureau of Industries began to compile statistics. There was also recognition for the "book farmers" at Guelph, who had long struggled in the shade.

For the leaders of the farm movements, if not so much as yet for the average farmer, the Ontario Agricultural College began to come into its own. In 1882 it was affiliated with the University of Toronto. By 1886 a board of practical farmers had been appointed to assist the faculty, and the government was providing scholarships available to farmers' sons. Summer classes began, using the months when sons could be spared from the land, and by the middle 1890s smaller schools and sub-stations, all administered by the college, were active in many regions.

Nothing changed quickly; the farm community, as always, was slow to accept guidance. Yet by the middle 1880s sugar beets and soy beans had been added to the list of crops, tobacco was becoming prominent in Elgin and Norfolk counties and the introduction of the silo had brought important benefits. With winter storage provided for feed corn and hay, livestock breeders and dairymen could operate the year round. With an increase of railway branches cattle could be carried live, packing houses took over more of the slaughter, and by the late 1890s refrigeration was coming. Noxious weeds and tree, plant and animal diseases were all gradually reduced; and inspection became stricter, though far from strict enough, in the larger creameries and dairies.

With the reclamation of land and the encouragement of diversification came a new attention to fruit growing and some of the kindred trades. The honey bee and the hive became the subject of legislation, protecting bees at flowering time from poisonous sprays and powders. There were government acts to encourage the planting of shade trees and Arbor Day was born. Southern Ontario agriculture, in spite of the diminishing farms, was branching out in sophistication and variety and yielding increased returns.

The Free Grant Districts, the newer lands to the north, were not yet a part of the prosperous picture. Much of the thrust of railway building had gone in that direction and had carried settlers with it. In addition to that, by 1896, the government could claim that it had built 4,567 miles of colonization roads and 82,339 feet of bridges at a cost of $2,500,000.00. In the broad northern belt that stretched across from the Algoma District through Muskoka to the upper Ottawa, 107 townships had been set aside for free grants and some 25,000 people had taken up about 3,000,000 acres. Yet the statistics were lean enough in proportion to the effort expended and the actual facts belied them. The farms that had grown with the lumber camps were dying as the camps moved on, without a market for their produce and withering on the thin soil. Of the 3,000,000 acres thousands were now abandoned, consigned with the stumps around them to returning bush and scrub.

In 1890 John Dryden succeeded Drury as Minister of Agriculture, and as such, the north was to engage his energies for the next fifteen years. The line of the CPR, slashing west from Lake Nipissing and above the Great Lakes, had opened a lane through newer forest regions. There, Dryden believed, there was sure to be good farmland, and by 1894 he had embarked on a search to find it. The timber man, however, soon followed by the miner, was to reap the first fruits. For agriculture, as yet, there was only hopeful rumour.

Both north and south the cities gnawed at the farmlands and industry bled away the strength of the farmer. He was part of a beleaguered class, mistrustful of new developments and often remote from their source. In spite of the Good Roads Branch, added to the Department of Agriculture in 1896, communications were difficult for the horse, the buggy and the wagon.

It is doubtful, (reported an inspector in that year) if there is a mile of true macadamized road in Ontario outside a few towns or cities. There are miles of road which are covered with dirty gravel or rough, broken stone and are popularly supposed to be macadamized. Today the majority are little better than trails. From the middle of October to the end of December and from the first of March to the end of May . . . by far the greatest mileage of the province is mud, ruts and pitch holes. There are at least two months when the roads are practically impassable.[7]

Yet the very fact of inspection was a recognition of need. The farming complex of the province was still the centre of its life, and the farms demanded roads. They would get them in good time because they were in a position to compel them. Ontario in 1891 produced three-fifths of the grain, half the hay and roots, half the sheep and cattle and more than two-thirds of the fruit, swine and dairy products sold by the whole Dominion. Fruits and great crops of vegetables added to the annual output. There was more mechanization, by the later 1890s, than in some of the northern American states. The binder, the cream separator and a whole range of improved horse-drawn implements were in steadily increasing use. The steam tractor was appearing and the farm-hand's powers were multiplying. It was estimated that one day's work would produce a bushel of grain which had formerly required a week. Money, science and machinery had come to the farmer's aid and however reduced in numbers he controlled a primary resource.

3.

In forestry, the Mowat government continued the old policies with little essential change. As the northern lands were surveyed the great pine stands were set aside as timber tracts to be leased to the highest bidder. The government received its revenues, the wood was cleared from the land and at the expiration of the leases title reverted to the Crown. In all, between 1877 and 1892, 4,234 square miles of provincial territory were disposed of in this way.

Yet the total leasings for the whole of that period were less than those of the year of Blake's regime.[8] For one thing, the areas already allocated provided years of cutting. For another, there was mounting criticism as the forests disappeared and were not replaced as hoped for with new farms. The miles of stumps stood, a testament to vanished wealth, on land that all too often would grow nothing to replace them. At each auctioning of timber berths the cry was raised that the sales were too large, that they were made preceding elections for the benefit of political friends, and that they were being made too quickly and at too low a price. More fundamental still were attacks on the flow of trade, which carried timber southward to be milled in the United States. Ontario was the hewer of wood while Americans reaped the profit on the sale of finished lumber.

To these arguments the government had its answers. Timber sales were open and were honestly conducted. Ground rents were increased and the "bonuses" on the auction of timber berths rose from $117.70 per square mile in 1872 to $3,657.00 per square mile in 1892. Sawmills in Ontario had a growing share in the consumption, and by 1893 only a third of the provincial timber cut was exported as unsawn logs. Export prices and methods both continued to improve, and there was no more trade in the wasteful "square" timber. If the answers were superficial, little emerged from the objections in the way of a new policy. The American market cried out to be supplied, and the axe was the best answer. Year after year the roar of great fires cutting avenues through miles of virgin forest, wiping out towns and villages and sometimes ringing cities with infernos of flame and smoke, enforced the argument that haste prevented waste. It was better to reap the timber than to let it stand and be burned. In addition to all that, the returns from the forest industry made up some 28 per cent of the provincial government's revenue. The advance of lumbering went on, much as it had done from the beginning.

Simcoe county, Peterborough county and the northern and eastern sections of the Huron-Ottawa Tract continued to be large producers through most of the 1880s. Colonization railways, built for the northbound immigrants as well as the southbound logs, veined the area with a proliferation of branches. Port Hope, Belleville and Toronto were all fed by the Midland from the shores of Georgian Bay. Toronto's own Northern, reaching on from Gravenhurst, was coming close to Lake Nipissing by 1886. J. R. Booth, greatest of the lumber barons, was pushing his Canada Atlantic from Ottawa toward Parry Sound. Colonization roads, moving beyond the railways, opened the way to camps still farther north. Each spring the familiar maze of lakes, rivers and streamlets, alive with leaping timber, contributed to the annual flood.

At the same time, with the building of the CPR, the westward extension began. Following the height of land and rounding Lake Superior, the line drew lumbermen after it to the region of Thunder Bay. By the early 1890s, with much of the pine exhausted in the Huron-Ottawa Tract, some of the older operators were beginning to phase down. But the camps of newer and younger men were north of Georgian Bay, reaching west through the corridor between the height of land and the Lakes, and opening the Rainy River District close to Lake of the Woods.

Meanwhile government action had improved some features of the industry. In 1878 the old freedoms of brush-burning and the casual ways of workers came in for limitation. In newly established "Fire Districts" no fires could be lighted except for essential needs between the months of April and November. New precautions were stipulated and new penalties imposed for the dropping of lighted cigars or burning matches, for discharging a weapon that might give off a spark or for running a locomotive with the usual belch of flame. In 1885 came a more effective step with the appointment of forest rangers. Thirty-three men, jointly paid by the government and the owners of timber tracts, were given control of the districts to see that rules were enforced.

The establishment of forest rangers was a preliminary to other measures that were to bear their fruit later. Up to 1890 operators reported to the government on the size of their annual cut and the values of wood sold. In that year, however, distrusting with some reason the statistics given by the trade, the Department of Crown Lands decided to inform itself. "Cullers'" courses were established in major lumbering centres to train estimators and assessors. Government licensed cullers, added to the forest rangers, became a knowledgeable and growing field staff in a matter of a few years. They were to be the nucleus of the Forest Rangers' School of the early 1900s, and provide knowledge and energy to promote reforestation. That work, however, by the end of the nineteenth century, was not much more than talk.

In 1888, at Georgetown, Ontario, there was a significant industrial marriage. The flow of the Credit River, passing over the turbines of a rudimentary generator, was transmitted as electrical energy to the plant of R.J. Barber, some two miles away. It was applied there, for the first time on the North American continent, to grinding pulp for paper. Water transformed to hydro-electric power had provided the tool for a major new industry.

Pulp had been replacing rags as an ingredient of paper-making from the early 1860s. Yet the process had remained difficult and the production very small. Spruce, balsam and tamarack, weeded out by the lumber camps from their cuts of better wood, had been sold to local mills. Hydraulic pressure in the mills, holding the stripped wood against the faces of revolving grindstones, had produced fibre at a great expense of water. The method was inefficient and strictly limited in scope. Only electric energy, transmitted from great streams could provide power on an economical basis. When that came, however, the other dynamic element in the continental economy arrived hard on its heels. American capital found its way to Ontario in the impressive person of Francis H. Clergue.

Born in Maine, Clergue was a lawyer, a promoter and a consulting engineer. He arrived at Sault Ste. Marie in 1890, on his way to Fort William where a hydro-electric power site had attracted some of his clients. At the "Soo," however, he stopped. There, at a narrow neck that was churned white by the rapids of the St. Mary's River, Lake Huron and Lake Superior were joined by an American canal. A Canadian canal was building, there was a link with the CPR and an international railway bridge crossed to the United States. The place bestrode the boundary as a nexus of transportation, and reaching north behind it lay the spruce forests of the Shield. There was, moreover, a power site in being, though somewhat the worse for wear. The "Soo's" city fathers, alive to its great potential, had begun a plant of their own. It was half-built and bankrupt, crushing the town with a burden of unpaid debt, and a caved-in section of river-bank had flooded most of the ruins. Yet water from Lake Superior, falling some nineteen feet, was still emptying itself into the St. Mary's rapids at a rate of 90,000 cubic feet per second. The engineer and promoter had seen enough. Acquiring the rights to the plant, to the vast relief of the town, he began negotiations with the provincial government.

The agreement came in 1892, the first of a long series in the disposal of Ontario's pulpwood. Again, as always in lumbering, only the wood was sold; land remained with the Crown. Clergue and his backers, who had already completed the power plant, received a twenty-one year licence to cut spruce, poplar, tamarack and jack pine at a rate of twenty cents per cord on any fifty square miles of territory "running back upon either side of one or more rivers flowing into Lake Superior and west of Sault Ste. Marie."[9] In return for that they were to spend at least $200,000.00 on a pulpwood mill to be completed before December, 1895, and employing not less than 300 men for ten months of the year. As usual in Clergue's case, he was better than his word. The mill began on schedule, twice its planned size, and by 1896 its average daily production was 150 tons. Surplus power from the plant was providing Sault Ste. Marie with light and water, and Clergue had only begun. A huge industrial complex, to be known by many names and to emerge as Algoma Steel, was just getting under way.

In the meantime to the south there had been sober second thoughts regarding the use of forest resources. The older timbering areas had been stripped of most of their pine, and some of the results were seen.

> The wholesale and indiscriminate slaughter of forests, (said the report of a Royal Commission in 1892,) brings a host of evils in its train . . . it turns plains into arid tracts, dries up springs and streams, denudes the soil and diverts life-growing rainfall into wasteful floods . . . the waste of one generation must be atoned for by the enforced economy of the next.[10]

There had been the same "merciless, ruthless and remorseless slaughter"[11] of game birds, animals and fish. For the coming generations, if old ways were continued, there would neither be forest wealth nor pleasure in forest life.

Arising from the bleak report came acts for the protection of game and an impetus toward reforestation. Both developed naturally into the concept of reserved areas maintaining the primal growth. In Nipissing district south of the Mattawa River there was a tract of virgin forest. Once part of the Algonquin tribal hunting grounds, it was about forty miles square, not suited to agriculture and not encumbered with settlers. It was a natural home for game and traversed by many rivers, several of which had their headwaters in the region. In 1893, recommended by a commission as the site for a forest reserve, Algonquin Park was established.

A year later, on Point aux Pins near the western end of Lake Erie, another and smaller tract came into being. Rondeau Park was less than 5,000 acres in area but it was a block of original forest and a favoured shelter for birds. Intended for summer holidays and as a place of recreation, it was to be another sample for Ontarians of an earlier and simpler life.

Preceding both these parks, and pregnant with more consequence, was the park at Niagara Falls. As a tourist attraction for the better part of a century, the whole region of the Falls by the middle 1880s had become a brash commercial fairground. The ideal of Mowat's government was to root out the commercialism, preserve the natural beauty and offer it as freely as possible for general public enjoyment. The park was a national treasure and would be so considered by Ontario if the national government was prepared to share the expense. Since the national government was not, an Ontario commission was appointed to see what the province could do. Sir Casimir Gzowski, the head of the commission, was a Polish-born nobleman who as engineer, railway builder and general entrepreneur had been a distinguished citizen of Canada for the previous forty years. By 1887 he had submitted his recommendations and legislation followed. Queen Victoria Niagara Falls Park was to be established and administered by a corporation with a fund of $525,000.00 raised by way of debentures which the province would guarantee. On May 24, 1888, the park was formally opened.

There had, however, been intervening developments. For one thing, the mere opening of the park had eaten up most of the fund and there was almost no money for continuing operations. For another, a large syndicate established across the river was preparing to use the American Falls for hydro-electric power. A third and linking factor was the prospect of American money for the impecunious Canadians if they were willing to lease their site. That hope, first dangled by a promoter in 1887, did not become a reality until 1892. In that year, however, with the approval of the provincial government, the commissioners of Queen Victoria Niagara Falls Park leased the exclusive right to produce power on the Canadian side of the river to the Canadian Niagara Power Company. It was a wholly owned subsidiary of the American group across from it, and would not produce power for a number of years. Meanwhile, with an annual rental of $25,000.00 and with the stipulation that all building by the Americans would conform to the beauties of the site, the Niagara Park was saved.

Power resources had been mortgaged but they remained the property of Ontario, by then a valued property. Between 1888 and 1890, as an almost casual afterthought to the work of a mining commission, the province had conducted an inventory of its lakes, rivers and streams. The resulting report had caught a glimpse of the future.

> The probability . . . is that in another ten years there will not be a village or even a homestead in the land that will not be in range of some one or other of Ontario's magnificent waterpowers. . . . It is thus a franchise in which the people at large, now and hundreds of years hence, are and will be deeply, nay, vitally interested. It is one, consequently, in which the rights of the Crown, or in other words of the people, are to be most jealously and carefully guarded.[12]

4.

The mining commission which had promoted the forest inventory and the altered view of waterpower was a prelude to other change. For a hundred years and more, silver, gold, iron and copper deposits had cropped up in the province and been worked with some success. That there was much more to be found was a matter of common acceptance, but the search for minerals was expensive, the returns all too rare, and the likeliest sites were far from roads or railways. The government approved of prospecting, but not as a public work involving public expense. The private man with his pick and the owner of private capital were left to develop the mines.

Since great risk was involved, encouragement had to be generous, a fact fully appreciated by Sandfield Macdonald's government. The prospector's licence required by the Mining Act of 1869 cost $5.00 and a proved claim could be purchased at the price of a dollar an acre. The land bought could be held in perpetuity, since it was agreed that practical necessity called for permanent tenure. Also the miner was absolved from royalties on the ore and minerals raised. Government was not in the mining business, it was in the business of promoting growth. Towns, trade, employment and the opening-up of the country would flow from successful ventures and provide the people's profit.

That kind of thinking prevailed generally in the province for the next fourteen years. In 1883, however, the tremors of change began. The line of the CPR, pushing west from Lake Nipissing in sticky August heat, had cut through the sprucewood forests and craggy folds of the Shield to a collection of huts and workshops that boasted the name of Sudbury. Three miles west of Sudbury, as the cutting moved ahead, a blacksmith working in the neighbourhood discovered some red-stained rock. It looked to him like copper, and there was enough confirming evidence to stir up local interest. By February of 1884 merchants, contractors and politicians of the area were stamping through woods and snowdrifts and acquiring blocks of land. Sold at a dollar an acre, usually in parcels of two or three hundred acres, it was little more than an intriguing speculation. Development required capital, and beyond the price of a claimsite there was none of that to be had.

A supply of capital soon appeared. S.J. Ritchie, a sharp Ohio industrialist with considerable funds in hand, was then building the Central Ontario railroad, which ran north from Trenton through the bog iron country around Marmora and Madoc. Its real functions for Ritchie were the acquisition of land grants and the search for mineral deposits, and with word of the copper finds both came to an end. He arrived in Sudbury in 1885 and was soon in touch with excited local speculators. Offering a generous profit on the prices paid for their claims, he acquired almost all of them for about $100,000.00.

By January 1886, Ritchie had completed arrangements with the Ontario government, secured additional capital from friends in the United States and organized the Canadian Copper Company with its head office in Cleveland. In May mining began. It would be some years yet before the full extent of the great find was known. The huge, oblong basin of copper-bearing ore, about thirty-eight miles long by seventeen miles wide, was covered with spruce and overburden in much of its eastern section. It would be revealed little by little as timber was cleared away and prospectors went to work. In the meantime, however, on the southwest rim where the first claims had been staked, the masses of reddish rock lay heaved up to the surface, hardly dusted with earth. There was no need to drill for ore; the machines and the pick and shovel men could simply scoop it out.

By the summer of 1886 the making and marring of Sudbury were both well under way. Most of the waste was removed from the quarried rock by hand sorting on long belts and tables. As sulphurous copper ore, it passed on to the roast yards for the removal of its sulphur content. Beds of spruce cordwood, cut from the surrounding forest, provided fire for the work. Glowing day and night under heaped-up tons of ore, they gradually ignited the sulphur and burned most of it away. Blast furnaces continued the process, melting off slag iron, and copper "matte" emerged as the finished product. Meanwhile the yellow fumes and the all-pervading stink went out over miles of the north country heralding the arrival of industrialization. The spruce trees cut for the fires came to the smelter already yellowed, vegetation withered over patches of open ground, the fish died in the rivers, and the bare rock pushed up. Sudbury's "lunar landscape" was in process of being born.

At the same time the birth pangs of a still greater development were felt. The first matte from Sudbury had been shipped to the Orford Copper Company, a large refinery in New Jersey, and the shipment had been refused. The ore was too hard; it contained an intrusive alloy. "Kupfer-Nickel" or "Old Nick's Copper" was known to the miners of Saxony as the devil's bewitched metal which defied ordinary working. It was not much better known to the whole civilized world, which produced a minuscule quantity that sold at a dollar a ton. To the resourceful Ritchie, however, the presence of nickel in his copper was the gate to opportunity.

New refining methods were being studied around the world, but it was Sudbury that impelled Orford to develop a new and highly valuable secret process. Of thousands of potential uses for a super-hard metal, there was one immediately at hand. The great powers were arming, battleships required armour, and the United States Navy was soon followed by others in creating a demand for nickel. By 1890, with a world market growing and prices steadily rising, Sudbury's ore production was 130,000 tons per year. The world's largest nickel producer and Canada's greatest mine had been sold at a dollar an acre. No royalties on all the ore produced came back to the province of Ontario.

That fact, by then, had come in for rueful notice. Yet the mining commission, reporting in 1890, was still disposed to accept it. The commissioners had travelled the province, convinced themselves that it had great wealth in minerals and recommended strongly that these be found, studied and used. They had many useful proposals for the general improvement of mining. Beyond that, however, at least in the commission's eyes, the old imperatives remained. Dollar-an-acre claims, land on permanent tenure and minerals free of royalties were conditions below the border. Ontario competed with Americans for the favour of the entrepreneurs, the high chivalry of commercialism, steeled to the great risks. If they were to be attracted north, and it was still felt that they must be, "a liberal policy must be followed; mining lands must not be less free here than in the United States."[13]

They were to become a little less free as different views developed.

T.B. Pardee, who had administered the Crown lands for fifteen years, died in 1889. Arthur Hardy succeeded him, and began some cautious changes. In 1891 the prices on sales of mining claims were increased and pro-rated according to the quality of the land. Speculation was checked by imposing forfeiture on undeveloped claims. More important still, against loud complaints from the mining industry, a royalty of 3 per cent was imposed on nickel, copper and silver ores, with a lesser rate on others. Yet a new mine, beginning to develop production, was to be exempt from royalties for a period of seven years, and there was an ingenious Canadian compromise on the acquisition of claims. Instead of outright purchase one could have a two-year option to buy, followed by a ten-year rental period. The option would cost the usual dollar an acre, the rent would be progressively reduced during the ten years of development, and the successful miner would have the title to his land.

In future, said Arthur Hardy, "the government shall not too readily part with the ownership of their public lands without receiving some adequate consideration for the general uses of the Province."[14] The Americans, he said,

> have given away their public lands, their pine timber; they have practically given away the richest coal mines known to exist in the world. They have given away their gold and silver mines, yielding to individuals wealth which the fables of the past do not approximate. We may well consider whether that is a system to be followed by a people having large mining interests still in their infancy.[15]

The consideration he spoke of was little enough in proportion to the prizes offered, and would be less so in future. There was no recovering the lost royalties of Sudbury, and that would be a sore for years. Yet a first step had been taken on a long and twisting road, and the work done by the mining commission was not without effect. The Bureau of Mines was established in 1892. The Kingston School of Mines, later affiliated with Queen's, came into being in 1893. In 1894 the government invested in diamond drills, one for the Bureau of Mines in its work of exploration and one to be rented by prospectors who could not afford their own. By 1895, in four special summer schools at Sudbury, Sault Ste. Marie, Port Arthur and Rat Portage, which was later to become Kenora, young miners and prospectors were receiving technical training.

Present needs were insistent but there could be some thought for the future. The discovery and opening of mines was a matter of great risk, of great expenditures of money and of new means and technologies which Americans largely controlled. All were still essential in the view of the government of the day. Americans must be encouraged to come but they should be persuaded to share returns, while Ontario went on to equip herself as the eventual senior partner. Canadian capital was sluggish, knowledge and skills were lacking and the industry still in infancy must be given the tools of growth. In that work at last the passive, paternal province was assuming an active role.

5.

Manufacturing and commerce, the children of the primary industries, grew up with them on the frame of transportation. It was a broad frame when the Mowat regime began, and in some of the central regions already overbuilt. Land grants and provincial and municipal subsidies had encouraged private builders since the early 1850s. Sandfield Macdonald's railway fund had been increased and supplemented by Blake. It was to be further supplemented by Mowat, particularly in the case of colonization railways. Yet before that, after twenty years of hasty and sprawling growth, came the solution of a major problem.

In 1873, though the provincial treasury was almost embarrassingly full, the municipalities were in trouble. For the past two decades, borrowing from a Municipal Loan Fund intended for local improvements, they had spent too much on railways. Their combined debt and interest burden was over $12,000,000.00, and it had left some of them strapped. A good many, including the city of Hamilton, had passed through the ordeal of bankruptcy and repudiation and were practically without credit.

Mowat's answer was to adjust the Municipal Loan Fund on a broad and generous basis. Out of the provincial surplus each city, town, county and district of Ontario was allotted an amount equivalent to $2.00 per head of its population. To municipalities which were not in debt the sum was a free grant, to be applied on existing loans, with the surplus funds, if any, also reserved for improvements. If the grant was insufficient to repay a loan in full, a municipality could issue debentures for the balance, repayable in twenty years. The debentures, however, were not to be held by the province but by the debt-free beneficiaries as part payment of their grants.

In all, some $3,300,000.00 was distributed throughout the province, including the new Districts of Algoma, Muskoka, Manitoulin, Parry Sound and Nipissing. The adjustment of the Municipal Loan Fund was an effective Mowat reform, providing not only relief but a new release of energy. The roads, bridges, harbours, town halls, schools and hospitals that had been lacking for many years could once again be thought of. Sidewalks, waterworks and fire-engines, parks, paving and playgrounds became immediate possibilities. Above all, with the support of later measures and the growth of local initiative, judicious subsidies to railways and encouragement of local industries could expand provincial trade.

From 1876, when the completed Intercolonial supplemented water transport, there was an increasing flow to the east. In the maritime provinces, England and other countries of Europe, Ontario farm implements were displacing those of the Americans. Sewing machines, stoves and other well-made products of the small provincial factories were meeting with the same success. Generally, however, the 1870s were lean years, with Ontario manufacturing dwarfed in the American shadow.

With the coming of the National Policy in 1879 there was a lively surge of growth. The completion of the CPR in 1885 extended the movement westward. Ontario factories that had built up eastern markets with the help of protective tariffs turned to a newer market in Manitoba. Ontario tools, implements, building supplies and lumber went out to equip the homesteads. Boots, shoes, textiles and a flood of household goods followed to supply the owners. From there they had gone on, along the extending axis sheltered by its wall of tariffs, to the prairies and the Pacific coast.

A reaction came in the late 1880s, as the National Policy began to lose its magic. The protection of home industry and the east-west flow of trade had been achieved at high cost. An aggressive United States, determined to force the continent into its own pattern of trade, was responding to high tariffs by higher tariffs of its own. Not only Ontario's factory products but its grain, cheese and dairy products were almost wholly barred from the American market. At the same time the Ontario consumer suffered. The protected manufacturer, whose high costs in Canada were reflected in higher prices, controlled the domestic market.

By the early 1890s the alternative to the National Policy had become the cry for Commercial Union, with all tariffs abolished between Canada and the United States. Mowat damped it down and the assenting province silenced it because the cry of the blood was stronger. Commercial Union with the Americans was an all-too-likely step in the direction of political union; and Ontario was to remain British. At the same time a massive shift of markets was taking place. The flow of agricultural produce, dammed up by prohibitive American tariffs, turned to the United Kingdom. By the end of the nineteenth century all but some 15 per cent of Ontario's export surplus was going to the British market. Prices remained low, however, and times hard for the farmer. They were hard, too, for the Ontario manufacturer but the east-west axis held, giving him the market stretched between the oceans. Assailed by the free traders, damning them and the Americans, he was still able to compete.

Too much Ontario timber still went to the Americans in the form of raw logs, and the same was true of pulpwood. Yet for all the continuing complaints, sawmills, planing and finishing mills increased in size and volume and hardware trades and building trades were growing up in proportion. Almost a hundred furniture factories used Ontario lumber, and about a third as many paper mills were using Ontario pulp. Carriages, wagons and bicycles, boots, shoes and clothing, complex new machinery and innumerable processed foods came out of the new factories or from old factories expanded. The tobacco habit alone supported some sixty plants, with expansion promised by the arriving cigarette. Goods passed from the hands of the manufacturer through an ever more complex network of jobbers, wholesalers and retailers to reach the ultimate consumer. Greatest of the beneficiaries of a high protective tariff, the limping trade in textiles became a major industry. By the middle 1880s new and well-equipped mills and dye houses were producing patterns and fabrics that rivalled the best imports in range, variety and colour. Ontario's plain "greys" had gone with the pioneers.

The iron industry suffered from a lack of primary resources. Ontario had no coal, the "bog iron" of Hastings county was poor and hard to mine, and great deposits in the wilderness still remained to be discovered. Coal could be drawn from the Maritimes by a long, expensive haul, but it was soft coal where anthracite was preferred. Dependent on Pennsylvania for most of its good coal and still turning to Michigan for its major supply of ore, the industry was one of the sufferers from protective tariffs. Nor had a system of federal bounties, supplemented by provincial bounties, brought much effective relief. The solution to the problem of iron awaited the discovery of better grades of ore, which was now not far in the future. Even then, however, a permanent feature of the business so far as Ontario was concerned, would be the province's lack of coal.

In manufacturing, wholesaling, and even the professional fields, rigorous competition and the quest for larger profits had induced the urge to combine. Stove makers and iron founders had had selling and pricing arrangements for a matter of twenty years. There had been a salt monopoly in Ontario since 1871, and however bitterly the railways fought they had set their rates in common. When the National Policy came, stimulating the protective impulse, there was wider recognition and a rapid realization of the strength of a common front. By the middle 1880s biscuit makers and confectioners, jewellers and wire and cordage makers, flour millers, oat millers, coal men, dairymen and makers of processed foods were all organized in tight industrial combines. Bankers, lawyers, doctors, dentists and insurance companies mobilized in separate groups. The wholesale Grocers Guild, with an iron hand and an eagle eye for price-cutting by jobber, wholesaler or retailer, controlled the distribution chain from the factory door to the consumer. It was said that the consumer's life, from Nestle's Food in infancy to the coffin whose price was set by the Dominion Burial Case Association, was in the hands of combinations of suppliers.[16]

Another effect of combines was a ruthless weeding-out of the weaker sisters. The consolidation of the textile industry on the whole Canadian scene was a prime example of the process. In Quebec, Ontario and the Maritimes, between 1879 and 1885, thirty-five cotton mills had proliferated with the National Policy to a total of fifty-four. A first move to combine, in 1886, had been broken up by the rivalries of older and smaller mills, lacking modern equipment and in savage competition with each other. Then the greater capitalists with the new mills and resources had acted with a strong hand. By the end of 1890 seventeen mills were left, and 70 per cent of their capacity was controlled by the largest two.

Toronto's industrial complex ran the whole gamut of production, from ships and marine engines through farm implements and rubber goods to pianos and silver plate. Spreading along the waterfront or pulling the city northward were food and allied industries for the needs and luxuries of the home. Seven lines of railway as well as the old waterways delivered the raw materials and fed the produce out. The timber trade that had once come to Toronto passed above it in the north, east by the CPR and west from the Huron watershed by way of the Great Lakes. Cattle had come to replace it as the trade in livestock grew; great, bawling transit yards crowded with beasts for export were clustered along the bay. Based on a wealth of old resources, opening the north and west and developing world markets, Toronto was unassailable in its standing as Queen City.

Hamilton, the burly rival, was as hard and muscular as Toronto and had managed to retain its looks.

Of all the places we had visited during our trip to the American continent, (an English visitor wrote,) the prettiest, cleanest, healthiest and best conducted was the city of Hamilton, Canada. (With) vast and varied manufacturing industries. . . 170 factories . . . 14,000 artisans, large capital invested and an immense output annually, (it was) well named the Birmingham of Canada.[17]

London, in the heart of the westland, was growing on the trade and industry that agriculture had brought. It had been ahead even of Toronto in its use of electric power developed by steam generators, and its street lights and tram cars were familiar features of the city. Yet the effects of change were round it. Homes, shops and factories, as they pushed out to the eastward expanding the city limits, were absorbing deserted farms and half-deserted villages. The wheat had ceased to grow, the sons had gone away, and there were still areas where nothing replaced them. Outlying North London, in the early 1890s was a desolation of decayed and empty farmhouses where stray cows and chickens nibbled among the weeds.

Through almost twenty-five years, in spite of provincial surpluses and the effects of the National Policy, times had been described as hard. They had been hard for many, but Ontario had pushed through them to the verge of the industrial age. She was not yet quite into it by the middle 1890s, nor as yet fully adapted. The declining farms complained of the growing cities and of the demands made by the sub-structure developing to support industry. Industry was as slow to civilize as the pioneers before it, with its sweated children in the factories, its distrust and fear of labour unions and its urge to combine and grab. Yet there were already salutary reactions and much to show for the work, good, bad and indifferent.

In the ornately panelled offices of a few modern executives the first typists in shirtwaists with their skirts sweeping the floors pecked at cumbersome machines. Slim telephone directories sat on many desks, and Hamilton, Toronto, Montreal and Ottawa were linked by long-distance. Gaunt poles of pine, disfiguring the city streets, carried wire for the telephones and the trams and electric lights. There were 'phones and electric lights in many of the private homes. Ontario had its parks, its new pulpwood industry, its hydro-electric power. Life was vastly changed, becoming in some ways better, and men and political forces were also changing with it. In 1896, during the course of the federal election, the redoubtable Sir Charles Tupper came to visit Berlin, the one-time sleepy hamlet settled by German farmers. As knowledgeable a politician as ever counted a vote, he was met by a parade of sixty men from a furniture factory, forty from a shirt and collar company, sixty from a felting company, twenty from a piano and organ factory and two hundred and forty others from assorted industries of the town.[18] He could hardly have had a doubt, as he beamed and waved from the platform, that the old Ontario of the farmlands was entering a new day.

Notes

1. George William Ross, *Getting Into Parliament and After* (Toronto: Wm. Briggs, 1913), pp. 190-192.
2. John Willison, *Reminiscences Political and Personal* (Toronto: McClelland and Stewart Limited, 1919), p. 103.
3. Evans, *Oliver Mowat and Ontario*, p. 14.
4. L. A. Wood, *A History of Farmers' Movements in Canada* (Toronto: Ryerson, 1924), p. 28.
5. Evans, *Oliver Mowat and Ontario*, p. 437.
6. O. D. Skelton, *General Economic History, 1867-1912,* in *Canada and Its Provinces,* (Toronto: Edinburgh University Press for the Publishers' Association of Canada, 1913), Vol. IX, p. 124n.
7. Jacob Spelt, *Urban South-Central Ontario,* (Amsterdam: Van Gorkum), taken from report quoted by G. P. de T. Glazebrook, in *A History of Transportation* (Toronto: Carleton Library, McClelland and Stewart: Greenwood, 1938).
8. H. V. Nelles, *The Politics of Development* (Toronto: Macmillan of Canada, 1974), p. 18.
9. *Ibid.* Also Margaret van Every, "Francis Hector Clergue and the Rise of Sault Ste. Marie as an Industrial Centre," *Ontario History*, Vol. 56, 1965, pp. 191-202.
10. Richard S. Lambert with Paul Pross, *Renewing Nature's Wealth* (Ontario: Queen's Printer, 1967), pp. 169-170.
11. Evans, *Oliver Mowat and Ontario*, pp. 465-466.
12. Nelles, *Politics of Development*, pp. 36-37.
13. *Ibid.*, p. 27.
14. *Ibid.*, p. 28.
15. *Ibid.*, p. 29.
16. Michael Bliss, *A Living Profit* (Toronto: McClelland and Stewart Limited, 1974), p. 40.
17. C. M. Johnston, *The Head of the Lake* (Hamilton: Wentworth County Council, 1958), p. 239.
18. P. B. Waite, *Arduous Destiny, Canada 1874-1896* (Toronto: McClelland and Stewart Limited, 1971), p. 273.

Chapter Five

Growth and Life

1.

When Mowat came to power in 1872 the bases of education had been firmly laid by Ryerson. Yet a first problem was the position of the man himself. An entrenched and aging autocrat, now entering his seventies, he was personally friendly to Mowat. His Council of Public Instruction was, however, an almost parallel authority to the provincial government and opposed many of its views. Little by little Ryerson's powers were diminished, and the end came with a gracious abdication. In 1876, at Ryerson's own request, the Council of Public Instruction gave way to a new department. Adam Crooks became the first Minister of Education. Provincial authority, direct and undiluted, was to bring the schools of the province "into harmony with the spirit of the times."[1]

Out of that spirit came a series of new departures. That same year, with encouragement from Crooks' ministry, the Ontario School of Art came into being. Two years later came the School of Practical Science, in close relation to the University of Toronto. It was an improved supplement to Ryerson's technical college, with courses in mining and mechanics, university lectures in chemistry and engineering and evening classes for tradesmen. Neither the advance in the arts, however, nor the advance in practical science, commanded wide support. Ontario, with its lower schools, considered its first wants cared for and often groaned at the cost. It was apathetic and penny-pinching even in the case of high schools and more so in the matter of extended learning. The new leaders, no less than Ryerson before them, had to cope with that fact.

One major problem was the training and supply of teachers. The two provincial Normal Schools could not keep up with demand, and the government recoiled from the cost of building more. It had to

73

think, too, of the expanding population, which was widening out with settlement to the new north and the west. No centralized establishment serving a single region would be in line with present needs. What was required was dissemination, accessibility and haste, and the answer came in 1877. It took the form of a system of Model Schools, small, widely-distributed and drawing teacher-candidates from areas near at hand. For all candidates there were to be thirteen weeks of training, with travelling expenses and part of maintenance provided; and graduates would leave as elementary teachers. Their Third Class Certificates would be a grade lower in standing than those of the Normal Schools, but they would be equipped to begin their work.

By 1878 there were fifty Model Schools operating in the province, with almost 1,400 teachers in training. Most candidates were successful, supply problems were eased, and Third Class Certificates became familiar in provincial schools. They became too familiar as the years passed and multiplied them, since for many holders they signified the end of training. Poorly qualified, badly-paid instructors remained as an enduring weakness in the elementary system. Hired cheaply by impecunious school boards, they reduced the level of salaries, delayed the advancement of standards and discouraged ambition in better qualified teachers. Yet particularly in newer districts there would have been no teaching at all if there had not been Model Schools. They were a necessary fact of life in nineteenth century Ontario, and a few were still in existence as the century came to an end.

With the early 1880s the old Mechanics' Institutes, the working men's libraries, came in for expansive change. Government, building on them, and supplying additional grants, encouraged municipalities to establish public libraries. Open and free to all, they were to have an additional function as places for resuming study. Libraries conducting evening classes for those who had left school were provided with special grants.

The step toward better programs for the education of the adult was accompanied by new development at the other end of the scale. The pre-school child, beginning to figure in the minds of modern thinkers, interested James L. Hughes, the Inspector of Toronto schools. Closely in touch with Crooks, he was a persistent voice for reform, and he was allotted funds for travel. In 1882 he returned from St. Louis, Missouri, alight with a new idea that blossomed the next year. As Crooks, threatened with a breakdown, was preparing for his own retirement, the first public kindergarten, and the second of its kind on the continent, was added to Toronto's schools.

George William Ross, fresh from the federal parliament and new to the provincial legislature, succeeded Crooks as Minister in 1883.

A teacher, a sometime-journalist and later inspector of schools, he was forty-three by then, bearded and black-haired, of Middlesex county parents and hardy Protestant stock. He was to grow grey and grizzled through the storms of the years ahead, but his liking for the deft phrase and his love of the good book would be unimpaired to the end. A fine speaker when he chose to be, always devastating in debate, he was a cool political realist and a lifetime advocate of temperance with a wit as dry as his taste. He knew the workings of the school system and was aware of its faults and needs. He was also aware of the ways of a cranky public and of the bounds set by the possible. Oliver Mowat, as usual, had chosen his man well.

Ross gave steady encouragement to the projects inherited from Crooks. By 1896, in place of the ninety-three Mechanics' Institutes existing when he took office, there were 356 free libraries. There were ninety-five kindergartens, which by 1900 had increased to 120, serving 11,000 children. Beyond that, meanwhile, in every area of the pattern of education Ross's hand was felt.

He moved steadily, often against much resistance, to raise standards, increase grants and improve methods in finance and administration. A new order of efficiency was enforced on local school boards. School holidays were set and bare schoolgrounds beautified by a generous planting of trees. A miscellany of old textbooks, largely British or American, was replaced by a new and "purely Canadian" series. In many localities not served by high schools a system of "continuation classes" was instituted. The student leaving lower school could take about half of his matriculation requirements without the expense of leaving home.

At the highest level, in 1891, a School of Pedagogy was established in Toronto for the advanced training of inspectors and the masters of the higher schools. In the same year, buttressing the base of the system, compulsory education became more widely extended. It was to be applied by a new law to all children between the ages of eight and fourteen, and cities, towns and incorporated villages were required to appoint truant officers to see that the law was enforced. There had to be exemptions, however, compelled by the needs of the farm and the thought of the farmer's vote. Rural municipalities, though they were given authority to make the same appointments, would not be required to do so for another twenty-eight years.

Through a long period of bitterly-fought politics Ontario led the Dominion in its work for education and was well abreast of the level in the United States. The World's Columbian Exposition held in Chicago in 1893 brought out a resounding tribute. The province, winning twenty-one prizes for its educational exhibits, was given a special award "for a system of public instruction almost ideal in the perfection of its details and the unity which binds together in one great whole all the schools from the kindergarten to the University."[2]

In reality the system had many practical flaws. Particularly at its upper level, it was far from generally accepted. By 1896, 25,000 students were enrolled in high schools, where there had been fewer than 8,000 in 1872. Over 500 students a year, as compared to the less than sixty in 1867, were matriculating to the university. This increase was large proportionately but it was pitifully small in relation to population. Too much of Ontario was still content with the bare rudiments of learning.

These were not as good or as much in demand as the leaders liked to proclaim. Ross's School of Pedagogy was denounced as "frills and furbelows" by many knowledgeable men. Third Class Certificates and meagre qualifications continued to be the plague of the lower system. The salaries of all teachers were still wretchedly low, with $421.00 as the annual average for men and $296.00 as the "beggarly pittance" for women. Attendance in the lower schools, no less than the quality of teaching, remained a nagging problem. In 1885, faced with the fact that 88,000 children did not complete the two set terms of fifty-five days each per year, Ross reduced requirements to a total of a hundred days. Improvement still dragged, there was still wide indifference, and even the compulsory measure of 1891 resulted from mixed motives. Labour groups in the cities, where adult jobs were threatened, had created much of the pressure for keeping children in school. Social leaders, also, were as much concerned with juvenile criminality as with juvenile education. They were a little afraid, in fact, of "over-education." The streets must be kept orderly but the masses must not be spoiled.

The school system, said Ross, echoing the praise of the Columbian Exposition, was "a unit from the kindergarten to the university." Yet if it led to the university it was inclined to stop at the door, with women grudgingly admitted. It was 1880 before women were accepted as medical students and 1884 before they could train in law.

In 1887, to meet the growing needs of the church-related colleges, an act was passed enabling their federation with the University of Toronto. Queen's held aloof and so did Baptist McMaster, but Wycliffe, Knox, Victoria and later St. Michael's became part of the larger body. The great fire of 1890 that gutted University College and destroyed many of its treasures forced reorganization along with much rebuilding. But there were problems of structure and status and larger problems of finance with which Mowat's government was not prepared to deal. It remained wary of the views of a rural constituency and of a newer labour constituency growing in the towns and cities. To these groups, who were cool enough toward the thought of supporting high schools, the university was still for the rich man's son. The rich man himself was often inclined to concur. The system of education might appear to be homogeneous, but Ontario itself was not.

2.

Always centred on the schools, though it complicated many questions, was the vexed relationship of Protestant and Roman Catholic. It infected politics, distorted the work of leadership and was as much a bane to the best elements of Conservatism as it was to Mowat's Liberals. The leader of the opposition William Ralph Meredith, a London lawyer and a broad-minded Anglican, had none of the qualities of the bigot. Yet he was driven by party pressures and by ranting in some of the press toward views he did not like and positions he could not hold. Mowat, faced with the same pressures, managed to reduce them a little without reducing himself.

During Crooks' time as Minister of Education there was not much serious discord between Protestant and Catholic factions. On both sides resentments simmered occasionally over the support of separate schools or the lack of Catholic high schools. Mowat as a Presbyterian and an oldtime Protestant Grit had his peace to make with Irish Catholic conservatism. He was frequently assailed by Protestants for his friendly relations with the Roman Catholic hierarchy, but it was not until the 1880s and the time of George Ross that serious trouble began.

The school reforms and the improvements in administration brought their own difficulties. "The separate schools," said Mowat, "are a fact in our constitution, and we have to accept it whether we like it or not."[3] Ross was of the same view; the separate schools should be administered and provided with grants and amenities as part of the common system. He was also prepared, as a mitigation of separateness, to allow the appointment of one Catholic each to the boards of public high schools.

The Catholic schools, however, were institutions apart; and they were so by their own choice, preserving their own differences. The nun or brother of a Catholic teaching order was assumed to be qualified by his own vocational training. Unlike the lay teacher, he had no tests to pass, no certificate to present. The boards of Protestant schools were elected by secret ballot, while the open election of Catholic boards, in the view of hostile critics, was subject all too often to the influence of the parish priest. The same influence, it was said, operating on municipal clerks, could sometimes weight the tax rolls in favour of separate schools. Catholics in some communities

77

preferred a public school, considering its standards higher, but they were assessed and taxed, it was claimed, with or without their knowledge, as separate school supporters. Finally the appointment of Catholics to the boards of public high schools came in for new attack. Why this special privilege for the Roman Catholic alone, this singling-out from other denominations? Why all these differences, these complex private procedures, these irritations and excrescences on the general body of the system?

On the other hand, in the view of the Catholic hierarchy, justice was still withheld. The Catholic student in Ontario should have the same privileges as the Protestant student in Quebec. As an ultimate goal he should have high schools, colleges and Normal Schools comprising a separate system. That system, moreover, supported by additional taxing powers and supplied with new facilities, should be administered by a Catholic deputy in the Ministry of Education.

It was an impossible goal in Ontario, overwhelmingly Protestant and equally devoted to non-sectarian schools. Archbishop John Joseph Lynch of Toronto, the senior Ontario prelate, was a personal friend of Mowat and on excellent terms with Ross, but he was aware of realities. The three men, notorious as the "Concordat" in the columns of the hostile press, manoeuvred on narrow ground. The Archbishop might ask and the government would grant what it could, within the bounds of the present system. There was a new, if measured, welcome for Catholics in the public service. There was accommodation in the matter of local school boards and local assessment procedures, but there was no essential change. To the request for a Catholic deputy to the Minister of Education the answer was a gentle "no," but an additional Catholic inspector was allotted to separate schools. Division could not be widened but efficiency might be improved.

Upon all this, and beginning innocently enough, came the storm of the "Ross Bible." In 1882 the Anglican, Methodist, and Presbyterian churches, supported by Protestant teachers, had requested that prayers and scriptural readings be made obligatory in the schools. Ross had complied in part with a collection of scriptural texts, approved by Protestant churchmen. The work was to be used in the public schools of the province, but there was no compulsion to do so. Teachers were permitted to refrain on conscientious grounds and children whose parents objected could be excused during the readings. Protestant leaders had agreed to this since 50,000 of Ontario's Catholic children were in the public schools or high schools. For the same reason, and again with Protestant assent, Archbishop Lynch had approved the texts and suggested minor changes.

In 1884, however, when the book went out to the schools, the well-intentioned work of the leaders ignited the grass roots. Protestants stormed at the provisions that exempted students and teachers, while Catholic bishops not as tolerant as Lynch thundered at "penal laws." Zealots found that their favourite texts were lacking and to the Tory Toronto *Mail*, at the head of irate thousands, the influence of the Catholic Archbishop was apparent on every page. Protestants intended to have, said one school trustee, "the whole damned Bible or nothing."⁴ Amid the bitterest controversy that had troubled the province for years, the Ross Bible was withdrawn.

By 1888 the Jesuits' Estates quarrel, a purely Quebec issue expanded to federal dimensions, had washed over to Ontario. To rancorous and aroused Protestantism, the French province and the Vatican had distributed the lands of the Order; Popery was invading Canada. In 1889 came the mobilization of the Equal Rights Association, with much laudable rhetoric and one essential purpose: "to eliminate the shameless traffic with the Roman Catholic Church."⁵ By 1892, as Quebec ultramontanism delivered its answer to that, a new movement had crossed from the United States. The Protestant Protective Association was soon a network of lodges, a threat to many Liberals, and becoming in spite of Meredith a wing of the Conservative party. "What we want," said one of the spokesmen, "is to meet the solid Catholic vote with a solid Protestant vote."⁶ With this firm ideal of sectarian political warfare went an equally firm platform. The goals proclaimed by the movement were to exclude Roman Catholics not only from public office but from all employment by Protestants, to boycott Catholic business, to tax church property, to force the secret ballot and rigorous government inspection on all separate school boards, and finally and most importantly to abolish the schools themselves.

The movement was the more dangerous because of another problem. The use of the French language, always linked with religion, was becoming a rising issue in the eastern part of the province. Here, close to Quebec, and particularly in Russell and Prescott counties facing along the Ottawa, the population was more French than English. Separate schools predominated, instruction was largely in French, and it was given by members of Catholic teaching orders usually educated in Quebec. It was English-speaking Catholics, for the most part Irish here, who were concerned about their children in school districts in which French members were beginning to predominate. They were being taught exclusively in French, usually from French textbooks, and not infrequently by teachers who had little English themselves.

As complaints reached the press and began to emerge in politics, Ross had produced some hasty measures of reform. Bilingual textbooks were tried in the schools, teachers were subjected to tests to determine their proficiency in English and courses in Model Schools were provided for those who failed. None of the measures met with much enthusiasm and change was slow to come. The French and Catholic aura, supported by priests and teachers, remained a prevailing fact. Only some sixty schools were actually involved, and the number was being reduced by the 1890s. The pace could not be forced, for children of either language were entitled to consideration. Yet patience and caution, the necessary ingredients of the process, were not easy to defend. There was no law protecting the French language as there was for separate schools. There was no excuse for delay in the imposition of English, except for hope in the province and the rationality of its mood.

In Mowat's last election, in 1894, the mood seemed to prevail. The Patrons of Industry, embodying farm protest, achieved significant standing as a new political party. The Protestant Protective Association, as a vehicle of religious discord, did little to help and much to weaken the Conservatives. Within three years it had faded from the political scene. Mowat with a few Patrons as early "liberals in a hurry" came back to govern again. He was to leave in two years with purely religious bigotry a lessening force in the province and the question of schools and languages threatening a major quarrel. For that trial, however, Ontario was content to wait.

Nor for all the bristling Britishness of some of its louder press was it wholly of one mind. "It would be a proud thing for Ontario," C.F. Fraser said, "if the educational system was equal to producing a generation that could speak not only English but also French and German."[7] As a Roman Catholic and a cabinet minister his views were perhaps suspect, but he did not hold them alone. *The Week* of Toronto spoke up for the compulsory teaching of the French language in all Ontario schools. *The Globe* at least concurred in the possibility. Mowat himself, in one casual aside, gave vent to a mild endorsement. "No one is the worse," he reflected, "for knowing two languages."[8]

3.

In a cabinet noted for its teetotalling Premier and its equally dry George Ross, Arthur Sturgis Hardy provided welcome relief. He was a Brantford lawyer with a hot and ready temper, a sense of humour on his good days in the House, and one of the thunderous voices for which Brant county was famous. To "Orlando Q. Guffy MPP." the fictitious legislator who wrote a column for *Grip*, Hardy was a friend to be relied on for the drop of comfort and support.

The Ontario government, as Guffy saw it,

seems to run a good deal on the principle of the ancient Persian mythology, in which the powers of good and evil personified by Ormuzd and Adrimanes, though in continual conflict, maintained an equilibrium. The representatives of these forces in the provincial microcosm are, of course, the truly good Premier and his abandoned colleague, Arthur S. Hardy.

Particularly when the temperance issue raised its head bringing in deputations of determined women, Hardy's role was to act

as the wicked partner which prevents the good and liberal-minded Mowat from carrying out reforms he has set his heart on, so it ain't to be wondered at if he has to brace up occasionally. The more wickeder he is, playing euchre and swearing and entertaining thirsty strangers, the brighter does the virtue of Mowat shine by contrast.[9]

When the new parliament buildings were opened in Queen's Park they were generally described as "imposing." They were, however, well away from the taverns and only imposing to Hardy, according to Guffy's report, because

it's imposing on human nature to suppose that us fellows can stay around here from three p.m. till all hours without a snifter . . . I ain't going to reveal no cabinet secrets, but I don't believe there's many better judges of liquor than Hardy.[10]

For all that, Hardy as Provincial Secretary for over twelve years was a leading figure in the government's work of reform. It was cautious work, always advancing slowly and with much reconnaissance ahead. The many Royal Commissions and committees of investigation were often attacked as means for evasion and delay. If they were that, as they certainly were in some fields, they were also made to serve their ostensible purpose. In its shifts of population from the farms to cities, in its social life and industrial life, its labour relations and family relations, Ontario was a changing province. It had new needs, the needs required to be investigated, and in most cases the information was used.

The expenditure of public money on the unfit and helpless was still grudged and resisted. For the *Globe* of the 1870s it was "true mercy to say that it would be better for a few individuals to die of starvation than that a pauper class should be raised up with thousands devoted to crime and the victims of misery."[11] Yet in spite of that, under Sandfield Macdonald and Blake, some money had been spent and some attitudes changed. A momentum had been created in the matter of social welfare, and it was not opposed by the official opposition. Meredith, in fact, on most social questions was a spur, rather than a brake. "Though a Conservative," Ross said of him, "he was more radical than the leader of the government."[12]

The ministry of Mowat, particularly in its early years, gave grounds for radical criticism. It encouraged private charities, improved some asylums and reformatories and reorganized the system providing grants to hospitals. Beyond that, however, it legislated good intentions it was not prepared to enforce. The Industrial Schools Act of 1874 was intended to provide homes and trades for orphaned, abandoned or otherwise destitute children under the age of fourteen. Yet the authority to establish the homes, which was conferred on city school boards, did not include compulsion, was not accompanied by an adequate system of funding and required much more in the way of staff and facilities than municipalities could supply. For ten years the act lingered on the statute books as a pious dead letter.

In 1884, however, the government shifted the burden. School boards were enabled to delegate their "rights, powers and privileges" to any incorporated philanthropic society. By 1893, out of private charity and with some help from government, two schools had resulted; the Victoria Industrial School for boys and the Alexandria Industrial School for girls, both in Toronto. They were good as far as they went, and influential in much later development, but they were far from the first ideal. Planned as "cottage" schools where children might live and learn in a home atmosphere, they were always overcrowded, undersupplied with teachers and lacking much equipment. The young inmates, jammed fifty to a cottage and under rigorous discipline, acquired some rudiments of training but hardly an education.

There were the same shortcomings in other of the planned good works. Through the middle 1870s jails continued to be bad, penal administration inclined to its old ways, and asylums insufficient in means and treatment. At the same time, however, devoted men supported by a few enactments, were achieving some results. In 1876, under Doctor A. H. Beaton, the asylum for "idiots" at Orillia was enlarged in size and radically improved in methods. Beaton studied the distinctions between forms of mental illness, separated the retarded child from the adult patient, and provided training for inmates according to their capabilities. By 1881 the rate of released and presumably recovered patients had increased by nearly a third. Through the next seven years there was growing American interest in the work of the Ontario doctor; and in June of 1888, when Beaton opened a training school for feeble-minded children, colleagues from the United States were assembled at Orillia in convention. The school itself, the first of its kind in Canada, was to have its difficult times, but it remained a force in the study of mental health.

John Langmuir, always pushing legislators and never content with results, could concede a measure of progress by 1881. Prisons were cleaner and better, and reformatories more humane. The right of women to be legal guardians of their children had been recognized. The drunken brute familiar to the lower law courts was no longer absolute master of his abandoned wife and home. He could be disqualified as the guardian but made to pay support, and he could be sent to jail if he defaulted. For most of those in jail there was better, more useful work, and more was done to keep the miserable out of the prisons. Ontario, Langmuir claimed, had "one of the most complete charitable and correctional systems on the continent."[13] Yet the words, if true comparatively, were far from a complete endorsement, nor did Langmuir so intend them. Almost a decade later, and close to the end of his career, he would still be at war with the nineteenth century conscience.

With him was J. J. Kelso, a Toronto journalist devoted to child welfare, whose work culminated in 1891 with the establishment of the Children's Aid Society of Toronto. It was given muscle and a degree of official standing by the Children's Protection Act, a first step in bringing provincial supervision and municipal contributions to the aid of private charity. In all fields, however, there was a great deal more to be done and many of the needs were linked. Mowat, in 1888, appointed a Royal Commission headed by John Langmuir to investigate the prison and reformatory system of the province. After two years of work the Commission came back with rather more than it was sent for. "All this system of dealing with criminals and offenders," said the report of 1890, "rests upon the exploded principle that crime can be prevented and criminals kept in check only by deterrent agencies."[14] It was not so, and it never had been so. Poverty, vagrancy, alcoholism, the emptying farms in the country, the new slums in the cities and thousands of children still ignored or neglected must all be dealt with too.

The report was a huge foreshadowing of the needs of the twentieth century. It had accomplished something by 1893 with the establishment of foster homes and the appointment of J.J. Kelso as Superintendent of Neglected and Dependent Children. A greater change, however, was in the matter of fiscal policy and that had been made a year earlier. For the first time, with the imposition of succession duties, the province accepted a measure of direct taxation. The tax was moderate and not required as revenue; it was to provide funds for schools, hospitals and asylums. It was hardly opposed at all for there were by then similar novelties in Great Britain and the United States, and succession duties affected few but the rich. All that, however, would be changed in due time. The pocket of the private citizen, once opened in the cause of social advancement, was not to be closed again.

4.

In 1872, with Blake as Premier of the province and George Brown a power in the Liberal party, a strike by the Toronto Typographical Union had precipitated confrontation with an arm of the working class. Brown, as proprietor of the *Globe,* had fought to the last ditch against demands for improved wages and a reduction of the working day from ten hours to nine. When the issues were brought to court a Toronto magistrate had found the strike to be an "indictable conspiracy" and the unions themselves to be "illegal combinations" in restraint of trade.[15] Neither the later settlement of the strike nor the removal of the stigma on unions by a Conservative federal government had helped provincial Liberals. Blake departed the scene, Brown died later, shot by an aggrieved printer, and Mowat came to office tarred with the earlier record. If he was to hope for the support of any section of labour he must act to repair the damage. With that thought, and with evidence enough about him of injustice and exploitation, he moved in his first session.

He met some immediate needs with three acts, pious and largely toothless. The Mechanics' Lien Act, designed for the worker who could not collect his wages, was to provide a legal weapon to enforce payment. It could be used against an employer, without recourse to the long procedure of lawsuits, for any claim that exceeded $50.00. Yet the minimum was too high, the procedures were still cumbrous, and defaulting employers soon discovered loopholes. For the most part labour was unimpressed.

The Trades Arbitration Act for the settlement of industrial disputes was as high-minded and empty. Employer and employees, with an arbitrator presiding, were enabled to discuss their differences. But they were not compelled to decide anything, and one subject was excluded. The right to determine wages, like the sacred rights of property in mid-Victorian Ontario, remained vested in the employer. So also did profit sharing, as the theme of the third act. Under its terms any company and its labour force were free to establish a system for the joint sharing of profits, but the employer kept the books and set the allotment of shares.

For all their ineffectiveness the acts were statements of intentions. They were slow in realization because Ontario was slow in chang-

84

ing, with the heartbeat of its economy still centred in the farms. Industrialization was growing but labour strength was not; the Toronto Typographical Union, as a local of one of the strongest American unions, was an exception not only on the provincial but on the whole national scene. To the politician of the middle and later 1870s the decline of agricultural strength was almost imperceptible, while labour seemed to be a confused, diminishing voice. The Canadian Labour Union, formed in Toronto in 1873, was disbanded two years later. Its thirty-one component unions withered without support. The working man's importance and the organization of labour awaited aggressive progress and the need for hands and skills.

That began for Ontario after 1879, with the bustle of plants and factories encouraged by the National Policy. By 1881, with labour in greater demand, it was assembling in new groups. The Knights of Labour, established in Philadelphia, became a feature of the Canadian scene. Almost a million strong in the United States, they were the great idealists of the movement with their goal the brotherhood of man. Bankers, lawyers and saloon keepers were not received in their ranks, but beyond that they made no distinction of trades. Spreading out from Hamilton through the industrial centres of the province, they had become a force in Ontario by 1883.

At the same time the more orthodox forms of trade unionism that were eventually to take over had begun to regain strength. In December of 1883, twenty-one unions with eight regional assemblies of the Knights of Labour held a convention in Toronto. Out of that came the Trades and Labour Congress which in three years was to include 109 unions. From that peak the movement seemed to decline for a time. In the United States the American Federation of Labor, structured according to trades, was engaged in absorbing the Knights. In Canada as well there was much wrangling and dissidence and a sharp decrease in the number of active unions. Yet for all that, while organization faltered, labour was growing at its base. The working man was making his needs known and some of them were being met.

From 1882 onward a long series of amendments to the Mechanics' Lien Act lowered the minimum for claims and widened their application. The protection for men in trades was extended to household servants. By 1896 there was almost no employer who could escape the provisions of the act, nor was there any under-the-table form of evasion. Agreements to waive claims, made in favour of employers by hard-up workmen or servants, were declared to be null and void.

In 1886 the Workmen's Compensation for Injuries Act put Ontario well ahead of the rest of Canada. Yet it emerged grudgingly from earlier partial measures and it had still far to go. The workman, who was entitled to three years earnings as maximum compensation, had to sue to collect his claim. He had to establish the fact that he had not assumed risk and waived his right to be compensated at the time he took his job. The onus was on him to prove that his injury came from defective machinery, improper procedures or negligent superintendence. It was 1893 before some of these hurdles were removed and compensation in the industrial field became more nearly adequate and enforceable. Even then, however, the measures were still partial and an enduring gap remained. Bowing to the strength of the rural vote in the province, Mowat exempted farmers from liability for their help. So did later governments. It was to be nearly seventy-five years later, in 1966, before the hired man on the tractor, harrow or combine was as well-protected as the city man in a factory.

By 1890 arbitration procedures had begun to approach reality with the inclusion of wages and hours as subjects to be discussed. The time for talk, however, without effective machinery, was rapidly running out. Between 1888 and 1892 there were twenty-two strikes and five lockouts in the province. By 1894, after its usual period of slow and careful groundwork, the government was prepared to act.

The Ontario Trade Disputes Consultation and Arbitration Act of 1894 was introduced after study of new legislation in Great Britain, France and New South Wales. It provided for three steps in the settlement of industrial disputes. The first airing of differences was to be held before a council of four, with two representatives each for employer and employees. If these could not agree the argument proceeded to a Council of Conciliation made up of equal numbers of representatives appointed by and acceptable to each side. In the event of failure there, final reference would be made to a Council of Arbitration established on a permanent basis. This council of three, each of whose members was appointed for three years, was chosen with the co-operation of all recognized bodies both of labour and the employing classes. The Lieutenant-Governor appointed one member on the recommendation of labour, one on the recommendation of employers, and the third member was to be named by the other two. The award of the Council of Arbitration was to be the last step in the procedure but it was not made compulsory. Mowat had resisted that in the face of considerable pressure. An enforced settlement in his view, if it were not acceptable to the parties, would be simply an added irritant or at least a dead letter. Arbitration in its essence remained a matter of ventilation, having only the weight of balanced advice and judgment after all grievances were explored. Yet the process seemed to be acceptable for labour endorsed the act, and it remained on the Ontario statute books until 1932.

The report of a federal commission in 1881 had revealed much about the conditions surrounding labour. In Ontario and Quebec particularly, hasty industrialization was taking a heavy toll. Factories were overcrowded and often wretchedly equipped with sanitation and ventilation neglected, no fire precautions and workers unprotected from dangerous and exposed machinery. Women worked with the men, sharing the filth and risks, or segregated in the clothing trades were left to slave by themselves, stifling in airless attics or shivering in dank basements. Children of eight, nine and ten, often forced by their parents, were being exploited in growing numbers as a source of cheap labour. The work week for all was normally sixty hours and frequently more than that. It was considered to be rather high, at least in the case of children, and there was some thought of a half-holiday on Saturdays. Yet there was fear of leisure for the working class as a trend toward "dissipation," and the industrialist saw an overriding need. Conditions for his own labour could not be so improved as to put him at a disadvantage with his foreign competition.

Ontario moved glacially but it was the first of the provinces to move. An act of 1884, which did not come into effect until December 1886, imposed conditions on factories with regard to sanitation, ventilation, cleanliness and fire precautions. The ten-hour day or sixty-hour week became the maximum for women and working children. A minimum age provision was imposed on larger factories. No establishment with a working force of more than twenty persons could employ a boy under twelve or a girl under fourteen.

In 1888 children were banished from smaller factories as well, and wholesale merchants and shopkeepers had a mild brush with reform. They were no longer permitted to work a boy under fourteen or a girl under sixteen for more than twelve hours a day or seventy-four hours a week. They were required moreover to add a touch of luxury by providing seats for the girls behind their counters.

By the 1890s, with the growth of a new industry, some regulation was applied to conditions in mining. Since they were worse here than anywhere children were better protected, and no girl was allowed to be employed at all. No boy under the age of fifteen could be given underground work, no boy under twenty could be placed in charge of machinery, and the working day in each case was shortened to eight hours. The same regulations, by 1896, had been extended to include quarries, oil, gas and salt wells and refineries for reducing ore.

The total improvement was small enough, and for a long time much was poorly enforced. Inspection was a great weakness, and so were public attitudes. A long working day was common to the farming province, and children had not been spared. It was difficult to rouse the farmer to the cause of children in industry. It was reported in 1887 that there were three factory inspectors for all Ontario while there were three liquor inspectors in the city of Toronto alone. After nearly ten years, however, the inching forward process began to produce results. The enforcement of compulsory attendance was drawing children to the schools. It had the support of labour unions who approved of education and disapproved of children as competitors for adult work. The factory inspectorate improved and became considerably more effective, notably with the help of one industrious woman. Miss Margaret Carlyle had been a factory hand in Glasgow and later on in Toronto before joining the government staff. She was well aware of conditions and apparently of the need for work. Her first report, for the last six months of 1895, covered 611 inspections.

Neither labour nor labour unions were as yet integrated forces in Ontario's public life. The working man, often drawn from the farm, was groping his way in the face of new conditions. So were his wife and child. Property was still absolute, capital and growth the much-desired essentials, and labour still a commodity that must find its price on the market. With all the strikes and disputes and legislation, the concept of a minimum wage or of inherent rights to security and a decent standard of life had not emerged. Where there had been actual inhumanities, in mid-Victorian terms, reform had been conceded. Beyond that labour was simply a cross-thread in an ever more complex pattern, another strand in the web of urbanization.

5.

During his first session as Premier, in 1873, Mowat was confronted with a bill for prohibition. He avoided action with the claim that the liquor traffic was a matter of trade and commerce under federal jurisdiction. Yet he could hardly have failed to realize that he was faced with a rising issue as well as an emerging force. In 1874 the Women's Christian Temperance Union, an offshoot of an American union, was formed at Owen Sound. It had been preceded by earlier movements from the middle of the century onward as a hard-drinking Ontario began to review its ways. Distilleries had grown with the grain fields from the first days of settlement and harsh, raw whisky had been an accepted staple of diet. Made locally, bartered locally and consumed without restraint, it had been the comforter of ailing children, the protector against the cold and the all-too-ready solace of the lord and master of the home. Beer, indigenous as whisky, had been used with the same freedom. The appalling consumption of the farm and rural areas, with its equally appalling results, had been merely increased and concentrated with the growth of towns and cities. Multiplying hotels and taverns and amalgamating breweries and distilleries had extended the hold of a great provincial industry.

Reaction came through the work of some of the churches, with Methodists, Baptists and Presbyterians in the lead. To these denominations, though not so much to others, the use of alcohol in any form was an evil to be blotted out. There would always be a religious tinge to the crusade for total abstinence, but supporters of the liquor interest could quote from scripture too. The Anglican and Roman Catholic churches, holding the ground of "temperance," could never be brought to condemn moderate use. Men of all faiths, even if their views were "dry," were often stopped by the real difficulties of the question. Large capital and employment were both involved in the trade. There were fearsome practical obstacles to suppressing thirst by law. There was philosophical justice in the right of the free man to drink or abstain from choice. All that, however, was dismissed as mere casuistry by the moral and social reformer. From the mothers of the broken homes and the women finding voice there was only a common cry: "Oh God, if only we could get rid of those accursed bars!"[16]

Already dying on the statute books was a measure passed by the old province of Canada in 1864. It empowered municipalities, if they could win the support of a majority of local electors, to forbid the sale of liquor and the issuance of liquor licences within their boundaries. The act had failed because it was totally ineffective. The few municipalities persuaded to vote dry had merely transferred the drinking trade to their nearest wet neighbours and later relapsed themselves.

The liquor question, however, was not one to be avoided. Mowat as a non-drinker, and even more as a sensitive politician, was prepared to reform what he could. A first obvious step, which later proved to be a large one, was the correction of local abuses. There were provincial regulations for the licensing, inspection and control of liquor outlets, but they were very loosely administered by municipally appointed officials. As a correcting move to provide better enforcement Crooks sponsored a measure that was later tagged with his name. On May 1, 1876, when the Crooks Act came in force, all control of liquor licensing and local administration was transferred from the municipalities into the hands of officials appointed by the provincial government.

It created at one stroke a new legion of minor local bureaucrats, distributed across the province, closely in touch with the moist political grass roots and loyal to the Liberal party. Yet it did improve enforcement, and in 1878 under the federal Liberal government of Alexander Mackenzie came another worthy gesture. The Canada Temperance Act, based on the earlier experiment of 1864, established "local option" for parliamentary constituencies. Any constituency, on petition of 10 per cent of its electors, might hold a referendum on the sale and licensing of liquor and vote to abolish the trade. Very few did, and fewer remained steadfast. Yet in 1878 when the Mackenzie government fell, provincial control of liquor licensing and the Canada Temperance Act were both in full effect. They loomed high on the Ontario scene for John A. Macdonald when he returned as Prime Minister.

The Canada Temperance Act he was prepared to accept and endorse, since local option flowed from the federal power. On the other hand, the control of liquor licensing by a Liberal provincial government was not to be endured at all. If liquor was trade and commerce then licensing was a federal affair, to be delegated to federal agents. The Prime Minister as a lawyer was firmly of that view and it was doubly reinforced for him as a knowledgeable politician. There were between five and six thousand licensed hotel and tavern keepers in Ontario. Each was under the eye of a provincial Liberal official, and each at a modest estimate might influence twenty patrons. The usurped powers of "that little tyrant, Mowat" involved control of 100,000 votes.

Mowat was quite open about his use of political patronage, and determined to retain the weapon. By this time, he was engaged with Macdonald in a great struggle over the scope of provincial rights. The Ontario boundary was in question, as was Ontario's claim to the control of its navigable waters. The use or abuse of the power of disallowance as applied by the federal government to acts of the provincial legislature was breeding hot disputes. All these were to ascend, amid clouds of political rhetoric, for decision by the Privy Council. Along with them went the liquor question, dragged up through Canadian courts from obscure local disputes. *Russell vs. The Queen*, the suit of a New Brunswick tavern keeper, turned on federal authority as the controller of trade and commerce to revoke a local licence. The Lords upheld the authority and Macdonald reasserted it with an act directed at Ontario. Under the Dominion Licensing Act, the federal government appointed municipal commissioners and inspectors superseding those of Mowat. They did not, however, replace them. The provincial men remained, side by side with the new federal intruders, in a state of maximum confusion. Mowat moved to increase it by way of a provincial act, making all licences issued by federal authority subject to a special tax. Macdonald's response to that act was federal disallowance, but events had moved beyond him.

The case of *Hodge vs. The Queen* had also followed the tortuous route to London. Mr. Hodge was the owner of a Toronto tavern which included a billiard parlour, where some of his drinking players had been discovered after hours. For this offence against closing laws Hodge had been fined the sum of $20.00. He had appealed the conviction on the grounds that the provincial government, having no power to license him, had no power to regulate. In this case, however, the Lords of the Privy Council adopted another view. Whatever the law relating to trade and commerce, provincial authority extended to the control of local establishments. Since this involved licensing and supervision of licensing, these powers in their "plenary and ample" fulness became provincial rights. "Within these limits of subjects the local legislature is supreme."[17]

The judgment came down in 1884, demolishing the effect of the pronouncement in *Russell vs. The Queen*, and from that year Macdonald accepted defeat. The right of Ontario to control its liquor outlets was not to be questioned again. At the same time the other, more basic problem, the use of liquor itself, stood up in stark relief. So did the new fact and the growth of the new force, liquor's relentless enemy. The long work for reform by church and lay groups had vastly increased its impetus through the work of aroused women.

Within a year of the founding of the Women's Christian Temperance Union the demand for female franchise had become a perceptible movement. At its very heart was the hope of prohibition and the rasp of angry impatience at the dilatoriness of men:

We women pray for better times
And work right hard to make 'em;
You men vote liquor with its crimes,
And we just have to take 'em![18]

The complaint was equally a threat, chilling to the political male. At each provincial election the temperance question raised a dangerous issue. Hardly a session passed in the Ontario legislature without at least one bill to abolish the liquor traffic. Introduced and evaded, the bills emerged in the federal House to meet with the same reaction. Leaders shifted and dodged, denying responsibility or denying practicability or consigning both to the other field of government. In both fields jurisdiction was clouded, legislation perilous and any measure of real practical enforcement was likely to prove impossible. Most of the men in both parties, whatever their personal views or habits with respect to liquor, were afraid of prohibition. But women knew no such fears and they were becoming more than the auxiliaries of determined male reformers. They were threatening to become the leaders by demanding the right to vote.

In 1882 came the first limited concession. Unmarried women with property in a municipality were given a vote in the case of local by-laws. Extended a year later, the right included a vote in municipal elections. In the same year the Toronto Women's Suffrage Club was formed, and by 1889 a notable leader had appeared. Emily Stowe of Toronto, who was then fifty-eight and a doctor trained in New York, had been admitted after a long struggle to the Ontario College of Physicians as the first woman authorized to practice medicine in Canada. Established and respected in her profession, she became president of the Dominion Women's Enfranchisement League, promoted the absorption of the Women's Suffrage Club and became the powerful enemy of an exclusively male franchise, the "relic of barbarism" which classed women with the "imbecile and insane."[19] By the 1890s bills for the enfranchisement of women were appearing as regularly in the legislature as bills for prohibition. Even in the outer rooms where Mowat received his visitors change began to be apparent. The annual deputations on behalf of temperance had a militantly feminist tinge. With or without votes, the growing influence of women was hardening an old purpose. The Presbyterian Premier, who did not drink himself and could not be brought to support a female franchise, was moved to do what he could.

It was again a clearing of the ground, reserving potential action. On January 1, 1894, with a provincial election six months in the future, Ontario was offered a plebiscite on the question of prohibition. About half the male electorate chose to vote, and over 60 per cent of them voted dry. The verdict was reinforced by some 13,000 different coloured ballots representing unmarried property-owning women. Yet it was obvious that prohibition as well as women's enfranchisement had still far to go. Sixty per cent of 50 per cent worked out to about a third of the male electorate, to be considered definitely dry. In the other colour of ballots, or rather the lack of ballots, there was equally cause for thought. Of the 5,000 women in Toronto who had held the right to vote fewer than 900 had used it.

On June 26, 1894, Mowat faced the Ontarians in his last provincial election. Reinforced by the plebiscite he promised them prohibition, if and when he had power to enact the law. When he was returned to office he moved to redeem his pledge, or at least to share his problem with the federal government. Macdonald was gone by then, and it was to Sir John Thompson as Conservative Prime Minister that Mowat addressed his questions: Did the province have power to prohibit the sale of liquor? Did it have power to prohibit the manufacture of liquor? Did it have power to prohibit the importation of liquor into the province?

The federal government, following the usual procedure, submitted the matter to the courts. On January 15, 1895, the Supreme Court of Canada answered each of the questions with a flat "no." There remained, however, the higher authority in London, and appeal was duly made. On May 9, 1896, five days after Mowat had announced his decision to leave provincial office and join the Laurier cabinet, the Judicial Committee of the Privy Council responded. Ontario, in the view of the Lords, had the right to prohibit the sale and manufacture of liquor within its boundaries "in the absence of conflicting legislation" and provided the operation were so conducted as to make prohibition merely a local matter. After that Delphic pronouncement, opening a universe to future legal conflicts, it answered the third question. The province did not have power to prohibit the importation of liquor since this would "probably trench" on Dominion powers.[20] It would certainly make Ontario the receiving pool for a flood of foreign liquor. Mowat left office with the question of prohibition dangling in mid-air, as it would long remain for his successors.

Nevertheless, the twenty-three years of manoeuvring about the great, intractable problem had not gone for nothing. For one thing the consumption of liquor was reduced. The shift from rural areas to the towns and cities, though it concentrated some evils, was tending to reduce them generally or give them a milder form. Toronto, which had had 290 taverns in 1875 for a population of 70,000, had 204 in 1881 for a population of 86,445, and the declining trend continued. During approximately the same period, according to the claims of Liberals, the number of licensed hotels and taverns in the province went down by about 2,000. For the whole of Canada, between 1871 and 1896, the consumption of spirits was halved though the consumption of beer was doubled.

More important still was the change in the attitude of women. It was prohibition that had brought them to political life, and they would "not cease to agitate," the *Globe* predicted in 1888, "until their right to vote on the same plane with men is introduced."[21] They were to wait too long for that, but their developing views and influence were already strongly felt. By 1896 the Women's Christian Temperance Union was concerned not only with alcohol but with tobacco and narcotic drugs. It was studying the environment of children and of working girls in the cities and demanding better wages and improved surroundings. It was a force in opening eyes to the barbarity of the endless working day and the degradations of the sweatshops. The non-observance of the Lord's Day Act, then seven years old, was another matter calling for complaint and action. If the motivation was puritan and the attitude still parochial it was nevertheless to be a powerful new factor. Women along with men, equal partners or not, were beginning to shape Ontario as the nineteenth century ended.

Notes

1. Evans, *Oliver Mowat and Ontario*, p. 14.
2. *Ibid.*, p. 404.
3. *Ibid.*, p. 165.
4. John Willison, *Reminiscences Personal and Political*, p. 99.
5. Evans, *Oliver Mowat and Ontario*, p. 198.
6. *Ibid.*, p. 214.
7. *Ibid.*, p. 232.
8. *Ibid.*
9. *Grip*, Toronto, May 20, 1893.
10. *Ibid.*, April 15, 1893.
11. Quoted in Splane, *Social Welfare in Ontario*, p. 16.
12. Ross, *Getting Into Parliament and After*, p. 194.
13. Splane, *Social Welfare in Ontario*, p. 49.
14. *Ibid.*, p. 56.
15. J. M. S. Careless, *Brown of the Globe* (Toronto: Macmillan of Canada, 1963), Vol. II, pp. 292-295.
16. P. B. Waite, "Sir Oliver Mowat's Canada: Reflections on an Un-Victorian Society," in *Oliver Mowat's Ontario*, edited by Donald Swainson (Toronto: Macmillan of Canada, 1972), p. 17.
17. Evans, *Oliver Mowat and Ontario*, p. 280.
18. Graeme Decarie, "Something Old, Something New . . . Aspects of Prohibition in Ontario in the 1890s," in *Oliver Mowat's Ontario*, ed. Swainson, p. 169.
19. Evans, *Oliver Mowat and Ontario*, p. 280.
20. *Ibid.*, p. 340.
21. *Ibid.*, p. 274.

Chapter Six

Empire Ontario

1.

The question of provincial status was as old as Confederation, and it had left Mowat an inheritance of standing quarrels. By the terms of the British North America Act the Lieutenant-Governor, an appointee of the federal government, presided over "one House, styled the Legislative Assembly of Ontario." It was not a "parliament" like the Dominion parliament nor was its official head, as in the case of the Governor-General, a representative of the Queen. He was, in the view of John A. Macdonald, a subordinate federal official; while the Ontario legislature had "in fact something the character of a Municipal body."[1]

Sandfield Macdonald's government, pliant in some ways, had refused to accept this view. The first gathering of members elected in 1867 had been referred to as the First Parliament, and the Lieutenant-Governor as head of it had been firmly linked to the Queen. He gave his assent to laws not as a federal agent but in the name of the British sovereign; and the legislature, though it retained its formal title in each of the bills it passed, assumed like the Dominion parliament authority direct from the Crown. "Her Majesty, by and with the advice and consent of the Legislative Assembly of the Province of Ontario," made each provincial enactment.[2]

The same parallel authority had been asserted in other ways, both by Sandfield Macdonald and Blake. The privileges and immunities of federal members of parliament had been claimed for provincial members. The right to appoint Queen's Counsel and to administer "escheats," or unclaimed estates, was assumed and used by the province. Ontario had claimed authority over lower judges and magistrates, though the federal government paid them. It had won some and lost some in a series of minor disputes, and the general public had not paid much attention. The intricate concerns of judges, lawyers and legislators did not come home to "men's business and bosoms." It was 1876 before Mowat settled the question of privileges and immunities; and 1883 before the Privy Council decided that provincial powers were inherent within their sphere and not a delegation of federal power.

The question of the Ontario boundary overhung the decade of the 1870s and was reserved for decision in the 1880s. Meanwhile Ontario, Quebec and Ottawa were involved in lesser struggles. The right to control liquor licensing enhanced provincial power. Similarly a battle of competing lumbermen over use of a provincial river became inflated by the Rivers and Streams Bills to the status of a major issue. Four times, by four acts in the legislature, Mowat asserted the right to control "navigable waters." Three of the acts Macdonald disallowed, only to be reversed on the fourth by the Privy Council. Quebec demanded subsidies for provincially-built railways on the ground that they provided service for the Dominion's main lines. On the same ground Mowat demanded control or compensation for the building of every branch in Ontario that served a national railway. He had lost out on that point and been driven to much heat amid the flare of other controversies. If Ontarians, he said in the legislature in 1882,

> could only maintain Confederation by giving up half their province, then Confederation must go . . . if their power of passing laws within their own legitimate sphere was to be subject to the whim of a minister or ministers at Ottawa, and if they could not demand the large amount of property to which they were entitled without the advantages of Confederation, then it was not worth maintaining.[3]

When he allied himself with Honoré Mercier, the flamboyant Premier of Quebec, he was not, however, notably successful. Somewhat dubiously, in October of 1887, he accepted an invitation to join in an "understanding between the provincial governments with a view to the organization of a system of common defence."[4] He had presided in Quebec as chairman of the first inter-provincial conference and had approved the passage of formidable resolutions for the curtailment of federal powers. They remained paper restraints, however, for Macdonald simply ignored them. The power of disallowance, greatest weapon of centralism, remained in federal hands.

Underlying the conflict of wills and the rivalry of politicians had been a clash of ultimate views. To Macdonald, the national leader, constitutional legalisms and disputes about rail and waterways had been petty-minded obstructions. He looked ahead for a century and saw the map filled in, with Ontario in its proper place. She would be one of many provinces of moderate and balanced size and comparable wealth and resources, each duly subordinate and unable to pose a challenge to the central government. As new territory was opened it would be divided in new provinces, matching the old in strength and perhaps occasionally reducing them. Statesman-like patching and piece-work were to complete the pattern of the nation.

It had not been the view of George Brown or Blake, and it was not the view of Mowat. To rising, pushing, westward-looking Grits there was to be no clipping or fitting in the name of some higher unity. Unity itself was suspect, as another word for control. The provinces of the Confederation were to grow from their own cores, expanding in organic freedom. It was largely Upper Canada that had framed and forced the union and she had not done it to reduce her size or standing. Ontario was to find her way on ground she considered her own. The determination of that ground and the clash of those views were the heart and centre of the question of provincial boundaries. When that was settled much else would be settled, for Ontario and the nation too.

2.

In 1873, when Macdonald's government fell and Mackenzie's Liberals replaced him, the dispute on the Ontario boundary entered a new phase. Blake had refused the first prospective award and the Conservative federal government, preoccupied with the Pacific railway and the later Pacific scandal, had not pressed for a decision. Yet there had been no pause in the opening-up of the territory. North along the height of land, from disputed Thunder Bay to disputed Lake of the Woods, lumbermen, miners and prospectors were pushing their way west. The gruelling chain of the Dawson Route, with its lakes, rivers, wagon roads and portages, was pulling settlement onward while surveyors moved ahead. In spite of the Pacific scandal and for all the change of government, they were tracing the route for a railway. The vast west was alive, throbbing with boisterous growth, and it required the hand of a proprietor who was sure in his own right.

The Liberal government in Toronto and the Liberal government in Ottawa were soon agreed on a reasonable course of action. It was easier because of Blake, who was now in Mackenzie's cabinet but remained a counsellor of Mowat and was dominant on both scenes. Since there had been no formal award there would have to be a new commission; that mass of yellowing manuscript, those maps, reports and treaties, would have to be reviewed again. For that purpose a new board was appointed, with a federal arbiter, a provincial arbiter and a third nominated by both. Meanwhile, foreseeing deliberations that might well go on for years, the federal government and the provincial government drew some temporary lines. The "conventional" boundary of Ontario, pending determination, was extended north from the Ottawa to the region of James Bay, from there west along the 51st parallel to drop south from a point on Lake St. Joseph to the tip of Hunter's Island. That tip, now in Quetico Park, was 200 miles to the east of Lake of the Woods. But it was to the west of Thunder Bay by some seventy-five miles. Ontario with that much gained, or at least provisionally conceded, could leave the rest to a friendly federal government until full justice was done.

By 1874, with the conventional boundary dividing their jurisdictions, the two governments were in a state of serene suspense. They combined benignly to see that life went on for the lumbermen, miners and prospectors, the trappers, Indians and settlers who still largely ignored them. Keewatin District, the district of the "north wind," was carved out by the Dominion in 1876 to delimit its claimed territory. Yet mining licences and land patents were issued by both governments, while Mowat distributed officials and asserted provincial authority as far as Lake of the Woods. Whatever the "conventional" boundaries, his hopes were pinned on the arbitrators and the event at last confirmed him. In the sultry August of 1878, after a long period of dormancy and a change of personnel, the commission announced its verdict. Ontario was to be extended northward to the line of the Albany River, well above the previous conventional boundary, and was to reach west to the famous Northwest Angle that enclosed Lake of the Woods.

The Ontario government, Mowat wrote in December, was glad to ratify the award and would be glad to learn that the federal government concurred. He was writing by then, however, to a different Prime Minister. Mackenzie's Liberals were out, shocked, sore and disrupted after the autumn general election, and Macdonald was in again. Too familiar in his ways, and quite of his old views, he was not to be changed by any Liberal commission. He distrusted its modes of procedure, considered its findings wrong, and was determined now in any case to appeal to the Privy Council. Meanwhile there was delay while the grounds for a brief matured. Papers were reported lost, select committees denied the authority of the award, and life went on in the territories with ratification withheld.

For two years, while the Dominion and provincial governments stood with locked horns, a confusion of jurisdictions prevailed in the North-West. It was increased deliberately by Macdonald in 1881 when an act of the federal parliament, extending Manitoba, located her new boundary to the east of Thunder Bay. The Prime Minister, at one stroke, had enlisted a provincial ally, imported a new authority, deprived Ontario of the lakehead and in effect reversed the award. Nor was that the limit of the offence, in the eyes of the injured party. The Canadian Pacific Railway, risen from the ashes of the first Pacific project, was then on its way west. Its road allowance by contract was forty miles wide, but it was looting the best of the timber stands for miles outside its limits. The federal government itself was looting timber for its friends by selling tracts to lumbermen at a fraction of their real worth.

Underlying all, moreover, was the threat of a greater claim. By the terms of the British North America Act, uniting the original provinces, Ontario owned the land enclosed by her boundaries, with all the timber growing on it and all the minerals beneath it. Manitoba, the newcomer, did not enjoy that right. Her natural resources, at the time she became a province, had been reserved as property of the Dominion. They were to remain so within her extended borders and Macdonald applied the same view to the lands claimed by Ontario.

> Even if all the territory Mr. Mowat asks for were awarded to Ontario, (he said in 1882,) there is not one stick of timber, one acre of land or one lump of lead, iron or gold that does not belong to the Dominion or to the people who have purchased from the Dominion government.[5]

In the North-West, overhung by these conflicts, the bush camps and the mining camps, the construction sites and the rough frontier settlements began to reflect a minor civil war. Chaos reigned in the woods over federal and provincial licensing, and liquor flowed in the towns through competing prohibitions. At Rat Portage, which was not yet Kenora, a municipal government, a police magistrate and a court were established by Manitoba. Since Ontario had done the same there were two arms of the law, wrestling each other for control. In 1883, on the same disputed territory, both Manitoba and Ontario conducted provincial elections. By that time as well, in the war of the two judiciaries, the zealous constables of one province were arresting those of the other.

By 1884 Mowat was brought to agree with Manitoba on the course prescribed by Macdonald. Each province as claimant, preparing its own brief, was to submit a case for decision by the Privy Council. In Ontario's view there was no case at all, since Manitoba was an extraneous third party. She had been introduced by Macdonald as a stalking-horse and trespasser on lands that had become Ontario's by the award of arbitration. Nevertheless, with the old arguments recited and the old documents to support them, Mowat went to London and received the judgment of the Lords. His first point was denied, as Macdonald had been sure it would be. The award of arbitration had not been ratified by parliament and was therefore found invalid. Yet with that matter disposed of, the crucial verdict came. In the view of the Judicial Committee the actual boundary lines as laid down by the commission were "substantially correct and in accordance with the conclusion which their Lordships have drawn from the evidence laid before them."[6] The thrown-out work of the arbiters came back stamped with authority as a decision of the Privy Council. Macdonald had won procedurally but it had cost him the whole game.

He was not yet ready, however, to concede total defeat. He had to assess the real dimensions of defeat, for his hope of manageable provinces had gone with the decision of the Lords. Quebec was now laying claim to its northern hinterlands, and so was a Manitoba that had been pushed back from the east. For four more years, with the field of manoeuvre narrowing, Macdonald imposed delay. Ontario's boundary could wait until all boundaries were determined, and with surveys still to be completed in much of the northern territory it was not yet time for that.

In the meantime there was the question of natural resources onto which, almost casually, the question of Indian rights came to intrude. What was the Indian's status, how did he hold his lands, and what was the effect of treaties that ceded lands to the Crown? All these questions, dissected by many jurists, had been travelling up through Canadian courts on their way to the Privy Council. They arrived there in 1888, with Mowat and Blake accompanying them, to plead for Ontario's view. It was flatly opposed as usual to the view of federal authorities, and it had grown like many others around a hard commercial core.

In 1873, while the boundary dispute was quiescent, the federal government and tribes of the northern Indians had made a treaty. Subject to the usual terms, and apart from a few areas to be held as Indian reserves, a huge region lying along the divide and extending westward as far as Lake of the Woods was ceded to the Dominion of Canada. Ten years later, though the land was part of the Ontario claim and the quarrel in full flush, the Dominion government had issued a timber licence. It was only one of many and for a comparatively limited tract in west Algoma, but it entitled the St. Catharine's Milling and Lumber Company to cut the stands of pine. The Company had cut some 2,000,000 feet, and had been promptly sued by Ontario for the removal of provincial property.

The tract of land in dispute, through the previous verdict given by the Privy Council, lay well within the new boundaries of Ontario.

The immediate question concerned only the timber. In the federal view the Indians had ceded the right to it along with the cession of the land. In the view of Blake, as senior counsel to Mowat, they had no such right to cede.

The lands concerned, said Blake, by decision of the Lords before him, had passed from the authority of the Dominion to become the property of Ontario. And within the boundaries of Ontario, by the terms of Confederation, every stick of timber, every acre of land and every lump of lead, iron or gold was provincial property. So much for the claim of the St. Catharine's Milling Company. There was more than that, however, for the future had to be thought of and the development of Ontario's north. "Half of the province is north of the height of land,"[7] and most of that was Indian land, not yet ceded to the Crown. Did the Dominion government control it, pending any such cession? Obviously it did not. Indian rights existed and would have to be dealt with some day, but they were all subject to the paramount title of the Crown. That title, through the verdict of the Privy Council, had passed on to Ontario with the determination of her borders.

Did that reduce the status or diminish the rights of Indians? Blake was eloquent to the contrary. The Dominion remained the legislator and the ward of native peoples living on tribal lands. It could influence the disposal of their rights, without self-interest of its own. It would be the impartial referee in provincial dealings with Indians.

> I contend that possibly, nay probably, the Indian position is by our construction of the Act materially improved; since the Dominion of Canada ... without anything to gain by making an advantageous or hard bargain with the Indians, is set up as the superintendent or guardian ... and the protector and vindicator of the Indian rights.[8]

However that might be, and whatever its implications for a long future, the argument impressed the court and was yielded to by the Dominion. The Ontario Boundary Act, passed by the federal parliament in 1889, extended Ontario in full possession of its resources and its remaining Indian lands north to James Bay and west to Lake of the Woods. For good or ill, the prospect of northern provinces moderate in size and balancing southern sisters was finally laid to rest. Through the next twenty-three years, by various successive acts, Ontario and Manitoba were carried to Hudson Bay while Quebec reached up to the east of them to front on Hudson Strait. By 1912, 1,000 miles in breadth, enclosing the Great Lakes system, opening out to the Arctic and commercial master of the west, Empire Ontario would have attained its full dimensions.

Within the expanding borders, politics, law and some aspects of religion were undergoing change. For the first time, in 1875, Ontarians voted with no fear of their neighbours by using the secret ballot. Elections were still the raw tussles of democracy, with the drink, the $5.00 bill and the hopes or threats of patronage as ready weapons. More and more, however, with the new privacy for the individual voter, they expressed the general will.

Through the next thirteen years, yielding to the pressure of wage-earners and labour groups in the cities, Mowat enlarged the franchise. He was aware and fearful of the shift to urban power, and confessed as much in the presence of friendly farmers. There was, he said, "a greater amount of political and other virtue in the country than in the town."[9] Nevertheless, in 1888, manhood suffrage came, passed by the provincial legislature without even a division. Every male in Ontario of the age of twenty-one, if he was a British subject resident for nine months and neither a criminal, a lunatic nor supported by public charity, was given the right to vote.

As a former lawyer and judge, Mowat was concerned with the courts and well aware of their shortcomings. The three divisions, Chancery, Queen's Bench and the Court of Common Pleas, had become entangled in tradition and increasingly confused functions. In addition to that there was the question of provincial statutes, multiplying in the law books since the time of Confederation. By 1873 there were about 1,200 statutes of newer or older vintage and of more or less effect. Some applied to the old province of Canada but had been continued unrevoked, while some made by Ontario had been either changed or nullified by succeeding legislation. To a barrister preparing his case the accumulation of statutes, unconsolidated and quite possibly conflicting, was a jungle strewn with pitfalls. He had to search through years of law-making to find an applicable rule, yet it might have been amended later or it might have been wiped out. He could never be quite certain, on the day he rose in court, that he had found his way through the wood.

By 1874 a commission had set to work, and in 1877 the Revised Statutes of Ontario made their appearance. In two volumes and 224 statutes, consolidating the 1,200, they embodied Ontario's code of common law. With the two decennial revisions which Mowat later provided, they remained monuments to his name; and on either side of the legislature in a House of many lawyers they were received with grateful thanks.

Reform of the courts went on in careful stages, with time to observe results. In 1873 an Act for the Better Administration of Justice attempted to distinguish the various jurisdictions and make them complementary. An act of a year later provided for the transference of cases from one court to another. Finally, in 1881, came the huge Ontario Judicature Act which revised all machinery. Both equity and common law were to be embraced by the jurisdiction of the High Court of Justice for Ontario, with recourse beyond that body to a provincial Court of Appeal. The High Court and the Appeal Court were to make up together the Supreme Court of Ontario, which delegated some of its authority to lower courts and magistrates. With functions redefined and all procedures simplified, the new courts of Ontario became essentially what they are today.

In the churches, as social needs were recognized with the growth of urbanization, doctrinal divisions narrowed through sharing in common work. The Roman Catholic church, much preoccupied with schools, nevertheless enlarged its homes and orphanages and established teaching hospitals in towns and cities. High Anglicans and Low Anglicans promoted the same work, though they tended rather to confirm than sink their differences. In London, in 1878, Western University grew out of evangelical Huron College which had been established in 1863 and remained in affiliation as a faculty of divinity. Wycliffe College in Toronto broke off from Trinity College, which had been founded by Bishop Strachan. As a centre of the low church movement which had grown since the 1840s, Wycliffe's basic purpose was "to promote the interest of a scriptural Christianity"[10] and to "associate the strength of an enlightened Protestantism against the encroachments of Papacy and Protestantism" which it saw in the high church. Yet it remained an internal movement within the body of the Anglican church, and if there were mutual strains there were also mutual benefits. Evolution confirmed itself in 1893 with the attainment of new status. By electing its own primate and providing for self-government, the Church of England in Canada became an autonomous daughter church. High and Low Anglicanism, the two ends of the bridge between Roman Catholicism and Protestantism, remained united and competitive in the work of social advance.

Ontario's Baptists, united only by doctrine but always socially concerned, remained much as they had been, with each church independent and managing its own affairs. Presbyterians, however, with Scottish quarrels behind them, had come to the end of division. In 1875 the various groups were merged as one body, the Presbyterian Church in Canada. Nine years later Methodism, always a great proponent in the work of temperance and reform, arrived at the same stage. With schisms healed and sectarian issues forgotten, the four groups of Methodists became the single

Methodist Church, and increasingly spoke out on social and other questions with a powerful united voice.

In all churches and particularly, perhaps, in the wealthier urban centres, there was a new mood of questioning and a discontent with practice. The tall steeples stood, the church bells pealed on Sunday and the faithful filled the ornate walnut pews. Yet too many had paid for the pews from a too large share of the goods of the world outside. The church needed their support, but was that the church's base? Want, ignorance and evil, distorted and deprived lives were all a part of the same Christian community. There was much in this that disturbed the thoughtful churchman. Familiar with jails and hospitals, daily visiting the poor, he was still dubious of some of the new ideas. Socialism remained anathema and trade unions suspect, yet more and more in synods, conferences and pulpits the tone of the churches sharpened while prosperous listeners squirmed. The minister, relaxed in dogma, became the critic of factory conditions, the advocate of the living wage and the voice of the voiceless children withering at looms and benches. "Christianity," said E. H. Dewart, editor of the *Christian Guardian*, is "as idle as a painted ship upon a painted ocean" unless its principles are "wrought out in life and character."[11]

In 1882 came the mobilization of the Christianity of the streets. Jack Addie and Joe Ludgate, two young Englishmen recently come to Ontario, met by chance in London at a prayer meeting of Methodists. They had become Salvationists in England, had carried the call with them, and were soon unfurling the flag. Through the first years, as the Army marched to its drums, its military ranks, its fervent street corner meetings and its over-enthusiastic followers brought ridicule in some newspapers and rebuke from staider churchmen. Yet Methodists, as foster fathers, were soon of another view. "There is," wrote E. H. Dewart, "even in our Canadian cities a rapidly increasing class who are not reached by ordinary church agencies . . . They are too low down in the pit to be reached by the rope let down by the Churches . . . It needs another length."[12]

Approving the Army as an auxiliary, Methodism itself was broadening its means and methods. In 1887 women came to the fore in the new Deaconess movement and two years later the Epworth League sent young men to the streets, trained in doctrinal studies but also in social work. By the middle and late 1890s, as Methodists moved through the cities rubbing shoulders with the rough, they had begun to shift in some of their older views. They could see Christ in a restrained and altered socialism, and they could give support to unionism in improving the worker's life. Always strong for Sunday as the inviolable day of rest, they could also plead for Saturday as a half-day of leisure. Liquor remained the enemy to be condemned in any form, but it was suggested in one assembly that dancing and games of cards, and the theatre, circus and racecourse should be "discountenanced" rather than "forbidden."[13] It was too much for the 1890s and the prohibitions remained, along with some deeper strictures. It was said, as it could be said of many other Protestants, that "if one scratched a Methodist . . . he would find a violent Anti-Catholic."[14] Among Catholics, too, the old prejudices breathed in a light sleep; and in all churches, though the stirrings of social conscience were undermining dogma, they did not prevent discord.

Beyond the cities and towns and older rural Ontario, another field of the churches was the opening North-West. Roman Catholics and Anglicans had been established on the Red River since the early 1820s, Methodists and Presbyterians had begun their missions around the middle of the century, and the Baptist churches had followed in 1873. For the Catholic church in the west, built on its Métis base, there were some elements of tragedy in the decline of a native people. The rush from Protestant Ontario, beginning in the 1870s, was burly, British and set on domination. Yet it also carried with it a quota of Roman Catholics, and among all faiths ministers were soon at work. In some ways, among a simpler, wilder people, divisions were sharper here, and fierce religious controversies had origins in the North-West. Yet not only the white settlers but Northern Indians and Esquimaux were gathered into a framework that presaged civilization. Resources in the east were strained as the missions reached the Saskatchewan and crossed the mountains to the Pacific. Social work suffered and good intentions languished from preoccupation with the west and from lack of personnel. Yet the churches, balancing needs and devoting much of their effort to those of the pioneers, were broadening out with Ontario to a larger place in the nation.

4.

Between 1871 and 1891 Ontario's population grew at an average rate of less than 25,000 per year; from 1,620,851 to 2,114,321. During the next decade it was almost static in numbers, though the shifts of urbanization still continued. The proportion of urban to rural population, which had increased from 30 per cent in 1881 to 38 per cent in 1891, was 42 per cent by the end of the century. Small towns that had once been centres of farmland became centres of manufacturing. At the same time, as industrialization and commerce opened the north and west, the centres of population became more scattered and diverse. Yet industry combined with railways and improving communications to maintain some common patterns.

West of Sault Ste. Marie, rounding the head of the Lakes and following the edge of the Shield, was the domain of the lumberman and the miner, capped by the unopened north. Hard men lived hard lives in the primitive camps that were opening up that wilderness, and it might have seemed to be a civilization of its own. Yet the "Soo" and the lakehead cities and the towns on Lake of the Woods were linked by rail and waterways and fed with brains and money supplied by the older east. Men, tools and vehicles, household items and foods and fads and newspapers came with the trains and boats. Hotels, banks, barber shops, lawyers' offices, pool halls, libraries, schools and churches were all tied by memories and all subject to the influences of the metropolitan centres. One knew what the east wore, one knew what the east thought. For the most part, beyond the large, obvious and superficial differences, one lived as the east lived.

Sault Ste. Marie, with its pulpwood mills and power plant and its huge plans for expansion, was a raw Toronto of the north. Port Arthur, grown and named with the coming of the CPR, was a fierce competitor of Fort William for Manitoba wheat. The arriving grain at both ports was fed to towering elevators through miles of railway shunting yards and fed again to ships. Mining centres, lumbering centres and nerve centres of transport, the twins were bitter rivals as western gates to the sea. On Lake of the Woods, by 1899, Rat Portage, Keewatin and Norman had merged to become Kenora. They were supply centres for timber camps, the sites of enormous sawmills and tourist meccas in summer. At the end of each June, as the schools in the east emptied and the boats and trains came west, the summer cottages opened and the populations doubled. Society went afloat, taking romance along, in moonlit steamer excursions and rowing matches and regattas, while band concerts and picnics enlivened the public parks.

Nor did life cease when the snow came and the summer guests were gone. Skaters, curlers, hockey players and horse and dog-drawn sleigh-racers were distributed in hardy hundreds over miles of windswept ice. In the steam-heated halls, often electrically lighted, Mr. Edison's gramophone or the Rat Portage Minstrels replaced the summer bands. Painting teachers and dancing masters had each their clientele, and concerts, lectures and variety shows exhibited local talent. The touring theatre companies had discovered the North-West, and the CPR brought them. Heralded for weeks by posters and arriving in clouds of frost-suspended smoke, the great names of New York, Chicago, and London were transmuted to flesh and blood. They stepped to the station platforms under the eyes of gaping watchers, but they were often hunched in the fur collars of their coats. The breath of the waiting livery horses rose in a white mist, the streets were pitted ruts and the smoke of mills and factories climbed in a northern sky. They were still cold and remote, these islands carved from the woods, and the dark forests of the Shield gloomed beyond them.

On the face of older Ontario, by the middle 1890s, the strong lines of maturity had begun to deepen. The large towns were cleaner and better places than they had been a decade earlier, with less garbage in the streets and fewer wandering pigs. Most of the old manure piles that had once disfigured the outskirts were gradually disappearing. Local hotspurs given to spattering pedestrians as they charged through muddy ruts had felt the hand of the law. A Provincial Board of Health, established by Mowat in 1882, had been given substantial powers. With other powers delegated to the municipalities, sanitary measures improved and infectious diseases were checked. Vaccination of school children had become compulsory by 1886, and by 1889 the Board of Health was operating a public laboratory. Infectious disease was no longer a private matter; the home must report to a health officer who could impose a quarantine. There were still ignorance and carelessness in dirty towns and villages, and the city slums were growing. By 1895, however, some of the worst was over. The Board of Health in that year was able to report that there had been no smallpox in the province, that typhoid fever had almost disappeared and that diphtheria was on the wane.

Police forces were larger and more efficient, though they still had enough to do, with drunkenness and prostitution as naggingly persistent crimes. Larger centres had fire brigades, usually a piped water supply, and sewerage and sanitation systems that were not always effective. Even in Toronto itself the more affluent and cautious citizens bought drinking water in bottles. Yet gas lighting was everywhere, electric lighting and tram lines were no longer feared novelties, and the hot air furnace, the indoor toilet and the shower bath had become socially accepted.

In the middle-sized towns of the firstcomers there was much of peace and grace. In Niagara-on-the-Lake or Guelph or Port Hope or Maitland there were still fine old buildings with low-pitched roofs and tall double-hung windows in Georgian or Colonial style. Other and newer towns were less eloquent of the past, but reflected prosperous growth. Behind the banks and grocery stores and the shoemakers' shops and harness shops lining the main streets were homes of frame or brick or of weathered, greying stone. Many had gone up by raising bees in lively gatherings of neighbours, and occasionally one still did. They had few pretensions to style but they had been built by good carpenters and they spoke of secure comfort.

107

Shaded by elms and oaks and the maple trees that were now cherished possessions, the wide lawns with their flower beds ran down to
the garden swing and around back to the stable. The cool interiors,
heavy with Victorian bric-a-brac dusted by the hired girl, were
redolent of good cooking and of dutiful content with life. One was
never far from a grain field or a dairy farm or an orchard, and spring
washed over the fruitlands in waves of scent and bloom.

It was 1893 before the first electric car was made in Toronto. The
gasoline-driven vehicle, first made in Hamilton, had to wait for five
years more. No one yet went anywhere by way of the automobile,
but for annual summer migrants there were established routes and
sites. Torontonians of means inclined to holidays in the Muskoka
country or along the shore of Georgian Bay. Port Stanley, Kincardine and Goderich were summering places for Londoners, and
Ottawans had the Gatineau Hills. Gananoque with the Thousand
Islands and the chain of the Rideau Lakes drew yearly hordes to the
east, and Algonquin Park its thousands more to the north. As leisure
came to the Ontarian he was learning to make the most of it.

Underlying the lives of the fortunate, however, were the strata of
other lives. Sweated girls and pallid children in factories were producing much of the wealth. Trade unions, the only hope of driven
and exploited fathers, were still discouraged and fought. The working woman was an unprotected drudge, and a nomad host of jobless
and hungry labourers drifted across the province.

> Toronto, (said the report of a commission in 1891,) is the chief
> winter quarters of the army of tramps that infest this province.
> During the summer they are scattered over the districts not too
> remote from that city . . . and as winter approaches they set out on
> their return, following, almost invariably, the same tracks.[15]

There were darker threads still in the pattern of provincial
agriculture, not only in the new north but in exhausted areas of the
south where failure and loss had taken their full toll. An official
report produced in 1905 was as true a decade earlier:

> There is no doubt that fifty percent of the inmates of Canadian
> asylums are drawn from the farming community . . . Socially they
> are isolated from the world . . . Imperfect hygienic surroundings,
> the monotony of their daily lives, a dietary that seldom varies,
> often the entire absence of bathing facilities . . . reveals a state of
> domestic life that no wonder often ends in despair.[16]

5.

It was said of some of the older towns of Ontario that they were "pale shadows of eighteenth-century towns abroad."[17] Where that was true, the ordered Englishness of streets, the serenity of public squares and the fine proportions of Georgian or Colonial buildings represented diminishing islands eroded by waves of growth. Towns were set on waterfronts where railways, warehouses and factories had followed the first small boats. Much of the early building, good, bad and indifferent, had been swept away to provide space for industry. Fire had taken its toll, as had time and decay, and when replacement came it was all too often nineteenth century commercial, shoddily-built at worst and at best pretentious and imitative.

Kingston felt the effects, but for the most part it clung to its good stone and its good manners in architecture. Hamilton Bay, for all its clanging industrialism, was surmounted by Dundurn Castle, relieving grandiosity with its square-built Scottish pride. In all the cities where large wealth had accumulated there was a looking-back toward roots. The best houses were Georgian or Jacobean, in a comfortable English style. The banks and financial houses, with the British respect for antique solidity, reflected Greece and Rome. Osgoode Hall in Toronto was a jewel of colonial building, the university and the colleges had drawn from the best of England; and the parliament buildings in Ottawa with the lovely circular library were as fine examples of late Gothic architecture as there were in North America. That, too, had found its inspiration in the Mother of Parliaments and the enduring British home.

In all the arts and many of the recreations a pervasive British influence competed with the North American. Culture had been imposed as the prosperous became informed, and though it was overwhelmingly English it had not sunk very deep. The sub-stratum was hard, rurally-based and tough, and not easily penetrated by changing tastes and ways. There was too much old religion with its stern distrust of levity, there were too many forms of dissent enclosed in loyal Britishness, and there was inescapable intercourse with the people of the United States. Sports came in easily and were soon rooted and branched, but even here there was a distinction of national influences along with a division of classes. Lacrosse was native Canadian, baseball native American, and along with British football they were sports of the commonalty. Hockey was much the same, though it rose a little in status in 1893 when the Governor-General donated the Stanley Cup. The preference of the higher orders was still for English cricket, with some much-derided fox hunting, skating, bicycling, "pedestrianism" and the delights of a good horse. Lawn tennis, when it arrived, tended to bridge the gap, and brought with it an expanding freedom for ladies. It came to be conceded, at least on urban levels, that the feminine tennis player should be allowed to dispense with corsets.

Journalism, fed from the grass roots of the province, reflected faithfully all its raucous divisions. There was much good writing in some of the larger papers, and authentic voices spoke in the country weeklies. Homely essays on pioneering life and dialect verse and ballads recounting old hardships stimulated a pride of achievement in English, Irish and Scots. Local editors promoted consensus on farm and town needs, always within the frame of the local viewpoint. Polite serialized novels, usually imported from abroad, were a benign approach to literature and a support of religion and morals. Everywhere Britishness prevailed, generally to the disparagement of Americans, but it was never without dissent. "Practically the only difference between the British aristocrat and the Yankee plutocrat," said *Grip*, speaking from Toronto, "is that, while the former had ancestors to do his stealing for him, the latter had to steal for himself."[18] For all newspapers, moreover, the great fodder was politics, and here politeness stopped.

At the head of the dailies of the province, all entrenched in support of a political party, were the Conservative *Evening Telegram* and the Conservative *Mail and Empire*, the last the product of a marriage of the two papers in 1895. John Willison was the great pillar of Liberalism as editor of the Toronto *Globe*. They and the lesser dailies in all the major cities were powerful influences on the thinking of politicians. They were influenced in turn, however, by the subscription lists that supported them, and prejudice created controversy which created circulation. The best of the editors were often responsible advisers, in touch with affairs in the province and sought out by leaders. Others, inevitably, were adventurers, sharing their readers' prejudices and dangerously inflated by power. An experience awaiting Ross when he came to succeed Mowat was equally characteristic of the 1890s. Edmund E. Sheppard, who passed through the *Mail's* news-room to become editor of the Toronto *News*, was much-travelled, hard-swearing and determinedly picturesque.

He habitually chewed tobacco, (wrote Hector Charlesworth, who was a former journalist himself), and on one occasion the late Sir George Ross visited his office on a political mission. . . Sheppard, with a view to convincing the Premier of Ontario of his brusque independence, practised this gift throughout the interview, occasionally ejaculating an unprintable synonym for buncombe which

110

has its origins in ranch life. Sir George was never in danger, but would jump nervously every time a quid flew past him to the cuspidor.[19]

For all their undoubted value as watchdogs and opinion-shapers, most Ontario newspapers were trying to fastidious nerves. To Sara Jeannette Duncan, a future novelist but then a *Globe* reporter, the image of the province presented through the press was of "one great camp of the Philistines" fed on "politics and vituperation, temperance and vituperation, religion and vituperation."[20]

Music had come with religion to Upper Canada, and still served as its handmaid. In the boats and wagons bringing the early settlers there had been harps, guitars, harmonicas and even occasionally a small hand-pumped organ. Though some of the sterner sects distrusted music, the weathered and travelled instruments accompanying familiar hymns were a precious link with home. They were an aid to the balladeer as the villages and towns grew, not only in preserving memories but in celebrating new achievements. "Acres of His Own" – "Up and Be a Hero" – "Young Canada, or Jack's as Good as His Master" – "The Man Who Came From Nothing"[21] – written by local poets and sung to the fiddle or guitar, told of wars with the forests or wars with Americans or Tories and enriched a folk tradition.

From 1820 onward the first homemade organs began to supply the churches and stimulate the growth of choirs. Native music for the church organ and the choir established a long tradition as some of Ontario's best. The organ in the prosperous home became an ornament and status symbol; and by the 1870s sizable factories in Toronto, Hamilton and Guelph and small establishments in London, Woodstock and Bowmanville were advertising "every size and description of Church and Chamber Organs, with all the modern improvements and in the best possible style."[22] The Nordheimers and Mason and Risch were making pianos in Toronto from the 1870s; John Fox, established earlier in Kingston and later to merge with Weber and Company, employed about a hundred hands and turned out more than 500 instruments per year; while Theodore Heintzman of Berlin, after an apprenticeship with Steinway in New York, established himself in Toronto with a smaller factory. By the late 1880s bugles and drums were being made in Waterloo, though string, reed and brass instruments were all mainly imported. Whatever the style, however, instruments were much used at sleighrides, picnics and garden parties and by innumerable town bands.

Church choirs and singing groups, common in all the towns, became philharmonic and choral societies in most of the larger cities.

Promenade concerts in the lamplit public parks enlivened Toronto's summer and encouraged local artists. The city's winter musical season, offering a rich variety, was crowned by symphonies and concert groups and grand opera from abroad. All this, stimulated by the founding of the Toronto Conservatory of Music in 1886, tended to foster and develop native talent. By the 1890s several Ontario composers were making a name abroad with work ranging from the popular romantic ballad through symphonies to grand opera. Clarence Lucas, W. O. Forsyth and Gina Branscombe Tenney were well-known in Europe and the United States; and in London in 1896 Lucas was mounting his comic opera "The Money Spider" for production the following year.

Ontario musicians, however, had usually taken their training or completed their final training in Europe or the United States. Often technically excellent and wide-ranging in subject and inspiration, their work was influenced by Europe and depended for its stamp of approval on British or American taste. Canadian composers had yet to discover Canada. A few unmemorable cantatas had greeted historic occasions such as the visit of the Prince of Wales in 1860 or Confederation in 1867, and Alexander Muir of Toronto had saluted the new Dominion with "The Maple Leaf Forever." A dubious anthem of unity, since it commenced Canadian history with Wolfe on the Plains of Abraham and entwined the thistle, rose and shamrock, ignoring the fleur-de-lis, it was described by a Toronto critic as a military quickstep which "appeals not to the aesthetic sensations or the imagination but to the motor system and the feet."[23] "O Canada," composed thirteen years later by Calixa Lavallée of Quebec, was to wait until 1901 to be heard in a Toronto hall.

In sculpture by the 1890s the lone outstanding Ontarian was Hamilton MacCarthy of Toronto, whose statues of Egerton Ryerson in the grounds of the Normal School, of Sir John A. Macdonald in Queen's Park, of Champlain in Ottawa and of the Sieur de Monts in Annapolis Royal are the work of a pioneer in a generally neglected art. In the fellow arts, however, the workers with paints and canvas were considerably more advanced.

From the Society of Canadian Artists, established in 1867, the Ontario Society of Artists had developed in 1872, to become the Ontario School of Art in 1876. The founding of the Royal Canadian Academy in 1880 gave Ontario artists, like all Canadian artists, an inspiration and a hope of recognition. Paul Kane, who had travelled through much of the west in the 1840s and published his *Wanderings of an Artist Among the Indians of North America*" in 1859, had attracted interest in Europe. George Theodore Berthon, as a landscaper and portraitist, and Daniel Fowler as a painter of still life, had

J. S. Macdonald (1867-1871)

Oliver Mowat (1872-1896)

Arthur Hardy (1896-1899)

George Ross (1899-1905)

J. P. Whitney (1905-1914) Sir Adam Beck

N. W. Rowell W. H. Hearst (1914-1919)

E. C. Drury (1919-1923)

G. H. Ferguson (member for Grenville, later Premier, 1923-1930)

G. S. Henry (1930-1934)

Mitchell Hepburn (1934-1942)

George A. Drew (1943-1948)

Arts and Letters Club, executive, Toronto (October, 1922)

Ontario Conservative Association Convention, Royal York Hotel,
Toronto (May 28, 1936)

Last Cabinet of the Frost Regime (November 2, 1961)

Normal School, London (*ca*. 1906)

Kingston City Hall and Market (*ca*. 1912)

University College, University of Toronto (*ca.* 1890s)

Metropolitan Wesleyan Church

Theological Hall, Queen's University (*ca*. 1900s)

Toronto Safe Works

been awarded medals for their work at the Philadelphia Centennial Exposition of 1876. William Notman, already famous as a photographer in Montreal, had opened a studio in Toronto in the late 1860s and become an important influence. With his partner, John Arthur Fraser, he had developed painting from photographs into a skilled popular art. The work had drawn together a group of younger men, practising techniques and earning their bread and butter while they dreamed of better things. The "genre" pictures began to make their appearance in such works as "Family Prayers" or "The Foreclosure of the Mortgage" which relieved lugubriosity with their homely skill and warmth. Portraiture improved at the hands of some of the group, shedding much of its old colonial formality, and Horatio Walker emerged as the master of landscape painting.

In 1882 the publication of *Picturesque Canada*, a collection of Canadian landscapes brought out in serial form and circulated to thousands of homes, brought recognition of a lively artistic life. Four years later a significant broadening came with the formation of the Toronto Art Students League. In part a product of and in part a rebellion against the influence of the Royal Academy, it was to mark the beginning of a search. Young men such as C. M. Manly, Charles W. Jefferys, John Wilson Bengough and J. E. H. MacDonald were soon embarked on walking tours, absorbing the Canadian landscape and recording some of their findings in new and native terms.

The new work, however, was to be slow in winning acceptance. The Ontario landscape, like most things Canadian, was still subject to foreign standards and teaching. *Picturesque Canada* had followed and had for its model *Picturesque America*, published in the United States. American artists had contributed some of the paintings and American craftsmen had helped with the reproduction. The authority of the Academy supported the tastes of Europe, and most artists not only complied but concurred. Homer Watson, painting in Waterloo county through most of a long life, achieved some lovely landscapes depicting the scenes he knew. But his sombre, windblown trees, his cabins and ploughed fields, were seen through the eyes of an artist trained in England. They were, said Oscar Wilde, with the oblique, patronizing authority applied to colonial effort, the work of a "Canadian Constable."[24]

Collections of valued books had been among the baggage of the Loyalists when they arrived in Upper Canada, and substantial home libraries had come with later immigrants and British colonial officials. The upper classes read, were well aware that they were living a great experience, and were soon supplied with writing in a new colonial vein. Pioneering in Canada, the War of 1812, the rebellion of the later thirties and the political strife surrounding it were all lively materials. They were locally developed for the masses in a growing provincial press, but their larger fruit was in bound volumes from Britain. Soldiers, settlers and travellers were often British gentry, educated, adventurous, literate and eager for a name abroad. Their letters home were collected to be published as books of travel; books of advice and warning were offered the prospective immigrant, and imagination in the wilderness gave birth to early fiction.

By the beginning of the 1830s John Richardson, soldier, traveller and chronicler of the War of 1812, had produced his novel *Wacousta*. John Galt, head of a colonization company, had returned to his native Scotland to write *Lawrie Todd*, first of a series of novels set in Canada. "Tiger" Dunlop, a Scottish military surgeon for all his formidable nickname, was producing breezy satire on the life of Huron county; while Susanna Moodie and her prolific sister, Catherine Parr Traill, were only two of many who were beginning to make their names. "I did not expect to find the Canadians an ignorant people," said a British editor arriving in 1833 for a brief experience of publishing in Upper Canada, but "I find them advanced in civilization beyond my expectations."[25]

By the time of Confederation Susanna Moodie and her sister, roughing it in the bush near Peterborough, and the intrepid Anna Jameson, travelling out from Toronto to remote Indian outposts, had produced a considerable literature on home life in the wilderness. They, like Galt, Richardson and other travelling novelists and writers of home advice, had achieved a market where they sought it. They were minor household names and much-consulted authorities among literate Europeans. But they were less so to the average Upper Canadian. Published abroad and popular abroad, they reflected all too accurately the imperial British viewpoint. Mrs. Jameson was brilliant but caustic on Canadian manners and highly critical of Toronto. Mrs. Moodie was a determined British snob, prepared for battle with the wilderness, but not for life with drab, colonial neighbours. Only Mrs. Traill, lighter, wittier and more adaptable than her sister, was brought to accept Canadianism on the best terms it offered. Her *Plant Life in Canada*, published in 1885, and *Pearls and Pebbles*, completed nine years later, were studies devoted to nature in a magnificent old age.

Agnes Maule Machar stands out among other writers as a symbol of changing ways. Born at Kingston in 1837, she lived there almost constantly through her ninety years of life. Poet, novelist, historian and prolific contributor to Canadian magazines, she was "a superbly representative and summary figure."[26] Daughter of the second principal of Queen's University, she concentrated within herself the strength of Presbyterianism, the colonial devotion to the empire, and the essence of the Upper Canadian who had achieved and valued the achievement. She could be didactic, insular, wearily and sternly moral; she loved, professed and promoted all things British, but she was at home in her own land.

It was less so with some of the better poets as the frame of mid-Victorianism and North American commercialism grew around them. Charles Sangster was born at Kingston in 1822 and Archibald Lampman at Morpeth in 1861, yet the two died within six years of each other in the 1890s. The older man, as an ordnance clerk at Kingston, a newspaper man at Amherstburg and a civil servant at Ottawa, traced out a pattern of uneventful life that the younger came to follow. Both were civil servants, friends and contemporaries for a while, and each in his way a fugitive, seeking escape in nature. For Sangster, the man of the earlier times, the basic cause was simple. He revered nature because he saw it as a gift of God, he wrote poetry because he loved the poetry he had read and he considered it the good man's mission to embrace and express beauty:

> And so I love my art; chiefly, because
> Through it I rev'rence Nature, and improve
> The tone and tenor of the mind He gave.[27]

The sense of religious duty, as well as the echo of Wordsworth, are both present in Lampman but are merged with other strains. A graduate of Trinity College, he was well-grounded in the classics and a lover of all things Greek. Of the English romantic poets dear to Sangster, his first devotion was to Keats. "I have an idea that he has found a sort of faint reincarnation in me."[28] Respectful enough of churches as he was of social order, he was not stirred by the God of the mid-Victorians. He read widely, was aware of social problems and he could dream of Utopias for the just. But he could not move to create them; he could only turn from the ugliness and turmoil round him and seek to find his own.

> Happy is he,
> Who, as a watcher, stands apart from life . . .
> He shall be quiet and free. To him shall come
> No gnawing hunger for the coarser touch,
> No mad ambition with its fateful grasp;
> Sorrow itself shall sway him like a dream.[29]

Isabella Valancy Crawford, dying at thirty-seven, had a shorter life than Lampman's and might have been a greater poet. In the best of her work there are rich moments when not only the Canadian landscape but the creatures moving within it become elements of mystery and passion. Yet time was too short for that talent to develop.

Duncan Campbell Scott and William Wilfred Campbell, though they were born contemporaries of Lampman and both long outlived him, remained derivative poets. They enriched their day and preserved for a longer future its scenes and the moods evoked. Yet neither escaped from the influence of English masters nor discovered from life in Canada the glimpse of a new society.

Nor was there much encouragement from society in the way of financial reward. Charles G. D. Roberts, most skilful of all lyricists but more the Maritimer than the Ontarian, subsisted briefly in Toronto and found the times lean. Pauline Johnson, daughter of a Chief of the Mohawks who were settled in the Grand valley, was the most conspicuously successful during the middle 1890s. Launched on a series of recital tours, she crossed the Atlantic in 1895, to be lionized in London drawing rooms and publish *White Wampum*, her first collection of verse. Yet "The Song My Paddle Sings," which had made her reputation, had been sold to *The Week* of Toronto for $1.00. A cheque for $50.00, arriving later from the *Youth's Companion* of Boston which had also been offered the poem, had had to be regretfully returned. It was a long remembered loss for Pauline Johnson, since in her entire lifetime the income earned from her poems was about $500.00.

In the major cities, the theatre was well-established. It was not an indigenous growth, however, and there was little of native drama. The *Tecumseh* of Charles Mair, one of the literati who had founded Canada First, was a rare and minor peak. Dealing with the Indian hero in blank, interminable verse, it was praised more than it was read and read more than it was seen. In the east as in the far west British and American touring companies supplied the Ontario scene, often with fine productions. There was an annual quota of Shakespeare, some durable touring classics and a flow of lighter material to amuse the lighter minds. "Oh it's just heavenly," said *Grip* of one performance, quoting the feminine reaction, "Four lovely murders, a delicious divorce case, a beautiful elopement, and the first act is not half over yet. It's too sweet for anything!"[30]

All literary taste and most literary production were dominated and overshadowed by the presence of Goldwin Smith. It was a tall shadow but a thin one, and of somewhat dubious effect. A Regius Professor of Modern History at Oxford and later a professor at Cornell, he had arrived in Toronto in 1871. With considerable means of his own, and promptly marrying well, he was immediately established in the best Toronto circles. Journalism welcomed his coming with admiration and awe, and literature accepted his standards as the ultimate goal of effort. Canada First in its young days was delivered into his hands. He transformed it to a rudimentary political party, provided it with literary weapons and turned the guns on his friends. In 1872 the *Canadian Monthly and National Review* appeared, founded largely by Smith. He was chief contributor to *The Nation*, by 1874, a brilliant journal of politics and the voice of Canada First. With John Ross Robertson he founded the *Evening Telegram*; and *The Bystander* and *The Week*, largely supported by his money, acquired their edge from his work. Nor was he liberal only to journalism in his acid zest for reform. Toronto's first welfare officer was installed at Smith's demand and paid with Smith's money for the ensuing two years.

Smith's writing, for its world-wide perspective and its sustained and caustic power, had no equal in Canada in its day. His mind looked out from the Olympian heights of Oxford and he wrote at his desk in the Grange, one of the finest homes in Toronto. Below him politics crawled, with its squalor and party wars. The procession of religious bigots, the horrors of social injustice and the black fruits of industrialism passed beneath his eyes. He despised, condemned and excoriated them, and a good deal changed through his work. He was not lost in a library, speaking with no effect. Ontario and Canada alike, if they had conformed more to Smith, would have had cleaner and better politics, fewer nauseous slums and more tolerance and taste. Yet there would have been small room for the Jew, less for the French Canadian and little for the Roman Catholic with his hope of separate schools. The grubby chore of voting would not have been imposed on women, and the justice due the working man would have excluded the right to strike. Smith's tolerance was selective, subject to fierce recall, and it did not embrace dissent from his own opinions. Yet deep dissent there was, on a major national issue, and it drew its strength in the province through roots deeper than Smith's. From the 1890s onward, stubborn, older, increasingly bitter, he was to attack the new imperialism that rejected continentalism.

6.

Canada First, as established in the 1870s, had been a movement of young men, of and for an elite. Its "Canadian National Sentiment" had been wholly a British sentiment, with no appeal for the French. What it involved in its five founders and the cluster of intellectuals who came to support or join them was a strong sense of identity and a link with old tradition. Inheritors of the first builders, the conquering British builders, the Canada Firsters were determined to carry on. London drew them, fascinated them and nourished their pride in empire; the sun shone from there. But it was to be a warming sun

117

only, fostering, rewarding, stimulating the growth of a native dream. Canadian national sentiment was to be formed by Canada's best, working in their own way. Life, letters, society, the whole structure of nationhood was to be shaped to their design.

In practical application the glowing hopes had paled. Canada Firsters distrusted the plodding masses and were walled off from the French. Their hope was in private influence applied from the top down. Secretive amateurs of politics, intent on nation-making, they had put their trust in the genius of Goldwin Smith. He had seemed British enough, he had no love for the French, and he had large hopes for the English-speaking peoples. They were as wide in ultimate reach as the old dream of Simcoe, embracing a return of the continent to the arms of the British mother. But the rational first step, as Smith came to see it, was to abolish protective tariffs between Canada and the United States. Magisterially and eloquently, altering his own course, he became a part of the politics that supported Commercial Union.

Canada First was dead by then, smothered in its patron's arms. Yet out of the tariff wrangles and the shifts of American trade, out of the very thought that there could be some rift in the empire, a counter movement came. The Imperial Federation League, formed in England in 1884, had had the broad idea of drawing colonies together for trade and mutual defence. It could hardly have been better timed, so far as Ontario was concerned. In June of that year the United Empire Loyalists celebrated the centennial of their coming to Upper Canada. It was the fiftieth anniversary of the incorporation of Toronto. As the city blossomed with its flags, parades and spectacles, Ontario's proud Britishness swelled up in a great wave.

It was mixed with many elements that were hardly strange or new, though some had grown with the years. The agricultural function and the conception of rural life seemed threatened now by the black smoke of factories. It had not been so in the past, and that past had been British. There were the rasping, clogging differences with the intractable neighbour province, whose French refused to be British. The Americans pulled southward, tempting the sons away, always threatening with one hand and offering bribes with the other. In the nostalgia of celebration there was a resolve to remain unchanged, to keep faith with the past, and beyond that a way was opened to the future. The Imperial Federation League, the theme of many speeches, was soon rooted in the province, supported by Oliver Mowat and becoming a growing force. Americanism sank and wavered under the assault of the new Britishness, and the hopes of all free traders went down with Commercial Union. "If that," wrote Mowat to Laurier on the last day of 1891, "is to be the policy of the

Dominion Liberal party, I cease to be a member of it."[31]

Imperial Federation, like Canada First before it, was a dream faced with realities that could not be overcome. It was essentially an Ontario dream and of the old loyalist Maritimes; the diverse west was cool to it and Quebec generally hostile. The time had passed for the vision of an ironbound empire ruled from its central source. The ideal of a great commonwealth was not yet over the horizon, and a parliament of many colonies could not be made to work. The practical Macdonald dismissed it, Blake toyed with it and gave up, and few men of actual power in England were inclined to take it seriously.

What could be taken seriously was the need to draw together in the face of new imperialisms and a world of arming powers. Colonial conferences brought their delegates to the mother country, opening up minds on both sides. Imperial penny postage came, and the oceanic cables spread out their world-wide links. They were less than fleets and armies, but they were to bear more lasting fruits. There was a far deeper movement here than there was in Canada First, and it was embraced by better minds. Imperial Federation in the Ontario of the 1890s was commencing a long course.

7.

Much of this was in train and much more ahead when Mowat cleared his desk for the last time as Premier. In 1896 he walked out of a parliament house that was no longer a rambling ruin facing Front Street. Three years earlier the great new legislative building, towering in red stone and relieved by white facings, had been opened in Queen's Park, with a huge cry at the expense and reluctant pride in its appearance. There had been years of backing and filling before it was even begun and citizens bemoaned the sacrifice of part of the beloved park. Yet the building stood with the trees and lawns about it, well designed and at peace, somehow bespeaking dignity, a sense of massive permanence and the large, sober magnificence of the great province itself.

"How are we going to fill them?" Mowat was said to have asked as he looked for the first time at the completed structures. On that point he had few grounds for worry. There would be problems enough in the future, requiring people enough. The bustle of business strained at the peace of the farms, the miners and lumbermen stormed at American tariffs. The Imperial Federationist pointed to a darkening world, and the nickel went from Sudbury to make the ships and weapons. Wrestlings, decisions, dangers would be a part of every day.

There were portents still unrecognizable, even on homely ground. In 1896 the same busy Berlin that had gathered to welcome Tupper also welcomed Mowat. The town was rich in money as it was in old traditions, and thousands came to its great summer *Saengerfests*, with choirs, soloists, orchestras and thumping German bands from as far away as Brazil. Bright-jacketed *lieder* groups marched or strolled through streets overhung with bunting, and crowds rose to their feet for the singing of *Die Wacht Am Rhein*. Mowat came for the *Kirmes*, the great harvest festival, held in the public park. He was ushered in with all the members of his cabinet through a gaily painted archway cut in a high board fence. Inside the fence a mediaeval German town lay spread before him, with sun gleaming on its roof-tops and the breeze rippling its pennons. The little Premier watched and beamed benignly, enjoying the brilliant spectacle and sharing the townfolks' pride. At the park gate, however, dominating the statue of Victoria and hardly noted or commented on, was a huge bronze figure of Kaiser Wilhelm I surmounted by the German eagle.

Other portents were hovering over religion as well. The ministers of many churches, concerned with factories and slums, were experiencing growing uncertainty about their beliefs. In 1896 it was just thirty-seven years since Darwin had published *The Origin of Species*. Since the 1860s the doubts had rippled across western society, eroding certainties that seemed the base of belief. For the church world and the learned world the late age of Victoria was the age of Matthew Arnold. Troubling every solitude and diluting every strength was the "melancholy, long, withdrawing roar" of the receding sea of faith.

Even so, there were burly strengths that the wise ones overlooked and strands knitted through the past that they would not see easily unravelled. There were curious memories and haunting evocations that they did not even know of. On a sunlit morning in July of 1876 Alexander Graham Bell and George Henry Martin Johnson had walked along with hammers in their hands and staples in their pockets through woods, fields, orchards and up and down slopes by the side of a country road, stringing the two miles of stovewire that led from the telegraph office in Brantford to the Bell farmhouse. Bell was twenty-nine, known for his success as a teacher of deaf mutes and for his ideas on the transmission of sound. Johnson was a Chief of the Six Nations Indians, whose reserve stood nearby and who had once owned this land by the Grand River.

There were important guests at the farmhouse curious to see the experiment, and they assembled for a noon banquet. Afterward they went out to a table, set between two trees, and Bell lifted his

120

telephone. The telegrapher in the station at Brantford let out an exultant whoop. "I can hear you splendidly, Professor!" A moment later, however, he was listening in much confusion. Words had been replaced by harsh, staccato gutturals, and all that came through the receiver was something like "Sago gatchi ska na ka" with what might have been laughter in the background. He was aware of the preceding banquet and suspected possible results. "Are all you fellows drunk up there?" The answer came from Bell, clear enough once more and again with jubilant laughter. "You've insulted Chief Johnson. He's been speaking to you in Mohawk." The Indian had sent his message through the instrument of the white miracle-maker: "Good greetings, cousin; how are you?"

Supper followed in the evening, a family supper in the farmhouse, with the Chief and his wife remaining. As they talked, flushed and jubilant over the event of the afternoon, Pauline, the Chief's daughter, looked in at the open doorway. The future poet was fourteen years old and still slight and shy. Bell rose, went over to her and drew her into the room. As she stood by him, the man who had said he would rather give speech to the dumb than invent the telephone, and who would do both and more, raised his long, delicate, staple-scarred hands over her head. She was neither deaf nor mute, but Bell's fingers were moving in the sign language. It went on rather long but the girl watched attentively and looked up to meet his eyes at the end.

"You didn't understand what I was doing."

"Yes, Professor. You were saying Our Father."[32]

Notes

1. F. F. Schindeler, *Responsible Government in Ontario* (Toronto: University of Toronto Press, 1969), quoted p. 82.
2. *Ibid.*, p. 87
3. Evans, *Oliver Mowat and Ontario*, p. 519; quoted from Toronto *Globe*, June 27, 1882.
4. Donald Creighton, *John A. Macdonald, The Old Chieftain* (Toronto: Macmillan of Canada, 1955), Vol. II, p. 472.
5. Morris Zaslow, "The Ontario Boundary Question," in *Profiles of a Province* (Toronto: Ontario Historical Society, 1967), p. 114.

6. J. C. Morrison, *Oliver Mowat and the Development of Provincial Rights in Ontario: A Study in Dominion-Provincial Relations, 1867-1896*, M. A. Thesis, University of Toronto, in *Three History Theses* (Toronto: Ontario, Department of Public Archives, 1961).
7. Ontario Archives, Blake Papers: Argument in the "Ontario Lands Case" (St. Catharine's Milling Case) July 20, 24, 1888, Blake Argument, p. 5. Case of the Respondent, p. 2.
8. *Ibid.*, p. 18.

9. Evans, *Oliver Mowat and Ontario*, p. 265.
10. Encyclopaedia Britannica: "Evangelical Alliance."
11. Hartley Dewart, quoted in *The Bulletin* (Toronto: Committee on Archives in the United Church of Canada in collaboration with Victoria University, Ryerson, 1969), p. 24
12. *Ibid.*, p. 12.
13. *Ibid.*, pp. 45-46.
14. *Ibid.*, p. 89.
15. *Growth and Character of Vagrancy*, Report of Commission on Prison and Reformatory System, Ontario, 1891, pp. 111-113.
16. Proceedings, Eighth Canadian Conference of Charities and Corrections, Toronto, November 15-17, 1905, pp. 22-24.
17. Eric R. Arthur, Encyclopaedia Canadiana, "Architecture."
18. *Grip*, Toronto, May 6, 1893.
19. Hector Charlesworth, *Candid Chronicles* (Toronto: Macmillan of Canada, 1925), pp. 72-75.
20. Quoted by Claude T. Bissell, "Literary Taste In Central Canada During the Nineteenth Century," *CHR*, XXXI, No. 3, September, 1950, p. 246.
21. Carl F. Klinck, *Literary History of Canada* (Toronto: University of Toronto Press, 1976), Vol. 1, p. 166.
22. Helmut Kallman and John Beckwith, Encyclopaedia Canadiana, "Musical Instruments."
23. J. D. Logan, *Canadian Magazine*, September, 1913, Vol. 41, p. 490.
24. Encyclopaedia Canadiana, "Painting."
25. Klinck, *Literary History of Canada*, p. 155.
26. Roy Daniells, *Literary History of Canada*, ed. Klinck, Vol. 1, p. 210.
27. Klinck, *Literary History of Canada*, p. 162.
28. Daniells, *Literary History of Canada*, p. 405.
29. *Ibid.*, p. 407.
30. *Grip*, Toronto, April 29, 1893.
31. Public Archives of Canada, Laurier Papers 2041, Mowat to Laurier, December 31, 1891.
32. Miss A. I. Grant Gilkinson, *Incidents Regarding the First Telephone Call (1876) Brantford to Tutele Heights*, (Ontario Historical Society Papers and Records, 1930), pp. 404-405.

Chapter Seven

Decade of Transition

1.

On July 14, 1896, Arthur Sturgis Hardy succeeded Oliver Mowat as the fourth Premier of Ontario.

> I need hardly say,(he wrote to John Willison of the *Globe* two days later) that there are a good many reasons, perhaps, why I should not have accepted the office ... but after a great many misgivings I concluded not to let it pass by. There are other good men who could have taken the place, and it would not have gone begging; but you know how very difficult it is in this wicked world to let high honours pass you.[1]

The words were honest and characteristic of Hardy, but they were not the declaration of a purposeful leader. Though he was to oversee some changes and make some basic decisions, most of his work was done. He was turning sixty, he was poor and looking to retirement, and neither he nor his government had the strength for new departures.

The provincial election of March, 1898, made this abundantly clear. Mowat's administration, by the time it was bequeathed to Hardy, rested on a diminishing base. The rural vote, the core of Liberal support, was becoming less important than the urban. Patronage, the great weapon, was under increasing attack. Worse still, while there were justifications for patronage and it was openly admitted and defended, electoral corruption on local levels had become an accepted fact. It was hardly new, and hardly a Liberal monopoly, but there was more money on the government side and it was used with increasing freedom. Even Hardy was used, if tales of the time be true. He was said to have left Toronto on a visit to Napanee carrying along as a favour to his man in the field a valise of

123

fresh laundry which was opened on his departure and found stuffed with "the needful."[2]

In any case the slim victory in the election was almost as ominous as defeat. Forty-nine Liberals, exactly the same number elected four years earlier, managed to retain their seats. But of the sixteen Patrons of Industry, who had become diluted Liberals, only one returned. The government sat in a House that was returning to two parties, and it faced the revived Conservatives with a bare majority of six.

By October of 1899 Hardy's strength was gone, and he took his departure from politics a poorer man than he came. He accepted, because he needed it, a small legal appointment as a clerk in Osgoode Hall and it was James P. Whitney, the leader of the opposition, who moved to have his salary increased. A year later a gift of money from friends in the Liberal caucus eased his financial worries but could do little for his health. In 1901 he died. Oliver Mowat by that time had returned from Ottawa as Lieutenant-Governor of Ontario, and his end was also near. Early in 1903 came word that the old man had fallen and injured himself while watching his grandchildren at play. Sickness followed, death came on Sunday, April 19, and a House turbulent with politics was quiet a few days later as a vote was passed to raise a statue to his memory. Of a Liberal triumvirate receding into history the only remaining member was George William Ross.

With his accession as Premier on October 21, 1899, not only a new century but a new era in politics was quickly under way. "For two years," Ross was to write later in a poignantly confused metaphor, "I grappled with my evil star."[3] Actually it was nearer to five years, for the troubles that were to overwhelm him were breeding when he took office. Able, astute, progressive and lucky in some of his initiatives, he was faced with all the problems of a party too long in power. He was also faced, as Hardy had been before him, with the rise of a formidable figure at the head of the opposition.

James Pliny Whitney, when he assumed the leadership of the Conservatives in 1896, had hardly the look of a Messiah. The dictum of John Ross Robertson, editor of the Toronto *Telegram*, was to be current for a long time: "You could throw a brick through the window of any country lawyer in Ontario and hit a better man than Whitney."[4] He was of average height, average build, and stubbornly clean-shaven in an age that bristled with beards. He wore his clothes to cover him but with no view to enhancement, and they had been bought at his local store. There was fire in the deep eyes and the strong features were handsome in a rough-cut country way, but they were set too often in a frown. The smile when it came was warm and the laugh could be loud and deep, but both were rare with Whitney.

Fifty-three years old when he came to the head of his party, he had been born on a farm in Dundas county and had gone to school in Cornwall. Since 1888, as a lawyer practising in Morrisburg and a Conservative member of the legislature, he had had a long and hard experience of provincial politics. He knew the ways of the trade, detested the ways of Grits, and was little known himself except as a good organizer. Yet he had caught the eye of former leader, W.R. Meredith, and he had some of Meredith's qualities, though they were embryonic as yet. The older man had been seen by Ross as a radical, and entrenched Toronto Toryism had the same opinion of Whitney. Like Meredith, he would have nothing to do with the strain of anti-Catholicism that ran through the Conservative party. Separate schools he accepted, though he disliked control by the church and deplored the neglect of English in some of the French districts. Prohibition, the eternal spectre in politics, was faced by Whitney with a cold and steady eye. Detesting windy eloquence and sanctimonious pretensions, he saw both in many supporters of the movement. Whatever he thought of temperance, he was a wholly negative pragmatist in the matter of prohibition; he would not have legislation that could not be made to work.

Farmer's son though he was, he was cool to the claims of agriculture, and cooler still to the limp Patrons of Industry whom he saw as Liberal tools. On education he was the practical man of Morrisburg and of the country districts round it; he was for improving the common and grammar schools, but there was "more than enough being done to aid education at the university level."[5] He began his career as a rural politician, distrustful of corporations, suspicious of vested interests and doubly suspicious of large provincial projects. Whatever their basic merits, they were all distorted in his eyes by Liberal administration. Waste, patronage, extravagance, and above all continual electoral corruption, were Whitney's prevailing themes.

Dangerous enough to Hardy, they were deadly themes by the time Ross took office; and Whitney had forged his party into a new and sharper weapon. He had Meredith to thank for much, since the Chief Justice who was also Chancellor of the University of Toronto, remained his guide and friend. Taking counsel of Meredith and studying his own problems, Whitney's views had broadened. He was a continually growing man, and he was also developing as a leader who could pull his forces together and find strategic ground. Slowly, little by little, and always with blunt honesty, he had toned down the rancorous party Protestants. In J. J. Foy, an Irish Catholic Conservative elected with Whitney's help to one of the Toronto constituencies, he had gained a strong lieutenant who attracted Irish votes.

125

He had tightened and cleansed the Conservative organization, attracted better men and even engendered the confidence that brought in party funds. By 1902, as Ross reluctantly approached his first election, Whitney was ready for the kill.

He appeared to have failed when the results came, but it was only delayed success. On May 29, 1902, Ross emerged with a majority of five seats. He was to remain as Premier for two and a half years, but even less than his predecessor in charge of a secure government. Conducting the public business and grappling with large issues, he moved in a murk of caution and desperation. Election protests came, threatening his slim margin, and there were no merciful saw-offs with Whitney in opposition. Deposed members and ensuing by-elections became matters of life and death. Scandals rocked his authority and spattered some of his leaders. The "Gamey Affair" erupted, implicating a cabinet minister in the buying-off of a former Conservative adherent who refused to stay bought. The *Minnie M.* sailed into the lagoons of history, a loud and lurid example of politics in the new north.

It centred on Sault Ste. Marie and the expanding Clergue industries, where support of Liberals at election time was a matter of fixed habit. The *Minnie M.*, as an ore carrier of the company, had been used to much advantage in the campaign of 1902. Fitted out with a team of Liberal organizers and a stock of liquor and refreshments, it had crossed to the Michigan shore, embarked some forty Americans and brought them over to the Canadian side where a special train was waiting. The train had moved through the constituency, stopping at several polls, at each of which the Michigan visitors had voted. That done, they had been returned drunk and remunerated to the waiting *Minnie M.* and deposited on their native shore.

The elected Liberal candidate, displaced when the scandal broke, was later returned to office by his hardened northern electors. The mood of the province, however, had become less forgiving. Even the Liberal *Globe* was declaring by 1903 that "barnacles" would have to be removed from the ship of state. He would rather have the barnacles, Ross had flared in reply, "than a pirate on board the ship." It was the answer of a captain, however, who had almost run his course.

2.

The South African War, spanning the last year of the nineteenth century and the first two years of the twentieth, had found the province in a mood for imperial adventure. Empire Day, established by Ross in 1898 while he was Minister of Education, had been one of the signs of the times. With its school holiday, its flag-raisings and its lectures on imperial achievements, it had been designed "to make Canadian patriotism intelligent, comprehensive and strong."[6] That patriotism, no less for Whitney than for Ross, meant an ever-closer involvement and an increasingly mature relationship with the concerns of the British mother.

The war was seen by the great majority of Ontarians and by both provincial parties as a matter of black and white. Crude, reactionary and brutal Dutch farmers were opposing the march of empire and abusing British subjects. An outworn tribal tyranny resisting law and enlightenment was to be disposed of as others of its kind had been. That there was a different view of the Boers, and of the diamond miners and gold seekers waving the British flag, was not an argument that carried weight in Ontario. Neither did the view of Quebec, which was heartily against the war. With Americanism rising to the south and Frenchness again asserting itself to the east, the British loyalties of the province welled from reopened springs.

Empire Day had been preceded by similar symptoms from the late 1880s. Ontario's quest for itself and for a new relation with the motherland had led not only to the founding of the United Empire Loyalist Association but of such bodies as the Pioneer Historical Association, the Sons of England and the British Empire League, all dedicated to furthering the British connection. More significantly, perhaps, it had led to the establishment of the Navy League and to wider schemes and ambitions for the employment of a Canadian militia. Ontario, as a province of a seriously divided Dominion, was firm on its own course in case of an imperial war. It should serve, and serve unquestioningly, since the empire's cause was one.

The calls were minimal from a reluctant federal government which was heavily dependent on Quebec. Laurier was hard put to defend the war in South Africa as a matter of Quebec concern or even of imperial defence. The imperial government, for its part, was more in need of a show of colonial unity than it was of actual troops. As war threatened, Colonel Sam Hughes of Lindsay, journalist, politician and frenetic amateur of the militia, had secured the signatures of 23,000 men whom he was prepared to lead to the Transvaal. He was promptly squelched by authority and involved in battle with British military professionals, but he had steeled Ontario's mood and he had served warning on the Dominion. Whatever Quebec's sentiments, there could be no escape from militarism for the daughter of a great empire. As other warnings multiplied and pressures built about him, Laurier yielded reluctantly and with many qualifications. The force, if sent, must be limited to 1,000 men, which was all the

British were then prepared to accept. It must be composed of volunteers. It would be equipped and transported by Canada but paid by the British government. For obscure official reasons it must not be described as a "contingent," and it must not be taken as a precedent for support in future wars. The 1,000 volunteers were assembled in two weeks and by October 30, 1899, under the command of Lieutenant-Colonel, later Sir William Otter, they were on their way to South Africa. Inevitably demands mounted and qualifications gave way. The Canadian government was soon paying its troops, who were discontented with the low rates of the British. War changed, defeats came, and the long, dragged-out business of guerilla fighting began. The first force, promptly described as a contingent, was followed by a second and third and by squadrons, batteries and lesser units recruited through private means. In all, during the three years of the war, some 8,000 Canadians went to South Africa, and more than a third came from Ontario.

It was a modest enough offering for a small and ugly war, yet its effects were considerable at home as the effects of the war itself were considerable in world affairs. In Ontario, as in all the provinces not excluding Quebec, the first "Soldiers of the Queen" had been sent off amid flags and cheers and public benefits and pledges that would become familiar to their sons. They had fought well, and with a lively, active disregard of orthodoxy, particularly against guerillas. Paardeberg became a name as the first battle of Canadians on foreign soil, where the cost was twenty-one dead and sixty wounded. Canadians fought at Bloemfontein and were among the first of the British forces entering Pretoria when the Boer capital fell. Canadian cavalry squadrons and mounted batteries ranged out in the long marches of pursuit, the short, savage engagements and the dismal wasting of farmlands that wore down Boer resistance. A Canadian and an Ontarian in another field achieved happier distinction. During the Riel rebellion of 1885 Colonel G. A. S. Ryerson, nephew of Egerton Ryerson, had been an ambulance driver flying from his wagon a white square of cotton onto which he had stitched two crossed strips of red cloth, making a first link for Canada with the international Red Cross. In South Africa in 1900, by then the President of the Canadian Red Cross, he had found funds and means, with little help from officialdom, to bring some order to British medical services.

As the troops came back to flags and public rejoicings and to gifts, benefits and promises of free land, Ontario met them with a pride which was shared by most of the country. It seemed then, in the early 1900s, to have been a rounded experience of war and a duty done for the motherland at not too great a cost. Of 712 casualties in all the Canadian forces most were due to disease; only 162 had been suffered in actual battle. The gain, moreover, seemed visible on every hand, in the strengthened bond with the empire and the sense of a new unity that pervaded English Canada. "The larger patriotism which has now taken possession of Canadians," wrote Principal G. M. Grant of Queen's, "cannot possibly vanish . . . we are henceforth a nation." A Christian reformer, a humanist and a lifelong friend and proponent of Imperial Federation, he had seen the rise of other and hostile imperialisms as he neared the end of his career. He envisioned the armed empire and the armed nation within it as civilization's answer to the age of the mailed fist. "We must make our militia force a reality; must organize a naval reserve; must defend our coasts; must attract Newfoundland into Confederation; and must do these things at once."[7]

Yet Grant had his own difficulties over the moral questions raised by the South African War, and other problems remained to plague the province. Politics had a new edge and a new bitterness as Liberal strength declined, burdened with Laurier's reluctance in supporting the imperial cause. Ontario and English Quebec lay divided from French Quebec, which more than ever distrusted the ways of empire. Deepest of all, and perhaps most damaging of all, was a new strain of doubt affecting the imperial mission. Goldwin Smith, in the twilight of years and influence, had opposed "this vile war."[8] and he had not been quite alone even in Ontario. His *Weekly Sun*, the last of his many newspapers, had been echoed by a few others, mainly in rural areas. Some of them praised the Boers as "a poor, pastoral people like ourselves, bravely fighting under a grim old Kruger who trusts God and keeps his powder dry." Other critics of this mind saw only aggressive hypocrisy in the British yellow press, and in Joseph Chamberlain, Cecil Rhodes and Viscount Alfred Milner who had "goaded the Boers to resistance."[9] Dissent was barely a whisper against the roar of the daily newspapers and the general voice of the province, but the thought lurked in the depths.

The decisive influence of the Boer War, (said one British historian,) was that it turned the tables of morality. Previously the Imperialists had had the best of the moral argument. The Radicals could argue that Imperialism was expensive, arrogant, interfering. The Imperialists answered by pointing to the abolition of slavery, to the creation of schools, railways, health services – in short 'the British mission' – and the answer was overwhelming. They tried the same answer during the Boer War when they asserted that it was being fought for the sake of the native peoples in South Africa. It was no good. The Imperialists had the mineowners of the Rand tied securely to their coat-tails. The war appeared a reversion to one

129

of the worst phases of barbarism . . . contrary to all our ideals of national political justice.[10]

It was not the opinion of Ontario in the early 1900s, but somehow quietly and subtly imperialism changed its nature. The claims of mission gave way to the claims of preservation, for world-wide strength and unity to confront the arming powers. Yet even the efficacy of that came to be doubted. The love and lust of empire would last out another war, but they would not rise from the ashes.

3.

On the question of prohibition the basic policy of Hardy and the real views of Ross were almost indistinguishable from those of Whitney. No law, and certainly not a provincial law, could wipe out traffic in liquor. A federal measure was conceivable if it expressed the national will, but for all the efforts of reformers it could not be made to do so. Laurier had permitted the attempt through the holding of a federal plebiscite in 1898, and had achieved little but new resentments and confusion. Ontario was prevailingly dry, Quebec prevailingly wet, and the other provinces had leaned enough to create a dry majority.

It was a majority, however, of 13,000 votes out of a total of half a million; and less than half the electorate had troubled to vote at all. "I venture to submit," wrote Laurier to the head of the Dominion Alliance for the Total Suppression of the Liquor Traffic, "that no good purpose would be served by forcing upon the people a measure which is shown . . . to have the support of less than twenty-three per cent of the electorate."[11] The beast was not to be killed; it could only be curbed and tamed, by licensing that controlled use, by rigid enforcement of licensing and by a gradual increase of restrictive legislation.

Yet prohibitionists in Ontario were strong, articulate, determined, and refused to accept defeat. By 1901 Ross had been forced to accommodate them, repeating Mowat's promise that he would "go as far as the definition of constitutional limitations would allow."[12] Following that, and a year of hard campaigning, came a provincial referendum in December 1902. Hedged in by conditions, it accomplished nothing at all. The Premier had stipulated a basis for determining a true majority and the result, though it was a dry plurality, was 13,000 short. Ross, personally the liquor hater, was to go on waffling to the end.

He claimed in 1904 that Liberal control of licensing had reduced the number of hotels in the province from six to three thousand. Since hotels represented bars it seemed a considerable achievement, but it owed much to changing patterns of traffic. The stage was no longer on the roads and the railways carried travellers with fewer stops for refreshment. In any case, and whatever the effects of Liberal regulation, they were not enough for Whitney. Though he fought down prohibitionism where it lingered in his own party, he attacked flabby Liberalism for weak and corrupt control. Liquor commissions and inspectors, as appointed henchmen of the government, came under his guns from the beginning. The laws were weak, the official enforcers venal; and Ross, for all his pretensions, was drifting before the wind.

He was actually caught in cross-winds partly of Whitney's making. When defeat came for the Liberals early in 1905, it was due in Ross's eyes "almost entirely to the combination of the liquor dealers with the temperance men."[13] The truth was that he went down with a worn-out government; but he bequeathed temperance to his successor much in its old state.

Nor was there much to claim for the advancement of social conditions since 1896. Funds had been increased for welfare, and factory conditions had improved with a growing apparatus of control and investigation. Yet with many annual reports and much annual discussion there was little substantive change. Woman's suffrage made almost no progress, for if Hardy and Ross were cool to it Whitney was ice-cold. Children were better cared for, the poor better provided for, and medical and penal conditions were at least subjects of study. By 1903, on the strength of government grants, the Superintendent of Neglected Children was functioning through local committees in each electoral district. Asylums and asylum procedures showed considerable improvement, and fewer criminals and destitute were mixed in with the insane. Houses of Refuge, encouraged in every county, were removing the poor from overcrowded jails. In larger institutions the idea of the prison farm was being mooted as a substitute for stone walls and dank and sweaty workshops. The law was made more accessible by some small expansion of the courts. In these areas, Hardy and Ross, jogged on by Whitney, followed the paths of reform. But they remained Victorian paths and they opened no new vistas.

How little had been done, at least in the slums of cities, was revealed by a Toronto official in his report for 1904. While prosperous suburbs expanded and fine homes were served by modern facilities, cancerous neglect and decay ate at the older sections. There were not yet even sewer lines for patches of desolation hidden behind new department stores and business blocks and hotels. Thousands of the ignored and forgotten, existing on factory wages,

131

lived in hovels or worse, amid the reek of garbage-strewn alleys and outdoor "conveniences."

> There is scarcely a vacant house fit to live in that is not inhabited, and in many cases by numerous families; in fact. . . respectable people have had to live in stables, tents, old cars, sheds (others in damp cellars where we would not place a valued animal, let alone a human being.[14]

Out of such conditions, all too close to the labouring man in the cities, the labour movement was growing and assuming a new attitude. The fight for a living wage became more than a battle with the boss; it came to be seen as part of a larger war. The corporations and industries, the ever-multiplying factories and the branching-out railways were all an apparatus that supported a capitalist class. Based and built on labour it remained apart and hostile, designed to exploit humanity as it exploited other resources. With such a view socialism was not far off, and it was soon infecting labour.

It was not much help to unionism, for the idea of political action brought out a host of parties, each at odds with the other. The common man changed slowly, and wages, jobs and working conditions remained his first concerns. While social theorists dreamed and bickered above him, their many quarrels diluted union strength. The structure of trade unionism and its provincial, national and continental relationships were further divisive problems. The great American unions invaded Canada, offering the benefit of funds and organization but pursuing their own aims. At Berlin in 1902, when the Canadian Trades and Labour Congress met with the American Federation of Labor, the only result was new and worse division. Most of Catholic Quebec, resenting Americanism, Protestantism and perhaps Englishness itself, broke off in a separate group. Ontario and the other provinces were left seriously weakened in a Trades and Labour Congress which accepted American standards and in effect American control. The labour movement, though it was steadily growing in numbers and in consciousness of needs and rights, was tarred with the American brush and distracted within itself.

In 1900, two years before the Canadian Manufacturers' Association was incorporated as a national body, Ontario established a new Bureau of Labour. Its primary function was "to collect, assort, systematize and publish information and statistics relating to employment, wages and hours of labour throughout the province . . . (and to assemble information) on subjects of interest to the working-men."[15] A second hope for the Bureau was that it might serve as arbiter and conciliator and generally ease relationships between the working man and the employer. Nine years later, however, though it had accomplished a good deal, it had hardly changed the Canadian manufacturer. "Unionism," said its official publication, "is undoubtedly a good thing, but like strychnine it must be taken in small doses."[16]

They were small doses indeed through the first years of the century, as the iron of Michipicoten began to flow from Algoma and new foundries and blast furnaces opened up in Hamilton. The new west was calling for Ontario products, the new north was feeding down the resources, and the proclaimed function of the capitalist, echoed by all promoters, was to turn them into wealth. Queen's Park concurred, sharing the same idea and assisting the same cause. So did rival towns, each competing with another in the range of good things offered. For the potential manufacturer there were tax privileges and bonuses and, often enough, the inducement of cheap labour. There was less inducement for the trade union organizer, preaching his dangerous doctrines and importing "agitation." He interfered with initiative and with the laws of economics as interpreted by provincial builders whose one philosophy was growth.

The same growth, moreover, was enhancing the rural aspect of the general social problem. As cities and towns grew the farm community decreased, fostering a mood that threatened to become portentous. Girls of the 1880s had had a song on the farmlands as young men left for the west:

I'll sing you a song of that plaguey pest,
It goes by the name of the Great North-West,
I cannot have a beau at all,
They all skip out there in the fall.
One by one they all clear out
Thinking to better themselves, no doubt,
Caring little how far they go
From the poor little girls of Ontario.[17]

By the early 1890s, out of the same resentments, farm scribes were depicting life in the cities:

Miserable is the lot of poor men labouring in the cities, poverty often denies them a proper shelter and they are ashamed to make their necessities known, others are seen crawling along the streets, their countenances so haggard by woe, hunger and cold as scarcely to give them semblance of humanity . . . others labouring under disease, destitute of sustenance and the commonest necessities of life, stretched on some miserable pallet in garrets or cellars, where damp, cold, dirt and vermin are their only companions, lingering out their hapless moments in anguish and hopeless despair.[18]

133

What truth there was in the picture reflected another truth: industrialization and agriculture were becoming forces at war.

4.

As the turn of the century came, the proportion of rural to urban population was 57 per cent. It had shrunk in ten years by almost 10 per cent, yet a majority of Ontario's people were still engaged in farming. Grain, livestock, dairy products, fruits, vegetables and lesser crops delivered an annual income of some $200,000,000.00. It was a return of 20 per cent on a total investment in land, buildings, farm animals and implements estimated at $1,000,000,000.00. The figure was considerably larger than the investment in manufacturing for the entire Dominion of Canada. The farm community in another way was still, as its spokesmen claimed for it, "the sheet anchor of the country." Most of its export trade, diverted by American tariffs, was now with the British Isles. The agricultural interest, though few farmers were imperialists, was an important factor in strengthening the imperial connection.

Improving quality in some fields was another factor of progress. While Ontario cheese and dairy products flooded the British market, Ontario stock and breeding animals were sought in the United States and imported in spite of tariffs. The province famous for its bacon was becoming famous for its beef as refrigeration promoted easier shipment. Ontario sheep were known and Ontario wool demanded, though most of the latter was reserved for home consumption. Horses bred in Ontario had been used in the Boer War, and more of the same were now sought in Great Britain. So were Ontario fruits, particularly Ontario apples; and, though the palm for wheat had passed to Western Canada, barley, flax and feed grains with increasing production of tobacco and crops of newer soya beans more than made up the loss.

In every branch of the industry there was effective organization, designed not only for progress but to enrich a way of life. Stock breeders, dairymen, grain growers, fruit growers, bee-keepers and a host of other specialists were allied across the province in separate associations. Almost as diverse and numerous as the variety of farm products, the groups worked for themselves yet maintained essential unity. Whatever the particular interest it was part of the general field, for all rested on the land. The tradition of farmers' meetings, joint discussion of problems and joint displays of products at the annual fall fairs was as old as the province itself. The Farmers' Institutes and the Womens' Institutes were another source of strength, fostering pride and a half-religious devotion to the ways of farm life.

134

Nevertheless, the sons were leaving for the cities. There was a sense of diminished place, of a steadily constricting future, of a changed, preoccupied government that was turning to new concerns.

It was hardly Ross's fault. He could point to the work of the Ontario College of Agriculture, not yet quite appreciated but yearly more effective. The long record of assistance that had begun in Mowat's time went on through many agencies supported by provincial grants. With Ross as with all his predecessors, the strength and value of Ontario's farm community was an article of political faith. Yet he was uneasily aware that farm strength was diminishing in proportion to urban growth. The Patrons of Industry were dead and the Grange was slowly dying, not through political influences but from lack of farm support. The hope of retail co-operatives that had quickened both movements was being killed by the new department stores in larger towns and cities. It was the same with farmers' insurance companies and the dream of farmers' banks; the pressures of centralization and the weight of urban capital were wearing them all down.[19]

The much-demanded railways, supplemented now by the occasional electric tramline, were diluting many of their benefits by a host of new encroachments. Freight rates on produce were set for the long haul and penalized the local shipper who supplied a nearby market. The trains that brought the newspapers with their endless columns of advertising were also bringing the mail order catalogue, draining off further money from the struggling country store. Even the new roads were creating new resentments. By 1904, as forty machines of the Toronto and Hamilton Auto Clubs began an intercity journey which only twenty would complete, the automobile itself had become an urban imposition. The legislature the year before, faced with many complaints of farm animals run over, horses frightened and Sabbath quiet disturbed, had imposed a speed limit of fifteen miles per hour on all vehicles travelling country roads. Yet the farmer was not placated, for whatever the rate it travelled at he detested the thing itself.

Taxation became a problem as other disparities grew. In 1899, for the first time in its history, the province imposed a tax on corporations, but this act, intended for rural appeasement, was negated by flat refusal of another emerging claim. The farmer shared his tax base with the towns of his municipality, and it was all too often eroded by grants of industrial land. The result in his eyes was less land for assessment and proportionately increased taxation; he was subsidizing the manufacturer. It was a dubious and fine-spun theory but it remained a standing grudge, for in this case Ross could not give way. He was beset by towns and cities competing for new industry and the tax privileges and land grants were part of the onward march.

Nor was Whitney very helpful in supporting the farmers' claims. Free of responsibility, he could carp at much that was done, yet his own programs were vague. For the most part they were a patchwork series of improvements on established Liberal policy. A constant critic of the Ontario College of Agriculture, he attacked its centralization. Yet his remedy for that was wider distribution, an expansion in plant and faculties and even in additional colleges, where many farmers were concerned at the cost of one. On the tax question, though he harped at Ross, he was almost eye-to-eye with him; inclined if anything to facilitate, rather than whittle down, the efforts of the municipalities to attract industry. What the farmer saw, as he watched a declining government and a rising opposition, was the need to look out for himself.

Goldwin Smith, perennial supporter of lost and losing causes, had emerged in his later years as a champion of the farmers' interest. He had rescued the *Weekly Sun*, the faltering organ of the defunct Patrons of Industry, and given it a new voice. In September 1902, again on Smith's initiative, a substantial group of farmers came together. They were opposed to unfair freight rates, to tax policies that gave the advantage to industry, and they were of Smith's view on tariff policies and free trade with the Americans. With these ideas as its base the Ontario Farmers Association came into being. Significantly it was looking to the west, where agriculture was everything. As the Saskatchewan Grain Growers Association began to arouse the prairies, the Ontario Farmers Association expanded in its own province. By 1905 it was beginning to absorb the Grange and the greater movement of the United Farmers of Ontario was only a few years off.

It was not yet a new political groundswell but it helped to defeat Ross, washing away his rural Grit bases. Liberalism went out with the ebb, Conservatism came in with the flood, while the old ways of the farmer, like the old ways of society, continued their slow change.

5.

Through Ross's time as Premier, and thanks largely to the tolerant views of Whitney, the issue of separate schools remained quiescent. So too, for the most part, did the development of the public schools. Standards and teaching were criticized, and there were demands for vocational training which remained largely unmet. The high cost of textbooks and the government's close relations with friendly Liberal publishers brought charges of a "school-book ring." The main thrust of debate, however, and the main course of progress was on the level of the universities.

In this field some long-standing controversies were approaching a culmination. Western University, established in London as a child of Huron College, had struggled for a quarter-century without provincial support. By the early 1900s it had little to show for its efforts but a stubborn western spirit. Its one building had been financed by private subscription, with professors taking shares. Sketchily-paid lecturers, with their incomes rising and falling in proportion to students' fees, maintained a faculty of Arts. Medicine, the other faculty, was without a staff professor, and was served only and irregularly by busy local doctors. Annual revenues fluctuated in the neighbourhood of $3,000.00, while a deficit of $1,000.00 remained the only constant. The university was poor, deficient in almost everything and had no official claim on provincial aid. There was local opposition even to its mere existence, yet there was more of local pride and local need. Students went to Western who could not afford Toronto, and a provincial government could not forget that.

Still less could it forget Queen's, in the eastern heart of the province. Here was the growing fiefdom of George Munro Grant, stubbornly independent, lingeringly Presbyterian, yet asserting undoubted claims. They were geographical, financial and educational, and they had been backed by more than words. The eastern Ontario student, in the view of George Grant, was entitled to a university that was near his own home. For that purpose, and largely by his own efforts, the principal had raised a quarter of a million dollars, and he had improved standards as rapidly as he erected buildings. By 1893, he had acquired government support for a School of Mining and Agriculture. By 1894 he had a faculty of Practical Science. By 1901, still in the cause of science, which could be divorced from Presbyterianism, the government had erected a mining building and doubled the annual grant.

Yet it was not enough in proportion to Queen's work, and Grant took a decisive step. His aim was a university wide as the fields of learning, and it was not to be treated by the province as a mere glorified trade school. The denominational stamp was the only barrier he recognized in the way of further support; and in his eyes it was not a barrier at all. For over ten years neither the trustees nor the staff had been required to be Presbyterian, and less than half of the 800 students were by then members of the faith. On these grounds Grant had proposed to the church that it dissolve its connection with Queen's, and the proposal seemed to be favoured. It was not accepted when he died, in May 1902, but the force of his argument remained. Why should not Queen's, which was doing about two-fifths of all the Arts teaching in the province, receive a proportionate share of government aid? "More than one college is needed," Grant had said years earlier in rejecting federation. "Why, then, if public support is to be given, should it be limited to one?"[20]

All this emphasized the central problem: the needs, nature and standing of the University of Toronto. The affiliation of religious colleges in the early 1890s had brought cohesion and strength. Victoria, once of Cobourg, was now established in its own buildings on the campus, strong, progressive and autonomous within the frame of federation. By 1904, faced with many necessities and with the impossibility of meeting them as a denominational college, Trinity had followed Victoria into federation. The great work begun by liberal secularists seemed to have attained its goal, and seemed to have been accepted.

> Every sect cannot have a genuine University, (Chancellor S. S. Nelles of Victoria had said during the heat of the early controversy preceding federation,) and the Legislature cannot recognize the claims of one sect over another . . . I can remember when a Canadian University could venture to issue its calendar with an announcement of a single professor for all the natural sciences, and with a laboratory somewhat similar to an ordinary blacksmith shop, where the professor was his own assistant and compelled to blow not only his own bellows but his own trumpet as well. We can hardly be expected to go on in that style now.[21]

But, speaking as Methodist minister as well as educator, he had also attached a warning. It remained in many minds, potent and long enduring.

> I have not agreed, (he said) and I do not now agree with those who think that the higher education of the country should be purely secular . . . (Without) the highest and most effective of all spiritual forces, . . . the power of the Christian faith . . . she will stand, like Niobe of old, through her irreverence and despair, at last hardened into stone, and holding, not indeed the New Testament but 'an empty urn within her withered hands.'[22]

Secular growth itself had been attended by secular problems. In 1895, more or less coincident with the establishment of a department of political economy, the University of Toronto had enjoyed a students' strike. It had been a first cutting of teeth for the young Mackenzie King, one of the principal leaders, and it had been based more on defects of communication than on any actual grievance. An aloof administration, accused of favouritism and nepotism in making faculty appointments, was able to dispel the charges when they came to be fully aired. The strike died, but discontent continued, for its real basis was money. Administration was defective because it was not adequately supplied.

In the face of the claims of Queen's, the needs of the western part of the province, and the generally grudging attitudes of farm and labour spokesmen, Toronto asserted its own claims as the "state" university. It was that, to the extent that it was endowed by the Crown, but it had no assured claim on provincial revenue. Blake in his years as Chancellor had made the reverse claim; the university, through living on its own means, maintained its independence. By 1900, however, Meredith as the new Chancellor was faced with the new century and all its multiplying needs. He had different views from Blake, and he had a formidable new agent. The University of Toronto Alumni Association, formed when he took office, expanded to seventeen branches in the course of one year. It soon joined Meredith, and a changed and vocal Whitney, in applying pressure to Ross. Increased state aid, with the ever-broadening vistas that were opening to education, had become a state necessity. It had become so in particular for the University of Toronto, which was entitled to the lion's share. The government could not detach itself from higher education, nor in actual fact did it even pretend to do so. It supervised, suggested, discussed the problems of faculties and recommended appointments, while its purse was kept almost closed.

Fact as all this was, it was truth among many truths for the beset Ross. The university was struggling, its administration was weak, and politics and inertia combined to impede progress. Yet old thrift prevailed in the general mood of the province. Changed attitudes were dangerous, a general reorganization might involve huge expense, and there could be only half measures in response to large demands. In 1901, with the passing of a new University Act, the government provided grants of about $25,000.00 annually toward the maintenance of science departments. Money for buildings followed drib by drab, with a final grant in 1904, of some $300,000.00.

Whitney, for his part, went into the decisive election as a man at Meredith's side. He had grown far, under the influence of that friend, from the parochial politician who had considered that "more than enough was being done to aid education at the university level." He was influenced by new needs, and he was more aware than Ross that they were creating new moods. Whatever the other claims, the University of Toronto stood pre-eminent; accepted, desired, demanded. "We must take a forward position on the university question or else consent to be left hopelessly in the rear with disastrous results, one of which will inevitably be that our young men will go elsewhere for higher education."[23] They must not be allowed to do that, and they must be given the best at home. The university could not go on as it was, badly organized within, forever unsure of its position, stranded on a fixed endowment or rescued by fitful grants. It could not be permitted to remain "suspended between heaven and earth, like the coffin of Mohammed."[24] Conservatism, when it came to power, was pledged to correct that.

6.

Through most of the nineteenth century Ontario had been crude and wasteful in its use of natural resources. Governments had decreed and legislated but enforced very little, permitting lumbermen and miners to follow their own bent. Reforestation was talked of but remained largely ignored. It was 1898 before forest reserves were established to assure timber for the future. It was 1901 before the first school of forestry was opened at Queen's in Kingston. Sudbury's copper-nickel had been almost given away and the administration of pulpwood, with the one exception of the Soo, was a record of loss and muddle. Between 1898 and 1903 eight concessions had been granted on the terms established with Francis Clergue. They did nothing to improve revenues and failed of their main intent, which was to produce mills and jobs. Three mills were begun and almost immediately closed in the face of recession in the industry and high American tariffs. The other five concessions, which had been simply grabbed by speculators, did not produce at all.

To the record of domestic shortcomings were added foreign factors. American capital and markets were both essential to Ontario, but they imposed their own terms. The American investor supported and the American buyer controlled much of resource development. He could affect the results of development as they applied to native industry. The extent to which this was true became sharply evident toward the close of the nineteenth century, and the extent to which it was endurable became a lively question. It was this question, linking some major battles and capped by one disaster, that resulted in basic changes.

The Dingley tariff of 1897 asserted American protectionism in new and arrogant form. Sawlogs, the raw timber of Ontario, could be imported free by mills in the United States. Sawn lumber, however, the product of Ontario mills, was to be shut out by a frankly prohibitive duty. American tariff-makers, looking at the map from their side, had produced an explicit pattern. The sawmills of Ontario, with all their attendant industries, were to be confined to the domestic market. They were not to compete with Michigan or

Wisconsin or Minnesota for the jobs and wealth to be had in the United States. Ontario was to stand confirmed in its role of grower and hewer while the profits of manufacturing went off with the export timber in a one-way flow to the south.

It became clear that the limits of the endurable had been passed. Yet the federal government of Laurier, negotiating with the American government on the whole range of tariffs, could not afford reprisals on Canadian timber alone. Nor could the Ontario government act without the risk of shattering loss. Older lumbering firms in the eastern part of the province had an established trade in sawlogs, unaffected by duty. If that trade went, through a provincially-imposed embargo, it would raise a furious outcry. There were doubts as to the power of the province to impose any embargo, and formidable legal problems as to the status of Crown lands. Where they had been leased as timber tracts they had been leased on set conditions, and no condition impeded the right to export. The decisive voice, however, came from the new northwest. All across that region, from Lake Huron to Rainy River, were younger firms that were building their trade on sawmills and looking ahead to pulp mills based in their own domain. They were in full voice within a month of the Dingley tariff, and they forced the government's hand. "It is a hundred times more serious a matter," said Hardy, "than the Canadian lumbermen who are interested think."[25] Nevertheless, and in spite of the risks, he brought his bill to the legislature in 1897. It was passed and became law on April 30, 1898, providing that all pine timber cut on the Crown lands of Ontario be sawn in Canadian mills. The "manufacturing condition" had been established.

The results were better than the government had dared to hope. The manufacturing condition was confirmed by Canadian courts and accepted by the Dominion government. Instead of American reprisals American mills began to move north of the border to be near where the timber grew. By 1899 pulp and the spruce for making it had become more important, as the sulphite chemical process improved and cheapened production. A new and confident Ontarianism reacted promptly to that. The United States, said J. R. Stratton, who was then Provincial Secretary, should have manufactured products "but not one stick of spruce."[26] The manufacturing condition as it applied to pine timber was extended to pulpwood. By the end of 1900 all milling and processing of the wood from Crown lands would have to be done in Canada.

The next move was natural enough and was stimulated by many developments already achieved or in sight. Francis H. Clergue, building his industrial complex at the throat of Lake Superior, provided an example of what the province could do, and do with its

141

own resources. American though he was, he was a nourisher of local pride: "I had made up my mind never to ask for anything that had to be procured outside of Algoma."[27] He had procured his hydro-electric power, built his mill and tramlines and given the "Soo" the advantages of electric light. He had invented a drying method, in the case of groundwood pulp, that reduced its bulk for shipping. The sulphite process came, requiring the use of sulphur, which was then imported from Sicily at a ruinously high cost. Clergue looked instead toward the domain of the Canadian Copper Company, overhung with its yellow cloud. "I went up to the works at Sudbury and found they were racing sulphurous acid gas off into the air at a value of $2,000 a day at an expense and loss."[28] Unable to persuade the mining men to attempt to reduce the gas, he bought claims in the region, uncovered ore deposits and shipped them off to the Soo. Smelting the ore there, he not only obtained his sulphur but a superior nickel-steel along with a copper residue, which he began to separate and use. For this work certain alkalis were needed, produced by salt from Goderich and by an electrolytic process which Clergue developed himself. Chlorine gas was a by-product of the electrolytic method and resulted in a plant for bleaching powder that was used to whiten pulp. Sawmills and a veneer mill, large enough in themselves, were merely casual outgrowths of the trade in other lumber.

In the meantime, in the Michipicoten area to the northwest of the Soo, Clergue had acquired an iron mine which he named after his sister. The Helen mine was estimated, with what proved to be over-optimism, to have a reserve of some 30,000,000 tons of the best hematite ore. It was for the moment without access, but in 1899 a grant of 7,400 acres per mile from the provincial government and $6,400.00 per mile from the federal government provided means for a railway. Chartered as the Algoma Central, it was to connect the mine with the steel mills of the Soo, but Clergue's assorted urgencies could not wait for its completion. By the end of the year the new Michipicoten Harbour had been built on Lake Superior and the first twelve miles of steel, running from there north, had connected the harbour with the mine. With a fleet of some twenty carriers moving on the Great Lakes, Clergue could deliver his iron ore as well as his other products. In 1900, as 50,000 tons went to his mills, he described the sum of his enterprises in sufficiently mild words as "An Instance of Industrial Evolution in Northern Ontario."[29]

There were other instances elsewhere, though not of the same scope. Iron and steel interests, beginning to grow at Hamilton on the support of generous bounties, were casting their eyes north. Sudbury loomed before them, an example, warning and irritant, with its wealth of copper and nickel ore that became American steel. Why should it? Why should the ore go out, royalty-free, to be refined in American refineries and line American pockets? The Canadian Copper Company, controlled by American capital, enjoyed a near-monopoly on the product of Sudbury mines. The Orford Company of New Jersey, by virtue of its secret process, had the same monopoly in refining. In all fields Ontarians had been shut out, and the Hamilton interests now proposed to get in. They had the support of S. J. Ritchie, the first promoter of Sudbury, who had quarrelled with his American backers and was now out for himself. They had the industrial strength and capital to mine Sudbury ore. They had a new refining process which they claimed was better than Orford's, and they were acquiring mills and blast furnaces for the making of nickel-steel. They were in the same position, they felt, as the lumbermen and the pulp men; capable of home industry but requiring aid from government that would give them the means to compete. That aid, in default of a federal tariff change, was the manufacturing condition.

As the pressures mounted on Ross, who had now replaced Hardy, the first complexities emerged. Timber and pulpwood logs were the product of Crown lands, owned and administered by Ontario. The mines of Sudbury, however, were all private property, sold for a dollar an acre in the much-regretted past. The exportation of their ore, though it might be controlled by tariffs which Laurier would not impose, could not be embargoed by any provincial fiat. The one recourse was a licence fee, and this came to be adopted. In April 1900, with the approval of the opposition and with loud howls from mining men, an amendment to the Ontario Mines Act was passed in the provincial legislature. All exported ore would be subject to a graded licence fee which in the case of nickel matte, Sudbury's principal product, would be $60.00 per ton. If, however, the ore was refined in Canada the entire fee would be refunded.

The year-long battle that followed was to provide many lessons for the future. One by one, with threats and delegations, with battalions of lawyers and great barrages of journalism, the mining interests and particularly the copper and nickel interests bore down on government. Canadian Copper and Orford, the mining-refining complex, attacked first in Ottawa. The enormous provincial licence fee meant virtual confiscation. It would destroy an industry that could not refine in Sudbury, for weighty technical reasons that experts gave at length. It was an entrenchment on trade and commerce, an invasion of the federal field, and if the federal government did not act the American interests would. They owned, they pointed out, untapped deposits of nickel and copper ore that were a world away from Sudbury. New Caledonia, the long, humpbacked island in the far western Pacific, could be opened up to replace the Ontario mines. The threat was real to the government, and still more real to the men at the mines themselves. Some 1,500 jobs, with the economy of the whole area, seemed on the way to extinction.

The protests came in waves from the mines and smelters. Toronto developed doubts about the ability of Canadian capital to mobilize a replacement industry. There was familiar talk of a flight of invested capital, American and British both, from a province that ignored contracts. On the political level, also, there were further disastrous signs. Laurier had seen the licence fee as "absolutely prohibitory,"[30] and nothing had changed his mind. By April 1901, with an opinion from his Minister of Justice that the Act was beyond the powers of the provincial legislature, he was prepared to disallow it. With the provincial government on a collision course which it was now desperate to avoid, Ross gave way at last. Early in May a compromise was reached which was less and more than it seemed. The federal government would wait, withholding its disallowance, while the Ontario government referred its case to the Supreme Court of Canada. Since Ross did not refer it, and did not intend to do so, the act was consigned to limbo, unproclaimed. It remained ignored in the records for another six years, to be repealed at length by Whitney.

By the end of 1902, though there had been one bruising defeat, the government had much to point to. The manufacturing condition had achieved its purpose, particularly with regard to timber. There had been a huge transplant of sawmilling from the United States to Ontario. In the Lake Huron and Georgian Bay areas Canadian mills were growing and American mills were springing up beside them. The mills of the farther west, in the Keewatin, Kenora and Rainy River regions, had once seemed large enough. They were being dwarfed now or stimulated to growth themselves by American-financed plants.

The pulp industry remained an uncertain quantity, hampered by speculation and by the open door of Quebec, which still shipped its logs to the American market. Yet there was Clergue's mill at the Soo and another at Sturgeon Falls, both predating the condition but leaping ahead from its effect. Smaller mills were growing from the same stimulus; and there was a new confidence in prospects that were certain to bring more.

With blast furnaces at Deseronto and Midland, and with a large and growing complex centred on Hamilton, there was a confident basic industry developing from iron and steel. Confidence sprang, above all, from the great smoke-covered Soo, where all industry was flourishing and all things seemed possible. In early 1902, with ore flowing from the Helen mine to its new furnaces and rolling mills, the Algoma Steel Company was organized with a capital of $20,000,000.00. It was one only, and only the newest member, of Clergue's enormous family. The names of the greatest members were all household words: The Lake Superior Power Company, the Sault Ste. Marie Pulp and Paper Company, the Nickel-Steel Company, the Canadian Electro-Chemical Company, Ontario Lake Superior Company, Algoma Commercial Company and Algoma Central Railway. The whole was tied together by a great holding company, the Consolidated Lake Superior Corporation, and it seemed as firmly based, as naturally sprung from the land, as the province of Ontario itself.

Unfortunately the Corporation was lubricated in all its workings and fed through all its veins by a flow of American capital which suddenly dried up. There were dark rumours of machinations in Wall Street, but the surface facts were clear. Clergue was over-extended, vulnerable to a sudden strain, and the strain duly came. Steel rails, the products of his new plant, began to be returned by railway builders who found them hard and brittle. Something was wrong with the furnaces or the blends or grades of ore; it was an incidental "bug." But it meant research and delay, a conversion of furnaces and processes and a shattering loss on contracts. Money was required immediately and money could not be found; the New York markets would not respond to the demand. In December of 1902, with an idled mill and 500 men laid off, the company postponed a dividend. Its reputation was damaged, its stock plunged on the markets, and the high capitalists of the directorate deposed Francis Clergue.

By the summer of 1903, with affairs deteriorating in a general financial shambles, the company had defaulted on interest payments, and was faced with a maturing loan of some $5,000,000.00 from commercial bankers in New York. Unable to meet the loan when it fell due in September, the directors also defaulted on the weekly payrolls. Thirty-five hundred men, turned out on the streets, returned on the 28th to attack the company's office, and for three days there was a series of minor riots. It was October 1 when troops arrived from Toronto, accompanied by Clergue himself. No longer general manager, he still remained the promoter and he came with news that promoted a semblance of peace. The provincial government, he said, had agreed to meet the payrolls and provide further assistance.

"I think it will be a case of Government ownership,"[31] said Whitney when proposals came to the legislature in April of 1904. It

145

was not to be quite that, but it was to be heavy government involvement in a badly-battered and diminished operation. All subsidiaries
of the Consolidated Lake Superior Corporation had been declared
insolvent, their combined assets had been written down from a value
of $35,000,000.00 to a value of $2,100,000.00 and were owned by a
queue of creditors with the New York bank at their head. There was
danger that the whole enterprise, with its ore, pulpwood, jobs, its
half-completed railway and its future prospects, would pass to
foreign hands. It would pass, moreover, with an ignominious loss of
foreign capital, damaging the credit of Ontario and discouraging all
investment. For the sake of its own name, and to retain control of its
resources, the province was forced to act. In return for a first mortgage on all the properties and a right to the appointment of two
directors to the board, it guaranteed a loan to the company of
$2,000,000.00.

For Ross it was a bad moment during his last year of office. All the
disputed grants, benefits and concessions, and all the boasts he had
made for the Clergue enterprises, were passed in long review by the
opposition. He stood up in the House with thirty-two years of
Liberal government behind him, and with the flagship of its resource
policy struck and floundering on the rocks. Yet even Conservatives
agreed that it had to be pulled off, and with the approval of the loan
arrangement the vessel was at least afloat. The reorganized corporation, shedding most of its subsidiaries, was to struggle on for a
decade as a maker of iron and steel, with more struggles ahead of it
on the way to secure status. The great originator, meanwhile, had
departed for other fields. Clergue moved to Europe, on to the Rus-
sian Caucasus as a negotiator for Shell Oil, and returned as an
industrial consultant to die in Montreal.

7.

A new provincial adventure immediately preceded the fall of the
Clergue enterprises. On May 12, 1902, at Trout Lake, some three
miles from North Bay, the first sod was turned for the building of the
Temiskaming and Northern Ontario Railway. A product of politics,
business pressures and demands for northern settlement it must, at
least at its outset, have been one of the luckiest railways ever built.

Coming to office in 1899, Ross found, as he wrote later, that "the
only striking policy offering itself was development of the district
between the CPR and Hudson Bay."[32] It was hardly a new policy and
the words seem listless and vague, but the resulting action was not.
Ten large survey parties, including geologists, foresters and
agricultural experts, were sent off in the summer of that year to ex-

plore the northern country from the Quebec boundary to the Lake Superior hinterland. When they returned and their reports were published Ontario's sketchy knowledge of itself became a dramatic new conception.

Around Lake Timiskaming on the Quebec border, a hundred miles to the north of North Bay, there were known and settled areas of good farmland. What was actually revealed, however, as the survey work went forward, was a region of over 1,000,000 acres of arable land to the west and northwest of the lake. It was a valuable find but it became known as the "Little" Clay Belt, since it was immediately dwarfed by a discovery sixteen times as large. The "Great Clay Belt," as it came to be pieced together from the sum of all reports, was a wide band of some 25,000 square miles extending northward along the height of land and westward from the Ontario boundary through the Nipissing and Algoma Districts into the District of Thunder Bay. Described by some of the experts as "an almost unbroken stretch of good farmland,"[33] it was considerably more than that; enough more, perhaps, that it might have carried a warning. The rich clay loam was watered by many rivers, broken by great outcroppings that promised minerals and ore, and interspersed and surrounded by millions of acres of forest. It was timber, pulp and mining country as well as farming country, and it hinted of old troubles. Nor was any of it wholly new; it had been known and settled in patches. What came, however, with the discovery of its real dimensions, was a gathering together of all hopes in the north. New Ontario, based on the height of land, looking toward Hudson Bay and almost three-quarters as large as the settled southern province, became a quickening fact of life.

Inevitably railway problems quickened with it. The CPR was the pride of Montreal; it was less loved in Toronto. "With all due respect for the C.P.R.," Francis Clergue had informed the Board of Trade, "so far as Ontario is concerned it had better never have been built."[34] It passed west below the slopes of the height of land, carrying immigrants to the prairies instead of the new north. At the same time it was threatening to drain the north, for a branch line to Mattawa was extending toward Lake Timiskaming and providing Montreal with direct connections. Toronto's grasp on the hinterland ended at North Bay where the old Northern, which was now the Ontario Northland, connected with the CPR. New lines were required, even in the present race with the eastern competitor, and the future promised a demand for still more. Some day, and soon, in the opinion of the well-informed, there would be a second major railway crossing the continent. It would have to cross Ontario well to the north of the first, and whether built by William Mackenzie and Donald Mann, the entrepreneurs of the west, or by the Grand Trunk, the old lord of the east, it should be made to serve Toronto as the CPR did not. It should be locked to the south by northward-groping branch lines, and the time to build was now.

There were these pressures and there was the older one for the advance of northern settlement. Farmers in the Timiskaming area, encouraged to establish there, had been demanding a link with the south for ten years. Veterans of the South African War, with their free grants of 160 acres, were determined to settle in the region. So were thousands of others who swarmed in on the land offices to purchase their tracts at 50 cents per acre. The Temiskaming and Northern Ontario was to begin at North Bay, run first to the Lake, and go on from there to open the Greater Clay Belt as time and money permitted. The press supported the government, the opposition concurred, and the usual talk of railway barons and bloated corporations could be left for another day. Making a virtue of necessity, since it could not find private builders, the government proposed to build the line itself. Its own Board of Commissioners, provided with a land grant of 20,000 acres per mile, was to appoint a contractor, supervise construction and manage the entire railway. The initial cash requirements of some $2,000,000.00 were supplied by way of a bond issue with a provincial guarantee. It was also the government's hope, long to be unfulfilled, that a federal subsidy would ease the provincial burden.

Laurier, like Macdonald before him, disliked the thought of a provincially owned railway. Yet his refusal to provide assistance was a minor disappointment and the work went steadily on. Having taken its major decision, the government had also decided that the road should be well built, not as a "colonization" line but as a carrier of heavy goods. The planners knew there would be plentiful timber and pulpwood, they suspected potential ore, and their purpose was to serve Toronto as well as to promote settlement.

From North Bay the line curved up along the course of the North River, hacking its way through bush, bridging stretches of muskeg and blasting grades through rock. The grades proved to be moderate, much of the virgin forest had been cleared on the southern stretches, and the provincial Board of Commissioners had chosen a good builder. By the end of 1904, with a little over a hundred miles of trackage and with townsites marked and pumps and water tanks installed, the road had trains in service. Haileybury, the centre for Timiskaming, was a major point on the line and the temporary terminus was New Liskeard, five miles to the north. The telegraph service would prove to be the one failure and later have to be replaced. That, however, was not known at the time. On January 16, 1905, nine days before the defeat of the Liberal government, the Board of Commissioners of the Temiskaming and Northern Ontario Railway formally accepted the "first division" as complete.

Work on a second division was under way, approved by the provincial legislature early in 1904. By that time, out of long wrestling on the federal scene, the plan had evolved for the National Transcontinental and the Grand Trunk Pacific. The two sections, when completed, would be operated as one railway and would be another and northerly line spanning the continent. The eastern section, to be built by the federal government, would cross New Ontario and connect with the provincial railway, extended north from New Liskeard, at a point near Iroquois Falls, later to be known as Cochrane. The Temiskaming and Northern Ontario would have reached the heart of the Clay Belt, joined the Transcontinental and be pointing beyond that. Above Iroquois Falls were the Abitibi River and a veining of ancient pack trails leading to James Bay.

Yet these achievements and prospects had been overshadowed by others. In August 1903 the line of the first division had been a little south of Haileybury, at Mile 103. The right of way was a gash through rocky country, cleared of most of its timber and strewn with second-growth bush. Two timber cruisers, James H. McKinley and Ernest J. Darragh, were passing along the raw face of the cut when they discovered glintings of ore. They remembered Sudbury and immediately suspected copper, but were cautious enough to keep their findings secret. A month later, Fred Larose, a blacksmith, was out on a nearby section. According to one legend he must have been working at night and he must have been carrying a hammer, for he threw it at some glints ahead of him that he thought were the eyes of a fox. There was no yelp of an animal but the hammer clanged on rock, and the resulting spatter of chips was again copper. Or so it was thought by all in on the secret until protective claims were filed. With that, however, authority entered the picture, and W. G. Miller, the provincial geologist arrived.

What he found there, as he scraped away moss and roots matted over ancient rock, seems to have left him a little breathless. Copper was present but Miller almost ignored it in the face of other signs. Four veins had been located, and on the weathered surface of three of them

> vein matter is coated with the beautiful pink decomposition product, cobalt bloom. The green nickel stain is also seen on some surfaces but is usually marked by that of the cobalt. The native silver occurs as films or leaves and fine threads of moss-like forms through the nickel and cobalt minerals . . . . One sheet composed

chiefly of silver attached to the rock surface had a thickness of nearly 0.375 inches and a diameter of about one foot.[35]

He came from those to the fourth vein.

> Here a perpendicular bare cliff of rock 60 or 70 feet high faces west. The vein, whose width averages not more than eight inches, cuts this face at right angles and has almost a vertical dip. The vein is weathered away leaving a crack in the face of the cliff two feet, in some places 4 or 5 feet, in depth. When I saw it first it had not been disturbed. Thin leaves of silver up to two inches in diameter were lying on the ledges and the decomposed vein matter was cemented together by the metal, like fungus in rotten wood.[36]

He looked about him, as he finished, at the beginnings of the station site. Mile 103, one of the party told him, was to be called Long Lake, and he grimaced a little at the sound. It would not do, not as a name for this place. He rummaged around in a clutter of fresh lumber and found a square of board. An hour later he had set the board by the trackside and painted COBALT on it. By 1905, as the Ross government left office, Cobalt's fame was spreading. All the railway land grant not allotted to settlers had been declared a mining division. Silver was going out, prospectors coming in, and the traffic on the railway was paying interest on debentures. The real rush, however, had not yet begun. That, with its promise and problems, was left to Whitney's care.

8.

Since 1896 the question of Niagara Falls and its hydro-electric power had been a thorn in the government's side. When Mowat left the scene Hardy had been faced with a monopoly that was sitting entrenched and idle. The Canadian Niagara Power Company, wholly American-owned, had sole rights on the Falls but was generating no power. Its parent company and its market were both on the American side, and it regarded its footing in Canada as a mere option on the future. It was obliged by the terms of its contract to have a plant built and operating by 1898, and to reserve half its power to supply Ontario demand. Yet the end of the term approached with no plant begun, no power available, and nothing to show but vague plans and promises. Ontario watched jealously from its own side of the river as transmission lines brought light and power to Buffalo and electrified New York state.

In 1897 Hardy began to move. By 1898 an Act Respecting Water Powers had been passed, enabling the Commissioner of Crown Lands to reserve from sale any water power or privilege and the land necessary for its development. There was an immediate and intended threat here to the dormant rights of the Niagara Power Company; and in 1899, out of much bickering and pressure, came the basis of a new arrangement. There was to be no monopoly on the Canadian side of the Falls. The Canadian Niagara Power Company, in return for an extension of its own agreement to build, would relinquish exclusive rights and compete with new developers. The way was opened for a second company, which proved a stimulus to the first. By 1902 the Ontario Power Company, a new syndicate formed by Buffalo industrialists, was breaking ground for a plant while the Canadian Niagara Power Company was hurrying to build its own.

Now, the beginnings of a coming storm were rumbling around Premier Ross. There was resentment of American control and fear of American diversion of Niagara's waters. There was rising criticism of corporations and monopolies, and a rising interest in hydro-electric power. In 1900 a committee of the Toronto Board of Trade had discounted the urgency of drawing power from Niagara since it concluded that electricity would remain a "secondary force" compared to steam. In 1902, however, there was a sharp change of opinion. Through a long summer the mines of Pennsylvania were closed by great strikes, and the lack of coal or the prohibitive price of coal were crippling threats to industry. The shortage emphasized the need for the "white coal" of Niagara, renewed jealousy of American use of the waters and stimulated the fear of large private developers who could charge whatever they wished. Nor were these moods and sentiments confined to Toronto alone. Through the whole southwestern peninsula they were suddenly finding voice.

The province's industrial heartland, apart from the capital itself, lay in the great triangle between Lake Ontario, Lake Huron and Lake Erie. Berlin and Waterloo, London, Guelph, Galt, Brantford and some thirty other centres were heavily dependent on steam or on steam-generated power. Wood was long gone as fuel to heat their boilers. The clearing away of the forests had diminished their sources of waterpower as it reduced the flow of streams, while coal with all its uncertainties was becoming more expensive. The towns competed with each other and they all competed with Toronto, but in vital respects their interests ran in common.

Most of them were short of power or could see a shortage coming. Most of them, including Toronto, were within a radius of a hundred miles of Niagara Falls. The power was there to be had, but it was serving American users. When it became available to Ontario it would be through American-controlled companies which would choose the most profitable markets and set their own rates. If it was a bleak prospect for the manufacturer in Toronto, it was worse still for the

151

men in smaller centres which were likely to be bypassed. Power somehow had to be set free. It had to be developed and used at the least possible cost, not for the benefit of avaricious syndicates but as a general public service. This great resource of Ontario must become "the people's power."

That irresistible slogan, as well as the broad idea, had a slow, pragmatic growth. The idea of the public utility on a small and local scale was not new in Ontario. By the early 1900s some hundred municipalities operated their own waterworks or tramways or lighting systems. Thinking on a larger scale had begun with the emergence of Niagara as a potential source of power. For some ten years Dan Detweiler of Berlin, partner in a successful shoe factory, had served as a part-time prophet. On his spare days and evenings he had become a familiar figure on the roads of the Grand valley, peddling along on his bicycle to preach public ownership and the coming of the electric age. He had seen an end to the sputtering oil lamp, the wood-chopping, coal-shovelling and much of the dim-lit drudgery that plagued ordinary life.

Yet it was not the cause of the people but the cause of the manufacturers that struck the first spark. In February 1902, E. W. B. Snider, an owner of factories in St. Jacob's, a few miles from Berlin, addressed a meeting of Waterloo's Board of Trade. He was a man of considerable status as a Liberal politician and had served with Ross through ten years in the legislature. That was behind him now, and he was pondering the question of hydro-electric power. It was going to be developed soon by the two American syndicates, but not for the smaller centres. Without some joint action they were as sure to be passed by as the larger cities were sure to be overcharged. He thought, Snider said, that the municipalities should group together to create a common market and join hands with Toronto in seeking government help.

The words seemed mild enough but they were followed by the great coal shortage, and that by a startling impetus for general mobilization. By June delegates from Toronto and manufacturers from most of the southwest region were holding meetings in Berlin. By August, through two committees, they had evolved proposals for government which Snider presented to Ross.

The municipalities recognized that to supply power was expensive. To achieve economies of scale they were prepared to band together to create a market. With that done, would the government supplant the American-owned syndicates by developing its own power? As a second choice, would it build and control the transmission lines required by the private companies, thereby controlling rates? Or, as a third choice, failing these alternatives, would it

152

reserve the remaining power sites for future public use?

The Premier was faced with a movement whose strength he could not measure and whose demands were disturbingly large. There was a threat here to the sanctity of private property and more than a hint of socialism. The attendant clamour in the press, attacking American monopoly on the Canadian side of the Falls, might well be the work of interested manufacturers. Some of the municipalities were less interested than others and would probably fall away. In any case there could not be a huge expenditure, shared by the whole of the province, for a limited public utility serving the southwest region. To the first and second requests the answer was a firm no. Nor could Ross see grounds for the reservation of power sites or the fear of American control. Each of the existing companies was in competition with the other, and the pervading tinge of Americanism was soon to be wiped out. In February of 1903 the government proudly announced the granting of a third power site to the Electrical Development Company, a native Toronto syndicate supported by British capital.

Ross had underestimated both the "rabble of municipalities" and the force of public opinion. The principals of the new syndicate were William Mackenzie, Frederic Nicholls and Henry Mill Pellatt. Mackenzie was the railway builder whose work with Donald Mann, and whose genius for acquiring subsidies from federal and provincial governments, was extending the Canadian Northern. Nicholls was a large industrialist and electrical engineer who had had much to do with steam in the generation of power. Pellatt was the social lion, promoter and financier who was to look down on Toronto a decade or so later from the battlements of Casa Loma. All three were well and unfavourably known for the arrogance and wretched service of the Toronto Street Railway and the Toronto Electric Light Company, both of which were monopolies and both of which they controlled. At the new prospect of hydro-electric power controlled by the same trio a fierce public outcry peaked in the southwest.

On February 17, 1903, sixty-seven delegates, including the mayors of Toronto, London, Brantford, Galt, Waterloo, Guelph and other centres of the region, met again in Berlin. Some of them manufacturers, all were responsible leaders, and they were all aroused and determined. The "Berlin Convention," as it came to be called in the newspapers, was an ornate name for the discussions of hard-headed men, but it led to immediate action. Within ten days Snider and eleven mayors were once more facing Ross.

The chartering of the Electrical Development Company, Snider assured Ross, had only aggravated the fears of the municipalities.

153

They were either to be starved for power or charged more than they could afford. If the government would not take action as the competitor of the corporations, would it reconsider the alternative? Distribution was the key to rate control. It required the building of transmission lines, which the government was asked again to undertake. This time, however, when Ross repeated his refusal he was met with another plan. The municipalities, if authorized by the government and backed by the approval of their ratepayers, would group together as a jointly-owned utility, build their own transmission lines and negotiate rates with the companies developing power.

For Ross, whatever his opinion of the real worth of the plan, it provided escape from a dilemma. He could not tax the whole province of Ontario to provide power for its southwestern section. Yet the newspapers were hammering him hard as the friend of the "private interests" and the Conservative opposition was supporting the municipalities. "The waterpowers of Niagara should be free as air"[37] was a favourite theme with Whitney. "The government at the switch, not the corporations"[38] was acquiring force as a slogan. Whatever the words meant, they did not mean government investment in the eyes of either party, but they impelled Ross to the safety of the middle ground. If the municipalities were determined on a risky joint enterprise Ross would pass the enabling legislation. He would sit down with his troublesome old friend, Snider, and draft the necessary bill.

The advocates of public power had passed their first milestone. "An Act to Provide for the Construction of Municipal Power Works and the Transmission, Distribution and Supply of Electrical and Other Powers and Energy" was approved by the Ontario legislature in the session of 1903. With that and supplementing it came authority to create the Ontario Power Commission, to be supplied with funds by member municipalities and conduct studies for the work.

On December 8, 1903, the Ontario Power Commission met for the first time, with E. W. B. Snider naturally sitting as chairman. It had appointed as its own consultants a Toronto firm of electrical engineers, and seven municipalities – Toronto, London, Brantford, Guelph, Ingersoll, Stratford and Woodstock – had agreed to contribute $15,000.00 toward the cost of the preliminary studies. There would be a long process of investigation and decision before a spade went into the ground. The power movement, however, had now the status of a legal public body, and it had more than that in reserve. Sitting with Snider on the Commission and beginning to loom over him was the formidable Adam Beck, successful manufacturer, mayor of the city of London and Conservative member of the legislature.

Neither Beck nor Snider nor the power movement as a whole had yet troubled the sleep of the great magnates. By early 1904 the Electrical Development Company had begun building at Niagara, confidently expecting preferment as the first Canadian competitor. It had acquired rights-of-way for transmission lines from Niagara around the head of Lake Ontario and was looking forward to Toronto as a valuable closed market. If Ross saw portents of change he did not give much sign of it. At the end of 1904, in the closing days of his regime, he conceded to the Electrical Development Company the last of the public water rights remaining at Niagara Falls.

He went into his final election on January 25, 1905, claiming "a magnificent record of business administration compared with Conservative inaction and stupid obstruction."[39] From the other side came the statement offered by J. J. Foy. The province, Foy said, was to be delivered from "the hands of grafters, heelers, rake-off men, thimble-riggers, robbers and thieves."[40] In either case the fireworks obscured the facts. Conservatives were all too active and their leaders were not stupid. Whitney disliked Ross but did not question his integrity, and there was little cause to question the administration. "I was for seven years in very close touch with the Civil Service of Ontario," Hector Charlesworth wrote, "and not in all that time did I hear of the misappropriation of one dollar."[41]

As the election results came in the province spoke for itself. Sixty-nine Conservatives were elected to twenty-nine Liberals in what seemed to the politicians a cataclysmic change. It was hardly that beyond the environs of Queen's Park. Some 204,000 Ontarians had voted to retain the government. Some 233,000 had succeeded in throwing it out. Conservatives were to replace Liberals and James Pliny Whitney was to replace George William Ross. Of more significance, however, though Ross had been slow to realize it, was a prophecy of the Toronto *Globe*.

> The twentieth century, (it had said in 1900) will be kept busy wrestling with millionaires and billionaires to get back and restore to the people that which the nineteenth century gave away and thanked the plutocrats for accepting . . . .[42]

Notes

1. A.H.U. Colquhoun, *Press, Politics and People* (Toronto: Macmillan of Canada, 1935), p. 61.
2. Charlesworth, *Candid Chronicles*, p. 181.
3. Ross, *Getting Into Parliament and After*, p. 219.
4. Charles W. Humphries, *The Political Career of Sir James P. Whitney*, Ph. D. Thesis, University of Toronto, 1966, p. 135.
5. *Ibid.*, p. 65.

6. Robert Craig Brown and Ramsay Cook, *Canada 1896-1921* (Toronto: McClelland and Stewart Limited, 1974), p. 31.
7. *Ibid.*, quoted p. 163.
8. Robert Craig Brown, "Goldwin Smith and Anti-Imperialism," *Canadian Historical Review*, Vol. XLIII, No. 2, June 1962, p. 96.
9. Carman Miller, "English Canadian Opposition to the Boer War as Seen Through the Press," *CHR*, No. 4, 1974.
10. J.S. Conway, "Anti-Imperialism Before 1914," *CHA*, 1961, p. 91.
11. Brown, Cook, *Canada 1896-1921*, quoted p. 23.
12. *Canadian Annual Review*, 1902, p. 375.
13. Humphries, *The Political Career of Sir James P. Whitney*, p. 320.
14. Brown, Cook, *Canada 1896-1921*, quoted, p. 100.
15. Edgar Middleton and Fred Landon, *The Province of Ontario, A History 1615-1927* (Toronto: Dominion Publishing Company, 1927), Vol. I, p. 552.
16. Brown, Cook, *Canada 1896-1921*, quoted, p. 108.
17. Quoted by George F. G. Stanley in "The Western Canadian Mystique" for Western Canadian Studies Conference, published in *Prairie Perspectives*, ed., David P. Gagan (Toronto: Holt Rinehart and Winston, 1970), p. 12.
18. Quoted in Russell Hann, *Some Historical Perspectives of Canadian Agrarian Political Movements* (Toronto: New Hogtown Press, University of Toronto, 1973).
19. Wood, *A History of Farmers' Movements in Canada*, Parts 1 and 2.
20. D.D. Calvin, *Queen's University at Kingston* (Kingston: The Trustees of the University, 1941), p. 102.
21. C. B. Sissons, *A History of Victoria University* (Toronto: University of Toronto Press, 1952), pp. 170-172.
22. *Ibid.*, pp. 173-174.
23. Charles W. Humphries, "James P. Whitney and the University of Toronto," *Profiles of a Province* (Toronto: Ontario Historical Society, 1967), p. 119.
24. *Ibid.*
25. Nelles, *The Politics of Development*, p. 73.
26. *Ibid.*, p. 86.
27. *Ibid.*, p. 59.
28. *Ibid.*, p. 58.
29. *Ibid.*, p. 56.
30. *Ibid.*, p. 100.
31. *Ibid.*, p. 138.
32. Ross, *Getting Into Parliament*, p. 211.
33. Middleton, Landon, *The Province of Ontario*, pp. 494-495.
34. Peter Mussen, *The Temiskaming and Northern Ontario Railway Before World War One*, Undergraduate Thesis, York University, 1973, quoted, p. 17.
35. Middleton, Landon, *The Province of Ontario*, Vol. I, p. 519.
36. *Ibid.*, p. 519.
37. Humphries, *The Political Career of Sir James P. Whitney*, p. 345.
38. *Ibid.*, p. 280.
39. Toronto *Globe*, December 21, 1904.
40. Humphries, *The Political Career of Sir James P. Whitney*, p. 314.
41. Charlesworth, *Candid Chronicles*, pp. 182-183.
42. Nelles, *The Politics of Development*, quoted, p. 253.

Chapter Eight

"Ontario does not think I am a great man"

1.

"Ontario does not think I am a great man. It does think I am honest. And honest I must be."[1] It was Whitney's assessment of his position after three years in office, but it was the measure of the man from the beginning. With little of spacious vision, he offered complete integrity and intended government to reflect it.

As a new broom, he swept out much in the way of electoral abuses and sharply reduced patronage. In 1908, through a stringent act brought in by J. J. Foy, it became illegal at election time to promise a government job or to use a public vehicle to transport voters to the polls. The liquor commissions and inspectorates, though personnel changed, became less blatantly Conservative than they had once been flagrantly Liberal. Old ways endured, haunting practical politics, but they were generally kept to sub-strata removed from the Premier's eye. On his level the familiar hunger of the ward heeler came in for short shrift. F. F. Schindeler tells of one occasion on which the brusque Morrisburg lawyer, wearing his old cap and riding the bicycle he favoured in fine weather, was overtaken by another breathless cyclist. The Sheriff of Manitoulin had died; could the petitioner have his place? "It's all right with me," grunted the Premier, "if the undertaker doesn't mind."[2]

The government came to office committed to "public power," and in Adam Beck as Minister without portfolio it acquired a great exponent of that doctrine. As yet, however, neither the vast expenditures nor the host of technical problems were even clear in outline. Ross had solved nothing with his Ontario Power Commission; he had merely delegated the solution to a group of municipalities. Snider's Commission had begun its investigation and could plan and recommend. But it could not generate power or even move to distribute it without provincial support.

The private companies could, and were now preparing to do so. They had invested capital, created jobs and encouraged the growth of industry on the strength of licences to develop. Under the terms of each contract half their total output could be sold to the United States. The remaining half, though it was more than ample for the current needs of the province, would certainly be sold to users at all the traffic would bear.

That fact, obvious enough from the history of private utilities, was an article of faith with Beck. He saw more surely than any man the real potential of hydro-electric power. It was more than a useful tool and more than a great resource. It was the key, for Beck, to the transformation of the province, and not an instrument to be left in private hands. Whatever the steps he took, and whatever the concessions forced on him in the initial stages, that conviction remained. "The public hand at the switch" was the gospel of Adam Beck, and it was entirely in the character of the gospeller that he saw the hand as his own.

Wealthy, well-married and a breeder of fine horses, Beck was by the turn of the century a public figure in London. By 1902 he was mayor of London and a Conservative member of the legislature. By 1903 he was supporting Snider in the power movement and gaining the ear of Whitney. He entered the Whitney cabinet, obviously a coming man, and as obviously displacing Snider. Forty-six years old, in the full prime of his handsome, craggy vigour, he lost no time in pressing views of his own. To his mind, as to Whitney's, the Liberal government of Ross had shirked its duty. The province itself must investigate the question of power and act with the municipalities in making any decision.

In July of 1905 Beck became head of a second commission, supplied with provincial funds and supplementing that of Snider. Beck's mandate, however, was much the wider of the two. He was to inform the provincial government, not only on questions of cost, demand and rates, but on the hydro-electric potential of all the waters of Ontario, on present and future requirements and on the best means of supply.

The gesture was ominous in itself, and certain to be directed first toward Niagara Falls. The three syndicates, which had been merely contemptuous of Snider, were soon alarmed by Beck. His Commissioners asked for plans and probed into rates and profits, the sacred corporate concerns. There was an invasion here of a new field of technology, a great preserve of capital, and it was met at first by a blank wall. The companies refused requests for information, damned snooping investigators and attacked the advance of socialism which was undermining enterprise. Yet the advance continued.

Beck found and informed the public, among many other findings, that the Electrical Development Company planned to supply power to Toronto at $35.00 per horsepower per year, while the fair rate of delivery was $17.00. He released other statistics, well in advance of his report, at great public meetings in the larger municipalities. At the same time, as his own enthusiasm grew, he painted a brilliant picture of the uses of cheap power. It would revolutionize life as well as transform industry. There would be clean electric trains, electrically operated agricultural equipment and a host of electrical appliances in city and farm homes. As the housewife listened with her husband the hopes of the manufacturers extended to embrace the people and the issue became a crusade. In April 1906, when Beck's report came down and was being debated in the legislature, 1,500 delegates from seventy municipalities assembled at Queen's Park in loud support of his cause. The Minister without portfolio had become the Minister of Power.

Actually Beck's report was less adventurous than Snider's, which had been submitted a week earlier. The older Commissioner had returned to his first idea, as originally proposed to Ross. He was for publicly-developed power, through government-built plants, in outright competition with the private syndicates. That, in the view of Beck, though his ultimate aims went quite as far as Snider's, should not be the present strategy. It would involve an expenditure of between nine and twelve millions and require at least three years for plants to be designed and built. The plants of the private companies were already well along. Although half their output was reserved for the United States, they could supply Ontario's needs for years to come. Why should money be spent and a long delay accepted, merely to produce a surplus? There would be control enough for the moment, and restraint enough on the syndicates, if government built the transmission lines and set rates of supply. The need of the municipalities was for available and cheap power. Beck offered it more quickly, with more authority than Snider, and it was his view that prevailed.

On May 7, 1906, an act introduced in the legislature established the Hydro-Electric Power Commission of Ontario as the framework of the world's first publicly-owned power system. Adam Beck was appointed to head the body. On January 1, 1907, the municipality of Toronto and eighteen other municipalities in southwestern Ontario voted to join it. By January of 1908 they had approved rates and contracts. Power had been secured, customers awaited its coming, and the transmission lines were being built. After two years of battle, increasingly desperate on the part of the private syndicates, the Commission was under way.

It had been established as the combining body of the member municipalities, and also the directing head. It could acquire by purchase, lease or, if necessary, expropriation, any lands, waters, waterpower or installations required for its own use. It could build transmission lines and additional installations, contract with private companies to obtain its supply of power, and contract again to supply power to consumers. It could fix the rates it would pay, as well as the rates it charged. With its debentures backed by a government guarantee, it was sure of adequate finances and equipped with formidable means. Beck, in opposing Snider's plan, had merely postponed his purpose, and the private companies manoeuvred in full awareness of that.

The two American syndicates had chosen to lie low, sensing their precarious position and intending to make the best of it. It was the Ontario Power Company, early in 1907, that made the first contract to supply power to Hydro, at rates that at least were better than expropriation. That club, threatening invested capital which came mostly from abroad, Whitney was loath to use. There was room for accommodation, he doggedly pointed out, and most of the press concurred. The province was not at present, or even in present intention, the competitor of the private companies. It was potentially their best customer though it stipulated fair rates. The act, said the Toronto *Mail and Empire*,

> leaves the private companies the opportunity to do all the business on the market; and so long as they are satisfied with a reasonable profit and deal justly with all customers, the Hydro-Electric Power Commission will not interfere with them.[3]

No such arguments prevailed, however, with the Toronto magnates of the Electrical Development Company. Fiercely attacked themselves by the advocates of public power, they struck back with hired and imported experts and journalists and pamphleteers. "Dreamers, visionaries and crackpots" were fumbling with the mysteries of power; raw, red socialism had raised its head in Ontario, threatening all investment. The angry capitalists turned to the English markets where most of their money came from, and roused bankers and financial houses to the fear of "confiscation." Attacking provincial credit while they continued to lose their own, they rejected Whitney's compromises, held to their old positions and were steadily beaten back. Fed up himself and spurred on by Beck, Whitney grimly legislated where he could gain no ground by reason. The way was cleared for other power to reach the Toronto market and for the establishment of a public utility to compete with the Toronto Street Railway and Electric Light Company. By early 1908, with no Hydro contract, with Beck brandishing the threat of expropriation and with its Toronto monopoly gone, the Electrical Development Company had its back pinned to the wall.

Stubbornly facing bankruptcy and only saved by a general reorganization, it transferred the fight to the field. Through the next two years, as Hydro began its building and the tall steel transmission towers lifted over the farmlands, agents of the Electrical Development Company preceded the engineers. Where they could dispute the right-of-way it was disputed to the last foot; land doubled in price, farmers' fears were roused. There were leaks in the high tension wires and flaws in insulation; electric power was dangerous when delivered by public means. Yet the farmers still demanded it, and the pleadings turned to the courts.

From the community of high finance, alarmed for vested interests and the sanctity of private contract, a flood of petitions went to the Dominion government. The Power Act was beyond the powers of the province and should be disallowed. Another flood of lawsuits broke almost simultaneously in the cause of the common man. Could a private citizen be taxed by the decree of a municipality for electric power he did not use or want? The question received its answer from the High Court of Justice: "The self-interest of the few must give way to the common interest."[4] There was as flat an anwer by the federal Minister of Justice to the claim for disallowance:

A Provincial Legislature, having as is given to it by the terms of the British North America Act, full and absolute control over property and civil rights within the Province, might, if it saw fit to do so, repeal Magna Charta itself.[5]

They were strong words, dangerous in their very strength, and presaging new alignments as Hydro did itself. The age of the great tycoon, though it was still far from over, was sloping down from its meridian. The sense of public muscle and the hope of public benefit were in confused but stubborn growth. They were not to be stopped by legalisms or innuendo or threat; not even by money. The long line of the towers marched out from Niagara and public power came.

It came first to Berlin. On October 11, 1910, Whitney rode through beflagged and bannered streets with Adam Beck beside him. Cheering crowds followed them into the dim afternoon half-light of the huge Berlin arena. A little girl with what seemed to be a crown of glass walked up to the platform. She was carrying a red pillow, trailing a long wire, and a switch rested on the pillow. Whitney took Beck's hand and guided it toward the switch. "Gentlemen," he said, seemingly as always forgetful of the women present, "with this hand tried and true, this hand which has made this project complete, I now turn on the power."[6] The arena blazed with light, so did the streets outside and the crown of the little girl became a halo of lighted bulbs. Niagara waters had entered the people's service.

2.

A priority of the new government was reform and re-establishment of the University of Toronto. In May of 1905 the need for buildings was met through a program which authorized an annual expenditure of $30,000.00 for the next thirty years and provided additional funds for the construction of a General Hospital intended to serve Toronto and be used by the faculty of medicine as a teaching institution. With that much done, Meredith was appointed as head of a Royal Commission to consider larger problems.

The report came down in April 1906, and legislation followed.

We have a right to assume, (said the Commissioners, prefacing their recommendations,) that in the years to come the University of Toronto will more and more assert its influence in the national life of Canada ... a scheme of government created today must keep in view the gradual but certain enlargement of half a century hence.[7]

The view prevailed in the legislature even among reluctant Liberals, and with the passing of the University Act of 1906 an annual statutory grant of $250,000.00 removed the uncertainties of finance.

At the same time the university was strengthened through a series of major reforms. The province asserted its powers by appointing a Board of Governors, but their authority was balanced by a Senate which included representatives not only of the federated colleges but also of faculties and graduates. University College retained its autonomous standing; there was to be a combined faculty of arts for all the colleges, and a Caput, or advisory committee was to have authority in discipline. Higher salaries were authorized for all teachers, security of tenure established for full professors, and the fields of work were enlarged. The School of Practical Science became a part of the University, and new schools of law, art, forestry and music were added.

One factor in the former conflict of purposes and confused administration was James Loudon, an able but difficult president who "carried his own black cloud with him."[8] In July 1906, on a definite hint from the Premier, Loudon resigned his office. The replacement required, in Whitney's view, was to be

162

fairly well educated, very level-headed, a man who knows human nature thoroughly and knows something of Collegiate management . . . a man of great force of will, not hasty in his decisions but firm as a rock . . . in fact the man whom I think is necessary might fairly be called an intellectual tyrant . . . if you take away any offensive meaning of the word.[9]

The search ended in April of 1907 with the appointment of the former principal of Pine Hill Presbyterian College in Halifax. Robert Falconer, as president of the university, was to set its new course.

In the lower schools the "school-book ring" which he had attacked in opposition was an early target with Whitney. Three major publishers who had enjoyed a virtual monopoly were soon bidding on tender and at half their former prices. The quality of texts improved, both in subject matter and treatment, as the government sponsored a set of new readers. "If we can't keep the prices down," said Whitney in 1908, "we will make the books ourselves."[10] That proved unnecessary; the publishing world was tamed. By 1909, the T. Eaton Company, as a new entrant in the field, was producing books at 49 cents as compared to the earlier price of $1.15. For hard-pressed heads of families, school-opening with its book-buying became less of an annual nightmare.

Under R. A. Pyne, the Minister of Education, teachers' salaries improved, qualifications stiffened, and Model Schools and Third Class Certificates were almost wholly eliminated. The government moved to consult, through an elective Advisory Council, with the whole body of the profession. Four new Normal Schools were projected in 1906, and in the high schools the Ontario College of Agriculture began to introduce a range of subjects closely related to farming. That work, as part of Whitney's pledge to expand the field of the College, was capped in 1912 by the establishment of the degree of Bachelor of the Science of Agriculture. Nor was Whitney's view of the practical wholly narrow. By 1912, while the encouragement of travelling libraries in rural regions was resulting in the distribution of some half million books annually, both the Royal Ontario Museum and the Ontario College of Art had been established in Toronto.

The Industrial Education Act came down in 1912, partly in response to the findings of a federal Royal Commission on technical education. It owed much in Ontario to the work of John Seath. Since 1906, as Superintendent of Education, he had seen students go out from provincial high schools with no knowledge of the technical subjects or the new skills and sciences required for the industrial age. He had been determined to have them taught, not as casual supplements to an old classical curriculum but as keys to modern life.

These new subjects have come to stay, (he had hammered home to his colleagues,) and it would be well for all of you – Classical, Mathematical, Science and Moderns men – to realize the fact and use the movement, as it may be used, for the proper ends of education.[11]

The new act at least embodied those aims. It offered grants to municipalities for the establishment of whatever type of technical school best suited the region. All grants would be on the same basis as those for ordinary schools. The government would set standards, provide for the training of teachers, and if necessary import teachers with skills that the province lacked. Urban boards could establish technical high schools or general industrial schools or schools in specialized industries or in fine or applied arts. Evening schools would be supported; and in all cases the money grants of the province would be in proportion to the number of students, the nature of the equipment required and the qualifications of the teachers. The Act depended largely on the initiative of the municipalities and would take time to be effective, but it opened vistas for thousands to whom the universities were closed. The base had been laid and much of the frame set up for vocational education.

3.

At the end of 1908, though language posed its problems in the separate schools of the province, the main issue seemed to concern taxation. Corporations and utilities, often with Catholic shareholders and serving Catholic customers, contributed a portion of their taxes for provincial education. Yet there was no system established to identify the contributors and much of the money of Catholics supported Protestant schools. It was a long-standing anomaly and a source of irritation which the government hoped to remove.

On March 10, 1909, a Conservative private member introduced a bill in the legislature which provided that all Catholic shareholders of a corporation or utility were to be considered as separate school supporters and their taxes were to be assessed accordingly. As an attempt to redress a grievance it revealed difficulties that would be more apparent later, and on Whitney's orders the bill was quietly withdrawn. He allowed it to reach the order paper during the course of the next session, but by March 1910 he was writing of an event that had "so complicated matters that we find it quite out of the question to deal with the subject thoroughly during the stress of the Session."[12] On that issue there was to be longer delay than he realized. Much else that had been seething beneath the surface was coming abruptly to a head.

164

French-Canadian nationalism, growing with Henri Bourassa from the resentments of the Boer War, had been heightened in 1905 by the creation of an Alberta and a Saskatchewan deprived of separate schools. It was growing again with the issue of a Canadian navy, broached in 1909. Laurier's projected force, independent and autonomous, was seen by British enthusiasts as a mere "tinpot" gesture. It was seen by the French as a new step toward imperialism, toward militant English dominance and conscription in foreign wars. The Catholic French Canadian, rebuffed in the new provinces, seemed to be threatened and isolated in a Dominion he had helped make. He fought back, demanding a place for himself. There was everywhere a reassertion of old and long-held claims, for language, religion, status and above all for schools.

The counterpart in Ontario was resentment of French recalcitrance and fear of French advance. Federally under Laurier, as under Macdonald before him, Quebec's voice had weight. The city of Ottawa itself, with its large French population and its always-zealous hierarchy devoted to separate schools, was often a source of truculent irritation. Nor was there much sign, in the schools outside the city and the counties bordering the river, of any growth in Englishness or desire for English instruction. As the habitant from Quebec crossed to the Ottawa valley he brought his priests with him and often many of his teachers. Quebec migration was spreading through northern Ontario with the timber and pulpwood industries and the opening of new mines. It was asserted in 1910, by a largely hostile press, that some 200,000 people, almost a tenth of Ontario's population, were of French and Catholic origin and served by separate schools. There was enough in that alone to arouse the fires of Orangeism, but it was not to be left alone. As the government pondered tax reforms for the assistance of separate schools it found itself in the midst of new antipathies aroused by a flamboyant challenge.

The "event" Whitney wrote of was a huge Congress in Ottawa which began on January 18, 1910, and concluded on January 20 with the founding of the *Association Canadienne-Française d'Education d'Ontario*. Organized and conducted to the accompaniment of great publicity, it had been attended by some 1,000 delegates from the French Canadians of the province, by Laurier and members of his cabinet, by high clerical dignitaries and by the Apostolic delegate. Opening its ceremonies with a solemn High Mass, the Congress had proceeded through the course of the next three days to formulate positions and demands.

They were not unfamiliar but the emphasis was subtly changed, with language dominating religion. The French language, it was claimed, was a legal and official language in Ontario and should be so recognized in the educational system. Bilingual education should commence in primary schools, continue through secondary schools and be provided for and supplemented by bilingual Normal Schools. The certificates of French-speaking teachers granted by Quebec Normal Schools should be recognized in Ontario. There should, moreover, be broad changes in grants and the distribution of taxes to make the reforms possible. In all ways and by all means the recognition of French as an official language of the province should be extended throughout the schools.

Almost simultaneously, as the demands went to Whitney, he was faced with a new explosion. The Irish Catholics of the province supported separate schools; they did not support French. They bitterly resented the defects of French teachers in providing English instruction. The feeling divided the school boards and divided the hierarchy of the church, and it found expression in Francis Michael Fallon. Then Bishop of London, he was a former Vice-Rector of the University of Ottawa where he had seen defective teaching and felt French antagonism, which he returned in full measure. French nationalism, he suspected, was the demon behind the scene, and it threatened not only schooling but the unity of the church itself. By May of 1910, as Bishop of London speaking to the Provincial Secretary, he was demanding not only the discouragement but the rooting out of bilingualism.

> Does not the nationalism of Quebec threaten to ruin the Catholicity of Canada? (he had asked a fellow Bishop.) We are playing a part in the making of a great English-speaking nation and so far as I am concerned I intend ... to take my stand on the side of the manifest destiny of Canada.[13]

It could hardly have been better expressed by an Orange Grand Master, and beneath the rhetoric there were reasons. The widening Irish-French quarrel antedated Fallon. Franco-Ontarian leaders, fearing assimilation and desperate to save their language, were dependent mainly on a group with small means. So were most of the Irish who lived in French communities served by bilingual schools. Where all teaching was poor there was poorer teaching in English, because the French had mobilized their resources and drawn help from Quebec. The nuns and brothers of the teaching orders had come mainly from there, and they had brought their views with them.

School politics and church politics, all centring in Ottawa, had become steadily more embroiled. There had been talk by vocal Irishmen as early as 1906 of a militant propaganda which has picketed around the City a cordon of French Institutions, foreign in sympathy, aims, and objects–but all cunningly designed to prevent the entrance from without of any aids to English Catholicity or Education (and) at the same time equipped to encompass the destruction within the City of those ideals that form the standards of English Catholic life.[14]

Exaggerated as the words were, they represented the problem posed to Whitney. Language rather than religion had become the disruptive issue, and as it divided the separate school system it threatened to divide the province.

By August 12, 1910, the Premier had prepared his answer to the demands of the Ottawa Congress. He had much information before him. In 1909 Dr. F. W. Merchant, the Provincial Inspector, had found bilingual schools in the Ottawa valley to be generally inefficient and staffed by inadequate teachers. Students left them, he said, without facility in English. Bishop Fallon from his diocese, which included the French of Essex county, had even worse to report. He had visited nine parishes with eighteen separate schools and over 2,000 children, of whom a total of ten had succeeded in reaching high school. In one district not a single child had succeeded over a period of twenty-five years. At a confirmation service for a group of children between the ages of eleven and fifteen their priest had told the bishop after the ceremony, "Half the boys you confirmed this morning . . . can neither read nor write."[15] There seemed to be enough here to arouse an English province, yet Whitney's reply was mild.

There were, he wrote to Senator N. A. Belcourt in Ottawa, the leader of the Franco-Ontarians, some 250 bilingual schools in Ontario out of a total of 6,344 elementary schools. Of the bilingual schools, 195 were separate and about 55 public. He believed the difficulties of teaching could be solved under the existing laws of the province, but he would not allow "the creation of a new, additional statutory class of schools organized upon a racial basis."[16]

There could be no recognition of French as an official language in Ontario. The larger demands of the Congress simply could not be met. Yet the Premier's very figures reduced the problem to perspective. There could hardly be a danger to the English, nor did Whitney seem to fear it, in more generous treatment of the French. A measure of gradual improvement at the hands of reasonable men might have saved Ontario a dozen troubled years. But the reasonable men were lacking, or their voices were drowned out.

On January 25, 1911, George Howard Ferguson, Conservative member from Kemptville, rose in the provincial House. Already known as a prominent back-bencher and a man with a keen nose for the set of a political wind, he had his issue now. He intended to move, he announced, that "no language other than the English language should be used as a medium of instruction in the schools of this Province."[17] On this Whitney, who was aware of Ferguson's abilities but never found it convenient to invite him into the cabinet, descended with a firm hand. The measure as it finally emerged for debate and passage by the House was little more than Ross's earlier prescription:

> That the English language shall be the language of instruction and communication of the pupils of the Public and Separate schools of the Province of Ontario, except where, in the opinion of the Department of Education, it is found impracticable because the pupil does not understand English.[18]

It was at best a palliative and stopgap that bought a little delay. It quieted neither the claims nor the fears of the Franco-Ontarians, while to the Orange Toronto *Telegram* it was "a gold brick of the yellowest variety."[19] J. J. Foy, Irish, Catholic and Whitney's principal lieutenant, was inclined to the same view, as were other members of the cabinet. A. G. MacKay, the transient leader of the Liberal opposition, was for "no language but English"[20] and from both parties and on all sides the same cry was rising. In the midst of it all through another year the Premier stood his ground, waiting for information.

In February of 1912 it came before the House in the form of another report from Dr. Merchant. He had reinvestigated the condition of Ontario's bilingual schools and he had not found improvement. There were still teachers with minimal qualifications teaching on temporary certificates. There was disorganization in grading and the classification of students, in many cases a neglect of English instruction; and in some schools during school hours Catholic doctrine was taught, contrary to provincial law. He commented on good discipline and the neat appearance of classrooms, but there was little else to soften his recommendations. In effect they were to harden the old rules and make them more explicit. French, where its use was essential, might be allowed in the primary grades; but by the Third Form, or the fourth or fifth year, English should be required to replace it.

The legislation that followed was based on that report. The government was prepared to open or expand training schools for teachers who lacked proficiency in the English language. It would assist the teachers to attend. It would be lenient and sympathetic in administering regulations. But it had been forced now to adopt a public position and assert provincial law. All grants to school boards would be conditional on the boards' ability to provide instruction in English. There could be no further use of unauthorized French textbooks. Nor could there by any further vagueness as to the program set for the child. Going well beyond the recommendations of Merchant, the government added Regulation 17 to the general list of the Department of Education:

> Instruction in English shall commence at once upon a child entering school, the use of French as the language of instruction and communication to vary according to local conditions upon the report of the supervising inspector, but in no case to continue beyond the end of the First Form (third year).

For the current year an extension might be conceded, but only "in cases of pupils beyond Form I who, owing to previous defective training, are unable to speak and understand the English language."[21]

After another stormy interval, with French communities threatening open resistance, Regulation 18 followed in October 1912. Its Draconian terms transferred the authority of school boards and the responsibility of teachers to the Minister of Education. He could withhold a grant from a board which failed to obey orders and summarily cancel the certificate of an inadequately qualified teacher. There could be no remission of taxes payable to the public system to any dissident ratepayers supporting private schools. Finally, as a guarantee that they would adhere to their new instructions, teachers were required to sign a formal pledge.[22]

The government had been swept too far by the mood prevailing in the province, and Whitney seemed to sense it.

> The newer regulation, (he wrote to Thomas Chapais, a Conservative leader in Quebec,) will, of course, be amended from time to time as our experience shows the necessity for a change ... Ontario will go a long way and will strain a point even in order to make sure that our French Canadian subjects shall receive fair play.[23]

Yet fair play was the sticking point.

> For me, (replied Chapais,) the bilingual school question is not a mere question of civil law; it is a wide and broad question of natural law, of general policy, of equity and freedom, a great political and national question.[24]

They were large words for the province and the Premier of 1912; and they struck no echo in Whitney through what remained of his life.

On December 27, 1912, a deputation from Ottawa claiming to represent 280,000 supporters of bilingual schools protested the regulations before Whitney, Pyne and other members of the cabinet. Whitney, as usual, was blunt enough in reply. He would not allow a third system of schools, which could only be "racial schools."[25] Yet he would go as far as he could to reduce practical difficulties. In August 1913 Regulation 17 was relaxed by conceding a year's extension of the earlier period of grace. French inspectors were appointed for predominantly French schools, but English inspectors remained, with authority over the French, adding to all the tensions and producing a new malaise.

By October 1913 the trustees of the Ottawa school board were divided into two camps and had taken their quarrel to law. The English were seeking an injunction to prevent borrowing by the French for the payment of salaries due bilingual teachers. The borrowing was made necessary because the Department of Education, in view of French recalcitrance, had cancelled the annual grants. In June 1914 the provincial elections came, adding heat to a worsening situation, and three months later Whitney himself was dead. The turmoil of schools and languages remained to haunt Ontario as it entered the First World War.

4.

Whitney's proclaimed policy in the case of natural resources was to "enlarge the people's share." In Frank Cochrane of Sudbury, at the head of the Department of Lands, Forests and Mines, he had a tough and able minister. Yet for the new Conservative government, as for other governments before it, words came more easily than deeds.

The conservation of the forest as a living, permanent resource had become an official concept. Yet it demanded care which the government could not afford and a degree of support which lumbermen were not prepared to give. The vast northern regions defeated protective measures by their very size and extent. Year after year, though legislation stiffened and increased demands on the industry resulted in more patrols, the cigar of the careless woodsman, the heaps of brush in the clearings and the sparks from locomotives resulted in sickening loss. In 1910 and again in 1911, the last two years of Frank Cochrane's regime, great fires at Rainy Lake and the Porcupine swept over miles of forest and took 115 lives.

In 1911 the County Reforestation Act provided funds and seedling trees to counties and individuals who were prepared to renew growth. Considerable planting resulted in denuded southern areas, and other areas where timber remained standing were set aside as

170

reserves. There was accompanying legislation for the protection of forest life. By 1914 Burlington Beach Park had been established near Hamilton, as had Quetico Park along the Rainy Lake watershed, and Algonquin Park had been enlarged. Yet none of these measures, with their nibblings at renovation and their hopes of conservation, impressed the barons of the industry or brought about much reform.

In the case of the pulpwood industry there were many problems to resolve. The first was inactive grants; a number of large concessions made by the Ross government had been allowed to remain idle. These Whitney cancelled, resumed the rights of the Crown, and offered the lands on lease again at double the former dues. The next phase was to counter the open door policy of Quebec, which still exported pulpwood in the form of raw logs. It produced much more than Ontario, supplied the American market and reduced the effects of the manufacturing condition. The solution came to hand, however, through another battle of tariffs.

The growth of American newspapers had been matched by the growth of a pulp and paper industry, but at the same time by the decline of American supplies. The United States, through the Payne-Aldrich tariff, introduced in 1909, established prohibitory duties on the importation of newsprint, in effect demanding pulpwood for the supply of its own mills. That boon, however, the Americans were not to get; for Quebec joined with Ontario in presenting a united front. While the press below the border howled at the lack of newsprint, the manufacturing condition was applied to Quebec pulpwood. It could be exported from neither province where it was cut on Crown lands; it had to be milled at home.

Through 1910 and 1911 the campaign for reciprocity brought an American retreat. A first offer was to lift duties on newsprint in exchange for a Canadian freeing of the exportation of pulpwood. Both provinces refused, since it was pulpwood mills they wanted, with the infusion of new capital and the creation of new jobs. These came at last in 1913. The American Underwood tariff, proclaimed in that year, gave free entry to Canadian pulp and newsprint with no conditions in return. The border had been reopened, the tariff barriers removed, and there was immediate transplantation to the northern source of supply.

From Minnesota the great Backus-Brooks firm of International Falls came across the Rainy River to open up at Fort Frances. In the Niagara peninsula the Ontario Paper Company, owned by the Chicago *Tribune*, established itself at Thorold. In the north, along the line of the National Transcontinental, other plants sprang up at Dryden and Mattagami and in the Abitibi country. By 1914, with demand seemingly unlimited, Ontario was overtaking the sister pro-

171

vince. Its total pulp production was about two-thirds that of Quebec, while it almost doubled Quebec's in the newer sulphite pulp.

While the pulpwood industry grew, the timber industry was pushed into the background. Yet it was still large, and at least in Whitney's intention, it was to be well-watched and controlled. There was to be open bidding on timber lands, he proclaimed in 1905, and not too much of that. Sales would be held "only as the timber was endangered by fire or for some other good reason."[26] Since fire was always a danger and reasons never lacked, it was not much of an advance on earlier conditions. Larger reforms, however, came down in 1909. That year, in the face of declining revenues, timber dues were increased and the collection system revised. Dues were to be paid in future, not on the acreage leased but on the volume of timber cut, and the assessment of that volume was to be made by government men.

The promise of better returns, however, was reduced by the problem of staff. Between twelve and fifteen hundred men were scattered throughout the province as timber cullers and estimators in part-time government employ. Yet they were also part-time lumbermen, often close to the companies and not inclined to check or dispute their figures. The new system, like the old, had its quota of loopholes that were quickly found and used. Widespread, rich and wasteful, polluting rivers, destroying game and leaving stumps behind it, the lumber industry for the most part went on in its old way.

Mining problems for Whitney were largely centred on Cobalt. With the first thaws of the spring of 1905, miners, prospectors and accompanying hordes of speculators poured into the region. By early summer the area was blanketed with claims, most of which were gambles and merely held for sale. The government closed that phase of the boom in August. Invoking a clause in the Mining Act which required discovery of ore, it cancelled the claims that were not based on findings. At the same time it despatched a corps of inspectors to confirm the approved claims. Mining of these got quickly under way, while on the released lands about them the actual working prospectors, freed of tagging speculators, were able to resume their search.

The next step was "to enable the people of Ontario to get something as well as the men up there."[27] It was a knotty issue that occupied more than a year, and produced some tentative measures. In 1906 a uniform system of mining districts was established across the province, and regulations were stiffened for inspecting and granting claims. The question of revenues from mining still hung in suspense, but there was no doubt that larger returns were expected. Whitney made that clear in his disposition of the major properties at Cobalt. They comprised ungranted sections along the railway right-of-way, the beds of two lakes and a stand of virgin pine some nine square miles in area which was known as the Gillies Limit. On these properties, with the exception of the Gillies Limit, the first annual rental terms were $50,000.00 for the concession, $500.00 for a building site, and royalties beginning at 10 per cent rising to 50 per cent on the ore taken.

The returns showed at least that lessons had been learned from Sudbury. The Cobalt property along the right-of-way was to yield $666,915.00 in royalties between 1906 and 1914. Kerr Lake brought in $771,833.00, and Cobalt Lake, under altered terms was sold to a syndicate headed by Henry Pellatt for a purchase price of over $1,000,000.00.

The Gillies Limit became a case by itself. The government announced that it would hold the land until October of 1906 to allow the timber to be cleared. Then, Whitney said, "we will not dispose of this valuable area . . . we will keep it and we will use it, develop and mine it, for the benefit of the people."[28] As a politician in the midst of the Hydro battle he was using familiar words, which the province interpreted for him. There was a huge wave of enthusiasm for the idea of a public mine, and it swept the government along. On October 1, 1906, Ontario itself became a producer of silver with the Bureau of Mines in charge.

Two and a half years later it was glad to make its escape. Seemingly rich veins had quickly petered out. Much industrious prospecting, encouraged by the hope of bonuses, had turned up little that was new. The government was half in the politics and half in the business of mining, with little practical experience of chancy, difficult work. In the spring of 1909, with a net profit of some $35,000.00 the land was auctioned off to private developers.

In the interval the Mining Act, after much intensive study, had been passed in 1907. To speed development and discourage speculation it taxed idle claims. Ore production was to be linked with the allied iron and metal industries by distributing a share of the revenue in the form of bounties. The essential change, however, was in the abandonment of the royalty system. Royalties charged on the quantity of ore raised, always difficult to determine and dependent on the companies' figures, were to be replaced by a tax of 3 per cent on profits.

Vigorously attacked by the mining interests, the tax gave promise of a larger and fairer yield. Yet the hope proved difficult to realize in the face of skilled techniques. Mining accountants discovered new expenses and hosts of legitimate deductions that reduced taxable profits. Mine owners and their lawyers had special cases to plead, and a government building industry and encouraging capital investment was usually inclined to listen. It would protest much in public, scold a little in private, but for the most part it would bend.

As silver production neared its peak in Cobalt, gold came into the picture. The prospectors ranging outward, combing the west and north, were making their first strikes. By 1914 both the Dome and McIntyre mines had opened up in the Porcupine. The future Hollinger Consolidated had staked out its property. The Lakeshore and the Wright-Hargreaves mines were developing at Kirkland Lake. The Temiskaming and Northern Ontario, as it reached north from Haileybury, was extending branches to Charlton and Kerr Lake, Timmins and Elk Lake, all in the service of mines. Transport, power and production were all in their early stages, but the value of gold delivered was approaching that of silver. Yet from 1911 onward, after a first substantial rise, public revenues declined. Through the five succeeding years, while mineral production in the province increased by 60 per cent the income returned to the treasury was actually cut in half. Getting the people's share, while encouraging capital to invest, remained the enduring problem.

In 1908 the first train of the Temiskaming and Northern Ontario came steaming into Cochrane. The second leg was completed on the road to James Bay and the third seemed to be in prospect. It was to be delayed for several years pending a federal subsidy, but in the meantime there was enough of other building. The Canadian Northern, Mackenzie and Mann's enterprise, was extending east from Winnipeg in the direction of Montreal and reaching down from Sudbury to make connections with Toronto. The National Transcontinental, linking up with the Grand Trunk Pacific, crossed through the bush and the Clay Belt north of the CPR. The great redundant network, not to be completed until 1915, traversed an enormous wilderness that was still lacking in people. Yet the provincial government was fervent in its belief that people would come, and was prepared to spend to bring them.

Out of the spending came a pattern of homesteads, radiating out from the rail lines. As settlements grew to towns they required connections with shipping points, and work on these commenced. Municipalities were organized, there were schools and promises of schools and in 1912, with the passage of the Northern Development Act, the beginnings of a major effort. In that year, after spending an average of $200,000.00 annually on colonization roads, the government appropriated $5,000,000.00 to extend a system north and south of the National Transcontinental and west for 200 miles from the

Quebec border. During the next two summers, in that country of bush and rock, between four and five thousand men were busy with picks and shovels, and when they downed their tools for rifles there was a sketchy grid of roads.

To encourage British immigrants Whitney established an Agent-General in London. He was generous to the Salvation Army and to other private agencies engaged in the same work. For those who came to the homesteads old provisions were revoked, and the settler acquired the right to his pine timber. The reservation of mineral rights was also eliminated. Cochrane, the promoter of northern development in the cabinet, left for the federal government in 1911, and was replaced by William Howard Hearst, an even greater enthusiast. Parties of distinguished visitors and influential journalists were taken on long excursions through the opening regions. Demonstration trains, loaded from older farms, travelled the southern province displaying the fruits of the north. Magnificent vegetable and root crops and early-ripening grains could be produced in some of the areas during the short, hot summers. Yet the lumbermen and the miners, who saw their territory encroached on, remained as consistent sceptics.

Dean B. E. Fernow, the head of forestry at the University of Toronto, was also among the doubtful. He had travelled the country for years in the course of earlier work, and had prepared a report on the Clay Belt after a trip in 1912. It was mere libel to the ever-ebullient Hearst. "With all due respect to the gentleman mentioned," said the Minister of Lands, Forests and Mines, "I know a great deal more about Northern Ontario than any professor in the country... there are millions and millions of acres of the very best agricultural land in the world."[29] For all that, Fernow's warnings remained. Among much land where "the outlook for agricultural development is undoubtedly bright" he had found areas of muskeg where "I could put a pole down nine feet before striking clay." There were larger areas with "merely more or less satisfactory drainage conditions" and another sombre caveat applied to the whole region: "average date of late frost in spring June 8 ... first fall frost September 14... growing season about three weeks later than old Ontario and also closing earlier ... sanguine expectations should be guarded against."[30]

But these expectations had been nourished for too long, and were too difficult to dispel. A flow of settlement trickled steadily north, carried by the roads and railways and urged by the propaganda. In 1914 Hearst pointed proudly to 2,200 "persons" established on 268,238 acres of free-grant land in that year alone. It was hardly an impressive figure, representing perhaps 500 families, but it was

175

always certain to increase. The north itself was larger. In 1912 the District of Keewatin had been divided by the federal government and the new District of Patricia awarded to the province of Ontario, extending it from Georgian Bay to the line of the Albany River and giving it a coastline of 600 miles along James and Hudson Bay. Quite apart from farming there were calls to the adventurous there, and in Sudbury, Cobalt, the gold mines, and a restored Sault Ste. Marie, where the loans made to the bankrupt had been easily paid off and the steel industry was back on its feet again.

"Five years from now," Whitney told Londoners on a visit to the imperial capital in 1911, "we're going to have a thickly settled country up in Northern Ontario."[31] He looked forward to seeing 1,000,000 people, and he was destined to be disappointed. Lumbering and mining men could wring wealth from the wilderness but not the man with the plough. Where agriculture was concerned the north seemed to be a sieve, emptying itself through abandoned farms as new farms were established. In the Clay Belt, though dairying began to be possible for the man with enough capital, the small farms declined into producers of hay and potatoes. From across the Quebec border came French-Canadian settlers, working their farms in summer and the pulpwood camps in the winter. They were less desired than English settlers, but more inclined to stay. The tinge of Frenchness was deepening on the eastern edge of the province, and in other ways the land was defeating the prophet. Ten years after Whitney spoke, across the whole of Ontario's north, from Kenora through empty Patricia to the Quebec border at Timiskaming, there was little more than a fourth of his hoped-for million.

5.

Southern Ontario agriculture presented a different face, and one seamed with problems too. By 1905 the Grange movement was dwindling into a group of respected theorists. What political strength there was lay in the Ontario Farmers Association, whose base was discontent. High protective tariffs built up manufacturing and restricted the export market for agricultural products. Urbanization and industrialism were reducing the farmer's influence. The old ideal of status, with its half-religious overtones, seemed to be threatened with destruction.

Such a condition, (said Ernest C. Drury, one of the rising leaders,) cannot fail to have disastrous effects upon the nation at large, not only on its material prosperity but on its political, social and moral life, the backbone of which is, and must be, the farm home.[32]

Threshing, Mount Pleasant (*ca.* 1905)

Barn raising, McDairmid's farm, Emo (twenty-two miles west of
Fort Frances, *ca.* 1915)

Making the James Bay Indian Treaty, Flying Post, Sudbury District (July 6, 1906)

Ontario Government Immigration Office, Toronto (*ca.* 1913)

Cobalt Mining Company (*ca.* 1910-1915)

Pouring gold, Hollinger Mine smelters, Timmins (1918)

Logs for Lockhart Mill, Seine Bay, Rainy River District (1915)

Laying track, National Transcontinental Railway,
Cochrane District (*ca*. 1910-1915)

Acton recruiting office and posters (*ca.* 1914-1918)

Armistice Day, King Street, Toronto, (November 11, 1918)

Incline Railway, Hamilton Mountain.

Dundas Station, Hamilton and Dundas Street Railroad.

Yonge Street Wharf (*ca*. 1902)

Pretoria Day, Yonge Street, Toronto (June 5, 1901)

Kew Beach, Toronto Lakefront.

Raid on "Blind Pigs" (Bootleggers), Temiskaming District (*ca*. 1920s).

That home was certainly changing as it was drawn within the orbit of the city. New conveniences came, many of which were welcomed. Life was easier in the kitchen, there was more efficiency in the barn, and implements brought in crops with fewer men. The growth of merchandising had practical benefits for the farmer. The automobile was beginning to tempt the prosperous, and better roads were provided for the prevailing horse and buggy. People visited more, it was easier to attend meetings, and the farm communities were knitting closer together. There was an increased consciousness of strength and common interest, but there was also more awareness and more discussion of loss. Steadily and undiminishingly sons, daughters, hired men and neighbours were flowing away from the farms. Many went to the west. Some gave up as old land was exhausted and joined the trek to the cities. W. C. Good, Dominion Master of the Grange, claimed in 1911 that 100,000 members of Ontario's rural community had been lost in ten years.[33]

It was the dark side of a picture that on the whole was bright enough. Agriculture as an industry was sound, flourishing and productive. It was bolstered by modern science and equipped with modern means. Yet it no longer held the place claimed by its leaders as "the tap-root of national vigour."[34] Even in the richest areas there was a perennial shortage of help; and in poorer rural communities where depopulation was worst education and religion showed decay. "Schools," said Good, which had once had forty children "now shiver with a beggarly half-dozen."[35] The better teachers left, discouraged by shrinking salaries, and only mediocrities could be scraped up to replace them. Churches closed, unable to support a minister, and congregations dwindled. Village groups of some faiths, scattered over wide areas, were served rarely and inadequately by a single hard-pressed man.

It seemed to the farmer in such places, as he walked through weed-grown fields and looked at deserted buildings, that malign forces were closing in about him. To the farmer everywhere, whatever his financial status, it appeared that the real enemies were the growing, grasping cities. The hostile interests gathered there to control and change his life; and more and more, at each provincial election, the causes the farmer cherished and the candidates he supported went down before urban votes.

In the farm view the remedy was a shift of power from the trusts and corporations, the railways and great industries that fattened on government aid. They had demanded and got a taxation system that was weighted against agriculture. It was their strength, concentrated in the cities, that was diminishing rural status. The sons went to the cities because they were drawn there by money, and that flow was directed by political power. It could be reversed or redirected if the farmer regained control.

The mood of the farms was a latent force in politics and a spur to government action. It was Whitney's settled policy, though he could never quite hold to it, to eliminate provincial bonuses and cash grants to railways. He did succeed in increasing railway taxes. He taxed the mining industry and extracted more for the treasury from lumbering and pulpwood men. He raised the taxes and stiffened the regulations controlling financial houses, and for the first time in Ontario imposed a tax on banks. As revenues increased, moreover, a larger share was diverted back to the farms. Better rural roads and the improvement of rural life became permanent features of expanded provincial programs.

The problem of abandoned land was attacked by extensive drainage measures and experiments in reforestation. The Ontario Agricultural College, with Edward John Zavitz who was later to be Provincial Forester as one of its leading spirits, embarked on a larger role. Forestry stations were added to its agricultural sub-stations and individual farmers were encouraged to plant woodlots. Instructors in forestry and farm work were supplied to many of the schools. By 1912 graduates of the college were teaching the elements of agriculture in 284 high and continuation schools; gardening and nature study were being taught in the lower schools and a one-year course at Guelph was available to teachers in training at provincial Normal Schools. Not only farm technology but the development of a taste for farming were becoming integrated parts of education.

By 1914 the government had powerful statistics to support its claim that agriculture was a well-supported, carefully nourished industry. The enlarged college at Guelph had 1,600 students, and 90 per cent of its graduates had returned to farm work. Annual provincial spending on agricultural projects had nearly tripled in a matter of ten years: from $475,678.00 in 1904 to $1,160,574.00 in 1913. There were seventy drainage projects, where there had been none ten years earlier. Dairying, fruit growing and livestock raising had largely increased. Cereal grain growing, which had declined heavily in the past, was once more on the rise with better methods. Fifty-six courses had been offered by the Department of Agriculture in 1913 for the improvement of stock and seed. "While in 1904 there was only one Inspector for Bee Hives there are now no less than 16 Inspectors at work under his supervision." Co-operation was closer between the government and the College of Agriculture which supplied the men in the field. "There were under the late Government only three graduates in the employ of the Department while at the present time there are about 50 graduates so employed."[36]

James Duff, as Minister, could point to a condition in agriculture of "quiet but steadily growing prosperity." The mortgage burden on all farms in the province amounted to only about 15 per cent of their value, and that figure was decreasing as mortgages were paid off. In the banks of many counties the savings of farmers were the large bulk of deposits, and "it was deemed safe to estimate the total amount of farmers' deposits in rural Ontario at $100,000,000.00."[37]

Milk, cheese and dairy products provided an annual return of some $40,000,000.00. Field crops accounted for $200,000,000.00, orchards and vineyards for $25,000,000.00; while the population of cattle, sheep, hogs, horses and poultry remained an asset to which no figure was attached.

> A point I want to make, (said Duff,) is that while the wheat crop of the whole of Canada was in round numbers worth $125,000,000., the field crops (including wheat) of the Province of Ontario were worth $200,000,000. That seems almost incredible but it is a fact.[38]

Yet the other fact remained: the declining influence of agriculture beneath the large statistics. Mechanization and science increased returns to the farmer, but they did not provide security for the farmer's way of life. He saw his numbers lessening and he looked ahead for his sons. They would not have what he had if present trends continued, nor would a world of expanding cities leave them even a choice. The old strength and moralities would go with the independence that had been built on broad fields; and in the consciousness of that danger there was a growing will to fight.

As the Grange declined the Ontario Farmers Association gradually absorbed it, under the leadership of J. J. Morrison and E. C. Drury. The Grange took no part in the Canadian Council of Agriculture when it was formed in 1909 to unite Ontario farmers with the grain growers of the prairies. Yet four years later, on the eve of the formation of the United Farmers of Ontario, there was a last word from the departing Dominion Master. It might have served as a declaration of war.

> Our national policy, (said W. C. Good,) has deliberately and persistently fostered urban industries at the expense of the rural. Our cities have grown with feverish haste, not because their growth provided advantages for the average city resident, but because it gave opportunity to the Big Industries and big landowners to exploit the labour of a large number of workers and to gather into their own pockets the 'unearned increment.' A class of idle rich has grown up in our cities, to whose love of ostentation commerce and

179

industry are now pandering. These enervated and miserable specimens of humanity rush about the country in great cars, flaunt their wealth in our faces, tear up our roads and cast their dust upon our fields.[39]

The Grange movement as it died was handing the torch along; and not only to the United Farmers who were organized the next year. The discontents of the farmlands were striking sparks in the cities as labour gathered strength.

6.

Whitney came to the Premiership at the age of sixty-one, and very few of his priorities were concerned with social change. Where he saw immediate needs and practical remedies he was prepared to break new ground. Where he did not he stood on the old, defending it as best he could.

He was contemptuous of the cant surrounding prohibition, and equally so of attempts to make it law. Even the "local option" that had dried up some constituencies on the vote of a bare majority Whitney would not accept. He required 60 per cent, or three-fifths of the electors; and the "Three-Fifths Regulation" was attacked throughout his time. The will of the three-fifths, when once clearly expressed, had unequivocal support. The liquor licence and inspection service, though never quite divorced from the taint of politics, became a formidable and respected force. Licensing and the control of licence holders became more rigorous each year. Liquor profits were cut by increasing provincial fees and there was a steady reduction of bars and other outlets. The liquor interests were left in no doubt that they were regarded as a disreputable menace by a large section of people. Each session of the legislature stiffened the forms of control; and each year through municipal referenda the dry constituencies increased.

In 1906, out of 844 municipalities in the province, 252 had prohibited the sale of liquor. By 1912 there were 444, plus 118 others who had voted dry by less than the required majority. These last remained wet because of the three-fifths ruling, and there were grounds in that for renewed assaults on Whitney. Yet there was grudging praise for the effects of government control, even from prohibitionists. The liquor licences in the province had been decreased by nearly a third, to a total of 1,800. They had been made more difficult to come by, less profitable when gained, and they were hedged with stern restrictions against abuse. It was as much for that time as politics could be expected to do. Newton W. Rowell, the latest of the Liberal leaders who had followed George Ross, was for "the wiping out at one stroke of the retail liquor traffic."[40] Whitney dismissed his views as "fiddle-faddle." Access to liquor remained, inalienable by provincial law, but the whole thrust of policy and of government administration supported the desire of temperance men to reduce a social evil. In Whitney's eyes the practicable had been attained.

He offered no encouragement to the movement for woman's suffrage, and in his day there was no visible advance. The spinster or widowed property holder could vote in municipal elections, and that was the extent of the right.

> The fact is, (said Whitney,) that spinsters and widows were given the right to vote in municipal affairs in order to represent property. The Parliamentary franchise does not rest on that basis. Hence it can not be used as a reason to give the Parliamentary vote.[41]

After countless deputations and years of resolutions proposed and lost in the legislature he remained of the same mind. In 1909 Dr. Augusta Stowe-Gullen, president of the Toronto Women's Enfranchisement Association and daughter of Emily Stowe, came to him at the head of 300 women and was "received with little favour."[42] By 1912, as the National Council of Women asserted its strength in Ontario and Liberals moved ambiguously to acquire the new support, three bills were proposed for various degrees of suffrage and all hoisted or lost. The Premier's stand was clear enough, not only in words but tone. If the question were ever to be settled, he said, "it will be by opening the flood-gates and allowing all the sisters in."[43]

In 1913, at the final session over which he was able to preside, three more measures were proposed and all shelved or defeated. A fourth proposal was for a committee of investigation, and that too was refused. Woman's suffrage in Whitney's time was rejected even as a matter for official study. If the private members' bills were significant straws in the wind, they gave no sign to the Premier of a storm building behind them. The National Council of Women had been supplemented that year by the Toronto Women's Liberal Association, and in the 700 branches of the Women's Institutes of Ontario there was evidence enough that rural women were active. Yet the total enrolment of the branches was 20,000 members, and suffrage in Whitney's view ranked low among their concerns. The question, he said as his last word on the subject, was "dull, torpid and dead."[44]

He was more receptive to women in the guise of social workers because he saw more to be done. During his first year in office when a deputation came to him from the National Council of Women urging better care of the insane, support for the aged poor, improved conditions for working girls and the establishment of a house of refuge for feeble-minded females, his answer was that "practical steps would probably be taken."[45] It was hardly an inspiring promise, but most of the reforms were made. The government of the blunt Premier, engrossed in large projects, had no resounding commitment to the cause of the common man. Yet where it saw needs that were within its frame of the possible it worked for amelioration.

Whitney had promised law reform on behalf of the smaller litigant, and that promise was kept. Appeals were made easier and cheaper, the jurisdiction of district and county judges was widened and procedures were simplified to reduce delay and expense. For women, though there was no suffrage, there was better care in maternity homes and a modest advance in status through grants for deserted wives. The Ontario Juvenile Courts Act, passed in 1910, was a more important departure. It established not only a court but a new corrective system that enlisted workers of the Children's Aid Society. These men or women, often closely involved, became entitled to serve as probation officers in charge of the young offenders.

Health care, child care, factory conditions, sanitary conditions and the insane, indigent and criminal were all the subjects of long annual reports. Equally familiar complaints were heard that not enough had been done, but grants were increased, new buildings were erected and in most cases "practical" steps were taken. By 1910, under a series of measures sponsored by W. J. Hanna, the brilliant Provincial Secretary, prison labour on contract had been largely brought to an end. The prison farm had come and hundreds of Hanna's "boys," whom he sometimes came to eat with, were at least out in the air. Around Guelph, Orillia, Brockville, and later Whitby, they were cutting thousands of fenceposts, opening up quarries and draining and improving swampland that had been lying waste for years. By 1912, with the reorganization of the health system, ten medical officers under the authority of the Provincial Secretary, had become responsible for separate districts. There were new teeth in the laws on vaccination, stricter measures in regard to sanitation and better training for nurses, particularly in mental homes.

In Toronto, in 1912, the old, dismal Central Prison and Asylum was sold for a million dollars and plans were made for a larger, modern building on a new site. The new General Hospital, associated with the great developments at the University of Toronto, was coming near to completion. Toronto itself, under the leadership of H. C. Hocken, its new and vigorous mayor, and James Simpson, its Labour Party Controller, was fostering expansive plans. There were more public parks and supervised recreation and there was vastly more of sport. Public baths were installed, the sewage system extended, and a program of public health nursing brought milk to infants in the slums. Between 1910 and 1914 the death rate from communicable diseases dropped from 114 per 100,000 to 27 per 100,000, and it was not the end of the changes. A minimum wage of $15.00 per week was established for all workmen paid by the City of Toronto. There was a first attempt at a municipal housing program and a municipally owned abattoir and cold storage plant were set up "to keep all the small wholesale butchers in business, and prevent the great meat trust . . . from driving out the small dealer."[46]

Toronto in all this, however, was well ahead of the province and considerably ahead of Whitney. He was often at odds with its "socialist" administration, and with Newton Rowell. In 1913, when the leader of the Liberals demanded "modern principles of factory regulation and inspection, so as more effectively to safeguard the lives, health and physical and moral well-being of the men, women and children employed in factories and shops,"[47] he drew a hot reply from the Premier.

> I don't care whether our (Factory) Act is up to date with other countries. So long as it is up to date with common sense I am satisfied. There is no country in the world where there is so little to complain of in regard to conditions of labour surrounding children as Ontario.[48]

This was not the view of labour which was better acquainted with the factories, with working conditions and with the stubbornly-persisting, ever-growing slums. Yet labour remained weak, unable to influence government or to do much for itself. The working age for children remained at fourteen, though unionists wanted it raised by two years. The eight-hour day, though it was tentatively considered and at first supported by the Premier, was rejected as "precipitate" change. It was to Sir William Ralph Meredith, still his adviser, that Whitney owed his best achievement for labour. As chairman of a Royal Commission, Meredith conducted a long and searching inquiry into the operation of Mowat's Workmen's Compensation Act, and produced a notable improvement. Manufacturers for years had been evading compensation on the ground that a workman voided his claim through some negligence of his own. There were pious pleas that such a provision was necessary both to induce care by the worker and protect other workers, but Meredith brushed them aside. "The manufacturers have been looking out for their own interests. They haven't had their workmen in mind."[49] With the completion of Meredith's report the legislation came, and Whitney lived to see the passing of the new Workmen's Compensation Act, on

183

May 1, 1914. He had removed the question of negligence as a barrier to compensation from the list of worries haunting an injured man.

With all that, a great deal was left undone. The Board of Health complained of the pollution of waters by an undisciplined industry. The reports still came of slaughter houses and dairies where conditions were "generally bad." Immigrants meant for the farmlands came crowding into city slums, to exist on starvation wages, live in tumble-down houses and add to misery and filth. Sewage disposal, if it had improved a little in Toronto, was wretched in many cities, and the inspection of foods was universally lax. The old Central Prison, sold but still in use, reported on "overcrowded, unsanitary buildings, poor conditions for women, bad ventilation." Feeble-minded children were still mixed with normal children in many of the lower schools. J. J. Kelso, the Superintendent of Neglected Children, continued faithfully at his work, with 1,017 charges to be "rescued, relieved, aided" on a grant for each of some $30.00 per year.[50] The unionism that was weak in the cities hardly existed at all among the great, far-off projects that moved in the van of growth. It was said of the worker on the National Transcontinental that

> apart from losing his personal liberty, a man would have been more comfortable, less molested with flies and mosquitoes, would have a real bed and much better sanitary surroundings if, instead of going for six months to railway camps, he had gone to Kingston penitentiary.[51]

In the eyes of the Victorian man who had lived through the Edwardian age to the brink of the First World War these were the minor shortfalls inevitably dogging growth. They would be submerged in new achievements and redeemed by the general advance. Yet Meredith saw, if the Premier himself did not, that the old pace and the old way could not be maintained much longer.

> It will be bad policy, (Meredith had said as he conducted the hearings on Workmen's Compensation,) to antagonize the workingmen in any just claim they may make at the present time. There is something in the air, not unreal, that may easily take front and force in an attack upon protected privilege.[52]

Notes

1. Willison, *Reminiscences Political and Personal*, p. 330.
2. Schindeler, *Responsible Government in Ontario*, p. 23.
3. Toronto, *Mail and Empire*, quoted in Merrill Denison, *The People's Power* (Toronto: McClelland and Stewart Limited, 1960), p. 57.
4. Denison, *The People's Power*, p. 78.
5. *Ibid.*, p. 85.
6. Nelles, *The Politics of Development*, p. 302.
7. Humphries, "James P. Whitney," in *Profiles of a Province*, p. 118.
8. *Ibid.*
9. *Ibid.*, p. 124.
10. *Canadian Annual Review*, 1908, p. 277.
11. Robert M. Stamp, "Educational Leadership in Ontario, 1867-1967," in *Profiles of a Province*, p. 202.
12. Franklin A. Walker, *Catholic Education and Politics in Ontario* (Toronto: Thos. Nelson and Sons (Canada), 1964), p. 227.
13. Brown, Cook, *Canada 1896-1921*, p. 254.
14. Walker, *Catholic Education and Politics in Ontario*, p. 231.
15. *Ibid.*, pp. 250-251.
16. *Ibid.*, pp. 246-247.
17. *Ibid.*, p. 258.
18. *Ibid.*
19. *Ibid.*
20. *C.A.R.*, 1911, p. 470.
21. *Ibid.*, pp. 266-267.
22. *Ibid.*, pp. 470-474.
23. *Ibid.*, p. 275.
24. *Ibid.*
25. *Ibid.*, p. 279.
26. Lambert, Pross, *Renewing Nature's Wealth*, p. 262.
27. *C.A.R.*, 1905, p. 266.
28. *C.A.R.*, 1906, p. 334.
29. *C.A.R.*, 1914, p. 359.
30. B. E. Fernow, *Conditions in the Clay Belt of New Ontario*, Report to the Commission of Conservation, December 28, 1912.
31. *C.A.R.*, 1911, p. 427.
32. Brown, Cook, *Canada 1896-1921*, p. 158.
33. W. R. Young, "Conscription, Rural Depopulation and the Farmers of Ontario 1917-9," *CHR*, Vol. 53, 1972, p. 292n.
34. *Ibid.*, p. 294.
35. *Ibid.*, p. 296.
36. *C.A.R.*, 1913, p. 353; 1914, p. 361.
37. *C.A.R.*, 1913, p. 354.
38. *C.A.R.*, 1914, p. 361.
39. Brown, Cook, *Canada 1896-1921*, p. 157.
40. Middleton, Landon, *The Province of Ontario*, Vol. 1, p. 452.
41. *C.A.R.*, 1913, p. 374.
42. *C.A.R.*, 1909, p. 360.
43. *C.A.R.*, 1912, p. 335.
44. *C.A.R.*, 1913, p. 374.
45. *C.A.R.*, 1905, p. 268.
46. Brown, Cook, *Canada 1896-1921*, p. 102.
47. *C.A.R.*, 1913, p. 383.
48. *Ibid.*, p. 372.
49. *Ibid.*, p. 365.
50. *C.A.R.*, 1914, pp. 358-359.
51. Brown, Cook, *Canada 1896-1921*, p. 114.
52. *C.A.R.*, 1913, p. 366.

Chapter Nine

"Ut incepit fidelis"

1.

The Ontario that Whitney left on the eve of the First World War was still a province that would have been recognizable to Oliver Mowat, or for that matter to Sandfield Macdonald or Edward Blake. There had been vast change and more change was in the making, but the forces at work had been known and the horizons of growth perceptible to the early leaders. Government was sure of its functions and of their comfortable limitations, and the governed seemed to accept them with the usual mixture of complaints. Hydro had changed something, but it was not yet clear how much; the farmers were threatening change and so was labour. Yet Ontario at forty-seven, as the twilight closed on an age, remained essentially the daughter of Upper Canada.

With the acquisition of Patricia District the province had reached and passed for a time the limits of manageable expansion. A huge, sprawling block of 412,582 square miles, Ontario stretched from the St. Lawrence to the coast of Hudson Bay, centred in the Canadian heartland and embracing within its boundaries over 15 per cent of the area and over 30 per cent of the population of the entire Dominion. Yet its own population, estimated in 1914 at 2,705,000, was clustered massively in the older, settled south. Over 16 per cent was in the Ottawa-St. Lawrence triangle that made up eastern Ontario. Over 54 per cent lived in the broad belt of cities, towns and farmland that bordered Lake Ontario, embraced the Niagara peninsula and continued to Lake St. Clair. Some 9 per cent was in the counties of the midwest, Huron, Perth, Waterloo and Wellington; while a little over 10 per cent was distributed in the horseshoe region that surrounded Georgian Bay, from Bruce county on the west to Parry

Sound on the east. There was a bare 5 per cent in the far northeast of the forests, mines and Clay Belts, and something less than 3 per cent in the whole of the northwest, including Patricia District. Ontarians drew much of their sustenance from the wealth of the new north, but most of them had never seen it. They lived, over 90 per cent of them, within the chain of lakes and rivers that had formed the boundaries of the province when Simcoe first came.

Nor had they changed much in their bloodlines, though there was some change on the way. Between the census of 1901 and the census of 1911 there had been disappointment with the results of immigration and worries over cross-migration between Quebec, Ontario and the west. Too many British immigrants had passed through to the prairies, and too many native sons had gone with them. Elements of a new foreignness were diluting older strains. The number of Ontarians of French origin had increased from 158,671 to 202,442, while the earlier groupings of German origin were now less than the French. No Poles had been listed in 1901; 10,000 were counted in the census of 1911. The 35,000 of Dutch extraction represented an increase of 50 per cent over the total in 1901. There were 21,000 Italians as compared to 5,000; 12,000 Russians as compared to 4,500; and 8,250 of Scandinavian origin where there had been less than 4,000 ten years earlier. A census which distinguished Jews among the international community showed an increase in their numbers from 5,337 in 1901 to 27,000 in 1911. Immigrants welcomed for railway building and for the mines, forests and new farms of the north, were less welcome as they came to settle in the cities. Yet if they added a ripple of strangeness and disturbed some social patterns, they hardly touched the basic nature of the province. With 884,000 English, 608,000 Irish, 424,000 Scotch and 9,000 Welsh, Ontario's pattern of peoples was 80 per cent British.

The community was balanced on a knifeblade between rural and urban interests, with the trend moving inexorably in favour of the towns and cities. In 1901 the ratio of rural to urban population had been approximately 57:43; by 1911 it was approximately 48:52; and by 1921 it would be 42:58. The farmer was crossing the divide; he was becoming part of a minority outside the urban circle.

At the same time the forces making for change were easing some of the effects; communications were reducing isolation. Railways spanned the province in an over-prodigal grid of some 9,000 miles. The roads of the "good roads" programs, built for the horse-and-buggy, had done much for their time, but that time was passing. The automobile, still bitterly complained of and hedged in by a bristle of regulations, was winning grudging acceptance as were some of its developing needs and accompanying possibilities.

187

If we had good roads in Ontario, (said Sir Edmund Walker, President of the Bank of Commerce, in 1913,) people would come in increasing numbers from the United States . . . there is no question of an increase in the number of motors so great that we would soon be issuing 20,000 licenses for cars . . . say at $25. each . . . $500,000. – quite a contribution.[1]

The mail came now to the box at the farmyard gate by rural free delivery. The party lines of rural telephone systems were in ever-increasing use. Hydro and Adam Beck, though they had not yet fulfilled the promise that "the poorest workingman will have electricity in his home,"[2] had accomplished much since the day of triumph in Berlin. By 1914 thirty-eight municipalities had been incorporated into the Niagara system and were serviced with light and power. Hydro was building the first of its own generating stations on the Severn River in Muskoka; plans had been made for another system at the western lakehead and for still another to supply eastern Ontario. In addition to that, while rates were scaled down and standards, methods and inspection all steadily improved, the campaign went on to increase demand and use.

The "Hydro Circus," touring the central province, was one of the most spectacular of the missions to the unconverted. A caravan of two horse-drawn covered wagons, one with motors and transformers and the other stocked with equipment for demonstration, made the rounds of reluctant municipalities, performing for Boards of Trade, showing what power could do. Quite often, on the road between rural centres, it wheeled into a farmyard and gathered neighbours for an impromptu demonstration. The dim interior of a barn would glow with an electric lamp, power hooked to a saw-rig would convert logs to firewood, a cow would be milked by a milking machine and cream separated by a separator, both electrically driven. An electric stove in the kitchen would produce a steaming meal, a room would be cleaned by an electric vacuum cleaner, and sometimes a week's laundry washed by an electric washing machine and pressed by an electric iron. Not infrequently Beck himself was present, adding his own eloquence to the appeal for better living. It was hardly necessary; the machines spoke for themselves. Here, conceived in the cities and reaching out from the cities, were fruits of an industrialization that could benefit every home. Yet for all that, with the new conveniences and advantages came the old sense of inferiority and displacement. The farmer looked at the city man with a mixture of fear and envy, suspecting the drummer of progress who took more than he gave.

The urban fabric developing with industrialization had its heart and centre in Toronto. Six of the national banks whose branches speckled the province were Ontario institutions with their head offices in the city. The Bank of Nova Scotia, though its official home was Halifax, had its general manager in Toronto. The four Quebec giants, the Merchants, Union, Royal and the Bank of Montreal, had regional headquarters on King, Yonge or Bay Streets. There was similar concentration among the trust, loan, mortgage and insurance companies; though some of these, in common with the Bank of Hamilton and the Bank of Ottawa, had other names than the Queen City's at their mast-heads. With them as with all others, when it came to the making of loans and the application of capital, Toronto directors exerting Toronto influence had usually the final say. The stock exchange and the mining and commodity exchanges reflected the reach of the city and the effect of decisions made there in daily ups and downs. British and American investment and the building of branch plants were usually the result of plans matured in Toronto. Wherever money flowed, from the mines of the far north to the industries of the southwest, much of it flowed through Toronto and returned its share of profit.

By 1914, as it widened along the lakeshore, Toronto had absorbed within its boundaries some twenty-eight of the minor communities and villages that had once been independent. Ambitious plans, coordinated with the federal government, were about to change the grimy chaos of its waterfront where the freight train reigned supreme. The lines of the entrenched railway companies, which were still protesting, litigating and disputing every foot, were to be moved to new sites. Yards, trackage, coal bunks, a tangle of dismal freight sheds and rickety ancient slips were to be replaced by concrete wharves, new access roads and by a boulevard along the water. The Toronto Harbour Commission was reclaiming marshy forelands and clearing and dredging approaches for a hugely enlarged port. The Welland Canal was to be deepened to permit passage from Fort William of the big ships on the Lakes and put Toronto in competition with Buffalo. And beyond that, as another plan, was the deepening of the St. Lawrence waterway from Toronto to Montreal.

> That this development is bound to follow, (wrote the Chairman of the Harbour Commission,) is now recognized ... large ocean freight vessels will carry their cargoes direct from old country ports to the docks in the capital of Ontario.[3]

The capital's population, which was approaching 400,000, had nearly doubled since the census of 1901, and so had the area of the city.

Electric railways were branching out to the suburbs, and in the busy central area as far north as St. Clair twenty-two miles of street car lines competed with horse-drawn traffic. The automobile was as yet a lesser problem, but the street cars made their own. They were part of a jerry-built system and a confused structure of rates that was an abomination for the passenger. With his ticket at 2 cents or 10 cents for six, he had no benefit of transfers and few direct routes. Two or three of the tickets and as many changes of cars were often required for a trip. Nevertheless, thousands came pouring out of the cars to offices, shops and factories six days each week. Recession and unemployment marked the year before the war, but they barely shaded the outlines of a decade of massive growth.

As a business, financial, administrative and distributing centre Toronto dominated the province. It was the greatest port and a hub of railway service, from the far west to the Atlantic and from the depths of the northern Shield country to the cities of the United States. At the same time it was by far the greatest of the manufacturing centres. All the old commodities, flour, whisky and food products, lumber, furniture, woollen goods and textiles, clothes, shoes, leather goods, an infinite variety of home products and a vast range of tools, machinery and implements were made in Toronto plants. They were more efficiently produced and yielded a better profit because village shops and craftsmen had been absorbed in the modern factories, often leaving the villages to wither away empty. In 1881 Toronto had had 10 per cent of the industrial workers of the province. By 1911 it had 27 per cent and the proportion was still growing.

A broad band of smaller centres repeated the same pattern. Ottawa, Kingston, Cornwall, Brockville, Smiths Falls and Pembroke, all in eastern Ontario, were centres of production for most of the familiar staples and had some distinctions of their own. Cornwall throve on textiles, Kingston was producing mining machinery and developing a chemicals industry, while Pembroke, "the sawdust town" of the old timbering region, was converting its wood to lumber and to crates, boxes and veneers. The unbeautiful Dominion capital, still far from becoming the "Washington of the North," remained a hub of the lumber trades and was growing on electric power. Its paper mills, supplied from the Chaudière, were the largest plants in the province.

In the Lake Ontario region east of Toronto Belleville had grown as a dairying centre and as a divisional point for the Canadian Northern Railway. It was now the great cheese maker whose cheddar was world famous, while Cobourg, Lindsay and Port Hope, with planing mills, woollen mills and the inevitable flour and grist mills, were producers of furniture and leather goods, largely for a local market. In Oshawa in 1907 Robert McLaughlin and his son, R. S. McLaughlin, had converted the family carriage works into a plant for automobiles. The town had grown to a city on the strength of McLaughlin vehicles powered by Buick engines, and the McLaughlin-Buick foreshadowed General Motors. The growth of Peterborough, however, had been the dominant feature in east-central Ontario. A milling, lumbering and farming town till the early 1890s, it had attracted the Edison Electric Company to the Otonabee River. By the turn of the century there had been pre-Hydro development, the Edison Company had become Canadian General Electric, and cereal makers, boat builders, factories, foundries and machine shops were gathering to the source of power. In a matter of fifteen years, with its population doubled and double that of any city in the region, Peterborough had become an industrial centre of 18,000 people.

West of Toronto was Hamilton, the nearest rival, the second industrial city and the second in population, with some 82,000 people. It fronted on Lake Ontario, it was served by the lines of three Canadian railways and products came and went from it by four American connections. The great distributor of the west and "the Pittsburgh of the North," Hamilton surpassed Toronto in steel and iron production and matched Toronto in its supply of electric power. Yet it remained securely dominated by the wealth and reach of the metropolis, while its smelters, mills and fabricators were plagued by defective ore. Neither the Helen mine nor any of the provincial sources had fulfilled their early promise; their ore was low-grade. It required American supplements and expensive blending processes, neither of which were covered in the view of the manufacturers by bounties wrung from the federal and provincial governments. Nevertheless, complaining, bustling, petitioning, yearly adding to its factories and the smoke from the spires of industry, the city forged ahead. Almost anything Toronto made, Hamilton made too, or felt capable of making.

South of Hamilton around the curve of the lake were St. Catharines, the garden city, Welland bestriding the canal, and Niagara Falls at the centre and source of power. To the west, beginning at Brantford lay the wide zone and the conglomeration of industry that was growing on the use of power. London was now the third city of the province, with 46,000 people. Berlin, Guelph, Stratford, Galt, Chatham, Woodstock and St. Thomas, all sprung from the farmlands, were manufacturing centres. Sarnia, begun as a lakeport, had grown on Petrolia's oil, the salt mines of Goderich and the trade in grain and timber. Windsor surpassed Oshawa as an automobile city, for Ford had arrived in Ontario ahead of General Motors. Incorporated in 1904 and establishing itself at Windsor, the company had built its hundredth car before the end of 1905 and was now numbering them in thousands. Fortunately, perhaps, for a province that was not yet geared to receive them, much of Windsor's production was distributed throughout the empire.

To the north round Georgian Bay was the zone of the older industries that still clung to their position. Meat packing and leather working were principal supports of Barrie, and the Hydro plant on the Severn was building up Orillia. Collingwood, Midland and Penetanguishene were great centres of saw milling which was still the largest employer of provincial labour. Owen Sound as a lakeport was moving ahead of Collingwood, though it had lost out in one respect to diminutive Port McNicoll. The village on Hog Bay, in preference to Owen Sound, had been chosen by Canadian Pacific Steamships as the site for the headquarters offices, freight sheds, machine shops, docks and roundhouses serving the Great Lakes fleet.

North Bay on Lake Nipissing was a city of 7,000, a railway centre and gate to the farther north. Sault Ste. Marie, at the throat of Lake Superior, had settled for something less than its early hopes. The vast industrial complex once foreseen by Clergue had dwindled now to centre on Algoma Steel. That industry, moreover, in greater degree than the smaller plants at Hamilton, was faced with the costs of blending imported ores and with ever-deficient federal and provincial bounties. For all its great beginnings the Soo's growth had been slow. It supported a population of less than 11,000 while Sudbury and Copper Cliff, neither of them yet approaching the status of cities, gave work to 10,000 distributed in the area round them.

Kenora remained the Muskoka of the far west, with its lakes, rivers and fishing camps and its hordes of summer visitors. Six thousand of its people were processing lumber and pulp, packing commercial fish, building boats for the tourists and manning the great new flour mills that tapped the western traffic. On the main flow of that traffic, added to old resources, Fort William supported 27,000 people, and Port Arthur 11,000. The bulk of their great storage elevators rising at the western gateway symbolized massive change. Wheat production in Ontario had declined by 40 per cent and barley production by 80 per cent in a matter of thirty years. Twenty-five per cent of all Ontario farmland was now converted to pasture, a territorial adjunct to the dairying and livestock industries. There was a welcome now in the rapidly industrializing province for the flood of prairie grain.

Where Canadian wheat was concerned Ontario had become

primarily the transporter, handler and miller. Yet it remained the producer and processor of timber, minerals and pulpwood, with its only rivals Quebec and British Columbia. It was more and more a supplier of manufactures to a national domestic market. Ontario had thirty-one of a total of seventy Canadian meat packing plants, ten of eighteen smelters, six of the eleven condensed milk plants in the Dominion, and 129 of its 147 establishments for the packing and canning of vegetables and fresh or evaporated fruits. The consolidations of the textile industry spanned several of the provinces, but of eighty-seven woollen mills Ontario had sixty-eight.

The 8,000 manufactories of the pre-war province ranged from such world-wide businesses as Massey-Harris in Toronto or the Cockshutt company at Brantford to town and village establishments of five or six men. Within the broad southern belt, moreover, a large proportion of the small ones was comparatively well distributed. Stubbornness, position, power facilities and access to transportation had enabled local industries to resist the pull of the centres. There were blast furnaces at Midland and Deseronto as well as at Hamilton and the Soo. Farm tools and equipment and the simpler varieties of machinery were made in shops within range of the farms that used them. Furniture making, food processing and meat packing often went on as usual close to sources of supply. Not all the fruit and vegetable canning and very little of the wine making had moved from the Niagara towns. Over much Ontario industry, for all the absorptions and mergers, there was still the homely touch of the local craftsman. Along with that, however, was the advancing march of Hydro, signalling the new day. One hundred and thirty-three plants, publicly-owned or private, were producing electric power, and twenty-seven factories were making electrical equipment and supplies. Nineteen automobile plants had been started by 1911, though only eight survived. Ford and McLaughlin-Buick, though they had begun with a long start, had seen the foreshadowing of rivals. The Durant, Star, Flint, Gray Dort, Reo and Studebaker had all made their appearance, some of them come to stay.

Of another industry as yet there was only an unpromising glint. At the Petawawa Army camp, on August 2, 1909, Casey Baldwin and J. A. D. McCurdy had flown their Silver Dart biplane for the benefit of some Canadian officers. The plane had broken its undercarriage as it came in for a landing, and generally left the soldiers unimpressed. They had been equally cool to the famous Count de Lesseps, who met with a similar accident in staging another show, and only mildly interested when the first inter-urban flight in North America was made between Toronto and Hamilton in 1911. The flying machine was becoming moderately familiar through the work of barnstorming pilots stunting at fall fairs. It had not, however, disturbed the sleep of the military or attracted capitalists to a new field of investment. That, with much else, the coming war would change.

3.

For its educational and social services the province could, and did, make many claims. The University of Toronto and its colleges as well as Queen's, Western, and McMaster were training grounds for leadership in the hands of a confident elite. Science was being recognized, and vocational schools were coming. Agriculture and the resource industries were permeated and benefited by the influence of special schools. For the Torontonian and the visitor prepared to seek it there was an enrichment of cultural life in the collections of the Royal Ontario Museum and the frequent exhibitions of the Ontario College of Art. There were travelling libraries for the country districts and assisted public libraries in most sizable towns. Continuation classes were a link for the town high school with the distant university. Grants to primary and secondary schools had been more than doubled in a decade, and teachers were better paid and better trained. The profession was advanced in status and, with the first beginnings of a pension fund, acquiring a new security. Medical and dental care were entering some of the schools, and the expenses of parents everywhere had been reduced by cheaper books. "All over this continent," said R. A. Pyne, "the example of Ontario is cited as a triumph in text-book policy."[4]

In Pyne's boast, however, there was an echo of George Ross, and beneath the claims and statistics were many of the old faults. The "better pay" of teachers was a strictly relative expression. It was noted in 1911 that the elementary teacher who received $400.00 in Ontario could earn $1,200.00 in Saskatchewan. In raw northern Ontario neither salaries nor qualifications adhered to any standard, and both were declining in the depopulating regions of the south.

Even in the richer districts there were always rumbles of complaint. The farmer who was short of help, and whose school taxes had doubled, resisted the advancing claims of education. He was reluctant to spare a son, and his wife to spare a daughter, even for attending high school. School attendance, particularly in the busy seasons, was always a nagging problem; and there were deeper problems for the concerned senior professional. The Normal Schools poured out their quota of teachers to the required specifications. They did not open minds, however, or produce graduates who did. The child in the expanding system was being too much taught by

194

rote and with all too much dependence on the dreaded examinations. Teaching was becoming rigid and education static as the formal framework grew. Structure had replaced quality, something was being lost to growth, as it was in many fields. Beyond that, moreover, in the field of the separate schools, the rankling issue of bilingualism created an ugly rift.

By 1914 the Toronto General Hospital stood completed, with a wing for medical research allied to the university, and a social service clinic. The province itself, divided into ten regions under District Health Officers, had 159 hospitals, public and private, including twelve sanatoria for the treatment of tuberculosis. It had seventy houses of refuge, thirty-two orphanages, two convalescent homes and three homes for incurables. The nearly 6,000 insane in its cluster of mental homes were generally better cared for than they had been in the long past, as were most of the prisoners in jails. Organization, inspection and considerable public outcry had done much for the ailing and the sub-strata of the miserable. Yet the shortfalls still remained, deplored and unrelieved.

Private and county hospitals, assisted by lean subsidies, were often lacking in staff and in all modern equipment. Other institutions included in the statistics were neglected, malodorous shelters in remote country districts where an inspector seldom came. In general sanitation, for all the work of the Health Officers, habits were slow to change. While the countryside improved, the city slum took over as a major problem; and in this as in all else Toronto led the way. Immigrant workers crowding to the central districts were garrisoned by sharp landlords in half-condemned houses, four or five to a room. "Their ideas of sanitation are not ours,"[5] and Toronto's standard was not high. Water had remained a problem until late in 1910, and it was only on the heels of a typhoid epidemic that improved filtration came.

It was only one improvement of many still to be made. A year later, as inspectors wandered helplessly among straggles of dank tenements, they found

> houses unfit for habitation, inadequate water supply, unpaved and filthy yards and lanes, sanitary conveniences so-called . . . which have become a public nuisance, a menace to public health, a danger to public morals and in fact an offence against public decency.

They found a dismal brick factory "under the morning shadow of the City Hall" with its top floor housing machinery and six families including forty workers crammed on the floor below. The whole place was served by an outdoor privy which the owner had boarded up, and beside the privy was the water tap with a tin pail beneath it. Another place "for which one of the best-known real estate firms in Toronto collects the rent" had for its sanitary facilities "the condemned and out-of-date privy pit" which had been overflowing for months and which adjoined a vacant lot.

> Into that vacant lot the husband of the poor woman who still struggles to keep that house decent casts, under cover of night, the 'night soil.' The same thing is done from seven other dwellings of which we have reports. In other words, what we have read of with disgust as having happened in the cities of Europe in the Middle Ages, happens in Toronto now before our very eyes.[6]

"There is," said another report, "a permanent population of at least 1,000 dependent children in Toronto." It was augmented, particularly in winter, by a drift of the indigent and imbecile and the diseased and unemployed. Churches and private agencies did what little they could, but all system was lacking. There was, according to the professional social worker, "vastly too much indiscriminate charity." Imbecile girls, particularly, occupied the social mind, and it was still a mind of late Victorian or early Edwardian turn. "It is a question whether medical skill should not be invoked to prevent the possibility of the propagation of the species."[7]

The provincial attitude to labour had been hardly more advanced. Under Mowat, Hardy, Ross, and equally under Whitney, there had been a general increase in wages and improvement in working conditions but there had been little change of view. The working man was a commodity necessary to support industry, and the needs of industry came first. Government machinery was evolved to assist in the placing of men, but they were placed on the employer's terms. A series of bitter strikes had left Whitney unmoved; he disliked the forces of unionism and he opposed the minimum wage. He was equally unmoved by the rising cost of living and the increase of unemployment; labour must fend for itself, find its place in the market. In 1913, as the ranks of the jobless grew, he did establish an unemployment commission. Yet he was in no hurry for its report, and there was nothing done in his time. After nine years in office, as the Whitney government prepared for its last campaign, only one item in its long record of achievements was addressed directly to labour. The claim for the workman's support was based on "investigation into labour conditions and the compensation for injuries question with pending legislation."[8]

Governments had been lethargic because labour had been divided; but the wars of competing unionisms and doctrinaire socialisms were slowly coming to an end. There was a stronger sense of direction, a determined gathering of forces and an infusion of new blood. Immigrants who had come to the promised land and found less than they hoped for were making their views known, some of them with practised skill. British experience in the work of trade unionism came with Englishmen and Scotsmen who were soon vocal as leaders. Russians, Balts and Slovaks were functioning as union organizers not only in the northern mines but in the packing plants of Toronto. John Ahlquvist, a Finn, became an officer of the Toronto Journeymen Tailors Union, formed in 1912. John Boychuk, a Ukrainian, was an organizer of the clothing workers, and Jewish leaders everywhere were surfacing among the sweatshops. They spoke with curious accents and were well-hated by employers, but they found receptive ears. The native labour movement, slowly pulling together, was building on hard times.

Across this the unresting temperance movement cut with a deeper swell. The prohibitionists in their long wrestling with Whitney had achieved a union of forces that widened the scope of their cause. The farm constituency, largely Protestant and largely Anglo-Saxon, was their oldest source of strength. It was confirmed now by many of the changes of the times. Drink had become to the voters in rural areas a part of the evils of the city and the fruit of urbanization. In the city itself, to the respectable, comfortable and church-going, it was the curse of the lower classes, the prime cause of the filth and misery of the slums. Prohibition stood first among the many causes of women. They saw the bar and the liquor shop as keys to the broken home, as nurseries of prostitution and as the first enemies of the wife, the family and the child. The social reformers trooped to the ranks of the drys, citing the police court blotters and the long trains of statistics that associated crime with drink. Sabbatarians complained of the neglected sabbath, and churches of thin attendance because of liquorous Saturday nights. It was easy to convince the defenders of an old way of society that liquor ate at its fabric.

It was not so easy to promote the conviction with labour. The working man liked his beer and he went less often to church. When he did go, and was subjected to long sermons, he was often resentfully aware of conditions among his betters. For the prosperous private citizen the liquor cabinet and the wine cellar went unreproved and accepted. The home brew of the farmer and the flow from Niagara's vineyards were not mentioned in the lectures. Bent on redeeming the labouring man whether he wished it or not, the voices of total dryness had an authoritarian ring, the old ring of the employer. Prohibition as a cause was becoming a class cause.

It was also becoming a protector of Britishness as the immigrants flowed in. The French and Germans of the province, always notably cool to prohibition, were at least native and familiar. It was not so, however, with the pools and clusters of newcomers. The foreigner who had come from the winelands or the lands of the week-long weddings was blandly, blankly indifferent to injunctions to mend his ways. He was a threat of change and danger, sinking his alien roots, watered too often with drink. The journalist walked through streets in his own Toronto, fascinated, repelled and fearful:

The pick-axe represents for you all the seething, sweating centre of the activity of the city's Lower End . . . There they are, a whole hundred of them, bare-necked, sturdy brown fellows forming a cordon in the middle of the street between the two rows of tumble-down shacks . . . the picks swing up, then down, then up again. Each swing is accompanied by some utterance, an unintelligible muttering or a snatch of song. And you think of the Italian operas . . .

A mob of children come screaming from a small side street somewhere. They are dirty little wretches . . . they seem to be heralding something . . . a man with a hurdy-gurdy and a dancing bear . . .

The big brown bear circles round and round . . . fat shop women come out of their doors and stand with hands on their hips. Big smiles appear on their faces and their eyes dance with enjoyment . . . the brown-armed gang of workmen have laid down their picks. The boss does not seem to mind. Everyone presses close to the howling hurdy-gurdy and the dancing bear . . .

You go your way along the street. You are now among the Jewish inhabitants of the Ward. Half a dozen tawdry women with scarlet shawls on their heads appear from a lane somewhere carrying shrieking chickens under their arms . . . they are on their way to the Rabbi's . . .

There is a side alleyway . . . the receptacle for the thousands of bottles which are gathered on the streets every day . . . beer bottles, whiskey bottles, medicine bottles . . .

It is almost evening. The odours of garlic and spaghetti come from the kitchens in the Italian district . . . the gang from down the street come lurching home with their pick-axes. . . well-dressed girls, newly released from work in the down-town factories, stroll along . . . beautiful girls they are, with olive complexions and eyes like glowing black pearls. They look curiously alien with their long ear-rings and much-coiffed black hair. Alien to the city in general, but much at home in the district of garlic and spaghetti. If it were not for the filth all around! . . .

The girls are pretty, the men alive. *Voilà*, what will you?. . .

198

There they live, huddled up in impossible little shacks, they laugh, dance, sing ... the Italian will remain contented, with more thought of his Chianti and a snatch of song than of all the sanitation sermons in the universe.[9]

Nor was all this stubborn strangeness festering only in the slums, or among the foreign born. Poisons were creeping upward, infecting the veins of society and changing the ways of the young. The "well-familied" friends of one gentleman's daughter had broken into his liquor cabinet and stolen some of his cigars, inducing sombre reflections.

Engagement, (he wrote,) has become to the debutante merely a proof of popularity. With her young friends she discusses it and the man as one might the new maid. In cold blood they compare chances, delve into 'thrills' and psychology and arrive at conclusions that would stagger their parents ...

New gods interfere with our religion, divorce courts laugh at marriage, festivity disturbs our homes, slit skirts and transparent waists violate the sanctity of the body, the tango shocks Terpischore, cubism shatters art, sex stories distort literature, problem plays defile the stage. Our music has become mechanical, our charity an advertisment, our worship a form ... turkey trots, tangos and theatres ... bunny-hugs... cooling-off joyrides ... that is not unusual even in Toronto the good ... and with it all life is a continuous Coney Island, a parent is but a bank, home a sleeping-place.[10]

If decay and dissolution were attacking the social order they seemed to the prohibitionist to be a wave washed up by liquor. If the immigrant was part of that, the immigrant must be kept out. If labour remained recalcitrant, labour must be compelled. Protestant and Anglo-Saxon, rural and middle class, the resentful forces of old, staid Ontario were gathering in new strength. Newton W. Rowell, the ablest Liberal leader since the time of George Ross, had infused his politicians with some of his own force. He had gained the support of women by endorsing the suffrage movement. He already had their support, as well as that of a great body of churchmen, for his stern Methodist convictions. There could be no temperance or temporizing in the matter of liquor control; Whitney's methods had failed. By January, 1914, out of the 835 municipalities in the province, 502 had declared for local option, but the majority of the population remained determinedly wet. Nothing had changed through regulation and licensing in the populous urban centres that outweighed the rural vote. Bars infested the cities with all their attendant evils; the

199

"treater" offered temptation and the rich drank in their clubs. The foreigner, the stubborn labouring man and the friends of vice and "the interests" were defeating a great cause, and it was a greater cause than it had been. Rowell spoke for it now in the name of women and religion and at last of the Liberal party, posing a well-worn question in terms of a new crusade. "Shall the organized liquor forces in this Province triumph against the forces of a common Christianity?"[11]

4.

By 1914 the *University of Toronto Quarterly* had joined the twenty-year-old *Queen's Quarterly* at the head of Ontario's scholarly publications. Science, medicine, the arts and domestic and foreign affairs were dealt with in other journals. The history of the province and the Dominion was being written by academics. William Kingsford's ponderous ten-volume work had appeared at the turn of the century. Between 1903 and 1908 William Lawson Grant, the son of George Munro Grant, had inspired and edited the Makers of Canada series, while George M. Wrong, with much work still ahead of him, had been one of the driving forces behind the Champlain Society, established in 1905.

It was said of the province that there was a good bookshop in every town of over a thousand, and Toronto had at least twenty. In these last decades before the advent of radio, the daily and weekly press was an unsupplanted power. Church weeklies and monthlies circulated in thousands of homes, and the *Canadian Magazine*, *Saturday Night* and *Maclean's* were more sophisticated purveyors to a widely receptive public.

The books in the shops were mainly British or American. The daily and weekly newspapers carried much syndicated "boilerplate" and attracted thousands of readers with their cheap serialized fiction from British or American sources. The Canadian magazines had prestigious British rivals in *Blackwood's, Chambers' Journal,* the *Illustrated London News* and many others. Over them all, moreover, washed the mass circulation of greater American rivals: *Ladies' Home Journal, Munsey's, Cosmopolitan, Collier's,* and the *Saturday Evening Post.* They were cheap and influential, and for much of the general public the source of tastes and standards. Their wide appeal diluted the pull of localism and their fees attracted authors. Ontarians read more and there was more creative writing than there had been at the turn of the century, but the growth of an indigenous culture was still perplexed and painful.

200

Among the poets, Charles Sangster had been dead for over twenty years, and Archibald Lampman for fifteen. They were "nature poets," now a part of the Victorian past. Duncan Campbell Scott and William Wilfred Campbell were leaders of a lonely few, heard by a select few.

> Canadians, (said one commentator in the year before the war,) devote their best and virtually all their energies primarily to economic industry and nation-building . . . Roberts and Carman and their confrères came and sang, but the Canadian people refused to create the leisure to listen to their singing, and so the First Renaissance in Canadian poetry died from public neglect.[12]

It was a premature obituary. The best of Lampman would survive under its turgid overburden. There would be something left of worth even by his followers and imitators, as one recalled another. When Pauline Johnson died in 1913 Isabel Ecclestone Mackay described the effect of her verse, at least on a receptive friend.

> First it brings a breath of the woods, warm and fragrant, a breath which clutches at the throat . . . the sound of swiftly-flowing water, the splash of a leaping trout, the dip of a paddle . . . And with all these lovely and familiar things it brings also something fainter, more remote, more primitive: the strain of an earlier, bolder, cruder race.[13]

The note lingered hauntingly among some who were still writing, but it was a diluted, thinning strain. Ontario's poets could not make peace with progress, nor interpret it nor find acceptance. Charles G. D. Roberts, turning from verse to prose and leaving Toronto for New York, had an acid word for his fellows:

> You've piped at home, where none would pay,
> Till now, I trust, your wits are riper –
> Make no delay but come this way,
> And pipe for them that pay the piper.[14]

In the two decades between 1890 and 1910 a cluster of Ontario novelists began to make their appearance, with Ralph Connor, Gilbert Parker and Sara Jeannette Duncan as major figures. Archibald McKishnie emerged as a writer of the great outdoors; and Edward William Thomson, less prolific than the others, surpassed most of them in portraying the older province. In much of lesser fiction there was the warmth of familiar life, with satire entering occasionally and more rarely social criticism.

Yet the novelist's trade was suspect, disdained by the intellectual, deplored by the evangelical and only considered to be justified by much didactic preaching. Many of the writers were clergymen with the cloth heavy on their work, and few of the more successful had chosen to remain at home. The Scottish-born Robert Barr, after years as an Ontario teacher, recorded his impressions in England, where he died in 1912. Gilbert Parker, once a curate in Trenton, had escaped from home-grown sanctions and was making his name abroad. The Reverend Charles Gordon, the Ralph Connor of the Glengarry stories and dean of the best-sellers, was to end his life as pastor of a Winnipeg church.

By 1914 Sara Jeannette Duncan, cool, astringent and urbane, had become Mrs. Cotes and was living in India. She had bequeathed *The Imperialist* to Ontario as a picture of her own Brantford, but she had written it after she left. Walking through the scenes she painted as an amused, observant tourist rather than an involved native, she had discovered the strains and contrasts in this British Ontarian stronghold among "democrats who had never thrown off the monarch – what harm did he do them overseas?" There was, she had found,

> a common love for the throne . . . a half-ashamed enthusiasm that burned like a sacred flame . . . arbitrary, rococo, unrelated to current conditions as a tradition sung down in a ballad, an anachronism of the heart, cherished through long, rude lifetimes for the beauty and poetry of it.

She had also noted on the Brantford front porch "the adaptability of Canadian feet to American shoes" . . . the "rocker" also American, the hammock made in New York and "upon John Murchison's knee, with the local journal . . . a pink evening paper published in Buffalo."[15]

There was similar conflict for most Ontario writers between the demands of the heart and the pull of wider markets. Nostalgic warmth for the province inspired much of their work, but it was a warmth hardly reciprocated and it did not hold them there. By 1911 a professor of economics who had himself paid for the printing of his first book had found a publisher for the second. The *Sunshine Sketches of a Little Town* had appeared, and Orillia was bound for fame as Mariposa. Yet Stephen Leacock, in his "angular overcoat, his missing buttons and his faded hat,"[16] occasionally exuding the genial aroma of alcohol, remained on the faculty of McGill. There was still too much truth in the complaint of Robert Barr, made at the turn of the century: "Toronto will recognize the successful Canadian writer when he comes back from New York or London, and will give him a dinner when he doesn't need it."[17]

The province saw much of good professional theatre but it was almost wholly from abroad, or written by Ontarians abroad.

James Forbes may have been born in Salem, Ontario, (commented one critic,) and he may have received his education in Galt, but he does not belong to us. The 'Chorus Lady' and 'The Travelling Salesman,' his most successful comedies, tell us that in spirit he has become an American dramatist, and so far as Canada is concerned he might as well have been born in Harlem.

It was the same with Edgar Selwyn who was making his name in New York. "There are no signs as yet upon the literary horizon of the arrival of our dramatist, but we are waiting expectantly for we feel that he should come now."[18]

His coming was not hastened by a contrasting department of letters. The William Briggs publishing house of Toronto, an organ of the Methodist church, was the most prolific in Canada. Strongly supported by the Woman's Christian Temperance Union and commended by public figures, it had published among much else an eight-volume "Self and Sex" series which permeated the homes and influenced the schools of the province. Endorsed by clergymen and medical men, the individual volumes were addressed separately to the sexes and to various states of life. The boy, girl, wife, husband and younger or older woman were taught what they ought to know and much they ought to avoid.

There were strong warnings against the "debasing influence" of the theatre. "The appeal to the amative and sexual nature is so universal in novels that . . . no young man or young woman should be permitted to read a novel before they arrive at the age of twenty-five." Temptation lurked and was to be avoided even in married life. Separate beds were better for the discreet partners and separate rooms were best, since they eliminated "the sexual excitement which comes daily by the twice-repeated exposure of dressing and undressing in each other's presence." The menopause should terminate, and be grateful release for the wife, from all conjugal relations. Alcohol and tobacco were to be avoided as sexual stimulants; and masturbation for the boy (not even thought of for the girl) led on to debility, insanity and complete moral disaster.

From 1906 onward the Canadian Purity Education Association, with the sex series for its text, had been sponsoring lectures by doctors. Arthur W. Beall, a former missionary in Japan, visited schools as the "Purity Agent" of the W.C.T.U. and continued his work to the early 1930s. He was remembered, according to Michael Bliss, as a

little white-haired man, dressed in a flowing red and blue cloak, the expression on his face of a benign Hindenburg, striding about their classrooms delivering what he ... called his 'eugenics lectures' – interesting young boys, it is thought, in masturbation for the first time in their lives.[19]

The place of music in the province was wide and well established. Toronto's Conservatory drew from all the Dominion and was known throughout the continent. A fine symphony orchestra was concluding its eighth season in 1914. The Great Mendelssohn Choir of 250 voices was considering an invitation, that would later have to be rescinded, to make a tour of Europe. Ottawa had a symphony orchestra, Hamilton, London and Berlin had permanent choral groups, and devoted teachers had fostered some good composers. Yet there were also quirks of taste, and old, unyielding provincialisms. Grand opera had failed both in Montreal and Toronto. The "O Canada" of Calixa Lavallée was a matter of national dispute rather than a national hymn, and the subject of a critic's lecture for its cold reception in Ontario. "Canadians instead of admiring and loving this finely composed, sonorous, dignified melody, become a spectacle to the world by quarrelling over the racial affinity and creed of him who composed it."[20]

To the same critic they were also guilty of under-valuing their composers. Clarence Lucas, W. O. Forsyth and Gena Branscombe Tenney, "the first native-born Canadians who have systematically essayed musical composition as a fine art," remained generally neglected. Lucas, by 1914, had completed some 140 works of which many had been heard in Europe and much admired. "Yet this Canadian Titan of the musical world is as unknown and unappreciated as if his glorious music were a far-off, seldom-heard echo."[21]

The Royal Canadian Academy and the Ontario College of Art continued to foster a large body of painting. The most interesting development, however, stemmed from another branch. The casual group of painters, etchers and illustrators, first banded together as the Ontario Arts Students' League, had continued to attract associates, produce annual calendars and generally expand its field. Magazine, newspaper and advertising work as well as industrial design had drawn young artists to Toronto and kept them busy at easels but had hardly satisfied their souls. Neither had the state of landscape painting as they branched out for themselves. There was still too much of Englishness or of the newer French impressionism; to their minds it was decorative importation rather than home growth. When they looked at the actual landscape they had a sense of something else, native and new. Joining in week-end sketching trips to the Humber and Don valleys and across the Niagara country, they tried to bring back what they saw. As the range of the trips extended, J. E. H. MacDonald, Tom Thomson and a number of kindred spirits became familiars of the north. Railway companies discovered them, liked their flaring posters, and A.C.R. 10557, a boxcar of the Algoma Central, became one of their favoured vehicles.

Meanwhile their serious work was breaking on a startled public with its rawness of tumbled rock, its harsh glitter of waters and its gloom of pine and spruce. In 1913, as a kind of culmination, *Northern Lake* appeared, painted by Tom Thomson. He was to be dead four years later, drowned in a northern lake, and the Group of Seven would make its name without him. In 1919, however, when Lawren Harris, A. Y. Jackson, F. H. Varley, Franklin Carmichael, Franz Johnston, Arthur Lismer and J. E. H. MacDonald held their first showing in Toronto, several of them shared his influence and all shared his philosophy. "Art," they said in the calendar accompanying their pictures, "must grow and flower in the land before the country will be a real home for its people."[22]

5.

The Queen City in its appearance, as well as in its ways and attitudes, seemed to summarize progress. Toronto's banks and business buildings had a new air of munificence, and even some of its factories were designed to please the eye. There were the ivy-grown walls of some of the fine old schools and the distinguished multitude of churches. The university and its colleges, islanded in green lawns, were alive with confident youth. Scattered throughout the city were parks, playgrounds, skating rinks and toboggan slides, and the Don still ran clear. Summer swimmers and picnickers filled Riverdale Park, and Scarborough Beach was crowded through long days in the sun. The bronze bells in the tower of City Hall, slender and Romanesque, had been striking the hour and the half and quarter hour for nearly fourteen years. They weighed some eight tons, and they had been installed in time to salute the twentieth century. Toronto agreed with Laurier, though it agreed with him in little else, that it was to be the century of Canada.

By 1914, with the long, grimy waterfront involved in a turmoil of change, Union Station was rising along Front Street. The Harbour Commission's chairman had revealed his spacious plans. There was to be

a waterfront boulevard and driveway . . . from Woodbine avenue on the east, along the lakefront . . . and along the western waterfront to the Humber River. This boulevard and driveway will have a total length of thirteen miles and will consist of broad con-

205

crete walks, driveways, bridle path and park areas, to a total width of 200 feet, making one of the handsomest waterfront boulevards on the North American continent.[23]

The plan was to be delayed by war, however, and the state of the waterfront was deteriorating. There were still the miles of trackage, the rumble and smoke of freight trains and the sprawling hulks of the undisplaced warehouses. Beyond them, moreover, widening the blot on the shoreline, were plants of the manufacturers who were racing for new sites.

> With no railroad accommodation, with very primitive water system, with no sewage system, and the land in an ungraded state, several factories are putting up with the inconvenience at the present time in order to be in favourable locations when the new development is carried out.[24]

In the city's centre the Canadian version of the skyscraper was beginning to assert its dominance. A new Eaton's building glared at a new Simpson's building across the breadth of Queen Street, with a Woolworth building at the corner. First proposals for a subway had been dismissed as "hare-brained," but the evening rush at the corner of Queen and Yonge streets was keeping the thought alive. Under buildings placarded with advertising signs and among a jumble of poles and wires, street cars, horse-drawn drays, automobiles and pedestrians linger in old photographs as a muddled mingle of impatience. The traffic jam was as familiar as the films at Shea's or Loew's, or as the jokes of the vaudeville comics imported from the United States. At the Royal Alexandra or the Grand Opera on Adelaide there were superior stage productions, of which many came from Britain. In the life of the commonalty, however, the emphasis was North American. It was often admitted ruefully, yet with a sidelong glint of pride, that Toronto looked like any American city.

There were other claims, however, and other evidence of success. "No city of equal size in America," wrote one local admirer, "contains as many substantial and artistic homes and so delightful a series of residential districts as Toronto." The good houses, moreover, many of them in "sumptuous Queen Anne style," were of brick, marble or stone. There was "not a single frame house of any note in the entire city."[25] The elderly elegance of Jarvis Street and sections of Avenue Road was being matched now by Spadina, St. Clair and Rosedale. And towering up on Davenport, dominating the Spadina escarpment, was completed Casa Loma.

For all his troubles with the Electrical Development Company, Sir

Henry Pellatt had amassed a number of millions, acquired a knighthood and become a figure in London. All this involved an advance in lifestyle. High connections abroad meant trans-Atlantic visitors; distinguished hospitality would have to be fittingly returned. "A house," Sir Henry was quoted as saying, "whose dimensions in most cases would be considered ample, could not permit of anything like the style of entertainment that is quite common in England."[26]

Casa Loma, two years in building at a cost of some $2,000,000.00, was intended to meet the need. A European chateau, designed by Sir Henry himself from his impressions of English homes, it had ninety rooms many of them floored with teak, with mahogany and with oak panelling, woodwork carved in England and enormous bronze doors made in New York. Its library had shelves for 100,000 volumes, its conservatory was marble-floored, and among its other amenities were a palm room, a swimming pool, a bowling alley and a rifle range. An electrically lighted and elaborately tiled tunnel led from the house itself, passed under a street, and opened out on the stables for Sir Henry's horses. The stables, in the words of a breathless journalist,

> give one the impression of a Norman castle. Inside they are tiled and carpeted . . . and dozens of badges won at horse shows are artistically arranged in decorative panels on the walls of the harness-room . . . for Sir Henry never does anything with a small or narrow view.[27]

For all that, Toronto had doubts of itself, and they were shared by a British visitor. The depressing thing, said the young Rupert Brooke, "is that it will always be what it is, only larger."[28] A native journalist, though he did not quite concur, had his own views and produced evidence to support them. Brooke's complaint, wrote R. C. Reade in the *Canadian Magazine*, was "part of the large and generous diatribe of modern idealists against modern pragmatism and materialism, activism, dynamism and every other ism of soulless ugliness." But its inference of total monotony was not quite correct: Toronto had many contrasts:

> It is only a step from the sky-scraper to the slum hovel... The house is of plaster that in parts has fallen away in horrible running sores through which a few blackened laths show like gangrened bones. It does not resemble a habitation. It looks like a Calcutta leprosy ... The interior is desolate and loathesome; but that is nothing. On the steps of the door leading into the hideous litter of the back yard a little eighteen-months child, its legs in the drip-

pings from a rain-barrel, its face covered with dirt, is greedily eating bread crumbs soaked in a bowl of milk from which a flea-infested slum cat is at the same time feeding.[29]

6.

Provincial status affected provincial interest, and Whitney like all his predecessors was a watchful guardian of that. He had quarrelled with the federal government over jurisdictions and subsidies; and in 1909, when the Boundary Waters Treaty was concluded with the United States, he had seen Ontario as a loser. The two American power companies operating at Niagara Falls had been exporting half their output under a provincially granted licence. That arrangement was confirmed under the terms of the new treaty, but a provincial undertaking, revocable at any time, had become an obligation assumed by the federal government. A proportion of Ontario's power supply had been mortgaged in the national interest. In fact more power was available than the province was able to use, and its negotiations with Ottawa had been fruitful in other fields. The principle of *per capita* subsidies had been established in Laurier's time and the question of provincial boundaries had been laid to rest in Borden's. Whitney was content with Borden and Borden respected Whitney; Ontario seemed comfortably established as the senior partner in the Dominion.

If imperialism was a waning force it was hardly apparent in government or in the higher circles of society. The "Round Table" movement, centred in London and among a British elite, had a powerful influence in Ontario. It appealed to the intellectuals who shaped the minds of the establishment, attracted and cultivated journalists, was supported by wealthy businessmen, and like Canada First before it distrusted the lower orders. It worked in a lofty underground that aimed to instruct instructors and "to create an immense nexus of influence and patronage for directing public policy in imperial and other matters."[30] It had its own legitimate impulse from the fear of war in Europe and the rise of a truculent Germany. As the Kaiser's navy grew the need for increasing British strength, for an imperial drawing-together of all the far-flung colonies, became obvious. That fact Ontario fully accepted, while her own loyalties and conceptions imparted a deeper base. With urbanization and industry, with Americanization and foreignness, had come an increasing "sense of power."[31] The great energies that were mobilizing in many distasteful ways must be directed back toward their source; toward strengthened participation and perhaps to eventual leadership in the work of the British empire.

Whitney was of that mind, no less than Ross and Mowat, though he preached like them to a tide that would not rise.

I think, (he said at the time of the naval debate,) that Laurier lost a great opportunity ... he could by declaring his intention to offer one or two Dreadnaughts to the Empire have made the outside nations sit up and take notice of what the Over-Seas Dominions are about ... More than that, by doing so he would have quieted perhaps forever all timidity and restlessness in the minds of French Canadians as to what his opinion is as to imperialism.[32]

From that view of Canada's duty to the empire, and from that misunderstanding of Laurier's position in Quebec, Whitney never retreated.

Strong-minded and hard-headed, he was also aware of the strength and value of symbols. Ontario's seal, "appointed by Her Majesty" in 1869, was a hasty, simplistic affair. In 1907 Whitney initiated work on a new design and in 1909 it appeared, authorized by royal warrant:

Know ye, therefore, that We of Our Princely Grace and Special Favour have granted and assigned and by these Presents grant and assign the following Crest, that is to say: 'Upon a wreath of the Colours A Bear passant Sable and the Supporters on the dexter side a Moose, and on the sinister side A Canadian Deer, both Proper,' together with this Motto: 'Ut incepit fidelis sic permanet' ... to be borne for the said Province of Ontario on Seals, Shields, Banners, Flags, or otherwise, according to the Law of Arms.[33]

The words of the motto, Whitney wrote to a friend, alluded to the founding of the province by the United Empire Loyalists. "A free translation," he added, "would be: As loyal she began, so loyal she remains' or 'Loyal in the beginning, loyal still.'"[34]

So she remained as the sixth of her Premiers came to the end of his work. In early January of 1914 Whitney suffered a stroke while visiting in New York. By the 18th he was in the Toronto General Hospital where George Ross, lying in another room, was to die on March 7th. By April Whitney was at home, with fair hopes of recovery and receiving deputations. He declined a grant of money from all parties in the legislature, but accepted a smaller purse offered by his own caucus "as a token of public sympathy and personal regard."[35] On May 1 he was able to visit the House and give some thought to the imminent provincial election. He lived to see his government returned on June 29, with eighty-four seats to twenty-five for the Liberals and the usual one for Labour. On August 4 came the declaration of war, and he spoke out as expected. It was plain to

209

Whitney, the Ontarian, what Canada's course must be. "That course is to exert her whole strength and power at once in behalf of our Empire."[36] On September 25 he died and the Premiership passed to William Howard Hearst.

Notes

1. *Canadian Annual Review*, 1913, p. 357.
2. Denison, *The People's Power*, p. 88.
3. Lionel H. Clarke, "Putting a New Front on Toronto," *Canadian Magazine*, December, 1913, p. 215.
4. *C.A.R.*, 1914, p. 371.
5. *Report of the Medical Health Officer Dealing With the Recent Investigation of Slum Conditions in Toronto, 1911*, 1-104, Vol. 5.
6. *Ibid.*
7. *Report of the Charities Commission*, 1911, p. 12.
8. *C.A.R.*, 1913, pp. 365-366.
9. Margaret Bell, "Toronto's Melting Pot," *Canadian Magazine*, July, 1913.
10. "Degrading a Generation," *Canadian Magazine*, April, 1914, Vol. 42, p. 611.
11. *C.A.R.*, 1914, p. 378.
12. Bernard Muddiman, "A Vignette in Canadian Literature," *Canadian Magazine*, April, 1913, Vol. 40.
13. Isabel Eccleston Mackay, "Pauline Johnson: A Reminiscence," *Canadian Magazine*, July, 1913, Vol. 41, p. 219.
14. Muddiman, "A Vignette in Canadian Literature," *op. cit.*
15. Sara Jeannette Duncan, *The Imperialist* (Toronto: McClelland and Stewart Limited, 1961), pp. 58, 128.
16. Encyclopaedia Canadiana, Vol. 6, p. 100.
17. *Literary History of Canada*, ed. Carl F. Klinck, (Toronto: University of Toronto Press, 1965): "New Forces: New Fiction," Gordon Roper, p. 260.
18. Fred Jacob, "Waiting For a Dramatist," *Canadian Magazine*, June, 1914, Vol. 43, p. 142f.
19. Michael Bliss, "Pure Books on Avoided Subjects: Pre-Freudian Sexual Ideas in Canada" *C.H.A. Historical Papers*, 1970.
20. J. D. Logan, "Canadian Creative Composers," *Canadian Magazine*, September, 1913, Vol. 41, p. 491.
21. *Ibid.*
22. William Colgate, *Canadian Art* (Toronto: McGraw-Hill, Ryerson, 1943), p. 82.
23. Clarke, "Putting a New Front on Toronto," pp. 205-215.
24. *Ibid.*
25. Michael Foley, *A Toronto Album* (Toronto: University of Toronto Press, 1970), p. 45.
26. Newton MacTavish, "Henry Mill Pellatt," *Canadian Magazine*, June, 1912, Vol. 39, p. 109f.
27. *Ibid.*
28. Bruce West, *Toronto* (Toronto: Doubleday, 1967), p. 215.
29. R. C. Reade, "Four Angles of a Futurist City," *Canadian Magazine*, September, 1914, Vol. 43, p. 447f.

30. Carroll Quigley, "The Round Table Groups in Canada," *C. H. R.*, Vol. XLIII, No. 3, September, 1962, p. 204.
31. Carl Berger, *The Sense of Power* (Toronto: University of Toronto Press, 1970).
32. Humphries, *The Political Career of Sir James P. Whitney*, p. 432.
33. George W. Spragge, "The Great Seals and the Arms of Ontario," *Ontario History*, Vol. LI, 1959, p. 36.
34. *Ibid.*
35. *C.A.R.*, 1914, p. 354.
36. *Ibid.*, p. 459.

Chapter Ten

The First World War

1.

As a young lawyer in Sault Ste. Marie, William Howard Hearst had been "chief of the volunteer fire brigade and hail-fellow-well-met with everyone."[1] He was a man of fifty, however, by the time he became Premier, and joviality had waned. His habitual manner reminded his critics and even some friends of the abrasive, self-righteous assurance of a Sunday School superintendent. He had had six years as a member of the provincial legislature and three years as Minister of Lands, Forests and Mines, replacing Frank Cochrane who remained his friend and patron. A strong Methodist and temperance man, utterly incorruptible, he had much of Cochrane's force but none of his political skill. In the work of northern development he had been vigorous and single-minded, so much so that he had occasionally drawn criticism for neglecting the interests of the south. Always close to the Premier, he nevertheless had few public enemies and had maintained a neutral image. It was said of him, in fact, that "he had taken no pronounced stands on anything."[2] That sheltered position as the able, loyal subordinate was to be inevitably and drastically altered on the day he replaced Whitney.

The change took place at a short meeting of the cabinet on September 30, 1914. Before the meeting was a letter written by Whitney, shortly before his death, in which J. J. Foy was named as the first successor. Foy, however, was not only a Roman Catholic but also a seriously ailing man. R. A. Pyne, though he had been named as second choice and was serving as acting Premier, did not aspire to the office. The claim of W.J. Hanna, whose work as Provincial Secretary might well have earned him preferment, was ignored. He was accused by prohibitionists of favouring the liquor interests, and he had been a check on Beck's enthusiasm for the headlong march of

Hydro. These facts, apparently, Whitney had kept in mind, though he had also ignored Beck. Other possible candidates were considered briefly and dismissed, and with the assurance by Pyne and Hanna that they would retain their places in the ministry, the choice descended on Hearst. He emerged from the meeting to be called by the Lieutenant-Governor as the seventh Premier of the province.

By December 22 he had completed the reshaping of the government, with one notable replacement in his former office. George Howard Ferguson was advanced from a back-bench to become the new Minister of Lands, Forests and Mines. It was a pregnant move foreshadowing much contention, but it was seen at the moment only as a good appointment; a coming man had been recognized, a strong government strengthened. That it was strong there seemed to be no doubt. Adam Beck had withdrawn, but he had taken his departure gracefully and with adequate explanation. He felt, he said, that the direction and development of Hydro would absorb all his energies and he should be freed for that work. If he feared and disliked Hanna or was jealous of Hearst himself, that was only a matter of outside gossip. Transition appeared to be accomplished and ministers acquiescent, whatever the inner tensions. With a majority of fifty-eight in a House it had securely dominated for almost ten years, the position of the Conservative party seemed much the same as before.

By this time, however, the functions of government had changed. Industry, faced with a massive redeployment, was reducing its normal output and turning men on the streets. Factories would have to be retooled and new factories built for shells, weapons and masses of war material, but only federal authority was able to set requirements. Toronto's stock exchanges, closed since late July, had reopened in September under federally imposed restrictions. Banks, threatened with panic, had only been saved by federal guarantees. The federal presence was everywhere, urging, exhorting, demanding, and asserting new necessities. It had brought out the bands and flags, drawn the thousands to the recruiting offices and marched them away for training. Strength was gathering to the centre and would have to be directed from the centre in the name of national need. There had been shock, wrenching adjustment, confusion and indecision, but there had been no doubt of the response.

On October 2, 1914, two days after Hearst became Premier of Ontario, a line of thirty transports moved down from Quebec to drop anchor at Gaspé. Tumbled aboard them helter-skelter in a vast tangle of unequipped or badly-equipped units were 31,200 men and 15,000 horses. They had been brought together through August by hundreds of special trains, rushed to a raw new camp laid out at Valcartier, Quebec, and after six weeks of the mud and dust of the parade ground hurried onto the ships. Colonel Sam Hughes of Lindsay, now the Minister of Militia, had assembled his first contingent. On October 5, at 3.00 in the afternoon, the long train of vessels had begun to move through the Gulf, eastward bound for Plymouth. Among the 31,000 men were 14,000 from Ontario, and the second of many contingents was already building behind them. The new government was directing a province at war.

2.

Through the course of that war Ontario contributed 242,655 men and women to a total Canadian force of 616,557. All but some 60,000 were enlisted prior to conscription, which came with the Military Service Act of 1917. By the war's end nearly a tenth of Ontario's population had been in uniform, four-fifths of that voluntarily. Sixty-eight thousand Ontarians had been among the killed, wounded or missing; later statistics showed the effect on the province. In the census of 1911 the proportion of the population between the ages of fifteen and thirty-four had been 36 per cent. In the census of 1921 it was 32.7 per cent. There had been a heavy tax on a generation of youth.

Other strains resulted from the giant effort. Widely distributed as it was, and embracing all classes, it nevertheless gave rise to sharp divisions. The inevitable internments of aliens and the hunts for potential spies added bitterness to anguish as the casualty lists arrived. "Young Canadians," the *Globe* had said in September of 1914, "must be Canadian in their sympathies but not anti-German."[3] The fight was to be against militarism, not against a people who were Canada's natural friends. "No Canadian cadet should be allowed to think of a German or any other man as a target for his marksmanship."[4] That mood quickly faded. The University of Toronto, hammered at by the newspapers for retaining German professors, was eventually forced to suspend them. Solid old Berlin, the symbol and centre of tragedy, saw families torn and divided and friends alienated from friends before it became Kitchener in 1916.

At the same time other differences were sharpened. In the first days of the war twelve entire militia regiments offered themselves for service. The rich bought military equipment, subsidized batteries and units, and were not niggardly with their sons. Almost every cabinet minister shouting for volunteers had one of his own to think of, and sometimes two or three. The universities, as the head and heart of the elite, carried their share and more. The University of Toronto contributed in all 3,832 officers and 1,591 other ranks, of whom 531 were killed and 867 wounded or missing. Yet through

1914 and early 1915, with much of industry depressed or in process of tooling-up, it was the unemployed who led the rush to the colours. They came mostly from the cities, or from the mills, mines and timber camps that were idled in the new north. However, it was noted even then that in the older rural districts, perennially starved for help, recruiting was inclined to lag.

By 1916, as the munitions plants and war factories joined in the cry for men, there was no more unemployment. There were instead the casualties to be replaced, the demands for women workers and, even more insistent, the demands for soldiers from the farms. Yet at the same time there were the incessant demands for food, for more grain and livestock, for everything the farms produced. The farmer, caught in the middle, clung grimly to the little help he had; he could not produce without it. Nor could he produce with "volunteers" in the way of high school students or clerks from city offices, who left with their white hands blistered at the end of a two-weeks' stint. He was offered loans for seed but he was starved for men at harvest time; high-paid jobs in factories drew the best away. He was intrigued but unimpressed by the loan of government tractors, offered in desperation in 1917. That year brought conscription, softened at first by a promised exemption for farmers, and striking with full force when the promise had to be withdrawn.

Yet still the production orators followed the recruiting officers, demanding food from the land. They came by then from a federal Union Government combining Liberals and Conservatives, and from both provincial parties who had struck a truce for the war. Food they got, and in overflowing measure, for the farmer somehow managed to carry on. But with the new ache of parting as his conscripted son left came the old sense of helplessness and freshly embittered grievance. Whether in Ottawa or Queen's Park, it seemed, government remained the same – bland, uncomprehending and speaking with the cities' voice.

The first gift of the province to the war needs of the empire consisted of 250,000 bags of flour. Following that, amid a vast confusion of formed and forming agencies, came a flood of other offerings. The Canadian Patriotic Fund sprang to life nationally, raising millions in money. The Red Cross opened its branches in cities, towns and villages, administering funds and supplies. The Daughters of the Empire, the Womens Institutes and the church clubs and social clubs mobilized Ontario women in hundreds of fields of work. Socks, sweaters and bandages went off in thousands of bales, while the care, comfort and entertainment of soldiers were never-ending concerns. There were funds and workers for the wounded and for soldiers' needy families; food and tons of relief supplies for all the allied powers, while heatless days and meatless days were endured without complaint. The common theme was sacrifice, money was somehow found, and it was applied to good effect.

Medical men were prompt in assessing needs and in persuading government to supply them. Ontario's principal military hospital, established at Orpington in England, was to end the war with a capacity of 3,000 beds. Several others were supported in part by the province, while in all the home hospitals military needs came first. The public revenues supplying funds to government were soon effectively supplemented. In 1915, in addition to new amusement taxes and taxes on large estates, a special war tax of one mill was imposed on all property, yielding some $8,000,000.00 and covering almost all of the special wartime expenditures. Yet there was much more from the private pocket of the province. Between 1914 and 1918, in addition to work and supplies that could not be reckoned in statistics, Ontario contributed through her various funds and agencies some $51,000,000.00. That was about $18.00 for every man, woman and child, and it still left money for the Victory Bonds, the great national loans. Ontario purchasers accounted for over $800,000,000.00 of the $1,710,000,000.00 raised by the five issues. The old imperialist province, in the war to save the empire, was free enough with her means.

She could well afford to be generous, for she had become an arsenal and supply source on the strength of war demand. The mines and forest industries, which had been slipping into the doldrums, responded swiftly and recklessly to a surge of new orders. Timber production climbed toward the greatest of the old heights, and pulpwood production doubled. Idled timber limits, quickly opened and exhausted, were replaced by huge new land grants, distributed with a lavish hand. It was the same with pulpwood limits as old mills reopened and greater new ones came. Trespassing on Crown lands, fraudulent use of mining claims and much smuggling of sawlogs were all tacitly ignored. The timberman and the pulpwood man, under Ferguson, the new Minister, returned to much of their old and unwatched freedom. The first needs were the war needs to be supplied at any cost, and beyond them the prospects of peace expanded. By 1919, with a grant of 1,500 square miles to the Abitibi Pulp and Paper Company continuing a series which had alienated nearly 7,000 square miles of Crown lands without any pretence at tender or a fixed agreement on price, Ferguson was dilating on his hopes: "My ambition has been to see the largest paper industry in the world established in the Province."[5]

Mineral production, which had been $53,000,000.00 in 1914, rose to $94,600,000.00 in 1918. Sudbury, which had closed down its mining and smelting operations in 1914 due to the "unusual dullness" of the season, produced in 1918 over 92,000,000 pounds of nickel matte valued at $37,000,000.00. There would be an aftermath for Sudbury as the demand for wartime metal plunged with the coming of peace, but nickel's other uses were by then becoming known.

There had, moreover, been compensating changes. Through 1914 and 1915 International Nickel, the great American INCO which had absorbed the Sudbury interests, exported its product as usual to refineries in the United States. The company claimed that it could not refine in Canada, and blandly ignored the charges that it was supplying enemy buyers. In 1916, however, when a German submarine took on two cargoes of nickel at an American east coast port, the British, Canadian and Ontario governments combined for drastic action. They proposed first to embargo exports from Sudbury, and second to encourage a new company with a superior refining process. Faced with the twin threats, INCO saw the light. Absorbing the embryo company and acquiring the new process, it rushed work on a Canadian refinery at Port Colborne. By 1917 after thirty years of trying, Ontario's resources of nickel ore were being refined at home.

Meanwhile the war's demands were transforming the industrial structure. To a large extent it was still a horse-drawn war, and the old requirements of harness, wagons and saddlery rose to enormous heights. Small makers with dwindling local businesses were abruptly flooded with orders, and as old shops expanded others sprang up beside them. Many remained small since there was no time for the complicated business of merging; but larger plants in all fields were doubling and redoubling capacity. Everything used in peacetime was somehow required for war in new, undreamed-of-quantities. Boots, shoes, blankets, woollen goods and textiles, furniture, tools and metal products went off from country sidings or rumbled away in trainloads from larger city centres. Motor vehicles and weapons began to be poured out as the technology of war advanced, and above all the munitions industry resulted in great new factories and hundreds of new trades. In the chemical and metal industries, in the making of machine tools and in the training of thousands of workers the advance and widening of techniques amounted to a revolution.

By 1917, as British experts arrived to make Camp Borden in Simcoe county "the largest aerodrome in the world,"[6] military aircraft were being assembled in Toronto. The hydroplane was familiar, hovering over the bay, and trainers were rising inland not only from Borden itself but from five less important stations distributed across the province. In 1914 the total value of all munitions exported from

Canada had been just over $28,000.00. By 1918 it had risen to $388,213,553.00, of which some 60 per cent came from Ontario. It was only one indicator of the massive changes of war. The province which had had 8,001 manufacturing establishments in 1911 had 16,438 in 1919, while the total value of its products had risen in the same period from $579,000,000.00 to $1,737,500,000.00. Bloating the great statistics were inflation, tragic waste and unhealthy mushroom growth, which would take their later toll. Yet, for all that, the industrial life of the province had entered a new era.

Ontario Hydro, tripling its services to supply the needs of industry, had built plants and bought plants as it expanded across the province. By the war's end it was generating, transmitting and distributing much of its own power. The remaining private companies existed only on sufferance, and the days of a power surplus had been replaced by a general shortage. Adam Beck, the driving master of Hydro, was evolving peacetime plans. The electrification of the home, the town and the countryside was to resume at a new pace. There would be huge demands from industry as it converted to electric power, and beyond that there would be a revolution in transport. New "radial railways," a network of electric tramlines, were to link towns and cities and branch out to their suburbs, replacing outworn roads and making steam trains an anachronism.

Everything depended on huge resources of power, which Beck proposed to obtain. By January 1917 he had mobilized the municipalities and pressed a reluctant government into authorizing the "Chippawa Project." This was to be the world's largest generating station built at the gorge near Queenston where Niagara's waters fall from their greatest height. It would not be in operation until 1922, it would cost four times as much as the $20,000,000.00 estimated, and it would earn Beck in his long war with governments the title of "Dictator of Ontario." But it would give the post-war province, by then badly in need of it, a half-million horsepower of new electric energy.

3.

"The war has changed everything,"[7] said Hearst in March 1916, and the words he used in that case with reference to prohibition applied to much else. The claims of provincial status were overridden by the demands of national unity; the provinces functioned largely as arms of the federal government. Their rights and powers were aligned in the general effort, and even their political parties came to terms for the duration. Like everything else in war, however, it was a bitter and costly process. The federal Liberal party, wrecked and partially absorbed in Robert Borden's Union Government, was to bear lasting scars. Conservatism, however, in Ontario as throughout the country, would bear the major brunt of the war's effects.

From 1914 until late in 1917 Newton W. Rowell, as the leader of provincial Liberals, supported Hearst in the prosecution of the war. Both men, ardent in the search for recruits, and in support of the empire, were at the right hand of Borden as Union Government came. In June 1917 Hearst and Rowell appeared together at great public meetings, advocating conscription. They did so not only in the face of Quebec but in the face of Ontario farmers, solemnly protesting the taking away of their sons "while leaving wealth exempt from the same measure of enforced service."[8] In October of that year, with conscription become a fact, Rowell entered the federal field but left a pledge behind him. There were to be no by-elections until after the end of the war, and no provincial election until the demobilized men were home and one session of the legislature had been held following their return. The truce imposed federally by the hammer of Union Government remained confirmed in Ontario. Political responsibility for the measures taken in war was shared tacitly by both provincial parties.

Temperance, imposed as a war measure, was almost a joint effort, though it was done in Hearst's way. He intended it to be Whitney's way, for he had accepted Whitney's policy and was never sure that the cabinet would go beyond it. Methodist and liquor-hater, quite as fervent as Rowell, he moved nevertheless with much of the old chief's caution, measuring his inclinations against the general mood of the province. In December 1914, while Rowell called for the abolition of bars, Hearst came down on the liquor stores, curtailing their hours of sale. The bar served all too often as a club of the proletariat where workmen came to enjoy a glass of beer. There was as much effect morally and less danger politically in reducing the bottle trade.

This was not enough for Rowell and it was only a beginning for Hearst. By 1915, subjected to congenial pressures, he was ready for greater change. The country was geared for war, it was in the mood for sacrifice, and it was accepting regulation. The liquor traffic, so evil to the prohibitionist, was being seen now by others as at best a needless waste. It consumed grain, it reduced industrial efficiency and it put temptation in the way of the young soldier. Churchmen damned liquor as they damned the atrocities of war, and sometimes named it as the cause. The alien voice was lower, the British voice was louder and it was becoming even in the cities a voice predominantly dry. Thousands of casual moderates who had defended the right to drink were prepared now for the sake of wartime discipline to see it taken away.

The government's response, in the session of 1915, was a drastic change in the mechanics of regulation. The control of liquor licensing was transferred from the office of Hanna, the Provincial Secretary, to an independent commission under the chairmanship of J.D. Flavelle. A prominent brother of Sir Joseph, the meat packer, financial magnate and driving force in the munitions industry, Flavelle was also a Methodist and a prohibitionist. At the head of the new commission he was a sign of formidable trends.

They were becoming irresistible, not only in Ontario itself but in most of the provinces. "We will have nothing to do with license . . . We are out to annihilate the trade,"[9] said Samuel Dwight Chown, General Superintendent of the Methodist church, and his views were shared by the liquor commission's chairman. Late in 1915, with Flavelle as a prime mover and Hearst an approving spectator, a new Committee of One Hundred became a powerful provincial force. Non-partisan, non-sectarian and with its one object the establishment of prohibition, it threatened not only "the interests" but the wets in Hearst's cabinet. By February of 1916 it had blanketed most of Ontario with 77 county or city organizations, 700 municipal organizations and 35,000 workers. On March 8, 10,000 of the workers marched on Queen's Park to present a monster petition. It carried 825,572 signatures of which, it was claimed, 348,166 represented eligible voters. Some 73 per cent of the total who had cast ballots in the last provincial election were now supporting the demand for prohibition.

On March 22 it was Hanna, the man tainted with wetness, who rose in the House to give the government's answer. It had been foreshadowed in the Speech from the Throne a week before the parade, but it was more even than expected. By the terms of Bill 100, which Hanna was introducing, all bars, clubs and liquor shops were to be closed for the duration of the war. No liquor could be kept in hotels, boarding-houses, offices or other places of business. Only the private home was to be exempt from supervision, and liquor could be sold legally only for "medicinal, mechanical, scientific and sacramental purposes."[10] The provincial liquor commission would be charged with administering the act, and it would be an act of the present House. Prohibition, on the responsibility of the government, would be in force for the duration of the war. Only when the soldiers had returned and been absorbed again in the electorate would the matter be submitted to the voters as a subject for referendum.

Hearst would not waste time, nor spend the required money for taking an immediate vote. It could be, he said, only a partial expression without the voice of the soldiers. He was sure enough of the province and he had subdued the wets in his cabinet. He was, he said, continuing previous policies; he was following the general will.

> My contention is, (he told the members of the legislature,) that if this bill would bring no benefit to the province from a moral standpoint, if the results that follow its enactment would add nothing to the health and happiness of our people – as a war measure, for the purpose of aiding economy, thrift and efficiency, it is justified – it is made possible – yes, it is demanded – by public opinion.[11]

If there was an echo there of the lingering doubts of Whitney, it was drowned in a wave of cheers. There was still dissent in the ministry, as Rowell pointed out, but it had been effectively silenced. Liberals jabbed at the government for its former hesitation, and took what credit they could for bringing it to see the light. Beyond that, however, there was only applause from both sides. The Ontario Temperance Act passed the House unanimously and the members stood together to sing God Save the King. By Sunday, September 17, 1916, except for distilleries and breweries who sold their products elsewhere and an inward flowing trickle from sources beyond its boundaries, Ontario was drying up.

Two months later, as all provinces approached the same condition, a federal Order-in-Council unified the effects. With the usual minor exceptions for medicine, science and industry, the manufacture or importation of alcoholic beverages was prohibited throughout Canada. Distilleries and breweries shut down, and no more wooden cases arrived with foreign labels. Ontarians could neither make nor legally import liquor. Only the long foresighted could have legal liquor in their homes, and only the native wine maker remained conveniently ignored. Except for them and the prescription at the local drugstore, the last loop-holes were closed; the great adventure in aridity was fully under way.

At the same time the cause so closely allied to it was being juggled by both the parties. Rowell had declared himself for women's suffrage, but he could not commit his followers. Hearst, as he became Premier had continued to talk like Whitney, worsening the effect with his own pious unction. He could not see, he said, that the grant of suffrage was a matter of compelling interest. He believed that the time might come for it, but the time was not yet. He was lost in admiration of the work of women in war, but he could not insult sacrifice by the promise of political reward. He was convinced in his own mind that for a large body of women "the franchise is a responsibility and burden that they are not called upon to undertake and that they have not the opportunities to freely perform, in view of their responsibilities as wives, mothers and guardians of the home."

Meanwhile the bromides came forth, echoing from the long past: "If every woman had a dozen votes she could never equal the influence which a Christian woman exercises in the community."[12]

Through 1915 and 1916, as the suffrage movement grew with farm and labour endorsement, each of the major parties continued its old tactics. The Liberal leader was firm in support of women but his party wobbled behind him. The government had its usual evasions for the delegations who came to it, and its usual answer to private bills in the House; the time was inopportune. Certainly in a way it was. The franchise granted to women would double the size of the electorate and make it unpredictable in the midst of the war's problems. Yet the very size of the problems and the range of women's work were sweeping the cause along. In February 1917, the vote having been granted in the four western provinces, Ontario's time came. The Liberals meeting in caucus before the opening of the session adopted women's suffrage as a plank in the party platform. The government in the Speech from the Throne avoided any commitment, but it was prepared for the inevitable. Ministers watched benignly as two Conservative members tabled private bills, the one granting the municipal and the other the provincial franchise.

The debate that followed was a dramatic scramble for credit under the eyes of militant women. They had crowded into the galleries, each wearing the daffodil that had become the symbol of the movement, and they had presented one to every member of the legislature. Daffodils sprouted in lapels along the rows of opposing benches but Hearst, the all-important, had left his symbol on his desk. He rose, still without it, masterful and enigmatic, to discourse on obstacles surmounted and on many that still remained. Nevertheless, he concluded under the steely eyes of his watchers, "the Government endorses the principle of the bill now before the House and assumes full responsibility for it, and I call upon all my supporters to vote in its favour, and I take the full responsibility as leader for what the bill will entail."[13] Then he resumed his seat, put the flower in his buttonhole, and nothing remained for Liberals but to add their cheers and votes.

Yet for all the effect of that scene Hearst had fudged too much, and still continued to do so. It was two years more before women holding the vote were entitled to stand for office. Nor, when the right came, did the earliest women candidates appear particularly grateful. They had won against grudging males, of both political parties, and they did not minimize the results.

> One thing you men cannot do, (said Mrs. G.A. Brodie, president of the women's section of the United Farmers of Ontario,) you cannot win elections without the help of women who now have

half the voting strength of the country. You think your wives will vote as you do, don't you? Don't be too sure of that. We have got you where we want you at last.[14]

4.

The bilingual schools question, a major irritant in peacetime, became a virulent distraction in war. Called to grapple with hundreds of new problems, the government was forced on this issue to maintain its old position. It was in no way softened in its attitude by the rise of Howard Ferguson, effectively vocal as always and building on Orange support. Even among moderate British, and more among Catholic Irish, the wartime feelings rose. At the same time the very strains of the period increased resentment in the French.

As conscription loomed and nationalism grew in Quebec, the propaganda of both sides took on an uglier slant. To the French priest and nationalist, assailed as traitor or malingerer, the Ontarian became the "Boche." The closed schools in Ottawa were seen by the French as the result of imposed Britishness, while they were asked to defend that Britishness by joining the armed forces. The recruiting officers who spoke of freedom and patriotism were linked inevitably with school inspectors proscribing the French language.

The provincial conflict came to a point nationally with Laurier's intervention. On May 9, 1916, with the pressures rising in Quebec, the Liberals moved their resolution in the House of Commons, asking the Ontario government to change its course on the schools. He was not supported by Borden nor by any of the western provinces; nor was there much help from his own party in Ontario. He was, he said, fighting the extremes of nationalism and the fear of conscription in Quebec. He asked Rowell and asked the editor of the *Globe*: "Will the English Liberals in Ontario fight Howard Ferguson and the extreme Orange element?"[15] The answer in both cases was a firm and regretful "no."

From 1914 to late in 1916, while some of the bilingual schools accepted the regulations, Ottawa remained the glaring focus of dispute. In 1915 its divided and litigious school board, deprived of government grants, was taken over by a commission. That body the French refused to recognize and took their challenge to law, while new chaos descended on the schools themselves. French-speaking teachers who were not qualified in English were denied entry to their classrooms and sometimes barred by force. By February 1916, in the midst of demonstrations which amounted to near riots, 122 teachers had resigned, leaving 4,000 children without their bilingual schools.

223

In late June, as a climax to the celebration of St. Jean-Baptiste Day, the youthful 4,000 were assembled to receive diplomas commending their "courage and discipline" in support of the French language. Quebec by then had entered the fight itself, with an act of the provincial legislature authorizing municipal grants-in-aid to Ontario bilingual schools. Little had been left undone, it seemed, to make the worst of the quarrel.

At the same time, however, other forces were at work. On September 8, 1916, Pope Benedict xv wrote to Canadian bishops dissenting from the position of Bishop Fallon who had opposed bilingual teaching. For those who desired it there should be adequate teaching in both languages, but that goal should be pressed for with legality and moderation. On November 2 came decisions of the Privy Council on two questions referred to it. In the Lords' opinion the guarantees of the British North America Act were on behalf of a religious rather than a racial minority, and therefore did not apply to the teaching of the French language. The government of Ontario, however, in suspending the Ottawa school board and setting up a commission, had acted beyond its powers. With the claims of either side upheld only in part, conflict quieted a little and cooler voices were heard. One raised already among a worried body of Ontario intellectuals was that of C.B. Sissons, of Victoria College. "The whole body of enactments and pronouncements on the teaching of language in Ontario," he had written Laurier in May, "is woefully impracticable, obscure and even contradictory."[16] It remained to be cleared up, with principle finding a reasonable ground for compromise; and beyond that as the real solution was good bilingual teaching.

That would be a work for generations to come, but in the meantime, by January 1917, there was formal assent to the law. This was enjoined at a meeting of bishops held in Ottawa, and the resulting pastoral letter spoke for peace. "We are confident," it said, "there is no desire or intention on the part of the Government or the majority of the people of Ontario to proscribe the French language."[17] By 1918, as the broad-minded and energetic Anglican churchman, Canon H.J. Cody, replaced the aging Pyne in the Ministry of Education, a new *modus vivendi* was beginning to take shape. In 1919, under the whip of financial necessity, the two factions of the divided Ottawa school board were formally reunited, with "good will and courtesy" reported on both sides. "The bilingual trouble, which for seven long years has practically disrupted the Separate School System of the city, and which has faced the schools with danger of bankruptcy, is now to all intents and purposes at an end,"[18] said the Ottawa *Citizen* in January, 1920. It was speaking "so far as the

English-speaking supporters of the schools are concerned" and it was over-optimistic; but the children of both languages were at least back at their desks.

5.

The Hearst government, which was by that time out of office, had inherited the problem of the schools and been torn between two factions, neither of which it could ever wholly satisfy. When the provincial elections came in 1919 it felt the effect on both sides. At the same time, on the larger issue of conscription, its support of Union Government helped to bring it down.

Through 1916 and early 1917, as the prospect of conscription loomed, both agriculture and labour had prepared to accept the inevitable. They had done so, however, in a mood of angry questioning and with specific new demands. The whole province, sick to death of the war and strained to the last muscle, was becoming veined with resentments which centred in these two groups. Farmers importuned for food, and requiring their sons on the land, were hearing the sons called slackers. Munitions workers and workers in other factories were seeing inflation eat away their pay. Called on daily and hourly for ever-increased production, they were met with preachings of sacrifice when they asked for better wages. Joseph Flavelle, a Czar of wartime industry, had refused a proposal made by the Dominion government that a fair wage clause be inserted in munitions contracts. Trade unionism was growing and bringing its quota of strikes, while socialism and Communism were running strong in the movement. Farmers and labour alike were all too well aware of the inflated profits of industry and of patronage and political corruption. For all the new income tax and other taxes proclaimed as curbs on profits, the millions continued to be made and most of the money kept. If there were to be any new sacrifice, particularly of flesh and blood, it would have to be balanced and shared. Along with the conscription of men must come the "conscription of wealth."

This was a vague phrase at the core of programs for sweeping social reform which were not necessarily compatible and which had no chance of implementation in wartime. In August 1917, in the face of mounting casualty lists from the great battles in France, the conscription of men came with no conscription of wealth. The trade unions, which had seethed for a while and threatened a general strike, subsided in angry helplessness, agreeing to obey the law. Farmers, equally angry but still pleading on the basis of their special needs, appeared at first to have won a major concession. Through a

225

pledge exacted in November, during the heat of the general election that confirmed Union Government, men of military age, if they were legitimately required on the land, were to be given exemption from service.

Five months later, however, just at the beginning of seeding time when men were most required, the promise had to be withdrawn. On April 19, 1918, with the last German offensive beginning to approach its height, Sir Robert Borden rose in the House of Commons to propose the Order-in-Council that cancelled all exemptions. He could find no other course, and he found no mercy in the farmers. On May 13, 3,000 of them gathered in the Labour Temple in Toronto, and they were a part of 5,000 from Ontario, Quebec and some of the western provinces who descended on Ottawa next day. In the Russell Theatre, where Borden's cabinet met them, they cited the election promise and repeated the familiar argument:

> We are not asking exemption from military service as a class. We realize that our blood is no more sacred than that of others, but we do feel that food production in Canada is as necessary to the winning of the war as service in the trenches in France. To take one skilled labourer from the farms ... removes from the land one who is in the position of being able to provide for six or eight others as well as himself.[19]

"We need men to hold the line."[20] Borden was not to be moved from that position. He could offer nothing to the farmers and he refused their delegates a hearing before the bar of the House of Commons. The Ontario men returned totally rebuffed and E.C. Drury, the rising leader of the United Farmers movement, seemed now confirmed in the stand that he had taken. He had seen no hope in either of the old parties, and less in Union Government. Defeated the year before as an independent Liberal in the federal general election, he had not joined in the farmers' march on Ottawa because he considered the gesture useless. Another observer, however, saw it in a different way. "Instead of being the end of a futile protest," wrote the journalist, Peter McArthur, "it may be the beginning of a movement that will shape the destiny of Canada."[21]

It was certainly to have its consequences for the provincial government of Hearst. He had not made conscription, but he had supported it at every turn. A man of northern Ontario, he had never been able to establish himself as a friend of southern farmers. Totally preoccupied with the war, he had neglected or denied grievances that accumulated year by year. In James S. Duff he had had a weak Minister of Agriculture and when Duff died, late in 1916, Hearst had improved nothing by taking the post himself, subjecting complaining farmers to "a diarrhoea of advice and a particularly acute constipation in the matter of help."[22] In 1918 he acquired a farmer Minister in the capable George S. Henry, but by then it was too late. Tied to a federal government which had become a Union government, Hearst was also tied to its old policies. The effects in the farmers' eyes were the high tariffs that protected the great industries, made possible the hated combines, and promoted urbanization and foreign immigration. Even before the war, in the view of rural Ontario, these were the policies that had helped depopulate the farmlands and foster the growth of cities, bringing about "the natural conditions for the creation of despotic government" and laying into the foundation wall of the old structure of the province "elements of vice and weakness and squalid helplessness."[23] Upon all this came conscription and war weariness itself, the last precipitating elements in the formation of a new party.

On June 7, 1918, over 2,000 of the United Farmers of Ontario met again in Toronto. They heard and denounced the results of the trip to Ottawa and began to apply its lessons. There were still the old idealists who spoke for the methods of the Grange, but the movement swung against them. The farmer acting for himself as a force outside politics seemed to have accomplished nothing. For all too many years he had protested, pleaded and philosophised, with his strength steadily diminishing and his voice continually ignored. There would be no change in policies, no electoral reform and no relief for agriculture until all were won at the polls, not through the Conservative party, not through the Liberal party, but through outright votes for farmers. In that mood the assembly went out to get them.

Six months later, at a provincial by-election in the constituency of Manitoulin, an independent farmer confronted a Hearst Conservative and managed to take the seat. It had been a safe government riding, uncontested by Liberals because of the wartime truce, and the Premier had expected a casual acclamation. "What excuse," he demanded indignantly as he was called to the ground to oppose the farmer candidate, "does this man make for forcing this election on the people with all its expense and inconvenience?" The votes that answered the question pointed to larger consequences only a year away. In October 1919, on the eve of the provincial election, the United Farmers of Ontario issued their manifesto:

Whereas: The rural population of Ontario has been declining for many years, being now 139,000 less than it was in 1881 . . .

And whereas: Rural life has been rendered difficult and trying and farm production has been checked.

227

And whereas: The present condition in rural districts is justly attributable to the unequal rewards of farm and town industry, owing to the dominance in Parliament and Legislature of privileged urban interests . . .

And whereas: Both of the old parties are responsible for this state of affairs.

Therefore we, the United Farmers of Ontario, deem it our duty to ourselves and to the Province to seek independent representation in the Legislature . . . [24]

Almost simultaneously the Independent Labour Party was mobilizing its own strength. In existence since 1907, it had had at least one member always in the provincial legislature, but it had been a wavering and uncertain force. By 1919, however, in affiliation nationally with the Canadian Labour Party, it was building city membership and in sight of new objectives. Its views in many fields were at odds with those of farmers, but the first clash at election time would be with the government of Hearst.

6.

As the war ended the problems of re-establishment came with the returning forces. Both the federal and provincial governments had made extensive plans. Medical care was good and counselling and placement agencies had been at work for two years. In Ontario up to September of 1918 some 24,000 men had been given vocational or convalescent training and over 7,000 of these had been helped to find work. Yet all needs soared with the completion of demobilization, while the closing-down of the war factories eliminated thousands of jobs. Once more in the cities, defeating the hopes of planners, were queues of the unemployed.

Much thinking had centred on a great return to the land. The soldier was to replace the immigrant as a pioneering farmer, and a new fund of $5,000,000.00 had been established for northern development. Ferguson, as Minister of Lands, Forests and Mines and a great enthusiast of the north, had been eloquent on what was offered.

(The settler gets the right for) everything from the sky to the centre of the earth – oil, gas, coal, gold, silver, anything he can find; also timber, except white pine. . . . We meet him at North Bay and we look after him until he gets settled on his land; we feed and care for his live stock and house his implements until he gets settled. We build roads for him; we locate him on good land and try to find him congenial neighbours.[25]

By 1917 five townships near Cochrane on the line of the Transcontinental had been set aside as an area reserved for veterans, and a training school, first established at Monteith, had been moved north to become a colony at Kapuskasing. Here Ferguson, with all his usual energy and considerable liberality, was creating a nucleus for expansion.

By 1919 some hundred veterans, including many with their families, were in frame or log houses or in a communal dormitory equipped with kitchen and dining room and with food provided at cost. They had a blacksmith shop, a planing mill, a laundry and other facilities, all built by the government. Roads had been opened up and a railway siding built to link Kapuskasing with the main line of the National Transcontinental. Each veteran had received $150.00 toward the cost of his house and a loan of $500.00 for his tools, implements and livestock. His transportation had been free, he had been paid for the work of clearing the first ten acres of his frontage, and he had been given training and instruction. Yet for all that the experiment was bogging down. What could not be given the newcomers was the climate of southern Ontario, nor the amenities of civilization, nor in many cases the inclination to farm. The wet summers had been followed by early frosts, killing the first few crops. Married men and single men, bickering through the harsh winters, had been ready to leave by spring. Some took off for the pulpwood camps, some went back to the cities, and a stubborn few remained. Hay and potatoes could be grown and eventually dairying would develop, but Kapuskasing as a great forerunner of settlement was already tagged a failure.

Meanwhile southern Ontario was renewing a perennial complaint: its farms were starved for help. Neither large plans for the north nor the old lands of the south seemed able to absorb the mass of the returning soldiers. They were drawn inexorably to the cities, increasing the problems there, while labour troubles and occasional foreign agitators sharpened an ugly mood. Ferguson, alert to such things, gave it pointed expression. The "alien in our midst," he told his constituents of Grenville, was threatening the fruits of victory. "He should be eliminated and deported to whence he came."[26]

The housing shortage in the cities aggravated all problems. "In wartime," wrote C.B. Sissons, "Toronto had ceased to be a city of homes."[27] Factory workers, crowding to the central districts, had flooded them with new lodgers. Other workers, forced to live in the suburbs, had been worn out by travel.

In Toronto, travelling northward on a Yonge Street car of an evening one jostled strapholders who had transferred from branch lines and who were again to transfer to the train at North Toronto station, wearily journeying to their night's work at Leaside.[28]

There had been nearly 11,000 marriages in Toronto during 1916 and 1917, while only 1,551 new houses had been built. By 1918, with returning soldiers and their families multiplying all demands, the government at last moved.

Following a first and not very successful gesture which established a fund of $2,000,000.00 for loans through municipalities, an Act For the Erection of Dwelling Houses passed the Ontario legislature in March of 1919. Supported by federal financing, it was intended to provide low-cost homes at a price approximating rental over a period of twenty years. The payments were high, however, and the act came very late. To a restless proletariat and to soldiers who had expected much from a grateful country, the homes not yet erected, and even the promise of homes, compared poorly with the palatial new Government House, completed in spite of the war at a cost of well over a million dollars. There was renewed notice of the increase in the Premier's salary which had been raised from $9,000.00 to $12,000.00, and there were other comments on taxation. The Wartime Property Tax had been promptly abolished with the budget of March 6, 1919, and the gasoline tax reduced. The amusement tax, however, still remained in effect. "The rich man got his gasoline cheaper," said the *Farmers' Sun* in one of its few sympathetic comments on city life, "but a man without a car still pays his War Tax at the picture show."[29]

With all this came the end of the political truce. By the late summer of 1919 the five-year-old government of William Howard Hearst was preparing to face the electors. It had been resolute throughout the war, and it had not wholly neglected the concerns of peace. In the high schools, and even in some of the lower schools, vocational and technical training had been pushed forward by Pyne and were becoming more widely extended under Cody, the new minister. The Central High School of Commerce, the first such school in the province, had been opened in Toronto in September of 1916. There had been an Act for Town Planning as well as an Act for Housing, and social legislation had at least been kept in mind. A Child Welfare Bureau had been established and was now operating, while bills for a mother's pension and a minimum wage for women had been tabled though not enacted. A new Department of Labour had been established but it remained without a Minister. That appointment, with the other reforms, was to be made after the election.

The Chippawa Project, though it was eating up its millions, was steadily moving forward. The plan for radial railways, the great companion scheme, had been throttled down considerably but approved in part by Hearst. He would stand before the electors, hardly as a friend of the ambitious Hydro chairman, but as at least a sharer in his work.

Road building had been much delayed by the war, but there was now a paved highway linking Hamilton and Toronto. Beyond that, designed for the automobile, a new system of trans-provincial highways was planned and under construction from Windsor to the Quebec border. The plans for northern development remained as large as ever. Ferguson, though he was constantly shadowed by scandal in his dealings with the timber barons, had fostered a considerable advance in conservation. Sixty-two wooden lookout towers now stood in thirty-four fire districts, each of which was supervised by a Chief Ranger. Light pick-up trucks which could carry portable equipment were patrolling in each district on a series of new trails.

Also in its beginnings was a lively and imaginative plan for the assessment of forest resources. In the early summer of 1919 a party of young students led by six graduate foresters went out to explore a large section of the bush, survey the trees in the region and return an inventory of their findings. As a first annual safari, it was to be repeated for a dozen years and cover most of the province. Each winter, as the reports came back to the forestry department, charts would be compiled by men of the permanent staff showing the location, quality and quantity of timber in specific areas. The work of the youngsters in training foreshadowed the work of the bush pilot, and the days of the aerial survey were only a step off.

With all this, accomplished or at least conceived of under the stress of a great war, the government stood on its record. It had realized prohibition, given women the vote and at least relaxed the tensions on bilingual education. There was little to fear from the Liberals who had not only lost Rowell but were waffling again on temperance. Under Hartley H. Dewart, whose leadership was still disputed and whose views were notably wet, the party would go to the polls either of two minds or of none. Women were a new element in the field of provincial politics and so were the United Farmers and the rejuvenated party of Labour. Around Ferguson, too, the dynamic force in the ministry, there was a continuing roar of rumour. Charges of corruption and collusion, flying at every timber sale, had become another of the factors to be counted in at the election. Hearst, however, conscious of his own rectitude and proud of his wartime leadership, was prepared to discount them all.

He had promised a referendum on the question of prohibition, to be held at the end of the war. He was not compelled, and was strong-

231

ly advised against it, but he decided that the referendum should be simultaneous with the election. On October 20, 1919, the voters came to the polls to be presented with two ballots, and a war-weary, demobilized and disenchanted Ontario spoke for its divided mind. It was in favour of prohibition, and it was crushingly against Hearst.

To Conservative strategists later one of the reasons was clear. Thousands of farmers' wives, voting for the first time, had gone to the polls in support of prohibition. They had marked their second ballot as prescribed by farmer husbands, and the result had been disaster. If so, it was a disaster duplicated in many of the towns and cities. The province had smashed the familiar pattern of politics in one massive upheaval. Twenty-five Conservatives and twenty-nine Liberals, even in combination, would be a minority in the new legislature. The United Farmers of Ontario, still leaderless and not yet a party, would have forty-five members. Labour had elected eleven and there was a lonely independent. "The result," said Sir John Hendrie, reflecting his own forebodings as Lieutenant-Governor of the province, "is a move away from party representation toward class or factional representation."[30]

The possibilities were awesome in their promise of future conflict. Farmers, as group theorists, detested the party system and wanted to abolish it. The same system, to the social theorists of labour, was a tool to be taken over. Each of the two movements had damned the old parties for waste, patronage and corruption. Both, in varying degree, were for control or nationalization of industries and communications. They were together against monopolies; they were concerned with widening the basis of provincial education; and there was a common urge toward government with the free thrust of democracy. Yet the one was rural democracy and the other that of the city. The wages and hours of the factory hand were not a cause with the farmer; he envied and resented both. Farmers were determinedly dry, labour inclined to be wet; and the farm and labour movements were flatly opposed nationally on the question of protective tariffs. In spite of differences, however, there were the essential reforming purposes and the indisputable fact. The farmer had almost vaulted into the saddle, and he would be there if labour would ride behind him.

Within a week the members of the Labour party had overcome their doubts; they were prepared to join the farmers. In the same week the farmers acquired a leader. Ernest Charles Drury, in spite of the fact that he had not stood for election, was the nearest thing in the movement to a working politician and he had become the obvious man. He accepted without enthusiasm, and he saw what success imposed. The United Farmers, with the largest group in the

House, were bound to act as a party and entitled to reach for power. Labour made that possible and placed the reins in his hands. On November 14, 1919, Drury was sworn to office as the eighth Premier of Ontario.

He would be facing Howard Ferguson as leader of the opposition. Hearst had been gracious in defeat, though he had hardly been treated graciously by the members of his own party. A gloomy caucus, meeting late in October, had pointedly discussed the election failure, hardly mentioning his name. In the same mood it had invited Ferguson to replace him, at least for the time being. The new leader was regarded without enthusiasm and would wait a year to be confirmed, yet the interval would change much. "I used to tell Hearst," Ferguson was said to have said, "that he never really understood the party game."[31] That flaw, at least, the Conservative party had repaired. Its own fortunes were low and Ferguson's would dip lower, but there would never be doubt at any time that he understood the game.

Notes

1. Hector Charlesworth, *More Candid Chronicles* (Toronto: Macmillan of Canada, 1929).
2. Brian D. Tennyson," The Succession of William Hearst to the Ontario Premiership – September, 1914," *Ontario History*, Vol. 56, 1964, p. 187.
3. Toronto *Globe*, September 22, 1914.
4. *Ibid.*
5. Nelles, *The Politics of Development*, p. 388.
6. A.D. Camp, "Canada Organized for Aerial Flying," *Canadian Magazine*, June, 1918, p. 150.
7. Brian D. Tennyson,"Sir William Hearst and the Ontario Temperance Act," *Ontario History*, Vol. 55, 1963, p. 241.
8. Middleton, Landon, *The Province of Ontario*, Vol. 1, p. 455.
9. Tennyson, "Sir William Hearst and the Ontario Temperance Act," p.236.
10. *Ibid.*, p. 241.
11. *Ibid.*
12. Brian D. Tennyson, "Premier Hearst, The War and Votes for Women," *Ontario History*, Vol. 57, 1965, p. 116.
13. *Ibid.*, p. 119.
14. *Canadian Annual Review*, 1919, pp. 660-661.
15. Public Archives of Canada, Laurier Papers, 191317-191318.
16. Walker, *Catholic Education and Politics in Ontario*, p. 307.
17. *Ibid.*, p. 301.
18. *Ibid.*, p. 310.
19. W. R. Young, "Conscription, Rural Depopulation and the Farmers of Ontario, 1917-19," *C.H.R.*, Sept. 1972, p. 305.
20. *Ibid.*, p. 311.
21. *Ibid.*, p. 314.

22. *Ibid.*, p. 301
23. *Ibid.*, p. 295.
24. *Ibid.*, p. 316.
25. *C.A.R.*, 1916, p. 485.
26. Peter Oliver, "Sir William Hearst and the Collapse of the Ontario Conservative Party," *C.H.R.*, March, 1972, p. 42.
27. C. B. Sissons, "A Housing Policy for Ontario," *Canadian Magazine*, July, 1919, Vol. 53, p. 241f.
28. *Ibid.*
29. Oliver, "Sir William Hearst and the Collapse of the Ontario Conservative Party," p. 49.
30. *C.A.R..*,1919, p. 666.
31. Oliver, "Sir William Hearst and the Collapse of the Conservative Party," p. 47.

Chapter Eleven

Farmer Government

1.

"All my life," wrote Ernest Charles Drury, forty-six years after he became Premier of Ontario and forty-three years after the electorate voted him out, "I have been a liberal. Liberal with a small 'l.'"[1] His father, Charles Drury, had been the first Minister of Agriculture in the government of Oliver Mowat. Mowat, the son remembered, had once "patted me on the head and said he hoped I was a good boy."[2]

With that example and injunction the twig had first been bent. Born at Crown Hill, some five miles out from Barrie, the boy grew up on 250 acres of fine farmland looking down toward Kempenfelt Bay. At twenty-two he had received a degree in agriculture at O.A.C. For ten years, as a scientific farmer and an agricultural activist, he supported the various farm movements and fought protective tariffs. Able, shrewd, articulate, and as firm for the temperance movement as he was for farmers' causes, he made a name in Ontario and emerged on the national scene. In 1911, as first secretary of the Canadian Council of Agriculture, he supported reciprocity and saw the results of defeat. In his own province "more than half the local Granges folded up."[3] Two years later, however, he became involved in the revival of the farmers' movement in Ontario.

> In early October of 1913 I received a letter from J. J. Morrison, the Secretary of the Grange and Farmers' Association, asking me to meet with him and two other farmers, W. C. Good of Brantford and Col. J. Z. Frazer of Burford, in Toronto . . . We were to meet at the offices of *The Farmers' Sun*, but this was on Saturday afternoon and when we got there we found the place locked and deserted. We went to a little hotel not far away (I forget its name) and ordered four beers and were shown to a little alcove off the bar room. Good, Morrison, and I were teetotalers, Colonel Frazer

was not. I don't remember whether he drank all four beers, but I think it possible. There in that little alcove the United Farmers of Ontario was conceived.[4]

Drury was first president when the movement came to be formed, and within six years it had made him Premier of the province. Yet he had never been wholly a part of it or at one with its other leaders. In 1915 he had resigned his post as president, though he remained one of the directors. In 1917 he had strayed away as an independent Liberal to contest a federal seat. He had come back in defeat, but not to provincial politics, and he had not stood at all in the election that toppled Hearst. He was a reluctant Cincinnatus who had been summoned from Crown Hill, and for all his strength with elected farmers in the legislature, he remained unsure of his base.

He could not accept the philosophy of men like Morrison and Good, who had been born of the defunct Grange and preserved its old ideals. Society remained for them a pattern of groups and classes, each with competing interests and entitled to separate voices that political labels only confused and muffled. In their view the first evil of politics was the party system itself. They groped mystically toward purer forms of democracy, with a faith in complicated procedures which Drury did not share. He was attracted mildly to Proportional Representation, which had had supporters in the province at least from the time of Blake. Beyond that, however, lay Initiative and Referendum and the long leash of Recall. Under the first process a group of a prescribed size, acting in any constituency, might initiate legislation that would go to referendum independent of the parties and of the legislature itself. A same or similar group, using the right of Recall, might haul back its duly elected member and move to revoke his mandate. These and similar proposals, threatening not only partyism but the end of parliament itself, Drury flatly rejected. He could work for his friends' goals, but not with his friends' tools. They were outside of parliament, condemning the idea of party. He was a politician pushed to the head of a party and he had undertaken to govern.

It was not going to be easy. He arrived at Queen's Park as a man who had never sat or tried to sit in the legislature. There were no experienced members and there was not a single lawyer among his fifty-five supporters. He was a stranger among bewildered strangers who had not expected power, and he was faced with by-elections as the first of many problems. He would have to be elected himself, he would require a lawyer for the post of Attorney-General, and his choice for Minister of Agriculture was also without a seat. Called to Government House, he was received with cool formality by a scep-

236

tical Lieutenant-Governor and was not particularly warmed by another imposing presence.

> While we were talking the Duke of Devonshire, the then Governor General of Canada, who was a guest at Government House, came into the room and Sir John introduced me to him . . . He was remarkably like Old Bill in Bairnsfather's 'Better 'Ole.' He shook my hand without a word, walked over to an armchair, lowered himself into it, and said 'Zzzzzz-z-z-z – Z-Z-Z' into his walrus moustache.[5]

It was clear enough to Drury that at least on higher levels the prospect of farmer government was not received with enthusiasm.

More than that was evident as he painfully shaped his cabinet, with its two labour members and its assortment of clashing aims. Coalition would be difficult and it hardly assured power. Farm and labour combined, facing Conservatives and Liberals, had a bare majority of one. There was small prospect of survival in the view offered by the House, and there was still less in the forces arrayed outside it.

> May we not hope, (Drury had asked his members as they gathered for their first caucus,) that this political movement, which has begun as a class movement, representing farmers and labour, may expand and broaden out until it embraces citizens of all classes and occupations and becomes indeed a People's Party?[6]

The answer he was to have from all sides, growing through his term of office, was a flat, resounding no.

A people's party was anathema to the industrial and financial interests. "Broadening out" to Morrison and the elders of the farm movement meant loss of group identity and diminution of strength. It was enough and more than enough to be a party allied with labour. "We believe," said Morrison, "in lessening the cost of production. . . . Labour men generally believe in increasing the cost of production by increased wages and shorter hours."[7] To that rigid fallacy labour outside the legislature had its own acid riposte. The aims of farmer government, whether professed or not, were to bring conditions in the cities "to the level of labour conditions in the back-lot farms . . . degrading the city worker until he will return to the farm to avoid starvation."[8]

In spite of the clash of theorizers government was carried on. Neither of the exhausted old parties was eager to seize the reins, and a period of readjustment with its unemployment and depression was a time to be out of office. The raw new ministry led by the farmer Premier was somehow held together and somehow made to work. It was totally inexperienced and seldom of one mind, yet it accepted responsibility and it learned the uses of power. It was to go down in three years to what seemed to be complete disaster, but there was no miracle in that. The miracle was that it had survived, that it had discovered joint objectives and that it left with something done. "Broadening out" became a part of dissolution as the farm movement and the labour movement resumed their separate ways. The fragmented people's party, reabsorbed in the old parties, confirmed a record of failure at least in political terms, but in other respects it had served a useful purpose.

> In a very real sense, (Drury had said at the beginning,) we represent not alone the 40 per cent of the people who are on the farms, but also the great bulk of the common people of all classes. .... Our success therefore, depends not on political manoeuvring but on the breadth and fairness of our policy.[9]

There had been breadth and fairness, at least in the Premier's purposes, and he had narrowed a dangerous gap. The working man in politics, if he was again separate from the farmer, was not so separate as before. And old rural Ontario, as its life changed inevitably, was drawn to an easier merging with the life of the towns and cities.

2.

"In our first two sessions," wrote Drury, looking back from retirement through the haze of forty years, "we enacted such a program of social legislation as Ontario and indeed all Canada and North America had never seen, or perhaps thought possible."[10] It is a quaint exaggeration that denies credit to the impetus of former governments and claims more than was performed. Yet it reflects the effort and the compromises of men on difficult ground. The ministry at best was a tenuous combination, divided by basic aims. The very drift of the times, the inexorable urbanization, opposed the farms to the cities. The first social necessities, so far as labour was concerned, were a reasonable working day and the assurance of the minimum wage. On neither of these, however, did it have the support of the farmer. A minimum wage in factories would increase the drain from the land, and increase the cost of goods. There was the same threat of new drain and disparity in the question of leisure time. "How could farmers who are compelled to work eighteen hours a day," asked Drury, "be expected to help the eight-hour day movement?"[11]

Other pressures were created by unemployment, which was one of the weary constants through the three years of the regime. Manning

Doherty, who had been a favourite instructor of Drury during his college days at Guelph, was a fine Minister of Agriculture. Walter Rollo, as the first occupant of the position that Hearst had left unfilled, was an effective Minister of Labour. Even so, the government's new Labour Exchanges, though they improved on the old system of private employment agencies, were undermined in their workings by the clash of the two men's views. To Rollo the man on the street was entitled to his old job, or to make-work help until he found comparable employment. To Doherty the obvious remedy, with the farms crying for help, was to send him off to the land. The undercurrent of differences not only divided the cabinet but divided the men in politics from the leaders of their own movements. For all that they discovered areas of agreement on some general needs and found means to meet them.

The exploitation of women was more apparent than that of men, and a decent wage in the sweatshops hardly threatened the farms. Out of that view came the passing of a minimum wage act, applying only to women, which had been a good intention with Hearst. There were also family needs, some of which Hearst had recognized, on which consensus came. The impoverished widow was at last provided with an allowance for the care of dependent children. Grown children of means, with aged and indigent parents, were obliged to share in their support. There was some remedy for the grotesque injustice of the past in an Unmarried Parents' Act, which made the father responsible for the support of the child and provided further that the taint of illegitimacy could be removed by subsequent marriage. More important and more effective was help for the orphaned child. The adoption process had been long, tedious and expensive, involving the passage of a private bill in the legislature. Under a new act prospective parents could apply to a county judge, who was empowered to grant adoption. Subject to approval by the Children's Aid Society, a child could be put in a home in a matter of a few days and at a cost of three or four dollars.

Under farmer government, and in the face of the farm movement, came pensions for the civil service. Since economy was his eternal watchword and he believed government agencies were hives infested with drones, Morrison was flatly opposed. He was for a drastic cutting of payrolls rather than increased security, and even in the idea of pensions he contrived to see injustice. "Superannuation and retiring allowances are class privileges, as we cannot all be civil servants."[12] Fine-spun theory, however, gave way to practical necessities; Ontario required the services and was soon to feel the benefits of skilled career professionals. The Workmen's Compensation Act, the cherished instrument of labour, was largely extended

239

and improved. The Board of Health, transferred from the Provincial Secretary's office to the office of the Minister of Labour, improved care in the schools, provided better facilities for the training of school nurses and was responsible for the first Division of Industrial Hygiene ever set up in Canada. Less officially, in one case, came help for medical research.

> One spring morning, in 1920 or perhaps 1921, (Drury recorded,) two young men came to see me. Their names were Banting and Best, they were graduate doctors, and they were working on what they hoped would be a remedy for diabetes . . . They had a work room in the top of the Practical Science Building and they invited me over to see what they were doing . . . It was a very warm morning, there were several dogs in cages, and a pile of sweetbreads on a sort of counter, and a meat grinder, and a big glass funnel filled with filter paper. The place smelled horrible. They explained to me at some length that the sweetbreads were the pancreatic glands of young calves, which produced a substance called insulin . . . I went back to the Parliament Buildings much impressed. The upshot of it all was that we placed an item of twenty thousand dollars into the estimates, and on this Banting and Best were able to perfect their world-famous discovery.[13]

There were familiar attitudes and familiar class differences in the field of education, all of which governed progress. In the case of bilingual and separate schools, although the level of conflict was lowered, no real improvement was made. The province generally was mellowing and in the view of the United Farmers "the claim of the French-speaking people of Ontario that their children should be educated in French as well as in English is natural and just."[14] With that sentiment the farmer government agreed, and it encouraged conciliation, but it could not find its way through the tangle of old rules, the entrapments of lingering prejudice and the shortage of present means to a new basis of agreement. Regulation 17, in force when Drury came to power, remained in force when he left.

Also darkening the horizon as a new and larger issue was the revived question of the distribution of taxes. It turned as usual on the contributions of corporations and utilities to the general fund, which supported secondary as well as primary schools. It was the claim of the Catholic ratepayer, with no secondary system, that his separate schools were deprived of their fair share. English, Irish and French bishops, all straitened for means, were again asserting claims that were admitted to be largely sound. Yet the mere prospect of any additional sharing brought out the Orange drums. The government in this dilemma, which extended to its last session, adopted familiar tactics. Faced with an imminent election, it consigned the issue to the courts.

There were problems not only with separate schools but with the working of the general system. The farmer's attitude in Ontario was still critical and suspicious toward higher education. Only 7 per cent of all students in the province went beyond public schools. The Adolescent Education Act, which raised the high school leaving age from fourteen to sixteen, was inherited unproclaimed as a measure of the Hearst government and enacted as law by Drury in 1921. He found it immediately a new bone of contention. For all the support of labour and all the applause of the cities, the farm leader had gone beyond his constituents. Again in the last session, and again in the face of political disaster, he was forced to exempt the sons required on the land.

In the primary system some new ideas were developing. The one-room rural schoolhouse, with its single teacher, its local board and its work prescribed and inspected by a remote provincial ministry, had now outlived its time. The multiplicity of boards in single counties and townships was a duplication of effort. The boards themselves, responsive to local taxpayers, were as concerned with paring expenses as they were with education. Teachers were poorly paid, usually with poor facilities, discouraged in all their initiatives and they worked in isolation. The remedy was consolidation, a merging of boards and schools, and Drury was prepared for that. He was beginning to approach the thought of regional grouping in which a single large school, better equipped, less wasteful and enjoying a measure of autonomy, would offer more to the student. The rural school of the future, he said, should be a kind of community centre "where concerts, movies, lectures and meetings of various kinds can be held in the evenings, as well as providing better facilities as a place of instruction during the day."[15] In that vision he was well ahead of the province, but he was able to lay a groundwork. The salaries of rural teachers, and the quality and the outlook of Ontario's rural schools, were all bettered in his time.

Vocational and trade schools and vocational training in high schools were regarded by the farm community with mixed views. Where they fostered industrialization they represented another potential drain from the land. Rumbles of complaint and renewed cries for economy were heard as the program begun by Whitney and advanced by Hearst in wartime continued to expand steadily. Yet the needs and the demands were there and the farmer government responded. By the time it left office some 40,000 students, taught by 1,000 teachers, were enrolled in sixty-nine day or evening vocational schools; and in fourteen cities of the province there were new schools being built.

For the universities, standing at the head of the system, there was a period of readjustment. They were not deprived of support but they were subjected to new scrutiny in the light of their basic functions. Were they as much a part as they might be of the life of the whole province, and was their growth commensurate in proportion to other varied needs? In 1922 the grants to the universities were larger than the combined spending on primary and secondary schools. This balance was questioned, and another question was asked. Would it not be possible to raise the standards of high schools to the equivalent of the first-year level set by the universities? The student would gain a year, the university would be saved the expense of teaching him, and the high school system would benefit from largely increased grants. It was a sketchy plan that would wait long for fulfilment but it signalled a growing mood. Not only the rural zealot but the urban proletarian was questioning the serene elite. "There are a great many people in Ontario," said Drury, "who have never seen and cannot see the inside of a university . . . we must meet the needs of Ontario in a manner to give due regard to all."[16]

3.

In its work for agriculture the government occasionally moved ahead of its own supporters. Few farmers were enthusiasts for reforestation, though the south was splotched with areas of dried-up, windblown land, long stripped of its cover. Some of these Drury moved to reclaim. He encouraged and supported Edward John Zavitz, who was then Provincial Forester, in the establishment of two large nurseries, one at Orono in Durham county and the other at Midhurst in Simcoe county. Farmers complained of the expense and regarded the nurseries with apathy, but they were to result years later not only in thousands of seedlings but in fine new stands of timber.

The energetic Doherty established junior schools of agriculture, stimulated the college at Guelph and devoted much of his effort to the improvement of farm finance. What emerged in three years was a system of provincial savings banks, popular not only with farmers but with labouring men in the cities. As competitors of the chartered banks, and offering higher interest, they were opposed with much solemnity by conservative financiers. In 1923, however, when the Home Bank had failed and shaken its stately *confrères*, the radicals had their say. The provincial system, in the view of the *Canadian Forum*, was successful and should be encouraged until the chartered banks "find it impossible to declare dividends and to state that their affairs are most satisfactory when they are really ready to collapse."[17]

A fund for rural credits, built largely on the deposits of the provincial banks, was established under an Agricultural Development Act and administered by an Agricultural Development Board. There were continual complaints that politics influenced the Board and it was hampered in some of its workings by disputes with the farm movement. By 1923, however, it had put out some $2,000,000.00, not only in loans to individual farmers but in assistance to co-operative stores.

Side by side with that effort, and also made more difficult by the attitudes of some farmers, was the attempt to improve standards. Particularly in the matter of dairying, improvement was much needed, for Ontario's poor butter was as famous as its good cheese. Yet a Dairy Standards Act passed by the Hearst government had been left unproclaimed, and when the Drury government enacted it there was a roar of farm complaint. Particularly in the 1920s, as farm prices went down after the boom years of the war, the farmer resisted expense and clung to his old methods. In wider areas of his interest, notably the co-operative movement, he could see far and could plan, but even here his dogmatism produced some drastic shortfalls.

The United Farmers Cooperative Company had been established in 1914 as an integral part of the United Farmers movement. In the conception of Morrison and Good it was to be a kind of commercial commonwealth, buying through a central office and directed by a general manager, but with each community administering its own store. Dealing first on a commission basis in binder twine, implements, harness, groceries and farm supplies, it had offered substantial economies and paid a dividend to thousands of farmer shareholders. By 1919, with an annual turnover of better than $2,000,000.00, it had turned to the marketing of livestock.

Its branch stores, however, had become a problem. Organized locally and managed by a local farmer, each branch was part of a federation with loose and clashing policies. In the view of the general manager, "a clean-cut, energetic young fellow"[18] named T.P. Loblaw, the time had come to centralize, to buy and warehouse from Toronto and unify control. The plan was approved by Drury but opposed by Morrison and Good, who were not for a great combine but for farm democracy in action. Loblaw complained, resigned and left to establish his own chain of stores while the farm co-operative went on.

In a number of fields it was successful. By 1920, it was shipping 5,300 cars of livestock for subscribing farmers, and had acquired a large Toronto creamery. It had a profitable egg and poultry department, a seed-cleaning section, and during the next two years it added a farm products department for the marketing of hay, straw, alfalfa, potatoes and mixed vegetables. Its co-operative retail stores, however, faced with hard times and with the growth of a competition they could not meet as units, were steadily dragging it down. Little by little they drifted out of business, and when the last were closed in 1923 they had cost the company two-thirds of its capital. It continued to market livestock and a number of other products but it faced reorganization and had years of struggle ahead.

4.

Roads and radial railways were linked problems that the government inherited from Hearst. In each case there were half-initiated plans, large areas of conflict between the farm and city view, and new factors created by the automobile. The farmer, always for economy, had wanted country roads, while the city voice was raised for provincial highways. Yet by the dawn of the 1920s both claims were merging. The farmer in 1922 owned more than a third of Ontario's 182,000 passenger vehicles. He required roads for his cars, and they would have to cover the province. A complete network built for the automobile was an obvious future need.

In the light of that, for the farmers at least, the view of radials changed. The city worker who did not possess a car saw the electric tramline as a key to life in the suburbs. The businessman saw rapid electric transit as the answer to many of his problems. Trams between large centres would be faster than the old trains, and they would often compete with the trains to reduce freight rates. Yet there would also be huge expense and massive duplication. The new electrified lines would simply parallel railway lines, already plentiful enough. The automobile would be racing beside the tramcar on new provincial roads. Why, the farmer asked, in view of existing facilities and the large planned additions, should radials be built at all?

The government's developing attitude was soon implicit in its program. Frank Biggs of Wentworth county, "a road enthusiast ... abrupt and dictatorial,"[19] was appointed Minister of Highways. He had no resources of tact and little regard for money, but he had a clear view of policy with which the Premier concurred. The roads of the Hearst program were already obsolescent. On the new paved highway joining Hamilton and Toronto cement was cracking under traffic. "Nothing had been done," wrote Drury, 'to curve right-angled corners. At one such corner there was a big elm that was known as 'Dead Man's Tree' because of the number of people who had been killed by overrunning the turn and crashing into it."[20] There would be no more roads like that, designed for the horse and buggy. Not only provincial highways but the supporting rural systems must carry the automobile and be built to meet its needs. The monster would dictate government spending, presumably returning most of it in a flood of new licence fees and taxes on gasoline. The provincial and federal governments would build the main highways, the great carriers of the future. The province would help as usual in all rural improvement, but not on the usual basis. For local road-building, the estimated volume of automobile traffic would govern the allotment of funds.

Out of that program, in the course of three years, came some 400 miles of new provincial highways and a transformation of much of the rural system. Biggs, the road enthusiast, and Drury became valued targets of Ferguson in opposition. They were, he said, the two "highwaymen" of Ontario, spending the province's money like drunken sailors. Outside the House the economizers of the farm movement were also in full cry. Still at war with the age of the automobile, they resented not only provincial roads but the extent of improvement forced on the rural network. Why should corners be rounded at the expense of good farmland, and bridges widened and strengthened at tremendous public cost? Why two-lane pavements, when a single lane with a passing-place had been enough for horses and wagons? The advance of the roads program, as it linked the farms and the cities, was to link the farmers with Ferguson in opposition to Drury. Yet the work seemed acceptable enough when a new government succeeded. Ontario, said George Henry, Conservative Minister of Highways, speaking within a year of Drury's departure, had now some 1,800 miles of provincial and suburban highways, 48,000 miles of county or township roads, and in all a total of 27,000 miles that were paved or surfaced with gravel and ready for the automobile.

Radial railways had seemed to be a project in being when the Drury government took office. Adam Beck, who had forced the Chippawa development, was driving it through to completion at enormously increased cost. He had also persuaded Hearst to approve the building of a first section of radial line between Toronto and Niagara Falls. Some $4,000,000.00 had been spent in acquiring rights-of-way, and the plans of the Hydro chairman, vociferously supported by many municipalities, went far beyond that. With new power in prospect and under the wing of Hydro, he was proposing a web of radials for the southern part of the province, a six-track line monopolizing the Toronto waterfront, and an electrified Bay Street subway.

Drury was faced with a proposal for the expenditure of some $200,000,000.00, strongly supported by labour and most of the city

245

newspapers, and advanced by a man whose political power was almost as great as his own. On the other side, however, were the views he had formed himself and the solid support of farmers. In July of 1920 he took up the gage with Beck. A Royal Commission, he announced, would investigate the question of radials before anything more was done.

Early in 1921 the Commission reported as Drury had hoped it would: against the proposed scheme. With that the government acted. It repealed the Hydro Radial Act passed by the Hearst government and revoked the guarantee on bonds for municipal funding. One exception was made in the case of the Toronto-Niagara Falls radial on which much money had been spent. If the electors still desired it in the face of the Commission's findings the government would meet their wishes. They would have to pronounce again, however, at the next municipal elections, which would be held on January 1, 1922. At the same time Toronto could express its views on the question of the waterfront radial line and the subway under Bay Street.

Meanwhile Chippawa went on, contending with rock and water and with competing investigations. Plans changed in the face of new difficulties, experts were called in and were countered by other experts. Drury summoned a firm of American consultants whose views were challenged by Beck and revised by his consultants. What emerged ultimately as the war of technocrats continued was an expensive new decision. The project designed to produce 414,000 horsepower at a cost of $73,500,000.00 should be redesigned, with more concern for long-range economy, to produce 550,000 horsepower at a cost of $89,000,000.00. To that Drury steeled himself as the work was driven forward. "I was signing treasury board warrants at the rate of a million a week."[21]

On December 29, 1921, came the formal opening of Chippawa with its first phase completed. As befitted the great occasion the Premier of the province was there, along with Beck and a crowd of lesser dignitaries.

> In spite of our many differences, and some things hard to forgive, (wrote the Drury of later years,) I liked Sir Adam and I think he liked me . . . Sir Adam's only child, Marion, was standing beside me. She was a very pretty girl of fourteen or fifteen, and since her mother's death a few months earlier was all the family Sir Adam had. When it came time for me to open the valve, on a sudden impulse I took her hand and placed it on the wheel beside my own, so that she had a part in the ceremony.[22]

It was a graceful gesture, recalling the gesture of Whitney at the first

246

Berlin occasion eleven years before. If it soothed Beck, however, it did not change the fact of his impending defeat. The electric train was not to replace the steam train or compete with the automobile. Three days later, on January 1, 1922, the municipal voters spoke. They were against the completion of the Toronto-Niagara Falls line and against the radials and the subway proposed for Toronto itself. "After this," wrote Drury, reflecting the mood of the province, "the whole radial scheme was as dead as a doornail."[23]

5.

In the development of northern Ontario the government appeared to reverse the attitude of Hearst. Its road program in the north dwindled to one of colonization roads. It was much more sceptical than Hearst of the possibilities of the Clay Belt and was soon investigating land grants and cancelling the claims of settlers where conditions had not been met. Dominated by southern farmers who had long complained of neglect, it was more concerned with restoring the potential of old lands than with taking risks in the new. The one mistake of his Ministry that Drury freely admitted was its authorization in 1921 of the extension of the Temiskaming and Northern Ontario Railway from Cochrane to Moosonee. The advance toward James Bay, which was to be eleven years in completion, was, he said, "the one project which might properly have been opposed."[24]

The cabinet was divided on the basic national question of tariffs. Farmers were for freer trade, while labour was firm for protection. Southern Ontario agriculture, with its constant cry for economy and its distrust of big business, was an opposing force to the powers ruling the north, the timbering, pulp and mining and large industrial interests. Sectional clash was inevitable and the clashes duly came. The cry was raised occasionally, as it had been since Whitney's time, for the division of the north and south into two separate provinces. Yet for all that, and in the face of some savage politics, the knitting process went on. Mines, forests, industry and big business were as much as part of Ontario as the older southern farms and demanded as much care.

That care Drury intended to give, but on a new and rigorous basis. He believed that the mining industry had been fattened by many privileges and he intended to change that. The corporations and financial interests were to feel the hand of reform. Above all, and as a first step, he intended to expose the work of Howard Ferguson who had created in his eyes "the rottenest system of forest pilfering that ever existed on the North American continent."[25]

As the presiding genius of the north through the tumultuous years

247

of the war, Ferguson was highly vulnerable. He was responsible for the soldiers' settlement at Kapuskasing, which was dwindling away in failure. He had barely held his seat at the time of the Hearst *débâcle* and was still shadowed by charges of electoral corruption. He was the half-distrusted leader of a half-dismantled party which had, in the opinion of one of the investigators when investigation came, "given away most of the north country, not already disposed of."[26]

The Timber Commission appointed by Drury on March 9, 1920, was to open the whole record of the Minister of Lands, Forests and Mines in his dealings with northern lumbermen. It began its hearings on April 12, 1920, continued for twenty months amid the full glare of publicity and the roar of political upheaval, and concluded on January 7, 1922. It did not "get" Ferguson, though it left him a besplotched man. What it did expose was the wartime chaos of the lumbering and pulpwood industries and the existing state of practice.

The government in Queen's Park, with its own records in the highest state of confusion, had directed a scattered field staff that was not infrequently corrupt and reduced to the point of impotence as it lost men to the forces. There had been trespassing on Crown lands, much abuse of mining claims for the purpose of removing timber, and some outright thefts which the government chose to wink at. Beyond that were the practices of Ferguson himself. He had dealt with the timber and pulpwood barons as a free and easy partner, forever favouring bigness, ignoring the law on tenders and distributing some concessions on shockingly low terms. In some of the worst cases the province had obviously been defrauded of hundreds of thousands of dollars, and much of this was recovered by later legal actions.

Nevertheless the revelations intended to destroy Ferguson could not be confined to his regime. There had been the same looseness of practice and the same affinity with bigness in the days of George Ross. They had continued through the days of Whitney for all his regulations, and the Ministry of Ernest Drury was discovering the facts of life. Even as the inquiry progressed the industry went on too, requiring its negotiations and impelling its quite talks. They concerned power and pulpwood, they involved the interests of the great E.W. Backus Company of Minneapolis, and in spite of the new government they followed a familiar course.

In 1914 the Backus company, which had practically made International Falls, Fort Frances and Kenora and contributed largely to the growth of Fort William itself, had acquired a concession in the region of Lake of the Woods. In 1919, with the concession still idle,

Drury had threatened to cancel it. The company, in return, had presented an impelling case. As the largest operator in the region, it was in a position to build a mill, increase provincial resources and generate new employment. It could, however, only justify the investment if it were assured of wood for years and also of a source of power. Since neither was provided by the present grant, it had proposed extending its concession in the direction of English River. It had submitted an offer by tender as the Drury government required and its tender had been accepted; everything in that transaction had strictly followed the law.

It was promptly discovered, however, that prior to the submission of the tender, the accompanying grant of a power site, indispensable to development, had been made in private in the office of the Attorney-General. There would have been no tendering for the concession without the certainty of a power site, and there would have been no use for expensive resources of power if the whole process of tendering had not been merely a form. It had been merely a form, in spite of the anguished protests of an embarrassed administration, since no company but Backus could have developed English River. Drury no less than Ferguson, and Ministers before Ferguson, had had to accept realities in dealing with big business.

The inquiry proved, politically, to be a near-disaster for the government. Ferguson, a master of counter-attack, acquired a new mastery of his party and a new and total confidence as leader of the opposition. Northern lumbering, mining and industrial and financial interests were reconfirmed in hostility to the party of farm and labour. Yet the glare of the spotlight turned on the forest industry did produce improvements. In Queen's Park itself the old procedures of book-keeping, "a disgrace to a country store," were set on a sound basis. The far-scattered field staff, with its thousands of inspectors and cullers, was improved by new additions and strengthened by new discipline. Above all, building on the work of Ferguson and impelled by the Commission itself which reported that in 1919 $1,800,000,000.00 worth of timber had been burnt – twenty times the amount cut – there was advance in fire control. After 1922, when Haileybury was wiped out, steel lookout towers began to replace the wooden ones and air patrols commenced.

Aerial survey had been initiated two years earlier, and the annual parties of students conducted by trained foresters still went out from Toronto. The great northeast and west were becoming better known and were interweaving their interests with the south and central province. Basic conflicts persisted and were augmented by the shifts of population. With its Finns and Scandinavians, its Austrians, Ukrainians and Italians, its surviving bands of Indians and its growing numbers of French, Ontario's north was becoming a mixed society. Half of it was still rural and half of it was still British, but these were the diminishing halves. The northern farmer, scraping less than subsistence from his patch of half-cleared land, was often a part-time railway worker or a hand in the pulpwood camps. The growth of the industrial complex drew men to the cities or strung them out in clusters that became urban communities around mines, mills or smelters. The urban centres were small, most of them with fewer than two thousand people, but they had almost nothing in common with the small towns of the south. They were wage-earning communities supporting a few professions, and they were often a grouping of several tongues and ethnic origins. They wanted more for their labour, they wanted improved conditions and they were often fiercely at odds with their great employers. Yet they were joined with big business by the bond of the weekly payroll. They lived by industrial production, by its growth, protection and expansion, and their hopes were built on that.

Before long, a great gulf had opened between the Northern communities and the ideals of farmer government. When Drury sought to regulate the forest industries he was attacked for slowing their growth. When he taxed the mines he was accused of overtaxing and creating unemployment. In both charges there was a fair measure of hypocrisy and he was largely able to withstand them. It was not true, as Ferguson claimed, that Drury was "the curse of the north," nor was it true as lumbermen claimed that his government "was endeavouring to drag the modern and well-equipped sawmills which waste nothing but the knot-holes down to the level of the old-style mills that had not the machinery to salvage odd bits of timber and convert them into laths or boxwood."[27] He did stand, however, for a homogeneous province developed on the pattern of his youth. The only way to pull out of depression, he said in 1922, supporting a program for British immigration, "is by placing an adequate number of settlers on the land."[28] He opposed to the main thrust of industrialized northern Ontario the old convictions of the south.

6.

At the end of 1919, some two months after the Drury government took office, the federal government repealed the War Measures Act and with it the Orders-in-Council affecting liquor. The Dominion of Canada itself was no longer officially dry; beer, wine and spirits could be manufactured or imported, and as articles of legitimate commerce they were restored to the flow of trade. They could be restricted within a province so far as use was concerned, but they were free to enter and leave.

250

By the beginning of 1920 Ontario was experiencing the revival of a trans-provincial trade. Liquor that could not be sold was piling up in bond warehoused for onward shipment. The United States in the age of Volstead was an inviting black market. Quebec's borders were open, and Quebec had moved with alacrity to restore controlled sale. Even worse than that, in the eyes of the prohibitionist, it was again legal for the Ontarian to import for private use. However strict the enforcement of existing provincial law, the man of means was enabled to stock his cellar. Outside the law, moreover, creating a volume of leakage that expanded month by month, were the blind pigs, the bootleggers and the accommodating physicians.

To Drury, and even more to W.E. Raney, the peppery Toronto lawyer he had acquired as Attorney-General, the enforcement of the Ontario Temperance Act was a first article of faith. But the system was hampered by new conditions and it lacked essential teeth. Liquor flowed through the province, or was stored in course of shipment, and the flow was certainly tapped. Police and magistrates were apathetic toward law-breakers. Hotels and clubs, ostensibly importing liquor for the use of private members, were offering it for public sale. J.D. Flavelle, still Chairman of the Board of Licence Commissioners, reported that 90 per cent of the prescriptions issued by doctors for quart bottles of liquor were not medicinally necessary. One physician in one month had prescribed for the needs of 2,005 sufferers, while another had treated 487 in a day.

Dry forces were in arms and divided among themselves as they clamoured for new restrictions. The question of native wines, often raised in the cities, was a sensitive issue among the farms and vineyards and still remained in abeyance. Nor could Drury, for all his own views, remove the right to the private possession of liquor. He would set his face strongly, he said, "against any legislation that would involve search of homes and spying upon the people and encourage a system of informers."[29] What he could do, however, was to plug the loop-hole opened by the federal government. A provincial law could replace the rescinded federal law forbidding importation. In April of 1921 the question was put to a plebiscite and received an affirmative answer. The legal inflow of liquor was effectively dried up.

The plebiscite, though it supported dryness, was considerably less emphatic than the one two years earlier. The provincial mood was shifting, particularly in the urban centres where the labour vote was strong. The working man, often a returned veteran, seemed determined to have his beer, within or without the law. The substantial citizen, if he could not legally import liquor, was inclined to get it where he could. There was a steady local drain-off from supplies

251

officially in transit – liquor came in illegally and bootleg liquor was made. The back-alley saloons and the illegal sellers multiplied and the prescription business remained. A steady ooze of alcohol was eroding the base of law. Even some of the temperance leaders, as they saw the effects of total prohibition, were inclined to have their doubts. The Moderation League, always for relaxed controls, and always damned as a front for the liquor interests, was gaining an improved image. Weather-wise politicians and honestly concerned men were moved by the growth of lawlessness to approach the moderate view.

This was not true of the government or of the more convinced of the drys. Drury was firm for enforcement and Raney eager to enforce. Legalistic, dogmatic and tireless in moral reform, the Attorney-General was true to himself in office. He reorganized the provincial police force which had been lax and inefficient, and supplemented it with special "liquor squads" directed from his own office. Tolerant local authorities were stiffened with a hard hand, their jurisdictions invaded and sometimes superseded by the authority of the Attorney-General. The blind pig and the bootlegger were driven to increased mobility, if not to reduced sales, and the hotels and the private clubs, with or without liquor, were under increasing threat. Suspicion could bring raids, the informer created suspicion, and Drury's theory of sacrosanct possession gave way to the right of search.

By 1921 physicians were limited to forty prescriptions a month, and the over-generous were prosecuted. By 1922 it was illegal to carry liquor on a provincial highway if it was intended for use in the province. Travel and the tourist traffic, both reflecting a decreased revenue from potables, were showing signs of decay. "In few of the smaller places," the Ottawa *Journal* complained, "are the so-called hotels of today fit for self-respecting people to eat in or sleep in."[30] By 1923 not only liquor but the "commercialized vice"[31] of race-track betting had felt the lash of reform. Churchmen allied with Raney were moving to attack tobacco, and not even the haunts of the privileged were safe from government enforcers. John Willison, now an aging pundit observing from the political sidelines, noted that the Jockey Club of Toronto had been fined $1,000.00 because people on its grounds during a race meet had been found drinking from flasks. "Governments," he commented dourly, "never were so busy with prohibitions that do not prohibit and regulations that do not regulate."[32]

There was no question as yet of the deeper feelings of a large majority in the province. They had detested the liquor traffic and they would never have it back, not in the old way. Nevertheless an uglier traffic was developing, with uglier methods of restriction, and they were not proving successful. Whitney's view was re-surfacing with much of its old force; some would always drink, liquor would always be obtainable, and the only course for a government was to control the means of sale. That view, spiked with its political dangers, was attracting wary notice from the parties in opposition. Hartley Dewart, leader of the provincial Liberals and not a man for temperance, attacked Raney in the most vitriolic language.[33] F. Wellington Hay, who succeeded Dewart as leader, was more inclined to waffle. The Liberal party, he said, would support the Ontario Temperance Act "as long as it is the will of the people,"[34] but obvious in that statement was a considerable measure of doubt. There were larger implications in the course of Howard Ferguson, manoeuvring the Conservative party. Well watched by the drys, and well aware of their strength, he shifted emphasis in legislation toward temperance. Policy would become "more generous,"[35] he said, when Conservatives came to power.

Through 1922, as Drury and Raney pressed the work of enforcement, a roar of dissension grew. The half-hearted police and the all too vigorous liquor squads were alike increasingly frustrated and subject to fierce attack. Raney was accused of hiring "thugs and criminals,"[36] some of whom were frequently drunk themselves. As the great thirst of the Americans waxed in the United States, liquor traversed Ontario, stopped in bond in warehouses and paid government tolls. "Beer by the truckload" was leaving Windsor daily bound for the United States, according to the Toronto *Star*.[37] Yet not all of it left and far too much of it returned. In September it was reported that nine carloads of beer, removed from a bonded warehouse, had been seized en route to Walkerville. Ontario government launches patrolled between Windsor and Detroit, cutting off "export" liquor that was bound for provincial ports. Beyond capture, moreover, was the hurdle of confiscation and the cold eye of a judge. Week after week magistrates were quashing charges arising from liquor seizures and denying the effect of provincial jurisdiction. The Ontario Temperance Act, declared a Toronto magistrate in November of 1922, "did not attempt to prohibit *bona fide* transactions between persons in the Province and persons in a foreign country."[38]

Ontario as a legal channel for the flow to the United States could neither impede the traffic nor prevent the growth of its local off-shoots. The government was spending what the Moderation League projected as the equivalent of a mortgage on the province of $150,000,000.00 to enforce unworkable laws. It was hypocritical, said Ferguson, since the liquor designed for export, much of which seeped out locally, yielded a substantial revenue. Beyond that, moreover, was the question of the will of the province and the will of the cabinet itself, both clearly divided. Since the beginning of 1922 the Ontario Executive of the Trades and Labour Congress had officially advocated the controlled sale of light wines and beer.

Prohibition was renewing itself as the great enigma and threat. The government rooted in the farms, however, was sure of the farms' support. In December of 1922 Raney came before a meeting of the Independent Labour Party to insist that the Ontario Temperance Act could be effectively enforced and was being effectively enforced. He left the stage to the accompaniment of resounding jeers, but it changed nothing in him and there was no change in the Premier. Prohibition, said Drury, had come to Ontario to stay. "There is no danger of reversion to the sale of legalized liquor in any way, shape or form."[39]

7.

Six months later the government came to its end. The opening of the fourth session, in January of 1923, had been the beginning of a political shambles. On February 6 a labour member, openly defying Drury, had announced his intention to move for another referendum on the question of prohibition. On February 20, a farmer member had supported a Conservative motion. On February 23, not only the government whip but two others of the once-united farmers announced their withdrawal from the party. The Premier, they claimed, had been secretly "dickering" with Liberals and betraying his own supporters in hope of a coalition.

Stung and furious, Drury had denied the charge, and in the face of evidence that stopped just short of proof had threatened to dissolve the legislature.[40] Cooling the next day, he had replaced the threat with another proposition. The government, he felt, had still the confidence of the House, but a June election was advisable. He proposed, therefore, to introduce three bills: one that had been long pending for a redistribution of provincial electoral ridings, one for proportional representation and one for the transferable vote. It was all too obviously an election move in search of Liberal support, and it was met by a Conservative filibuster that stormed along for a week. On April 19, with Ferguson dominating the legislature and all three bills withdrawn, the parties went to the people.

The vote in this election was small, (said the *Canadian Forum*, commenting on the results of June 25, 1923,) and the enthusiasm negligible. Evidently those who were opposed to prohibition turned out to vote, and their numbers were augmented by those of the prohibitionists who despaired of the enforcement of the Ontario Temperance Act or who were prepared to take a chance on Mr. Ferguson.[41]

It was a measured and reserved comment by an organ friendly to Drury, but it dealt less than adequately with the skill of his prime opponent.

Ferguson was rising to his full height as a political strategist. He had attacked the government for its administration of the north, its antipathy to big business and its running battle with Beck to control the expansion of Hydro. He had even gained Beck, who stood as a Conservative candidate. At the same time the enormous cost of Chippawa, the large expenditures on roads, even the agricultural measures and some of the school reforms, had gained him ground with farmers. This government pledged to economy had more than doubled provincial liabilities. It had over-built on roads, it had over-restricted farmers in the matter of dairy standards, it had favoured the cities and industry in promoting electrification, and it had advanced the school leaving age to pull more sons from the land. It had stood opposed to labour on the question of unemployment, and still more obviously and openly on the question of prohibition. On that issue, still advancing with care, Ferguson had remained an enigma till the very eve of the election. Then, with the wind set and smelling strongly of dampness, the great pronouncement came. A Conservative government, he said, would enforce the Ontario Temperance Act till it was changed by a referendum, but "not in the spirit of fanaticism."[42] Those words and their timing had proved to be the master stroke.

In reality it was more than determined dryness and more than political stumbling that brought the government down. When Drury's "broadening out" was condemned by the United Farmers he had seen the writing on the wall. "I came to the conclusion that our chances in the next election would be very slim."[43] If there were to be no People's Party there would be no new party at all. Farm and labour members, once installed in the legislature, were faced with the task of administering the whole province. Every government policy, shaped by conflicting interests and balancing conflicting needs, was itself a broadening out. It was as much a series of compromises as the programs offered by the old political parties, and it drew men back to their positions. Group interest was sacrificed in the view of the rigid Morrison, and the farm party in politics had proved to be a flat failure. So had the labour party in the view of its doctrinaires. By 1923 the membership of the United Farmers had dwindled from 60,000 to 30,000, the labour movement had suffered comparable decline, and both officially were out of the political arena.

As group support melted and voters returned to their old political allegiances, Drury had pinned his faith on gaining Liberals. Liberalism after all, provincially as well as federally, was his first political home. He had not "dickered" to the extent of trading promises, but there had been much friendship in the legislature and considerable negotiation. There had been no betrayal in that; it had been recognition of realities and stark political necessity, but it had failed with his own supporters. He had hoped to divide the vote with well-intentioned Liberals through his proposed electoral reforms, and he had failed in that too. He was left with a United Farmers party separating again from labour and deprived even of a base in its own movement.

> Most of us think well of Mr. Drury, (wrote John Willison in April,) and are perhaps not greatly moved by the attacks that are made upon his government. But it is certain that the people of Ontario have not found any virtues in Farmer-Labour government that were not possessed in equal degree by Conservative or Liberal governments.[44]

With that view the province crushingly concurred. The war mood was forgotten, the aftermath was ending and Ontario was on the verge of better times. They were not times to be dominated by men speaking for the farms, preaching their old moralities to the blaring age of Jazz. Unemployment was lessening, industrial confidence returning and Ferguson himself was a symbol of the mood of a new boom. Drury went to the country leading United Farmers who had no support from their movement and with a campaign fund of some $1,500.00 largely raised by himself. By the night of June 25 he was defeated in his own riding and seventy-five Conservatives were to be the new masters of the legislature. "And so Howard Ferguson became Premier of Ontario and I returned to my farm."[45]

Notes

1. E.C. Drury, *Farmer Premier* (Toronto: McClelland and Stewart Limited, 1966), p. 197.
2. *Ibid.*, p. 36.
3. *Ibid.*, p. 68.
4. *Ibid.*, p. 72.
5. *Ibid.*, p. 88.
6. *Ibid.*, p. 87.
7. Peter Oliver, *G. Howard Ferguson: Ontario Tory* (Toronto: University of Toronto Press, 1977), p. 129.
8. *Ibid.*, p. 130.
9. *Canadian Annual Review*, 1919, p. 668.
10. Drury, *Farmer Premier*, p. 108.
11. John David Hoffman, *Farmer-Labor Government in Ontario 1919-23*, M. A. paper, University of Toronto, 1959, p. 39.
12. *Ibid.*, p. 59.
13. Drury, *Farmer Premier*, pp. 111-112. (On one point, Drury's memory is defective; Best did not become a medical doctor until 1925.)
14. *C.A.R.*, 1921, p. 602.
15. *C.A.R.*, 1920, pp. 593-597.
16. Edward Elmslie Stewart, *The Role of the Provincial Government in the Development of the Universities of Ontario, 1791-1964*, Ph.D. Thesis, University of Toronto 1970, p. 352.
17. *Canadian Forum*, September, 1923.
18. Drury, *Farmer Premier*, p. 83.
19. *Ibid.*, pp. 113-114.
20. *Ibid.*, p. 113.
21. *Ibid.*, p. 136.
22. *Ibid.*, pp. 137-138.
23. *Ibid.*, p. 123.
24. *Ibid.*, p. 151.
25. *C.A.R.*, 1920, p. 504.
26. Oliver, *G. Howard Ferguson*, p. 215.
27. Lambert, Pross, *Renewing Nature's Wealth*, p. 268.
28. *C.A.R.*, 1922, p. 587.
29. *C.A.R.*, 1920, p. 612.
30. *C.A.R.*, 1922, p. 595.
31. Oliver, *G. Howard Ferguson*, pp. 118-119.
32. John Willison, *Canadian Magazine*, September, 1921.
33. Oliver, *G. Howard Ferguson*, p. 206.
34. *C.A.R.*, 1923, p. 574.
35. Oliver, *G. Howard Ferguson*, p. 138.
36. *C.A.R.*, 1922, p. 592.
37. *Ibid.*, p. 593.
38. *Ibid.*, p. 594.
39. *Ibid.*, p. 591.
40, *C.A.R.*, 1923, p. 530.
41. *Canadian Forum*, July, 1923.
42. Oliver, *G. Howard Ferguson*, p. 139.
43. Drury, *Farmer Premier*, p. 107.
44. John Willison, *Canadian Magazine*, April, 1923.
45. Drury, *Farmer Premier*, p. 160.

Chapter Twelve

"Business Methods in Administration"

1.

The ministry of George Howard Ferguson was sworn into office on July 16, 1923, and dissolved through the resignation of the Premier on December 15, 1930. During those seven and a half years the continuing effects of the war gradually worked themselves out, federally as well as provincially and in moral and social attitudes as well as in economics. Yet it was not a time of solutions. The Ontarian like all Canadians, in a world more shattered than he knew, groped for elusive "normalcy" and found that it would not return.

In Ottawa, up to August 6, 1930, and except for a brief three months under the government of Arthur Meighen, Mackenzie King's Liberals dominated the national scene. They absorbed the agrarian protest movement, reduced labour to nothing as an effective force in politics and managed the country's business through the boom years to the crash. All this Ferguson duplicated in Ontario, and he was still in power when Mackenzie King went down.

During his time in office he fought two elections and emerged from the second seemingly unassailable. No election in provincial history had produced such a triumph as that of October 30, 1929, which returned ninety-one Conservatives to face a combined opposition of twenty-one members. The Liberal party was reduced to bewildered impotence, the divided remnants of the farm movement had a total of six seats and the Labour party had one. Ferguson, when he resigned as Premier, was leaving by his own choice for a post of his own choice. He was to go to London as High Commissioner for Canada, appointed by R.B. Bennett, the Conservative Prime Minister he had largely helped to elect. In Queen's Park, as he handed the reins of power to his friend, George S. Henry, he was crowning his own record of dazzling political success.

It was hardly Ferguson's fault that the story of the seven years was more chequered for the province itself. He was not responsible for the moods of the post-war period, or for the boom of the mid-twenties or the collapse that came with the thirties. He was dealing as did every Premier with always-competing demands, balancing claims and choices. It had been the same for Sandfield Macdonald, for Blake, Mowat, Hardy and Ross, for Whitney, Hearst, and Drury. Any one of them might have been glad to adopt his slogan of "Business Methods in Administration."[1] No one of them would necessarily have seen farther through the murk of changing conditions. Certainly in his own way this country lawyer from Kemptville with his quarter-century in politics was as representative of his province and as much alive to its needs as any Premier had been. Yet he did represent change, and it was not change for the better.

He came to office known and accepted for what he was. A survivor of scandal himself, he was soon exhuming scandal from the records of the Drury government. He viewed the foibles on both sides with a cheerful, folksy cynicism as part of the stuff of politics. So did much of the province, or much of the press that spoke for it, in the years of jazz and boom and bootleg liquor. Howard Ferguson was refreshing after the grey austerities of Drury and the rampant righteousness of Raney, particularly since the former ministry had been found to have its warts. His popular image was conveyed by one reporter through putting words in his mouth.

This idea that there are to be no rewards for political service, (he imagined Ferguson as saying,) is all buncombe ... I'm not running a Sunday School class or a standard hotel ... politics is politics. Do you expect men to work for you and then see somebody else get all the offices? ... Get office by promising people what they want. Try to give it to them if you can. Make friends. Hold on to office. ... Having won one election your chief business is to win the next. To that end the policies of the Government generally ... must be directed.[2]

Fictitious as the words were, the man largely confirmed them. "Fergie" got things done; he was feared, followed and respected as a skilled political mechanic. Along with that as corollary was a darker cast of thought, which he later expressed himself:

As a matter of fact the public has no intelligence. No election was ever won by logic or arguments. Educated, intelligent people ... are in a hopeless minority. With our Utopian, wide-open franchise the mob rules. The problem is to capture the imagination of the mob.[3]

259

This was the philosophy he bequeathed to Henry, and it foreshadowed the ways of Hepburn who was soon to follow. It hovered over the province through Ferguson's years in power. Shrewd, capable and decisive, he channelled provincial energies in line with his own directions. Even so, the goals were limited by the character and betrayed too often by results. More might have been done and much have been done better.

2.

Mines, timber, pulpwood and all the resources of the north were administered by Ferguson's government with a flair that Drury's had lacked. The new Premier had hardly been installed in office when he set out for James Bay. Travelling with a distinguished party by rail, foot and canoe, he arrived at Moose Factory near the mouth of the Abitibi and crossed to Moosonee. Here was the projected terminus of the Temiskaming and Northern Ontario, and the visit heralded the railway. The actual coming, however, was to be diverted by a new enterprise and would wait for several years.

In the Rouyn-Noranda area, to the east of Lake Timiskaming, gold finds had rewarded the search for copper. The region lay in Quebec but Ontario money was involved and Toronto interests were vigorously seeking access. As a railway problem it was not particularly difficult. The Temiskaming and Northern Ontario, postponing its northern building, could simply be extended east through Swastika and Larder Lake for approximately a hundred miles. Much of the mileage, however, would cross Quebec territory and conflict with Quebec ambitions. Alexandre Taschereau, who was then Premier of the province, intended Rouyn-Noranda to be connected with Montreal. He had moved first, moreover, by enlisting the Canadian National, and the line was already building when Ontario work commenced.

For two years, while interprovincial legalities were fought out in the courts, the railways crawled toward the mines. On the Ontario side, however, there was a lengthy interruption. The Temiskaming and Northern Ontario, as a provincial undertaking, was not empowered to cross Quebec territory. Foreseeing this, it had acquired the Nipissing Central as a subsidiary with a federal charter that carried the right of passage. When it reached the Quebec border and found passage refused it took its case to law. While the courts delayed the CNR pushed on, and by October 1926 it had completed its branch to Rouyn. Mining magnates in Toronto and the government in Queen's Park were forced to await a decision of the Privy Council. When it did come, however, it opened the gates for Ontario and

Quebec accepted the verdict. In November 1927 the first train out of Toronto by way of the Temiskaming and Northern Ontario turned east at Swastika along the line of the Nipissing Central and entered the Rouyn gold-fields.

By that time, some 800 miles to the west, new gold in Ontario was restoring the flush of a boom. Red Lake in Patricia District near the border of Manitoba had been the scene of a great find. A thousand miners and prospectors were opening up the wilderness, planes were flying supplies and equipment from Toronto and some of the unemployed were trooping north. There was every assistance from government and many concessions to mining men, for a generally depressed industry was in need of rejuvenation. Silver production was declining year by year. Ontario's low grade iron ore, in spite of government bounties, was hardly being mined at all. Nickel production, stimulated by new uses and helped by decreased taxation, was only beginning its recovery from the depths of the post-war trough. Red Lake and its prospects, quickening all mining, were keys to better times.

The great risks, the great profits and the whole climate in which mining was carried on appealed to the ministry. Ferguson, the friend of the north, was friendly to its entrepreneurs, and so was Charles McCrea, his Minister of Mines. Under their hands there was co-operation for the capitalist, a sympathetic attitude on the question of taxes and royalties and many special privileges which were duly noted and attacked. At the same time, however, with a new thrust in promoting the search for minerals, came improvement in administration and some stiffer regulation.

Government geological parties continued to explore the province, while training classes for prospectors increased the number at work. More help was provided for men already in the field. Speculation was checked by reserving potential minelands; and a free assay service speeded the placing of claims. The government tightened its grip and improved order in the mining districts by raising local commissioners to the status of quasi-judges. It forced reluctant mine owners to some first steps for the reduction of silicosis and indemnified victims of the disease under Workmen's Compensation. It was energetic and watchful over the whole range of the industry, and the results generally were good. The annual value of mineral production rose from $72,000,000.00 in 1923, to $117,000,000.00 in 1929. That growth, mainly supported by gold, was to continue throughout the depression and ease some of the effects. Great private developers had been encouraged to go their way, reaping huge fortunes and returning only a fraction as part of the "people's share." That fact would be complained of as it had been in the long past, but the other

261

fact remained in a tough and thriving industry and the creation of thousands of jobs.

In the administration of the forests there was the same pattern of drive, coupled with increasing care. By 1924 sixteen flying boats of the Ontario Air Service, based at Sault Ste. Marie, were on regular patrols across the northern woods, surveying, mapping and finding and fighting fires. On the ground a new inspection service improved the work of the timber agents, and rough-and-ready lumbermen came in for a closer watch. The increase of staff and the evolution of policy culminated in the Forestry Act of 1927 and the Provincial Forests Act of 1929. Real effort, by way of money and men, was enforced on the private operators in conservation, reforestation and fire protection measures. More land was withdrawn to be held as provincial reserves under the authority of the Provincial Forester. All land was classified, and a Forestry Board was appointed to engage in research and planning.

At the same time, with the classification of land, came a first yielding to one reality of settlement. Failure in some areas had been due to the fact that grants were unfit for agriculture; and where that was proved the government was prepared to redeem it. The farmer who wished to leave was offered a new grant, with assistance and compensation for the cost of transfer. Forestry policy and farm policy, at last and very tentatively, were beginning to merge on the Shield.

In a largely augmented field force, morale, equipment and efficiency came in for much attention. The big mechanical fire pump began to replace the hand pump, and hundreds of miles of hose lay coiled by the scattered stations. With the air patrols and a fleet of trucks and vehicles came new and liberal spending on effective communication. By 1927, 1,500 miles of telephone lines connected the 135 wooden and 42 steel towers of the lookout network. Wireless telegraphy was used for the first time and experiments with airborne radio began two years later. With 1930 came the first two-way traffic between flying boats of the Air Service and ground-based patrols. As fire losses were reduced conservation was enforced, and even dissident lumbermen were forced to concede its value. There were still lapses and shortcomings and the usual government tendency to wink at large transgressors, but the mechanics of preservation had definitely moved ahead.

Pulp and paper, however, dominated government thinking and stimulated large ambitions. Ontario and Quebec together accounted for some 90 per cent of all Canadian production, which amounted in 1920 to 867,000 tons. That figure, which had trebled in seven years, was more than trebled again in the course of the next six. Ninety per cent of the production went for export, and ninety per cent of the exports went to the United States. The two central provinces, still increasing their output, were providing the American market with some 2,000,000 tons. By 1926 fourteen large pulp mills were operating across Ontario and several of these were expanding. New plants were hurrying on construction and the daily output of newsprint was about 2,600 tons.

Demand seemed to be limitless. The United States, reserving what still remained of its own supplies of pulpwood, was turning more and more to the Canadian forests. Newspapers, the devourers of newsprint, were looking anxiously ahead. Some had invested heavily in Canadian pulpwood companies, while others were signed to large, long-term contracts. About 80 per cent of all Ontario mill capacity was then fully employed, and even full production was less than projected needs. Mills in the United States, farther away from their supplies and older and less efficient than the newer mills in Canada, were gradually closing down. To pulpwood operators and to the provincial government, eventual Canadian control of the American market seemed a reasonable prospect.

Within that framework the Ferguson administration established policy. Grants to the clamorous pulpwood companies would be expanded but not on the old terms. No land would be alienated to be stripped and left abandoned or allowed to remain idle. Instead, the holding company would act as a provincial tenant, administering a provincial asset. It would establish planned production, cut at an agreed rate and gradually renew its limit through reforestation. Heavier dues would be charged, stricter practices required, and with good forest management there would be wood in perpetuity. There would also be more mills and more jobs for Ontarians since no pulp could be exported except in the form of newsprint. The new measures, when they were announced in July of 1926, foreshadowed an increase in production from 2,600 to 4,500 tons per day, an investment of $80,000,000.00 by the various pulpwood companies and new employment for 14,000 people.

This was a broad-visioned program for an industry that was surging forward and a north alive with growth. Its essential premise, the ever-expanding market, was, however, a myth of the peaked boom. What followed in the next three years was an almost doubled capacity, a growing surplus of newsprint and a steady slide in prices. By 1929, as old mills expanded and new mills came into production, newsprint which had been selling at close to $80.00 per ton in 1924 was offered at less than $50.00 and much of it was going begging. Murderous competition had forced a move toward cartels, but among companies desperate for volume and staggering under fixed charges, no agreement could hold. The business had no order and the government could not compel it. The province was as closely involved as any one of the companies, for growth, development and payrolls hinged on the mills' success. Thousands of men, hundreds of camps and towns, a great segment of the whole northern community, depended on the sale of newsprint.

Quebec was in the same dilemma, but neither province had friends in the United States. Their one solution was to enforce pro-rating of production and the establishment of a fixed price. In 1928 they persuaded most of the operators to agree to that measure. The partial truce in Canada, dubious enough itself, was almost instantly destroyed by manoeuvres from below the border. The powerful American publishers' lobby howled at the Canadian combine. Importers turned to Norway as another source of pulpwood and idled American paper mills began to resume production. The prospect of the great, essential customer as a self-sufficient neighbour seemed imminent. In the face of that the Canadian mills, cutting prices savagely and losing money consistently, returned to their old way.

Through 1930 the downward course continued, with government as the senior partner doing what little it could. Even in its own aims it was forced to be contradictory. The larger, modern mills, more economical and efficient, could supply all the newsprint that present markets would take. Yet when the companies moved to consolidate by closing their smaller mills, Ferguson turned them back. He had to think of employment and of the government's undertakings; each mill supported its own community. Both small and large mills were operating when he left office, at drastically reduced capacity, with fewer and fewer men, and with loans, mortgages and bankruptcies as overhanging clouds. The great Backus Brooks Company was already into receivership; so was Abitibi with its new mill at Cochrane; and other companies were reorganizing or threatened with liquidation. The pulpwood camps were emptying, the unemployed were multiplying and a great industry in shambles lay sprawling across the north.

3.

Hydro-electric power, as a native source of energy, remained of consuming interest. By 1923, in spite of the development of Chippawa, new demands were threatening to outpace supply. Eastern Ontario, far from the Niagara system, was plagued by increasing shortages and complaining of high rates. The industrialization of the north, particularly in the case of the mines and the pulp and paper mills, imposed huge requirements. Rising over the horizon and foreshadowing new needs were the electrification of the farms, the growth of new factories and the conversion of existing factories from steam to electric power. Moreover, the attraction of new industry was dependent on increased resources.

"This government," said Ferguson when he came to office, "must see to it that if we are in the power business we have power to sell."[4] He had Adam Beck at his side, still chairman of Hydro and reinstalled in the cabinet. He had also a host of difficulties and various competing options. Coal and steam generators could produce electric power. Quebec had surplus power which it might be prepared to rent. There was still water available for expansion at Niagara Falls if the United States concurred. Yet these were limited, temporary measures, each with its disadvantages.

Coal for electric power meant continued dependence on the Americans. Quebec might withdraw the rented surplus power when her own needs required it. The United States, while it was prepared occasionally to discuss expansion at Niagara, was actually allowing Chicago to divert water from Lake Michigan, lowering the level of the whole Great Lakes system and decreasing the eastward flow. The "steal" was being protested and might eventually be stopped; meanwhile Ontario had developed its own plan for a compensating diversion. A part of the Albany River system in the Hudson Bay watershed could be turned south toward Lake Superior and the Falls. That scheme, however, as a work in the remote north, was of rather frightening dimensions. The real solutions, while large enough and beset with their own difficulties, were much nearer to hand. There were great resources of power still to be developed on the Ottawa and beyond that, dwarfing those possibilities, the power of the St. Lawrence itself.

As far back as 1918 Beck had been considering the St. Lawrence. From the Quebec border to Kingston the river ran as the boundary between Canada and the United States. In this "International Section," with Ontario lying on the north bank and New York state on the south, the stretch of islands and rapids between Morrisburg and Cornwall invited the thought of power dams which became the "Morrisburg project." Since it concerned a province, a state and an international river it would have to be a joint work, in which the Canadian government, the American government and the Ontario government co-operated. Behind the plan, when Ferguson came to office, were years of negotiations which he hoped to bring to a head. In January 1924, appearing for the last time as a great public mobilizer, Adam Beck led the representatives of 350 Ontario municipalities to Ottawa, asking for federal support of the Morrisburg project. By June Ferguson had passed an Order-in-Council

265

authorizing Beck, on behalf of Ontario Hydro, to apply formally for Dominion government approval. The work could not be begun without approval by the United States, but the Premier's goal was a clarification of positions.

For Canada and the United States the development of the St. Lawrence as a seaway was of overriding importance. The deepening of shallow stretches and the building of canals and locks could clear a passage for deep-draught ocean shipping to the head of Lake Superior. Within that frame there were large national questions and conflicting national ambitions which had been discussed before the war. Studies postponed by the war had been begun in 1919 through a Joint Engineering Board established by the two countries. Nothing had emerged as yet in the form of plans or agreements, but there was little doubt in Canadian minds that the seaway would ultimately be built.

Navigation was one question but it was linked with the development of power and with a federal-provincial argument that went back to Mowat and Macdonald. Clearly interprovincial waters were subject to federal control. The issue was the use and ownership, apart from navigation, of the beds, banks and riverflow that were within provincial boundaries. That right, casually claimed by the Dominion, had been long resisted by the province. At sites along the Ottawa federal leases had been granted to private developers which Ontario refused to recognize. Millions of future horsepower and untold millions of dollars had always hinged on the dispute. The question had been of much concern to Beck but would not be so much longer, for he died in 1925. It was to concern Ferguson for most of the next six years. From the issuance of his Order-in-Council in 1924 it was to be his principal battle, mainly with Mackenzie King. In season and out of season, Ferguson claimed for Ontario the right to develop power on its own stretch of the St. Lawrence "so long as the province does not interfere with the paramount use for navigational purposes."

Overhanging the long struggle and providing some of the alternatives was the attitude of Quebec. Within its borders was the "national" section of the St. Lawrence, wholly on Canadian territory. It had a surplus of power and no desire for the seaway. The magnates of Montreal, a railway centre and terminus for ocean shipping, did not relish the thought of enlarged ports in the interior and traffic passing them by. Quebec was cool to Ontario and cool to the Morrisburg project, which was linked inextricably in federal minds with development for navigation. All Quebec power was produced by private companies and the province had discouraged outside sale by imposing a tax on exports. In the case of the Ottawa, however, it was as much concerned as the sister province to establish provincial rights. If the Dominion government could dispose of leases and power sites Quebec would lose too. The Ottawa was a shared river dividing the two provinces, but it tended ultimately to join them in opposing federal claims. In the meantime, pending formal alliance and strengthening Ontario's position by supplying her interim needs, there might be sharing of power.

Standing in the way of that were the Quebec export tax, the high cost of transmission lines that Ontario would have to build and Quebec's continuing resentment over the question of bilingual schools and Regulation 17. The latter obstacle, however, Ferguson gradually disposed of, since he was Minister of Education as well as Premier of Ontario. "Quel beau rêve, "Taschereau mused in public during the course of negotiations, "si nos pouvoirs hydrauliques devenaient l'usine qui fait la paix et qui ouvriraient grandes aux petites enfants Canadien-français de l'Ontario les portes de leurs écoles françaises."[5] With broad hints from Ferguson that there would be an opening of doors, other difficulties faded and a new inducement rose. An appeased Quebec, if it supplied Ontario with power, might lessen the need for Morrisburg and postpone thought of the seaway.

By 1926 Quebec was not only renting power to Ontario but considering a joint development along the Ottawa. This had not, however, stilled the question of the seaway. The Joint Engineering Board had pronounced favourably on the project, Canada and the United States were engaged in negotiations, and Ferguson was pressing Ontario's claims at Morrisburg. These involved not only legal arguments but practical difficulties raised by the engineers. Power development at Morrisburg, whether or not it was within the rights of the province, would require the building of dams. A free channel and a canal system would be required for navigation; would the dams interfere with that? Ontario claimed they would not; the federal government was inclined to think they would, or was at least inclined to delay. In 1927, while the question of legal rights was before the Supreme Court, Mackenzie King took action to review the technical problems. A National Advisory Committee was appointed to investigate and report on the best method of proceeding with the entire seaway.

The report, brought down in April 1928, was a disastrous verdict for Ontario. It recommended that development of the St. Lawrence seaway begin first on the national section lying within Quebec. Where and when it was feasible to develop power the work should be done by private Quebec companies, authorized by that province. Quebec would control the building, the companies would control the power, and Ontario would have to buy from them at whatever price they would set.

The United States concurred with the committee's findings, but Ferguson's vocal outrage brought matters to a dead stop. There would be no development, he said, with Ontario's co-operation, until Morrisburg was reconsidered and provincial rights conceded. Quebec, moreover, whatever its views on Morrisburg, gave firm support to his position. That province could afford to wait for power, wished to delay the seaway and was concerned with rights too. On that question, in February of 1929, an answer came from the Supreme Court of Canada. To Mackenzie King the Canadian Court's pronouncement seemed as oracularly vague as any of the Privy Council and he "could not make head or tail of it." He "seemed to glean," however, "that the Dominion has no right to go into the navigation business for power purposes as such, that power belongs primarily to the provinces."[6] Yet if the Prime Minister was shaken he was far from fully converted. In January 1930, when Ferguson and Taschereau together pressed him for a declaration "that the Federal government recognizes the full proprietary rights of the Provinces in the beds and banks and waterpowers of all navigable rivers,"[7] he still refused to sign. The fifty-year-old argument had not been quite concluded.

In spite of that, Ferguson had changed the power picture in Ontario. In 1926 Hydro signed its first agreement with Quebec, providing for the delivery of a maximum of 250,000 horsepower annually from the Gatineau Power Company. This required the building of a transmission line some 230 miles long from the Quebec border to connect with the Niagara system, but it was far cheaper than the alternative of steam-generated power. By 1930 other contracts had been signed with Beauharnois Light, Heat and Power Company and the MacLaren-Quebec Power Company. In addition the Quebec and Ontario governments were considering a joint project at Carillon on the Ottawa River, while Hydro was extending its facilities, absorbing private companies and stimulating growth in the north. If growth had stopped for a time it did not lessen the achievement.

> We must look away ahead, thirty, forty, fifty years, (Ferguson said,) if we have confidence in the future of the Province ... It behooves us, therefore, to secure every horsepower we can on proper terms. ... Twenty-five years from now, I venture to think we will pay a great deal higher price for any power we might require to buy.[8]

He was right enough in the short view and he would be right again when it came to the long future, but in the interval there would be some stormy years.

4.

For southern Ontario agriculture the problems of the middle twenties were relieved by advancing prices. Between 1923 and 1929, with generally larger returns on an increased variety of grains, fruits, vegetables, dairy products and livestock, the farmer tasted prosperity. He was disenchanted with politics and cooling to the farm movement but he was getting more from his land. He was increasing the production of new staples to replace some of the old. The tobacco plant, which had come to Ontario early in the nineteenth century, was now of major importance. By 1923 some 35,000 farmers in southwestern Ontario were producing half the tobacco grown in Canada. In that same year the number of rural property-holders was reported to have increased significantly. A sign of growth in the province's rural community, the statistic was not much, but it indicated stabilization. The drift to the cities seemed to have slowed a little.

Yet there could be no change in the larger trends affecting rural life. The age of the automobile and the age of electrification had both come for the farmer. By 1928 Ontario had over 430,000 passenger cars, nearly as many as the other provinces combined. Tourist traffic no less than internal traffic had imposed huge demands and become an essential source of revenue. The province had added nearly 1,300 miles of paved provincial roads to the mileage built by Drury, and though it had eased the costs of building for rural municipalities the farmer still complained. He also demanded the roads, for he drove his own car. In the same way he was drawn to the use of hydro, with all that that entailed. Main rural transmission lines had been financed by the Drury government, but there had been no loans to the farmer for his private installation. These Ferguson provided, and the rush of change began. By 1930 some 6,000 farmers annually were bringing power to their barns and electric light to their homes. The one-time luxury of the city had become a new necessity of the farms.

For mechanization, drainage work and the improvement of farm properties the Agricultural Development Board continued to provide loans. The new government, like the old, assisted co-operative marketing, and was more active in promotional work to stimulate world demand. At the same time, particularly in the field of dairying, it renewed the attempt to foster regulation. The Dairy Standards Act, passed in 1926, provided for improved grading, compulsory pasteurization and better packaging of all export products. It was as stubbornly resisted, however, as it had been a few years earlier and remained largely ignored. The real answer to the problem was a grouping of dairies and creameries in large, efficient units. Yet this would mean for the small man eventual elimination, and Ferguson no less than Drury recoiled from imposing change. It was left to the agricultural colleges branching out from Guelph to educate local dairymen in cleaner and better methods, while government exhorted from the sidelines with advertising and advice. In 1929 the enlargement of the Markets and Co-operation Branch of the Department of Agriculture pointed toward improved techniques in manufacture and selling. By the end of 1930, however, faced with declining prices and increasing competition in diminishing world markets, Ontario's cheese and butter makers were still resisting change.

There was a firmer touch in dealing with northern agriculture. Official faith in the Clay Belt still remained unshaken and Ferguson was vigorous as always in promoting and directing growth. By 1926, through a Department of Northern Development, the government was distributing funds with a lavish hand. For the newly-arriving immigrant, as well as the long-established, more paternal assistance was offered than before. The pulpwood companies were encouraged to buy the settler's timber and the mines urged to employ him through the months when he could leave his land. Large drainage projects reduced the bogs and muskeg, agricultural experts inspected and advised on crops and the ubiquitous automobile came into use as transport. Colonization roads were widened from trails to highways; raw towns and mining centres were linked not only with each other but with southern civilization. Communications were reducing isolation, new claims were advanced for the future of the northern farmer, and in some of its milder areas the face of the Shield seemed tamed.

By 1929, however, the glowing picture of progress was flawed by increasing doubts. "Optimism in many forms of Canadian development and activity," said a writer in the *Canadian Forum*, "has gone crazy." Pointing discreetly and without naming it to one of the older regions of the Clay Belt, he reported on a recent visit:

The superficially observant stranger could motor through this district today and leave with the impression that it is prosperous. Cars are thick upon the roads; almost every farmer with a road has a car of some sort. At the time of writing the fields carry good stands of timothy and grain, and even the brilliantly green bush springing up all over the burns and uncultivated land lends an appearance of richness . . .

But honest and more exact observation will immediately detect something of the true state of affairs. There is something lacking in houses and buildings, in fences, in the number and quality of the livestock . . . a significance in the many empty farms, in the heavy preponderance of hay-fields over grain-fields . . . Across two or three settled townships, the farms having adequate barns and sanitary livestock accommodation can be counted on the fingers of one hand . . .

On many properties the owners are non-resident wholly or for the greater part of the time . . . perhaps a boy or two in the mines or on the railroad . . . a man able to leave his family in charge for short intervals or all winter, while he earns good wages on distant mining or lumbering jobs . . . These are the more fortunate ones; but it is not farming, nor does it help out those who have not got these advantages . . .

A fact which should not be lost sight of is that the much advertised assistance to settlers in the shape of opportunities of casual employment on roads, in the mines and woods, has about the same relation to improvement of the agricultural situation as the dole to English unemployment. It enables those who can take advantage of it to exist, but it gets them nowhere . . .

The limitations of agriculture in the northern claybelt must be realized . . . Corn is an impossibility; so apparently is alfalfa. There is a narrow enough margin – sometimes none – in ripening grain before frost. Since the removal of the sheltering woods red clover suffers from the lack of winter covering. The larger fruits and maple products . . . are absent . . . In the easier, richer south the farmer's trade yields least for the most work and greatest investment of all industries. In the north, handicapped by climate, by debt, by lack of available markets and the general inability to grow crops, is it any wonder that he cannot make it go? . . .

Many of those who are in difficulties are the pioneers, the people who, in the early days of the century, went in over dangerous canoe routes, and carried heavy packs for miles and miles through a trackless wilderness. They started in to hack farms out of a spruce and elder tangle with a faith that, looking back on, is almost incredible. . . They and those who followed in the next few years have laboured hard through the extremes of heat and cold, cut timber and driven the rivers, cleared land and built up homes. Their womenfolk have known loneliness on the isolated farms, and sickness in the family when medical aid was out of the question. They worked hard all winter to earn money for a grubstake, and to clear more land, put up more buildings, buy more machinery, more horses and cows – all to no better

271

result than to be worse off than when they started, and twenty or thirty years older.[9]

The report was denounced as vigorously as were earlier reports and warnings. It was far from being the complete story of the north. Yet for all the years of effort and all the millions spent, it was the story of thousands of Ontarians on the verge of the great depression.

5.

In Ferguson's view the Ministry of Education was the nerve centre of politics, and he reserved the post for himself. Generally he was a cautious innovator where he attempted change at all, and the primary and secondary school systems went on much as before. Some needs were recognized and adequate funds provided. Teacher training improved, courses were realigned and the range of instruction widened. Administration was more professional and efficient but there were few radical departures.

Where there was imagination and vigour and the authentic Ferguson touch it was applied mainly in the north. Correspondence courses for children in remote regions and a system of part-time classes for those who had left school were established and in operation by 1925. By 1929 four special railway cars had become schools on the move. Each fitted with a classroom and with living quarters for a teacher, they usually carried a doctor and sometimes a dentist as well. Traversing the bush and the pulpwood camps on a circuit of some 600 miles, they were far less than was required but a boon wherever they went. As they rumbled in to a division point, hooked to a northern train, they were shunted off to a siding. Students flocked to the stopping-places from wide, surrounding regions and there was no doubt of their enthusiasm. "They want to work day and night," one teacher reported; and an inspector told of an Indian boy who "came by canoe thirty-two miles up the river with a hamper of food to last him a week."[10]

In the south the problem of autonomous local schools, widely scattered, poor and fragmenting total enrolment persisted. Fifty-five per cent of all the rural schools had less than twenty pupils each, over 1,300 had less than fourteen, occasional schools had one pupil, and over a hundred had not more than five. Hearst had seen the problem, Drury had approached it tentatively, and Ferguson did little more. The obvious remedy was to expand the size of units. In 1925 a bill providing for the establishment of township school boards which would absorb many of the local boards was introduced "for discussion." It was quickly withdrawn, however, when discussion turned against it. The farmer's attitude had not changed through the years. He liked his little red schoolhouse, trusted his own school board and was not prepared to relinquish local autonomy. He was in no hurry for bigness or the sophisticated education that might draw his children to the city; nor did he want the cost of transporting them to a township school. By 1930 the one change in the status of rural school boards affected supervision. The province assumed the right to appoint county inspectors.

By 1928, forty-two vocational schools in the province had 20,000 students and a part-time enrolment of several thousand more. The Apprenticeship Act, which was passed in that year, improved on the old system, widened the range of training and related the work more closely to specific industries and trades. The number of night schools rose to sixty-one, with 30,000 adults enrolled in courses. New Canadians were offered instruction in English by forty other schools; and 6,000 children, handicapped or retarded, were being taught in special classes. In all these undertakings the social needs of the province were gradually being dealt with. The pace of the work, however, fell well short of requirements in almost every field. The provincial government responded where municipalities demanded, but it did not encourage initiative and was not too generous with funds.

In one field of policy Ferguson, like Drury before him, sensed the need of change. The universities were absorbing a large proportion of the general allocation for education. To the Premier it seemed too large and he was disturbed at the size of the grants, particularly to Queen's and Western. He suggested meaningfully in 1926 that they should draw on other resources; "they should look around for some money."[11] Nothing he said resulted in much curtailment, but the idea mooted in Drury's time, and even in Hearst's before him, became an actual proposal.

Why could not the universities, by transferring their first-year work to the junior colleges and high schools, reduce their own expenses? This would result not only in an expansion of the secondary system, but in a general knitting-together on both levels. Canon H. J. Cody, who was by then Chairman of the Board of Governors of the University of Toronto, had been Minister of Education in the Hearst government. In 1921, during the Drury ministry, he had recommended the change in a report on university finances. He was a respected friend of Ferguson who warmly approved the idea; and he had also considerable support from his president, Sir Robert Falconer.

Neither they nor the government nor the idea, however, could change the stand of the university community. Higher learning seemed determined to go on, constantly extending its reach, constantly straining its resources, but preserving itself in splendid isolation. It was only to be worn down, by hard years, the depression and the threat of restricted grants, to a first limited concession. In 1931, after Ferguson had left office, the University of Toronto yielded first. Senior matriculants of high schools with adequately improved standards were accepted on a par with freshmen who had completed their first year.

For all his old pronouncements and his Orange affiliations, Ferguson manoeuvred skilfully on the issue of bilingual schools. He approached the question, moreover, with the same shift of bias that was taking place in the province. Through Drury's regime, though there had been no formal change, there had been much development in practice and a vast improvement in mood. Franco-Ontarian citizens had paid for their own schools where they were deprived of provincial grants. At the same time and in the same schools they had advanced the teaching of English. With lessened recrimination but with ever-increasing persuasion they had driven their case home: they were friends and brothers of the English – English-speaking brothers – but at all costs, and in addition they would have their mother tongue. That right, when it was seen in that way, almost all Ontario was now prepared to concede.

With this knowledge, and with his need of Quebec power, Ferguson drew nearer to Taschereau and the realization of the dream. By 1925, though still deflecting proposals for any legislative change, he was informing the House that the government was "not wedded to Regulation 17."[12] In August of that year, under the long-experienced Dr. Merchant who was now Chief Director of Education, an intensive survey of all bilingual schools was begun. The report two years later, though it discovered little that was new, was a triumph for common sense. "No rule," it said, "which prescribes the medium of instruction for different forms or grades of a system can be applied impartially to all schools within that system."[13]

It was the signal for flexibility, which was all the government required, and as much as the French could hope for. There was to be no renewal of war over Regulation 17. It would remain on the books as a declaration which no French educator disputed: every Ontario child must be taught to speak English. Under the same terms, however, through changed methods and machinery, instruction in French would be given more importance. It would rank with English instruction in the amount of time allotted to it, even at the occasional expense of other subjects. Teaching in each school would be examined on its own merits by a Director of English Instruction and a Director of French Instruction, both reporting to the Chief Provincial Inspector. English local inspectorates, always fiercely resented, would be ended. To delighted Franco-Ontarians the intent and effect were clear; tolerance and good faith could be restored to all teaching. There was even room for extra-legal adjustment. The University of Ottawa, which was staffed by the Oblate Order and trained teachers in French, was quietly given the status of a provincial Normal School.

The changes came and were accompanied by the familiar Orange outcry, but its volume was sharply diminished. Ferguson had won Quebec with a substantial share of its hydro-electric power, and he was a trusted Orangeman himself. Many of the other Orangemen, altered as much as he was, were prepared to go his way. By 1929 the Ottawa *Journal* was echoing the *Citizen's* optimism of nine years earlier: "There is no longer a language issue in Ontario!"[14]

There was certainly a separate schools question, but it had been damped down by the courts. The Supreme Court of Ontario, the Supreme Court of Canada and finally the Privy Council had rejected the claims advanced by Catholic ratepayers in relation to schools and taxes. They were not entitled under the terms of the British North America Act, as interpreted by all the judges, to their own secondary schools, to relief from taxes supporting Protestant schools, or to any amended sharing. Protest still went on, agitation was building, but by the end of 1930 it was only a forming cloud.

6.

On the temperance question Ontario was moving with glacial inexorability but more than glacial speed. It had passed Drury's position, changing government in the process, and the momentum seemed to be increasing as Ferguson assumed power. The mass remained an enigma, however, with its weight of old convictions, its experience of recent years and its mix of clashing forces. All policies were dangerous, and the Premier chose to wait. The province was officially dry, he was head of the province, and his first responsibility was to administer existing law.

He surprised wets and delighted the temperance forces by appointing a prohibitionist to the post of Attorney-General. Under W.F. Nickle, not only were laws enforced, but stronger laws were made. The authority of the police was widened; a suspected bootlegger could be arrested without a warrant and any vehicle carrying illegal liquor was subject to confiscation. The prescription business of doctors and the patent medicines of druggists came under rigid control. The dry province, with each oasis tracked down and eliminated, was to learn what dryness meant.

It was also to have, as promised, a chance to change its mind. The decision to hold a plebiscite was announced in the Throne Speech at the opening of the first session in February of 1924, and the voters went to the polls seven months later. The long interval had been provided to allow for the assessment of conditions and the crystallizing of opinion, but the result was baffling. On October 23, 1924, some 551,000 Ontarians, mainly in the larger cities, voted for the sale of beer, wines and spirits "in sealed packages under Government control."[15] Against them was the will of 585,000, mainly in rural ridings and the smaller towns and cities, who were for the full retention of the Ontario Temperance Act. Balanced on a hairline majority of less than 35,000 votes, the electorate had forbidden change.

It was obvious, nevertheless, that change was coming. British Columbia and Quebec were enriching their provincial treasuries on a controlled liquor traffic and the thirst of American tourists. The three prairie provinces had departed the dry fold. Ontario was running a deficit, depriving itself of an important source of revenue and living a contradiction. It still served as transit ground for a leaky export trade. Some 2,000,000 gallons of its own native wine were produced without obstruction. Private stills were active and home brew was ignored. For all Nickle's efforts, as for those of Raney before him, liquor continued to flow. It welled up through thousands of illegal outlets, returning nothing in the way of provincial income.

All this the plebiscite tended to support. In five years an enormous dry plurality had shrunk by 90 per cent. The wave of the future was set and becoming acrid, soured with old complaints. Amid the fragmenting forces of temperance the British and the native born were again assailing the immigrants and including with them the province's French and Germans. The arid bigot denounced the liquorous Jew, the foreigner and the Roman Catholic. The deprived of the cities pointed to the hypocrisy of the farms, with their native wines and stills. Wet communities, sure of their own opinion, called for a return to the days of local option. The drys would not have it, not with the automobile. Local constituency boundaries could not seal off the roads, or contain the thirsty traveller. The government of a mobile province must make the law for all.

By the beginning of the second session in 1925 it had absorbed the lessons of the plebiscite and determined on its next step. Experiments "laboratorical and otherwise"[16] had convinced the authorities that beer with an alcoholic content limited to 4.4 per cent was nonintoxicating and might therefore be offered for sale. "Fergie's Foam" came in, to be attacked by *The Christian Guardian*, chief organ of Methodist prohibitionists, as a product of "one of the most barefaced and unpardonable pieces of political apostasy that the history of

Canada has yet revealed."[17] Nor was there much compensating gain from the forces on the other side. Near-beer to the drinker was also a barefaced fraud, non-satisfying, non-exhilarating and generally a waste of time. It was not a political answer, and the answer had to come.

By 1926 Ferguson was prepared to face it. Enforcement was the usual nightmare, the liquor problem on both sides was becoming a provincial obsession and there was little doubt where the weight of opinion lay. To consolidate that weight the government "hived" the dries, transforming nine mainly rural seats that had gone for prohibition into ten tinged with urbanity that were more likely to be wet. In the opinion of J. J. Morrison of the shrunken farm movement, power had been gerrymandered "into the hands of people in the congested centres of population, many of whom have no stake in the country."[18] The parochial whig, however, had become as flat as near-beer, even to many of his own. The government was in need of revenue and was now sure of the people. With the controlled sale of liquor as a principal plank in its platform and with the cry of "Booze or Bankruptcy"[19] echoing along the sidelines, it called a provincial election. On December 1, 1926, with the assurance that there would be no bars and that government control would be rigid over all packaging outlets, the province gave its response. Fifty-six per cent of the electors voting returned the government to carry out its program.

On March 10, 1927, the bill was introduced in the House that established the Liquor Control Board of Ontario. On June 1 the government liquor stores were opened, under formidable regulation. There could be no advertising of spirits, wines or liquors, nor could they be served with meals in any hotel. The purchaser required a permit and must be over twenty-one. Each purchase was recorded and the privilege could be revoked if over-used. Any dry constituency, if it chose to refuse a store, could do so through the use of local option. "We are not here to push the sale of liquor," Ferguson said, "we are here to restrict it within reasonable bounds."[20]

He was echoing the tone of Whitney and he had caught the prevailing mood. The effect on the provincial budget was soon a reinforcement. By the end of 1927 an eight-year series of deficits had been concluded and a new trend established with a surplus of $2,000,000.00. In the election of 1929, with prohibition largely a non-issue, Ferguson's government was overwhelmingly returned. Booze had averted bankruptcy and was not to be displaced again. It was hardly yet respectable and for many thousands in Ontario it never would be. There was still scandalized outcry, there was still authentic protest, but the new directions were set.

Ontario in the later 1920s, for all its difficulties and shortcomings, had been alive with confident growth. It was to be a very different province in the decade of the 1930s. Ferguson stood at the dividing point with much to claim for his work. He had befriended business, promoted industry and changed a provincial deficit to a growing surplus. He had initiated the Morrisburg project that would lead eventually to the seaway, assured Ontario a supply of electric power and asserted rights in relation to the federal government that would not again be questioned. For all his earlier record and his view of practical politics, his ministry had not been touched by major scandal.

In Toronto, after two years of imaginative and vigorous effort, the Ontario Research Foundation was established. Government had persuaded industry, and in some cases dragooned it, into large joint expenditures that promised much for the future. Good scientists in well-equipped laboratories were experimenting with improved methods and widening the range of products for provincial manufacture. Private companies, which supported the work with funds, were still inclined to use it to outrun their competition. New uses were emerging, however, for some of the old resources and the province was becoming less dependent on American-controlled research. More scientists were employed, and more young Canadians were recruited from the universities. Long-sighted and determined in his "business administration" Ferguson had broadened the base of secondary industry and was keeping brains at home.

He was not a man to be haunted by all that had been left undone, the cracks that had been papered over, the doubts that were beginning to appear. As a lifelong man of politics he had proved himself a master. His Conservative provincial government, whose mandate had been renewed, was at least in apparent power the strongest the province had known. "There are only two absolute monarchs in the world," said the thirty-three-year-old Mitchell Hepburn, who seemed to be the one spark of life that was stirring in the Liberal party, "Haile Selassie and Howard Ferguson."[21]

During the summer of 1930, his last year in office, the Ontario Premier turned to the national field. Rather too openly and rather too well-organized, the Conservative machine in the province, supporting R. B. Bennett, provided help to swing the federal election. In his own view, if not entirely in Bennett's, Ferguson had become a king-maker entitled to due reward.

When the reward came, as an appointment by the federal government to the post of High Commissioner of Canada in London, it was wholly congenial in form. On his annual trips to England, and even more in his returns, the shrewd Kemptville lawyer reflected Tory Toronto and its commercial and social elite. Ontario House, newly opened in London, symbolized his work in promoting the imperial idea, in fostering British trade and Britishness in immigration. He was ice-cold to the creation of the new Commonwealth; he was for tightening the bonds of empire by means of trade and tariffs. He was equally strong for other bonds that went with the old traditions. Provincial roads became known as the King's Highways, and the Ontario Premier favoured the return of titles.

In Ferguson's time relations with Quebec improved. The two provinces in a new posture of alliance imposed some changed positions, or the consideration of change, on a reluctant federal government. The always-troubled questions of federal grants and subsidies and federal and provincial powers were given a modern urgency and expanded to new dimensions. Highway building, resource development and urbanization with its host of social problems demanded huge expenditures that were beyond provincial means. However centred in a province, they were not local in extent; they were actually national concerns. By what division of tax fields and allotment of funds and powers were the new needs to be met? That enormous question, with its financial, constitutional and political implications, was to wait long for a solution. Ferguson, however, invoking the help of Taschereau, had made it a live issue.

Nevertheless he had not really closed, or even attempted to close, the older, deeper fissures dividing the two provinces. In the case of bilingual schools he had suspended animosities, but he had conceded little to Frenchness and less to Roman Catholicism. He feared the foreign immigrant and distrusted the labour movement as fruitful sources of Communism. He discouraged the French Canadianism flowing from across the Ottawa as a dilution of the British strain. Opposed to the idea of autonomy within the loose-linked Commonwealth, he was of the mind of R.B. Bennett and at war with Mackenzie King, ultimately at odds with Quebec.

Social progress did not have high priority with the "business" administration. For the working man there was no minimum wage. Unemployment insurance, federally as well as provincially, was still a political football. The autonomous municipalities, responsible for welfare payments, were hard-pressed for resources as the 1930s were ushered in. The Dominion and provincial governments, with much mutual wrangling, were forced to concede support. Across the province, with the opening-up of the soup kitchens, old rhetoric returned: the immigrant should be kept out, the unemployed city man should find a job on a farm. The provincial government, said

Ferguson, could do nothing more "so long as the Dominion pays no attention to our views."[22]

Other social agencies had functioned smoothly enough, but they ran in old grooves. There was very little expansion and there was less of new thinking. The pressures generated for improvement came from within the system, and an unresponsive government claimed more than it achieved. Hospitals, prisons and factories were all duly inspected; but the intervals between visits lengthened and the conditions in all deteriorated. There were not enough inspectors to cope with increasing needs; all were poorly paid and inevitably a few corrupt. Health care in the schools, the treatment of juvenile delinquents and the protection of children and dependents were all outrun by needs. Less was budgeted for children's aid than in Drury's day. Insulin was provided free to the needy diabetic, and another development in medicine at least was foreshadowed. The government announced, in September of 1930, that it was opening a centre in Toronto for the treatment of cancer. The institution, however, had only advanced to the planning stage when Ferguson left office.

Since 1926 the Ontario government had watched without enthusiasm a federal effort to establish old age pensions. In 1927, after a first rejection by the Senate, the Dominion Act was passed. Under its terms, to any province that accepted and was prepared to assume its share, the federal government would pay one-half the cost of a pension of $20.00 per month to Canadians over seventy with an annual income of not more than $125.00. Ontario resisted this munificence until 1929, when a government nearing election was moved to open its heart. It did so with a maximum amount of prudence and minimum generosity. There would be, Ferguson announced, a pension of $240.00 per year to all those who were eligible. Of this amount 50 per cent was to be paid by the Dominion government and the whole pension would cease in the event of federal default. Of Ontario's half share 20 per cent was to be paid by the municipalities. Also, the Premier noted, since a prospective pensioner would have to be over seventy, a Canadian citizen for twenty years, an Ontario resident for five and nearly indigent as well, most of Ontario's aged would not qualify. What the innovation would mean, he said, addressing himself as a business man to those of the business view, was a tax increase equivalent to 80 cents on a house valued at $5,000.00.

In the same late months of the year, and again in face of an election, the government appointed a Royal Commission on Public Welfare to investigate conditions in hospitals, jails, children's homes and mental institutions. The report when it came down, with the election well behind it, did nothing to revoke a great political triumph. Nor did it necessarily reflect more on the work of the Ferguson ministry than on that of some of its predecessors. It told much, however, of conditions allowed to develop over a period of many years and unremedied in the past seven.

Private agencies, said the report, contributed some half million dollars annually to the work of the Children's Aid Society. The provincial government contributed a tenth of that. Hospitals, jails and mental homes were all overcrowded. They were unassisted by research in the field of preventive medicine and starved for people who were trained in social work. One provincial officer and two assistants were responsible for an inspection service intended to cover nearly 400 hospitals, nursing homes and correctional institutions. The service, not surprisingly, was found "scandalously inadequate." Particularly in the jails and mental hospitals there was such an "unassorted, unstandardized, unstudied system of commitment," such a mixture of "normal, mentally deficient, light and very grave offenders and unplaceables,"[23] that some of the commissioners revived an old proposal. Since much crime was due to bad heredity and transmitted mental deficiencies, Ontario might yet be driven to consider sterilization.

Confronting the Ferguson government through its last few months in office was the Commission's recommendation for an expenditure of between twenty and twenty-five million dollars. The money was required for a mental hospital in the north, the enlargement of those in the south, for a cancer hospital, a psychiatric hospital and for increased facilities of all kinds in existing institutions. Nor was this a program to provide for the long future; it was a remedy for past neglect. Its recommendations, said the Commission, "are assertions of present needs. . . . If every institution or construction spoken of were in existence tomorrow, all of the accommodation should be filled up next day."[24]

It could not be done at once, nor was it likely to be done soon. All needs were a part now of the steadily darkening picture. Factories were standing idle or running on part time, the pulpwood industry was in chaos, many municipalities were wholly or nearly bankrupt and there were thousands of unemployed in the towns and cities. Ontario's administration, though not responsible for the great world-wide shambles, had followed the way of business and followed the world down. From all this, after the way of politics, Ferguson escaped through timely elevation. By the late days of December, 1930, he was on his way to London with gaudy views of his status as High Commissioner. It was the solid, stolid, enduring George Henry, his former Minister of Highways, who would have to weather the depression.

Notes

1. Oliver, *G. Howard Ferguson*, p. 157.
2. *Ibid.*, pp. 108-109.
3. *Ibid.*, p. 430.
4. *Ibid.*, p. 174.
5. *Ibid.*, p. 182.
6. *Ibid.*, p. 354.
7. *Ibid.*, p. 363.
8. *Ibid.*, p. 356.
9. *Ibid.*; and E. Newton White, "What is Wrong With Northern Settlement?" *Canadian Forum*, 1929, pp. 410-412.
10. Oliver, *G. Howard Ferguson*, p. 324.
11. *Ibid.*, p. 241.
12. *Ibid.*, p. 252.
13. *Ibid.*, p. 284.
14. *Ibid.*, p. 334.
15. *Ibid.*, p. 163.
16. *Ibid.*, p. 165.
17. *Ibid.*, p. 165.
18. *Ibid.*, p. 167.
19. *Ibid.*, p. 168.
20. *Ibid.*, p. 278.
21. Neil McKenty, *Mitch Hepburn*, (Toronto: McClelland and Stewart Limited, 1967), p. 33.
22. Oliver, *G. Howard Ferguson*, p. 316.
23. *Ibid.*, p. 318.
24. *Ibid.*, p. 319.

Chapter Thirteen

Decline and Fall

1.

On December 17, 1930, two days after Henry's accession as Premier, Mitchell Frederick Hepburn replaced the stolid and unimaginative W.E.N. Sinclair as leader of the provincial Liberals. The man who was to dominate the thirties had now appeared on the scene. In good times Conservatives might easily have disposed of Hepburn, and without him they might have survived the depression. The combination, however, was too much for their leader, and in four years he was out.

George Stewart Henry was fifty-nine years old when he succeeded Ferguson. A Bachelor of Arts, a lawyer and a graduate of the Ontario Agricultural College, he had almost every credential that appealed to established Conservatism. He was the owner of a well-run farm, the president of a large dairy company and a substantial Toronto figure in life insurance and finance. A member of the provincial legislature since 1913, he had won his spurs with Hearst and been a power beside Ferguson through seven years in office. Affable and well liked, he brought with him to the Premiership the views of a man of money and an aura of times past. Too close to business for a man so deep in politics, he was to suffer from that connection. Henry carried the weight of the years of social apathy that had distinguished Ferguson's government, and in a time of vast new needs he could not find means to meet them. Neither could anyone else on the federal or provincial scene but Hepburn found the slogans.

Born on the prosperous farm of "Bannockburn" near St. Thomas, Hepburn had blown up his schoolroom stove with firecrackers at the age of eight. He had left high school under the threat of expulsion, accused of throwing an apple at Sir Adam Beck's hat. With his

283

education concluded, he had gone next to a bank and was of age to enter the air force toward the close of the First World War. The young trainee, however, was late for active service, and the demobilized former bank clerk did not return to his ledgers. Hepburn's post-war years were spent on the family farm, which he improved, diversified and expanded with unrelenting vigour.

At the same time a family taste for politics began to assert its influence. Entering the U.F.O. as a radical-minded farmer, "Mitch" was soon known. He became more widely known during the dying years of the farm movement as a Liberal champion of reform. In 1926, standing for Elgin West, he was elected to the federal parliament as a supporter of Mackenzie King. Thirty years old, a brilliant, witty and charismatic campaigner, he seemed to be valued by King and he survived the fall of the party. In the election of 1930, though R.B. Bennett's Conservatives were swept to federal power, Hepburn kept his seat as a Liberal in opposition.

In the same year, and still a federal member, he replaced Sinclair at the head of the provincial party. He was cooling to Mackenzie King and he was discontented with his prospects in the federal opposition. As Liberal leader in Ontario, though he was still in opposition, he was a new, dynamic force. Through the next four years, without a seat in the legislature and declining all that were offered, he mounted an assault on Torydom that revived his own party. Through the same years the struggling Henry challenged him to accept an acclamation, enter the provincial House and "quit shouting from behind the barn."[1] When Hepburn emerged, however, he had chosen his own time. The fate of the Conservative party was written broad on the north, on the gloomy rural south and in the grey drift of misery that blanketed the towns and cities.

2.

On the southern farms, as the blight of depression settled, all prices fell. By 1931 the farmer's return for his products had decreased by 50 per cent from the level of five years earlier. There was no money for implements so mechanization stopped. The back payments on old implements and the instalments due on mortages became the farmer's nightmare. The moratoria began, holding off the creditor and preserving the family farm; but piling debt on the future. The land remained fertile; Ontario was free of the savage drought in the west, and meat, cheese, vegetables and carload shipments of apples went to the stricken prairies. Yet they were a disposal of surplus products, a denial even in themselves of the value of work and land. Southwest rural Ontario, the luckiest part of the province, became straitened, resentful, static and diminished in all its hopes.

From 1930 to 1933 the north seemed to be emptying itself of angry and workless people. The demand for all minerals, with the one exception of gold, declined with the demand for pulpwood. The timber output in some areas fell by 70 per cent and employment was reduced by half. For those who remained in the camps, working conditions deteriorated as employers cut their losses. Huts became older and filthier, rations meagre and bad and hours of work were lengthened in defiance of regulations. Through three winters, from 1930 to 1933, "jobless camps" established by the provincial government were strung out along the lines of the northern railways. The workers lived under canvas, eight men to a tent, each tent with a board floor and a stove. To the claim of the opposition that it was employing slave labour the government replied that the men did not complain. By comparison with many others, they had few grounds for complaint. They were paid better and were fed better than the gaunt men with families subsisting on the dying farms. For these there was evacuation, the hope of pick-and-shovel work with one of the southern road gangs or the weekly voucher for relief.

Between 1929 and 1939 the drop in value of manufactured products was over 50 per cent, from $2,020,000,000.00 to $958,000,000.00. Wholesale trade, retail trade, the work of selling and the work of distribution followed the statistics down. The sickening slide, though it was worst in the larger centres, extended gradually to all. As the wheels stopped in one plant the workers took to the streets, to be met by "No Help Wanted" signs at other factory gates. Some of them left for new towns, often riding the freights, and found no welcome there. Wherever they went the queues of clerks and factory hands and shabby former businessmen were somehow there before them, resenting those with work, resenting the strange outsider who had come in search of work and doubly resenting those with foreign accents. Most of them were waved off, day after dreary day, united by the bond of hunger. By the end of 1933 Ontario had 400,000 people on direct relief, subsisting on an average weekly food allowance of $4.22 per family. "The meat voucher serves for only one or two meals; hence the relief recipients are practising vegetarians most of the week."[2]

In those years almost 12 per cent of Ontario's population descended to helpless want. They were to be more years in recovering, though the turn for the better began in 1934. They did not suffer in health if statistics can be believed. The general condition of the province was reported better than before. In 1933, however, the birth rate fell to the lowest point recorded. Men were away at work camps and women caring and worrying over meagrely fed children in flats, hovels and tenements that were not repaired or renewed. The confident years of progress had come to a dragging stop. In 1933, in twenty-five Ontario cities, the number of building permits issued was one-eighth the total of 1930.

Around the mass of the workless was the flow of normal life, curtailed but going on. The privileged complained of taxes and bemoaned the reduction of dividends, but dined and played as usual. With reduced prices and living costs the people who remained at work, even on lower incomes, were not so badly off. Some were better off. Yet they lived in fear of the workless who were rivals for the same job and overawed by the employer who had the job at his disposal. The employer feared too, for his business, profits, position and the old order and security that the times were eating away. Communism and socialism, those foreign indistinguishables, had come to Ontario in the wake of the First World War, and were here again with the depression. New and strange men were muttering to the men in queues, talking on stumps and street corners and even in universities. They were being listened to by the young, who were emptied out of the schools or sometimes kept in the schools because they were the least wanted of all. Fear, frustration and anger were infecting provincial life, and their breeding-place was the mass at its lowest level. The 12 per cent were a society within society that reproached and strained the whole.

They were set off from workers and they were linked not only by the bond of hunger but by common humiliation. The recipient of a relief voucher had first to surrender his liquor permit and his licence plates and driver's licence if he had managed to keep his car. In most cases his telephone was disconnected. Nothing was allowed to the man for cigarettes or tobacco or haircuts or a newspaper; still less to the woman for such frivolities as lipstick. If the sink in the kitchen stopped or coal or wood or a doctor's care was needed, a grudging welfare office must be persuaded to supply the voucher. Any job taken, a job offered and refused, or any discovered dribble in the way of outside earnings brought instant stoppage of relief.

The tensions dividing society fragmented the workless families.

There are innumerable quarrels and bickerings, (wrote Hugh Garner, speaking of Toronto's Cabbagetown,) drunken fights, sordid tragedies. There are the quarrels of worn-out parents with their idle and blasé sons and daughters who, unable to find work, must needs lie about the house all day sunk in cynical boredom.[3]

Children were kept from school for lack of clothes, or went ashamed and mutinous in hand-me-downs from the agencies. Nor were those agencies themselves, though they supplied basic needs, contributors to human pride.

There are benches around the walls where shoes may be tried on. These are unnecessary as none of the shoes ever fit. The attendant ties up the order in brown wrapping paper and the recipient hurries from the office and down the street, looking straight ahead until he is clear of the neighbourhood.[4]

The T. Eaton Company, generous in supplying welfare to straitened members of its staff, made sure that the help was needed. Piecework wages were cut, the girls clocked by stop-watches, and disciplined or laid off if they could not maintain their output. With one line, where the price paid to the girl for producing a single piece came out to 33¾ cents, the fraction was lopped off in favour of the company.[5] Even so, it was not only at the department stores or among the great employers of the cities that meanness added to division.

"The eats are so high that a poor man can not afford it." The letter was one of thousands descending on R.B. Bennett, and it came to the Prime Minister from once-rich Lincoln county:

Do you know it is just a fright here in Grimsby the way the poor people are used. When they do get work from farmers which is not very often all they will pay is 10¢ an hr. But now it has got so you can not get a job anywheres. The farmers will offer a married man to keep his family on all is 1¢ for picking up apples a pack, it has got to be something done as people can not live on that ... why not put some of these foreigners and Indians in their own country and give a white man some show ... if we have any government at all why not they look into it as our country is overrun by foreigners ...[6]

As poignant and less thought-of was the case of working women, fewer in numbers than the labouring class, above the level of the factory girl and past the resilience of youth. A one-time secretary-stenographer of a company that had gone bankrupt wrote to Bennett from Hamilton:

I have applied for every position that I have heard about, but there were always so many girls that it was impossible to get work. So time went on and my clothes became very shabby ... first I ate three very light meals a day; then two and then one. During the past two weeks I have eaten only toast and drunk a cup of tea every other day. In the past fortnight I have lost 20 pounds ... Today I went to an office for an examination and the examiner just looked me over and said – I am afraid, Miss, you are so awfully shabby I could never have you in my office.

I was so worried and frightened that I replied somewhat angrily – Do you think clothes can be picked up in the street?

Well – he replied – lots of girls find them there these days.[7]

287

What happened to the lone woman or the apple-picker in Grimsby no one knows today. They were merged with the many thousands for whom faith in Conservative government, or faith in any government, gave way to reckless cynicism and a distracted cry for change.

3.

The drab record of agriculture through the years of the Henry government was relieved by one advance. In 1931 the reorganization of the dairy industry, long opposed and delayed, began with the establishment of the Ontario Marketing Board. By 1932 there was a five-year plan in being and the farm co-operatives were determined to make it work. With world markets restricted and competition increasing, higher standards were required. So were better cattle, better production and packaging and controlled economies in shipping. There was no hope of that while independent farmers and smaller milk producers went on in their old ways, poorer than they ever had been. They were to be helped with government loans but they were to be forced to improve their herds, comply with sanitary and other regulations and deliver their milk to the board. The transformation was slow, difficult, expensive and it was made in the face of the depression. As usual, it was much complained of and fought hard at the time; but the result in a few years was a more efficient industry based on larger plants.

In the north, between 1931 and 1934, something like $15,000,000.00 was spent in support of the old policies of encouraging and maintaining settlement. The Temiskaming and Northern Ontario was completed to Moosonee, partly to provide relief work. Neither the arrival at James Bay nor familiar calls to the homesteader nor pleadings with the unemployed could bring many to the north; the increasing drift was southward. Northern agriculture, moreover, plagued by soil and climate, was only part of the vast general dilemma. It was linked with the bankrupt paper mills, the idled mines and pulpwood camps, the declining traffic on the railways and the sullen thousands on relief.

"Never in the history of the great forest products industry," said a government report for 1931, "has there been more wide-spread discontent and uncertainty."[8] Sawmills closed as the timber cut declined, and the yards of dealers were piled with unsold lumber. Government revenues were reduced from $4,000,000.00 in 1930 to $1,000,000.00 in 1933, and all forest services went down at the same rate. Research work was halted, reforestation delayed and fire protection cut to the bare bone. The result in 1933 was 2,073 fires – the worst year on record – yet there seemed to be no breakout from an increasingly vicious circle. The rate of loss was appalling, but the government was spending on the forests a third more than it received.

The pulpwood picture was blacker still. By 1932 Henry was sombrely reporting that the United States could supply itself with all but some 600,000 tons of its newsprint requirements. The Canadian export market had been more than cut in half, and there were potential foreign competitors even for what remained. Canadian pulp and paper mills, almost all of them close to the edge of bankruptcy, fought for the dwindling orders, fought to decrease their payrolls and fought to increase efficiency. They were blocked, however, on every hand by the economics and the politics that had brought them into being. The closing of small mills meant death for the communities they supported, and that course the government could not accept. Efficiency in large mills meant new modern equipment, but labour-saving devices reduced the number employed. Men who were out of work and men on reduced pay were a seething mass of trouble across the whole of the north. The one possible remedy remained what it had always been: to accept the reduced market, combine and pro-rate production and agree on a fixed price. But it was no remedy at all to mills fighting for their lives; there was always the American pressure to drive prices down. Pro-rating agreements and agreements to hold prices were forced on companies and accepted and broken as soon as made.

Upon all this, intruding in a new aspect, came the ever-evolving issue of hydro-electric power. In 1932 the Conservative federal government revived the question of the seaway and prepared to approach the Americans. First, however, it approached the Ontario government and settled the question of power rights in line with Ferguson's principles. In July 1932, when the St. Lawrence Deepwater Treaty was signed though not ratified by Canada and the United States, it would have been a great victory for Ontario in terms of the 1920s. Henry was able to announce that when the St. Lawrence seaway was completed it would give the province an additional 1,000,000 horsepower of hydro-electric energy.

By that time, however, the problem was not with shortages but with a rapidly accumulating surplus. Ontario, in addition to her own production, had been provided with 750,000 horsepower which she was drawing at present from Quebec. Henry, moreover, had relieved the bondholders of the defunct Abitibi Pulp and Power Company by taking over their power site to produce another 300,000 horsepower for the industrial development of the north. He had looked "way ahead" as Ferguson had advised in his day, but Ferguson's day was past.

It was now Hepburn's day, at least on the provincial stumps, and he pointed to the effect of the depression's onset. From the beginning of the 1930s, as power potential rose, consumption had begun to decline. Industrial growth, the expansion of municipal services, and the electrification of the farms were all steadily reduced. Demand estimated in the glowing terms of prosperity became halved in actual use. Between 1931 and 1934 municipal consumption ran at about 65 per cent of what had been projected. In 1932 it was estimated that 30 per cent of the electric motors in Toronto were standing idle.

To Hydro engineers the condition was difficult but temporary and would soon correct itself. To Hepburn's Liberals, however, it was an irresistible issue. Ontario was importing power for which there was no present use, under long-term contracts made when the price was high. It could not reduce the inflow, and for all Henry's efforts it could not get lower rates from the Quebec companies. It had joined with the federal government in the St. Lawrence seaway project, which would flood the province with new power and load it with more debt. Worse than that, the Premier himself had been one of the rescued bondholders in the deal with Abitibi. Under Hepburn's hands, when the government went to the polls, power policy presented itself as folly tinged with scandal.

4.

The social work of the depression years centred on the problem of relief. Workers from closed factories were walking the city streets, desperate to feed their families. Single men were drifting from town to town, restless, resentful, dangerous. Concern for health, working conditions or general standards of life gave way to the first necessity of providing food and shelter.

In the year 1931-1932 over $25,000,000.00 was spent in Ontario to provide direct relief, with the Dominion and provincial governments contributing half the amount. The remaining half was to be paid by the municipalities, but they could not carry the load. Of 900 Ontario municipalities some 550, wholly or partly on relief, were required not only to support their own needy but to provide for a flow of transients. The stranger looking for a job became more and more the outcast, frequently ushered to the town or city limits. Where he was provided for at all he was required to register as an alien at the charge of his home community. Inter-municipal billings for the support of each other's workless became a new source of quarrels and continuing aggravation.

By 1933, though nothing more could be wrung from the federal government, the province's share of relief payments had risen from a quarter to a third. It was never enough, and it was administered with a stricter hand. To get his monthly allowance of $16.00 per family for food, clothing and shelter the recipient was required to produce a residence certificate. Nor was that to become available to any new arrival; he was to be set on the road again. Municipal borrowings on debentures, merely to pay relief, had become an authorized practice. Hundreds of towns and cities and thousands of Ontario citizens were mortgaging the long future to maintain a dismal present.

"Back-to-the-land" movements had been tried and had largely failed. For the most part it was road-building that maintained the army of the idle. Through 1931 and 1932 some 40,000 men worked for varying periods on Ontario sections of the Trans-Canada Highway. In 1934, as election time approached, Henry announced that another 20,000 were to be taken off the relief rolls and handed their picks and shovels. He was prepared to pour new millions into a Provincial Recovery Scheme that as usual would build roads. This was a grey hope, however, in comparison with Hepburn's promises, and a government without ideas was opposed as well by the CCF.

The Co-operative Commonwealth Federation, born in Calgary in 1932, had commenced its invasion of Ontario. It had joined forces as it came with a creation of the universities, the League for Social Reconstruction. Many forces were merging, or at least attempting to merge, in this gathering of farmers, socialists, trade unionists and intellectuals who saw government as the prisoner of private industry in a continuum of greed and grab. Though it was flatly opposed to Communism, the CCF seemed an equal threat to businessmen, and to the businessmen in government, with its program for a "planned and socialized economy in which our natural resources and the principal means of production and distribution are owned and controlled by the people."[9]

Hepburn, for his part, was the very voice of the cresting rage of the depression. He echoed and evaded Communism, picked and chose among the plans of the CCF, and few of his own purposes had any form at all. Yet his words seemed clear enough, and were satisfying enough to his listeners. The overturning of the old order was to precede the building of the new. A swollen civil service was to be cut by 50 per cent. He would help the municipalities with relief funds from Ottawa, cut taxes with one hand and balance the budget with the other. Unemployment, the stubbornest of all problems, was somehow to be wiped out. "There will be no more Lieutenant Governors in this province . . . until we get out of the present period of depression."[10] People's government would return with all its stern simplicities, and the luxurious ways of legislators be curbed with a hard hand. "If we are elected we are going to line up all the limousines at Queen's Park and sell them to the highest bidder."[11] Pudgy, charming, bibulous, and already in frail health, he professed to be storming the walls of privilege on behalf of the locked-out.

The government was faced, in Henry's mind, with a triple-pronged attack, by enemies he lumped together. "We are passing through a critical period in our history . . . which has destroyed in many countries the basis of credit and engulfed the world in a vortex of disorder." The CCF, as revolutionary as Communism, advanced a program "that might have been framed in Russia." From all sides the demands and the new ideas left Henry breathless. Delegates from the unemployed had "demanded of me in my office" such grotesque impossibilities as family allowances of $20.00 per week, unemployment insurance to yield an equivalent sum and "relief to everyone, citizen or not."[12] The demands, the Premier calculated, would mean an annual expenditure of some $80,000,000.00 against a revenue of $54,000,000.00 and they were made by "a section of the community whom, apparently, Mr Hepburn would take under his all-embracing wing."[13] In the face of that, when the parties went to the hustings, Henry called for the return of stable government. He was to find on June 19 that he had sounded the call in vain.

5.

Two other issues figured in the provincial election, and the already-doomed government had contrived to make the worst of them. Liquor consumption, as a result of hard times, had fallen off by more than 20 per cent. There was a rising cry, however, for beer and wine by the glass, to be sold in taverns and hotels. The drys resisted as usual, while the wets claimed that if cheaper and softer beverages were made more easily available the sale of the hard package goods would be still further reduced. If Henry had any view, on either side of the argument, it was not clear when he acted.

During the final session of the legislature in March of 1934 he introduced his measure. It provided for the sale of beer and wine by the glass, but reserved decision for the people. All constituencies were to pronounce by local option and no change would be effective until the new policy was confirmed, by way of a provincial election. When the election came in June wets and drys were almost equally aggravated, and Hepburn met the straddle with a regal gesture of contempt. The government, he said, was making "a desperate effort to becloud the more important issues confronting our people." The "beer and wine act," if he became Premier, would be proclaimed without amendment.[14] He did become Premier, promptly redeemed his promise, and liquor retired through his time to the fringe of public affairs.

The many-faceted schools issue was equally damaging to the government. Through Henry's years, as depression stalked the province, grants, salaries and teaching staff were all drastically reduced. Secondary schooling suffered and consolidation in the primary system came from sheer necessity. The smaller rural boards were forced to close their schools and gradually merge in larger township groupings. By 1934, with attendance generally declining and teachers looking for employment, Normal Schools were reducing their annual output. The stringent years, moreover, always worst for the separate schools, renewed familiar claims.

By 1930 the Catholic Taxpayers Association had become a movement supported by bishops and led by the "brilliant and choleric"[15] Martin J. Quinn, an Ottawa lawyer. Its demands for a secondary school system and a redivision of taxes circulated throughout the province and were echoed from many pulpits. It was claimed that a quarter of a million Catholics were mobilized behind the movement while the diminishing forces of Orangeism, always opposed to change, were set at 50,000.

Both figures were Quinn's, and were subject to some dispute. Whatever the number of Orangemen, they had thousands of other Protestants standing in strong support. Nor were all Catholics united. A good many of them, it was said, tired of the endless controversy and now sceptical of improvement in their own impoverished system, were "hoping that the separate schools will peacefully die."[16]

That solution, however, could never be accepted by the church, nor by the majority of Catholic laymen nor the vocal Martin Quinn. Henry, battered from both sides through his four years in office, was finally driven to adopt the well-worn course. On March 30, 1934, in the last hours of his last session, he announced that the issue of tax sharing would be embodied in a series of questions and submitted again to the courts. Hepburn, out on the stumps, had one large banality in answer to that manoeuvre. "I'm a Protestant, a Mason and a Knight of Pythias, but I do believe in fairness to our Catholic friends."[17] The friends on election day responded to some effect, as Henry noted later. "The entire north," he wrote, "has deserted us under the influence of the Church. In fact, in our group of seventeen which we now muster, there is no representative of the Roman Catholic Church."[18]

Notes

1. McKenty, *Hepburn*, p. 51.
2. Hugh Garner, "Toronto's Cabbagetown," *Canadian Forum*, June, 1936.
3. *Ibid.*
4. *Ibid.*
5. Michiel Horn, ed., *The Dirty Thirties* (Toronto: Copp Clark, 1972), pp. 122-126, quoting evidence from the Committee on Price Spreads.
6. As quoted in L. M. Grayson and Michael Bliss, eds., *The Wretched of Canada* (Toronto: University of Toronto Press, 1971), p. 58.
7. *Ibid.*, p. 83.
8. *Canadian Annual Review,* 1932, p. 141.
9. *The CCF in Ontario: A Party of Protest,* unsigned term paper in files of Peter Oliver, p. 2.
10. McKenty, *Hepburn,* p. 55.
11. *Ibid.*
12. *C.A.R.*, 1933, pp. 135-136.
13. *Ibid.*
14. *C.A.R.*, 1934, p. 176.
15. Walker, *Catholic Education and Politics in Ontario*, p. 354.
16. *Ibid.*, pp. 369-370.
17. McKenty, *Mitch Hepburn*, p. 56.
18. Walker, *Catholic Education and Politics in Ontario*, p. 410.

Chapter Fourteen

"Interesting times"

1.

On June 10, 1934, Hepburn was sworn to office as the eleventh Premier of the province. He came to a pruned legislature, reduced for the sake of economy from a hundred and twelve to a total of ninety members. Of these ninety Hepburn had sixty-six. Allied with him under Harry Corwin Nixon, who had been Drury's Provincial Secretary, were four survivors of the United Farmers movement, now Liberal-Progressives. There was one remaining member of the UFO itself, an ambiguous Independent; and the CCF "busy around the clock, our evenings filled with speeches, our days with executive meetings and pamphlet writing," had one seat for its work.

"We are in for interesting times," said the defeated George Henry, and he did not stay long to endure them.[1] His seventeen Conservatives, as the official opposition, were a numb, fragmented rump, disillusioned and rebellious. By 1935 the Liberal win in Ontario had been followed by a federal victory and Mackenzie King was back. William Earl Rowe, who had sat for Dufferin-Simcoe and served in Bennett's cabinet, became available for the provincial field. At forty-two, as a farmer and a cattle-breeder and a man with business leanings, he appealed to old Conservatives as a safe but younger Henry. In 1936, elected to replace the leader, he took the unenvied place.

Liberals came to office with the worst of the depression over, but the long, dragged-out aftermath obscured the promise of statistics. Recovering primary industry had huge losses to make up, factories reopened slowly with their staffs cut to the bone and thousands were still on relief. The idle were more impatient as other men found work, more rasped by long waiting and long unfilled needs and more than ever inclined to the strong solution. Yet it did not come with Hepburn. The Liberals proved to be conservative in their total rejec-

295

tion of Communism, their close rapport with business and their contempt for the CCF. The great promises of the stumps were redeemed with new economies and minor pyrotechnics. The limousines of cabinet ministers were duly auctioned off and the civil service reduced. Game wardens, bee-keepers, clerks and high officials were drastically weeded out, and even the Lieutenant-Governor, H. A. Bruce, put on notice. Chorley Park, his official residence in Toronto, was to be evacuated within three years, and Ontario House in London closed its doors at once. When groups of "Hunger Marchers" arrived at Queen's Park, they were met with a hearty welcome and provided with food and blankets, but they returned to homes and families in the same straits as before. The new government, like the old, was faced with enduring facts. It had not the funds and no plan for effective social assistance. By 1935, with the return of the federal Liberals, the dribble of funds from Ottawa to assist municipal relief was increased, but it was hard won and small. The real relief of the workless would come with improving times.

In 1934 Hepburn announced flatly that he was opposed to the St. Lawrence seaway. The view was convenient at the time, with a Conservative government in Ottawa, but it only hardened to a challenge with the return of Mackenzie King. Hepburn's dislike for King was born of contrasting temperaments, his manners were all his own, and like every provincial Premier facing local issues he resented federal authority which always seemed to intrude. Relief and unemployment, the power question and the seaway question created a mass of difficulties inviting co-operation. They were met instead with developing animosities and mutual exasperation. The quarrels begun by Ferguson were open and near at hand, and time was fruitful of others. By 1937, as major problems festered and rhetoric replaced planning, a federal-provincial war divided the Liberal party.

2.

Within the province, as life crawled back toward normal from the depths of the hard years, there was some renewal of spirit. Hope began to stir, pride to assert itself, and once again as in Whitney's day it was possible to think of symbols. On March 26, 1937, the legislature passed an Act asserting that: "The flower known botanically as the trillium grandiflorum and popularly known as the white trillium shall be adopted as and deemed to be the floral emblem of the Province of Ontario."[2]

It was one of the last acts of the last session before a provincial election. In October of that year the Hepburn government went to the polls again and received a second mandate, not much changed from the first. The Conservatives gained six seats but only three from Liberals; the major change was at the expense of minor parties. The CCF was deprived of its single beach-head and Nixon's Liberal-Progressives reduced from six to two. The province seemed to be regrouping itself behind the two older parties, and was obviously inclined at the moment to support the one in power.

In agriculture generally, and in the reorganization of dairying, the farm co-operatives and the government had worked well together. In 1938, faced with a rising cry from urban centres, they combined in a new step. The pasteurization of milk, compulsory for export products, was also made compulsory for deliveries in the domestic market. The measure increased production costs for thousands of small farmers, and again like earlier advances was fiercely opposed for a time. Yet within two years, it was said to have reduced deaths from bovine tuberculosis by something like 20 per cent.

Gold production in Ontario continued its steady rise, and the output of 2,378,503 fine ounces in 1936 became over 3,000,000 in 1939. It was the bright spot in a generally uncertain picture, and was seen as such by Hepburn. The great gold magnates, lightly taxed and always with the ear of government, became the Premier's too-close friends. Iron mining, also, was helped by some force-feeding in 1936. Substantial bounties reopened the Helen mine, revived Algoma Steel and gave it a voice with government that rivalled the voice of gold. Copper, nickel and silver remained wavering factors, with the hopeful advance of one year followed by retreat the next.

In northern settlement there had been one decision, all too long delayed. "We are going out of the business of colonization," said Hepburn in 1935. "It is unsound in principle and simply throwing good money after bad."[3] The same economies of necessity were imposed on the provincial forests, with a cruder hand than Henry's and still more drastic results. The air, forestry and inspection services were all cut down to the point of demoralization. The fires of the 1936 season, another of the worst on record, were met with a budget halved from its former level. Politics intervened, replacing seasoned officials with Liberal party hacks, who shifted and fired experienced men and added to the downward drift. It was 1941, with the demands of a new war imposed on a dying government, before the trend was reversed and reorganization compelled.

The wrecked pulp and paper industry had been the crippling fact of the decade. Hepburn and Duplessis, the new Premier of Quebec, had as little success as Ferguson, Henry or Taschereau in coping with that problem. The real solution would await the coming of war and the surge of war demand. Behind the mills, however, were the

297

unemployed of the pulpwood camps, a reserve of idle men. In their case Hepburn was more effective.

Cancelling inactive grants, he threw the limits open to anyone prepared to cut. The thirty-year-old "manufacturing condition" had already had to be abandoned; pulpwood taken from the Crown lands of Ontario could once more go unprocessed for use in the United States. The protective barrier was down, American mills were demanding wood again, and there was an immediate rush to supply them. Between 1934 and 1936 the number of pulpwood operators in Ontario rose from 149 to 227, the number of camps from 282 to 557, and the number of men at work from 11,184 to 23,140. To that extent the discarding of older policies had reduced unemployment. It had also reversed the growth and eroded the very base of a large segment of the industry. With huge capacity idled in the province's own mills, the pulpwood camps were building up competitors. Conditions were back to those of the 1890s; Ontarians were cutting the logs, Americans were making the paper.

3.

As workers returned to the industrial plants and factories the labour movement itself began to revive. Within it by the middle thirties were the scars and memories of the depression, a considerable tinge of Communism and some of the hopes for socialism that were offered by the CCF. Above all was the hope of a stronger unionism that would be able to force change. Workers returned to their benches disgusted with the old order and hoping for better things. They were opposed by a farm community that was barely reviving itself, and more directly opposed by most of their own employers. Business was hard-pressed, fighting its way through still stagnant conditions and inclined to insist on "sacrifice" as a means to full recovery. For a little while, at least, wages should be kept low, working hours long and workers should remain unorganized in sturdy independence. On these grounds Communism, socialism and unionism were indiscriminately fought, while labour stubbornly reacted.

To demands for better wages the Hepburn government responded with one of its best acts. Arthur Roebuck, Attorney-General and Minister of Labour, and David Croll, Minister of Welfare, were strong ministers in the cabinet and both were friends of labour. In 1936, under their auspices, the Industrial Standards Act was placed on the statute books as the first approach to a minimum wage for men. It required a co-operation between employers, labour and government which was never fully effective but did promote advance. In selected large industries groups of the major employers, meeting with groups from their labour force, were empowered to negotiate wage and hour settlements and prescribe conditions of work. Once these standards were agreed to they were to be imposed with the authority of government on the whole body of the industry. Agreement was hard to come by and discipline often failed, but the sweatshop fringe of many Ontario industries was gradually pruned away.

Even as the act came in, however, the hope of peace with labour was well on the way out. From the northern industrial cities, where it was growing in the United States, the Congress of Industrial Organizations was seeping across to Canada, more by casual osmosis than by any set design. Workers in Canadian plants, attracted by the internationalism and the power of the C.I.O., were forming their own locals and claiming affiliation. They had occasional help from responsive American organizers, and a good deal more than they asked for from the Communists of Tim Buck.

> Our party, (Buck recorded,) had trained and developed a whole cadre of people who knew about unions and how to go about organizing them . . . the party men, even though they didn't work in the industry, would go out distributing leaflets, helping to organize the union.[4]

By 1936 Ontario was feeling the effects. In Cornwall that summer, at the textile plant of Courtauld's, there was a six-week strike by 1,800 men. Trouble followed at Kitchener, where there were tire and rubber plants, and worse trouble at Stratford. In February 1937, 1,500 furniture workers at a dozen points in the province walked off their jobs, closing some twenty factories. A month later at Sarnia a sit-down strike by foundry men brought violence and pitched battles. The rural south of the province was aroused, indignant and fearful, and the watchful eyes of industrialists detected a planned "invasion." Pulp, paper and mining men, and above all the gold barons, had fears of rampant unionism disrupting plants in the north. So had the Liberal Premier, the Bannockburn radical, who was still the friend of the farmer but even more of Bay Street. When the next strike broke at Oshawa it found Hepburn ready.

On March 31 Charles Millard, as president of the recently-formed Local 222 of the United Auto Workers, presented General Motors with a list of ten demands. They included the adoption of the forty-hour week, time-and-a-half for overtime, the recognition of shop stewards and the acknowledgment of Local 222 as an affiliate of the C.I.O. On April 8, when the demands were not granted, the men walked off their jobs.

On wages, hours and several of the other conditions the company had been willing to talk. The sticking point was recognition of the union. It had recently been formed in Oshawa and the president and chief organizer was a company employee. No fault was to be found with Millard's credentials; he was as vigorously anti-Communist as General Motors itself. What he represented, however, was acceptance by a major industry of the presence of the C.I.O., and the lines were drawn on that.

"We know what these agitators are up to," said Hepburn on April 9. "We were advised only a few hours ago that they are working their way into the lumber camps, the pulp mills and our mines. Well – that has got to stop and we are going to stop it."[5] So was George McCullagh, his rich young friend who had bought the *Globe and Mail*, with money made from gold. As a counsellor at Hepburn's elbow and a man with the public ear, McCullagh spoke for industry:

> The strike at Oshawa is minor compared with the national potentialities of its success. It is no secret that along with the motor industry, steel plants, pulp mills and the mines are in the contemplated line of march. If the Lewis agitators get a foothold this country will pay dearly.[6]

The fear of Communism was real enough and pervaded the whole province. It was linked quite inevitably with fear of the C.I.O. Tim Buck's agents, whether invited or not, were aiding and abetting the movement wherever they could elbow in. The real spectre, however, was that of collective bargaining, imposed by aggressive unionism and having the force of law. In the minds of the large industrialists there could be no truce with that, and the Premier shared their view. Spectacular, unpredictable and shouting for the people's cause, he prepared to put down the strikers.

He would use, he said, if necessary, "the full strength of the Provincial Police."[7] The force available proved to be seventy-five, and at Hepburn's urgent request a hundred mounted police arrived from Ottawa. They were still not enough but a second request was refused, and the rebuffed Premier returned the first contingent. With a new federal quarrel added to a lengthening list, he then proceeded to recruit his own army. Some 300 students and various assorted idlers were gathered in impromptu barracks awaiting the command to march. Talk of "Hepburn's Hussars" began to fill the newspapers, to be answered in other papers by talk of the "Sons of Mitches."[8]

Meanwhile, however, in Oshawa Millard and General Motors had resumed their prorogued discussions. While assembly lines were stalled and the men surly and idle, orders were arriving steadily. After seven lean years the prospect of lost business and competitors gaining ground was too much for the company. It was becoming too much for union men, to whom strike pay was unknown. On April 23 there was a partial meeting of minds; the Hussars demobilized in Toronto, the pickets withdrew in Oshawa and men went back to work.

They had won the eight-hour day and established a minimum wage. Time-and-a-half for overtime was also part of the agreement. On the larger issues, however, they seemed to have been beaten back. There was no acceptance of shop stewards or of formal organization. Charles Millard was recognized only as an employee who had been given leave to negotiate and speak for his fellow workers. It was incidental in the company's view that the workers had formed a union, and there was blank and total silence regarding the C.I.O. It remained the disreputable parent, foreign, American, Communist, not to be named in documents or acknowledged to exist in Canada.

The political and military antics appealed not only to industry but to most rural voters. They assured the Liberals of victory in the October provincial election. They also divided the Conservatives and diminished Earl Rowe, but they cost Hepburn two of his best ministers, since Croll and Roebuck both were dismissed from the cabinet. Working people, said Croll:

> have a right to form their own associations for the purpose of collective bargaining ... have the privilege of joining the lawful union of their own choice ... if they, in their wisdom and their knowledge of the conditions under which they work, consider that they should make the final resort to a strike, then that too is their right; and having struck, they shall not be molested if they picket peacefully and within the law.[9]

It was the new note that emerged in the later 1930s, heard in the Dominion parliament and demanding Hepburn's concurrence in spite of his federal feuds. Not only collective bargaining but unemployment insurance became law in his time. The C.I.O., divesting itself of Communism and recruiting Charles Millard, resumed and widened its advance. Oshawa, like Bannockburn, was a battle with large consequences, but they weighed out eventually on the side of labour.

4.

Earl Rowe, who had lost a provincial election and been vaguely sympathetic to the claims of the C.I.O., went down as a political casualty in 1938. Conservatives turned to another man who appeared to be in tune with the times. George Drew, even before the election, with his broad, inclusive antipathy to Communism, socialism and unionism, had seemed closer to Hepburn than he was to his own leader. He had actually been close enough that, hoping to enlist Drew in his war with Mackenzie King, Hepburn had proposed a coalition of parties. That was not to be, but it remained a thought in the background and a confusing current in the House as Drew succeeded Rowe.

George Alexander Drew was two years older than Hepburn and a world away from the other man in tastes, talents and character. Born in Guelph of an old Loyalist family, he had followed the route of the elite, through Upper Canada College and the University of Toronto to take a degree in law at Osgoode Hall. He had entered the army at the beginning of the First World War, distinguished himself as an artillery officer and returned with a serious wound. That, eventually recovered from, served to enhance the background. His post-war rank of colonel, his accustomed air of command and his red and blue artillery tie were sign and symbol of the man. The inescapable aura was of a military stuffed shirt but it was worn by a fighting soldier.

Mayor of Guelph by the time he entered his thirties, Drew was a man of old central Ontario and revealed some of its strains. He disliked separate schools, opposed the claims of the French and was inclined to stand on familiar Protestant grounds. As an army man who approved of army methods, he was an authoritarian and a centralizer and a believer in the firm hand. Though he was soon prominent as a Conservative party organizer he disliked the disorder of politics, with its backslapping, its bootlicking, and general inefficiency. The stumps that Hepburn loved, Drew thoroughly detested; well-groomed and immaculate, he kept his distance from the mob. In the case of the Liberal leader he kept his distance too. Hepburn soon recognized, and was not allowed to forget, that in spite of new expediencies there were two parties in the House. That fact, even before Rowe's departure, Drew had helped make clear.

Hepburn provided an issue in his handling of the Catholic taxpayers and the claims of separate schools. He had come to office in 1934 with the hopeful support of Martin J. Quinn. If he had not rejected the help, however, he had promised nothing in return. "I have never been asked to make, nor have I ever made, any pledge to them."[10] As the Ottawa lawyer presented his election bill he was met with the reasonable response of a man in office. "I will hear the other side of the story before acting."[11]

Action came, however, in 1936, and it was at least vigorous enough. "An inequality exists,"[12] conceded Hepburn, and two portentous bills descended on the legislature. One provided for a

Catholic secondary school system, the other for a revised sharing of corporation taxes, and the second was debated first. By the time it was passed at the end of a six-day battle, the secondary schools proposal had slipped unheard to limbo. In the House, the parties and the province there was already noise enough.

The tax-sharing bill was not merely divisive but complicated beyond belief. Corporations, required to allot their taxes, were now obliged to distinguish between Catholic and Protestant ratepayers. If they had no knowledge of the beliefs and status of their shareholders the bill compelled them to obtain it. Thousands of shareholders were disinclined to give it. Where there could be no classification there would have to be a municipal assessment, determining the status of ratepayers and dividing the taxes of shareholders between Protestant and Catholic schools. Obviously a lawyer's dream and an accountant's nightmare, the bill brought down on Hepburn the wrath of the opposition and a threat from George Drew. Clumsy, utterly unworkable and wrong in its basic purpose, the act would be expunged from the books when the Conservatives came to power.

In the event the Liberals forestalled them. Within eight months, while the slippage of votes from the party became more and more apparent, thousands of appeals and counter-appeals entangled the tax collectors. The wild complexity of the provisions not only distracted school boards but defeated the act's intent; even some of the separate boards complained of reduced income. Martin Quinn and his supporters raised the cry for revision, but throughout the province generally the dominant mood was clear. On March 24, 1937, Drew's prediction was anticipated. With eighty members in the House, a subdued Hepburn joined Liberals and Conservatives in a unanimous vote for repeal.

Through the rest of Hepburn's regime there was no more schools' legislation. In 1939, to the general relief of the bishops, Quinn resigned as head of the Catholic Taxpayers and cooler heads took over. Still with an inadequate tax base and no support for secondary education, Catholics moved to regroup themselves and pursue limited objectives. Improvement of existing schools was a first essential; and means were gradually provided through increased provincial grants. Between Protestant and Catholic educators, though principle remained an issue, attitudes became more flexible and there was a search for common ground. By 1942, as effective liaison developed between the church, government and school boards, recognition came. An able priest and teacher, charged with the supervision of all Catholic schools, became a provincial official in the Department of Education.

When Hepburn came to office Ontario had surplus power and was committed to the St. Lawrence seaway. By the time he left he had reversed both conditions. The threat of waterborne transport as a competitor to roads and railways had been staved off for a time. Ontario was paying less for power imported from Quebec. She had, for what it was worth, asserted her independence in the face of federal authority. But the mix of many factors, like the mixed motives of the achievement, left her development stalled.

In 1934, having deposed Henry's Conservatives, the Premier rejected the seaway. In 1935, with the Power Commission Act, he revoked the contracts made with the Quebec companies. The act, though not proclaimed and highly questionable in law, was intended as a club to enforce reduced rates. It was successful with one company but the others stood on their rights, and by the end of 1936 the Ontario courts had upheld them. The province was faced with judgments totalling over $4,000,000.00 and was still accepting power that it professed not to want.

By 1937, though another of the smaller companies had been forced to reduce its rates, the judgments on the two larger ones had been sustained by the Court of Appeal. Nor was the legal decision the worst of the emerging problems. The chameleon of electric energy supply was changing colour again. Business was picking up, motors and wheels turning. Once more, as an inconvenience to industry and a political disaster to the government, there were hints of a power shortage.

Concealing that prospect as a state secret, Hepburn called and won the October election. Within another month, back at the bargaining table in a considerably sobered mood, he gave a little and gained a good deal more. Out-of-court settlements removed the weight of the judgments, and all the recalcitrant companies agreed to a new price. The reduction, generally, was from $15.00 to $12.50 per kilowatt hour, and it was claimed by exultant Liberals that over the life of the contracts it represented a saving of some $78,000,000.00.

The settlement, however, merely reversed the dilemma and opened a wider quarrel. With all supplies assured Ontario was over-bought; in spite of recovering industry she had substantial surplus power. The northern American states, close to the Niagara system, were always a receptive market, and late in 1937 Hepburn informed Mackenzie King that Ontario wished to export 90,000 horsepower.

This was an international affair requiring negotiation, which King as usual deferred, thus infuriating Hepburn. On January 21, 1938, the Premier returned to the charge with a formal application to export not 90,000 but 130,000 horsepower. Since he had secured the support of Premier Maurice Duplessis of Quebec beforehand, and since the two central provinces were the ones directly concerned, he had made it difficult for the Prime Minister to refuse. The American government, however, made the refusal for him. The shocked Hepburn, forever after suspecting an intrigue by King, was informed that the United States would not allow the importation of power on the terms offered by Ontario. Nor would it consider any agreement that did not include the seaway.

Back of it all were questions of larger scope. Ontario had continued its studies on the feasibility of diverting water from the Hudson Bay watershed into the Great Lakes system and so going "back to Niagara" for new resources of power. The Americans, however, had made their studies too. To the United States the only acceptable power plan must include the development of inland navigation and must deal as a unit with the Great Lakes, Niagara and the entire St. Lawrence basin. There would be huge expense in the project for a still-depressed Ontario which wanted to develop power at its own convenience and pace. It was already burdened with debt and over-burdened with railways, the competitors of water transport. Hepburn had some reason, apart from personal pique, for being wary of the scheme.

Nevertheless, the future was taking shape. In May 1938, Cordell Hull, the American Secretary of State, submitted a draft treaty which was generally approved by King. Under its terms both the Great Lakes system and the St. Lawrence River basin were to be developed jointly for navigation and power by Canada and the United States. Ontario's rights were respected and she could delay spending on her own works until new demand required it. The United States, moreover, was prepared to import Ontario's surplus power, to permit diversion from the Hudson Bay watershed and to stop the "Chicago water steal" at the southern end of Lake Michigan. It was a generous series of proposals, later to prove too generous for some of the states concerned, yet the large hopes of the plan were encouraged by the President himself. In August 1938 Roosevelt travelled to Kingston, opened the Thousand Islands Bridge at Ivy Lea and spoke out for the seaway, rebuking "prophets of trouble." Hepburn, however, was not there to hear him. He was "not going to be swept off my feet by ballyhoo and propaganda"[13]; he could snub Roosevelt as effectively as he usually snubbed King. The seaway project he would not even discuss.

With that attitude the province entered the war. "There can be no power development along the St. Lawrence River," said Hepburn, "unless all the governments consent, and there will be no consent from my government."[14] By that time, however, the ailing, failing Premier had shrunk to a diminished obstacle. The demands of the war emphasized what future needs would be, and the seaway loomed as the one available answer. By the war's end, with that fact impressed on it, a power-starved Ontario would be urging the inception of the project.

6.

Inextricably involved with the power and seaway issues were other disputes in federal-provincial relations. Some rose out of the depression, some were part of the natural frictions of government and all reflected a federalism that was coping with new strains. To their real difficulties, moreover, was added the personal feud. Hepburn's political objective became the destruction of King, King's eventually to rid himself of Hepburn, and the national interest suffered. Few solutions were found, and the greatest problem was shelved.

Some imperative changes were made, forced by the needs of the depression. A sharing of personal income tax and a rearrangement of grants combined to relieve the tottering municipalities. Pensions for the blind came in as a federal-provincial measure. On unemployment insurance, proposed as a national scheme, Hepburn stood immovable, holding the provincial keys. "It is clear," he wrote to his good friend Maurice Duplessis on February 14, 1938, "that with the western provinces hopelessly bankrupt, any national scheme of unemployment insurance will have to be borne by the two central provinces."[15] He could well understand, he added, "the advantage it would be to the other provinces for them to raid the Federal treasury, particularly when Ontario and Quebec contribute 80% of the revenue."[16]

Allied with Quebec on the seaway question and adopting her views on others, he was then involved with an even larger issue. On August 14, 1937, the Dominion government had established by Order-in-Council a Royal Commission which was to undertake "a re-examination of the economic and financial basis of Condederation and of the distribution of legislative powers in the light of the economic and social developments of the last seventy years.[17]

Formidable enough in outline, the work involved a probing to the very roots of federalism. War, depression, social needs, and the growth of the industrial economy had created enormous changes and new demands. They were common to all provinces and they involved responsibilities that were beyond provincial means. In the matter of relief alone, between 1930 and 1937, the federal proportion of all funds distributed had been 46 per cent. It was more for the poorer provinces, less for Ontario and Quebec, but in all cases there was a vast tangle of book-keeping, a duplication of services and a blurring of old distinctions between federal and provincial authority. The general effect, moreover, was to establish a trend toward massive centralization. The source of money, becoming the source of power, was diluting provincial rights. It might be a necessary change, it was certainly a profound change, and there was more of that in prospect. Unemployment insurance had become a national necessity, as had national roads and nationally funded pensions, and glowering along the horizon were a host of new demands. They could not be met in the way of the founding fathers. The poor provinces demanded as much as the rich in social rights, security and living standards for their people. They could not be left forever to scramble for federal grants. Nor could even wealthy Ontario, in the light of the long future, exist on her present means.

The dilemma was posed to the Commission in its terms of reference. "Either new revenues must be allotted to them (the provinces) or their constitutional responsibilities and governmental burdens must be replaced, or adjustments must be made by both methods."[18] For Newton W. Rowell, now in his seventies and Chief Justice of Ontario, the attempt to solve the problem was to be a last public service. It was to be the same for Joseph Sirois, a distinguished notary of Quebec: and drawing from the universities as well as the civil service, it involved the work of some of the best brains in the country. The Rowell-Sirois Commission was to produce a famous report, almost as seminal as Durham's of a hundred years earlier. Out of it eventually were to come the transference of tax fields and the principles of equalization that would tend to strengthen and justify the whole federal system. It was not to bear those fruits, however, on the eve of a World War, nor in the time of Mitch Hepburn.

In May 1938 the Commissioners came to Toronto to hear Ontario's brief. They were met by a bristling Premier who had readied his ammunition. The provinces had not been consulted before the inquiry was launched. They were partners, not subordinates, allied in a federal pact which it was not necessary to change. Tax fields and methods of administration were within provincial domain, not to be interfered with by federal equalization:

> If it is proposed that readjustment be in the form of assigning more duties to an already overburdened central government, more power to a government that has already departed from the well-thumbed practices of parliamentary institutions, then ... we have but to look across the Atlantic to read the destiny of the Canadian people ... we are a stupid people if we imagine ourselves immune from the consequences of concentrating power in a few hands.[19]

In the rising shadow of Hitler and Mussolini, Hepburn detected King, rising beside them. He had decided the fate of the Commission, so far as Ontario was concerned. By 1939 the sick and aging Rowell was forced to resign as chairman and leave the work to his colleagues. The complete report appeared in May 1940, vast, compendious, challenging and lost in the fog of war. By that time, if there had been any hope of considering it, there was certainly no will.

Hepburn had reduced his government to a jumble of rancorous confusion and his own status to that of a national nuisance. Fretful, impotent, ill and often drinking heavily, he talked of joining the forces and sought appointments in England, a man looking for escape. For three years he had pursued an alliance with Drew, pursuing his war with King. He had recruited Alberta's William Aberhart, the Social Credit Premier, promoting ideas that cost him his friends on Bay Street. In January 1940, with no encouragement from Conservatives and to the vast dismay of Liberals, he had made his final cast.

Rising in the House across from Drew, he openly attacked King, his own national leader. In the terms of a resolution which he had scrawled out on a piece of yellow paper, he committed the government of the province to regret "that the federal government at Ottawa had made so little effort to prosecute Canada's duty in the war in the vigorous manner the people of Canada desire to see."[20]

To that move there could be only one response, and it was welcomed by Mackenzie King. Calling a general election, he returned with a smashing mandate which divorced Hepburn from any semblance of power. The Prime Minister, with the Premier of Ontario disposed of, could proceed to his own disposal of the Rowell-Sirois Report.

That came on January 14, 1941, when King sat down for discussions with all the provincial Premiers. He expected little and got less in the way of implementation. The huge complexity of the problems and the need for intensive study were actually the major obstacles. Hepburn loomed as another, but he was one in a field of many. Duplessis was in eclipse but Quebec remained herself, the province of the French minority, distrusting central power. British Columbia's T. D. Pattullo was much of Hepburn's mind and "Bible Bill" Aberhart, the rebuffed redeemer of Alberta, was by then his open ally. At the end of the second day the conference stood adjourned, with the recalcitrants claiming victory and King the master of the field. Whatever came to be implemented would be done by the federal hand, equipped with its wartime powers. Two days later Joseph Sirois died, Newton Rowell died the following November, and the report went to the vaults.

The federal-provincial discussions seemed almost irrelevant in the midst of total war. Ships, squadrons and divisions were scattered around the world, and hearts and minds went with them. Vast needs and urgencies, clearing men from the streets and drawing women from their homes, revived Ontario industry and extinguished unemployment. Machines and student workers, supplementing normal manpower, were driving the farms toward new peaks of production. There was no sparing of effort, there was better planning than there had been in the earlier war, and once again there was the grasp of centralization. Recruiting, training, arming, plans, policy and finance were all in the hands of an expanded federal government. By 1941 unemployment insurance was a national institution. By 1942 Ontario, like the other provinces, had ceded rights and tax fields. Personal income and corporation taxes were all to be collected by Ottawa, with a portion returned annually by way of fixed grants. It was the prescription of Rowell-Sirois, softened only by the condition that it was not to outlast the war. "We have reached," said Hepburn glumly, "the status of a county council."[21]

He was close to the end himself, and the federal-provincial warfare had disrupted his provincial party. Yet it had not helped Drew nor the Conservative party federally nor Arthur Meighen, the newly-elected leader. In February 1942, at the height of the first phase of the conscription crisis, dramatic evidence was provided of the return of a third force. The imposing Meighen, resigning his place in the Senate to obtain a federal seat, stood for a by-election in supposedly safe York South. Unopposed by Liberals, he was roundly and soundly beaten by the unknown Joseph Noseworthy, standing for the CCF.

By September 1942 the confusion of world alliances and shifting national policies seemed fully reflected in Ontario. With Russia a wartime partner, Communism was approaching respectability in some quarters. While George McCullagh stormed at the claims of socialism and Bay Street fought to defend the established order, Hepburn sat on platforms with the friends of Tim Buck. Drew rose in the middle, strong for national unity as the immediate first essential. His gorge rose at Communism and the socialism of the CCF, but he found much in their programs that could be given another name. He despised Mackenzie King but was prepared to damn and endure him while he wielded national power. Drew respected authority, approved of centralization and he was a man with time on his side. That, obviously, the present Premier was not.

On October 21, 1942, with no warning or consultation with the party, Hepburn resigned his post. Sweeping aside his caucus with imperial unconcern, he handed the leadership to Gordon Daniel Conant, who was then Attorney-General. He himself, however, was to remain as Provincial Treasurer, still on the trail of King. "We shall," he wrote Aberhart in one of a flood of truculent manifestos, "fight this King conspiracy to a finish."[22]

For six months the war within the war went on, distracting the sober Conant and fragmenting the Liberal party. The Treasurer sat in the cabinet or came and went as he chose, gradually coming to see himself as a treacherously displaced leader. On March 3, 1943, after a long series of complaints, invective and abuse, he informed Conant that he had gained the office of Premier through "the Hitler policy of setting up a Quisling government in Ontario."[23] That same day the Provincial Treasurer was out.

An election was now inevitable, but it was not to be fought by Conant. The party's choice, at a convention held in April, was the solid Harry Nixon, another of Ontario's cattle-breeders and a man of common sense. For a little over three months he was the new leader and Premier. He was not, however, the man for the mid-war years, still less for the future. The mind of the province under the distractions of politics was moving toward new conclusions. They were hardly formed as yet, but the trend was unmistakable. The CCF and its socialism, unacceptable to the farm movement, anathema to the older parties and long rejected by the trade unions, was once more gaining ground. Depression and vast inequities, war and wartime planning, had diluted the taint of Communism and the fear of social change. A "new order" of some kind had become the promise of the day. Ontario, like most of Canada, was asking the dangerous question: why should democracy be saved, the old democracy of the rich, powerful and privileged, if it was to remain the same society that had made the pre-war world?

The parties heard the question and Drew had evolved some answers, but they were barely answer enough. He proposed change and reform and an advance in social justice, but so did the CCF. It came out of the provincial election on August 4, 1943 as the second party in the province.

Only the vote of the farms had prevented it from being first, and nothing had saved the Liberals. The wrecked party of Hepburn would still have fifteen members, of whom he himself was one. But Drew with thirty-eight and the CCF with a total of thirty-four would be the new arbiters of change.

Notes

1. Oliver, *G. Howard Ferguson,* pp. 409-411.
2. Statutes of Ontario, Chapter 26, 1 Geo. VI, p. 92.
3. Nelles, *The Politics of Development,* p. 54.
4. Irving M. Abella, *American Unionism, Communism and the Canadian Labour Movement: Some Myths and Realities in The Influence of the United States on Canadian Development,* ed. Richard A. Preston (Durham N.C.: Duke University Press, 1972), pp. 213-214.
5. Richard M. Alway, *Mitchell F. Hepburn and the Liberal Party in the Province of Ontario,* M. A. thesis, University of Toronto, 1965, p. 117.
6. *Ibid.*
7. *Ibid.,* p. 114.
8. McKenty, *Mitch Hepburn,* p. 110.
9. Alway, *Mitchell F. Hepburn and the Liberal Party in the Province of Ontario.* pp. 124-125.
10. Walker, *Catholic Education and Politics in Ontario,* p. 404.
11. *Ibid.,* pp. 416-417.
12. *Ibid.,* p. 420.
13. Alway, *Mitchell F. Hepburn and the Liberal Party in the Province of Ontario,* p. 222.
14. McKenty, *Mitch Hepburn,* p. 153.
15. Alway, *Mitchell F. Hepburn and the Liberal Party in the Province of Ontario,* p. 244.
16. *Ibid.,* p. 245.
17. Donald V. Smiley, ed., *The Rowell-Sirois Report* (Toronto: McClelland and Stewart Limited, Carleton Library, 1963), p. 2.
18. Alway, *Mitchell F. Hepburn and the Liberal Party in the Province of Ontario,* p. 239.
19. *Ibid.,* pp. 249-250.
20. *Ibid.,* p. 298.
21. *Ibid.,* p. 342.
22. *Ibid.,* p. 353.
23. *Ibid.,* p. 361.

Chapter Fifteen

"There must be planning"

1.

Drew had carried his election in a province geared for war. Some 350,000 of its people were in the armed forces, the major part of its work force was producing military supplies and its life was governed by a federally-planned regime. Meat, butter, sugar and other goods had been rationed; there were no new automobiles, or stoves, refrigerators or home electrical equipment, and home building had stopped. Regulations and restrictions kept the peace in industry, controlled labour mobility and prescribed the supply and pricing of every article for sale. Yet unemployment was gone and a curtain of gloom was lifting, though there were bloody months ahead. The great campaign on the Atlantic had swung in favour of the Allies and the convoys were getting through. Armies, ships and airfleets were being assembled in England for the great return to France. The war was being won in Russia, it had already been won in North Africa; and the same radio that carried the clatter of politics was telling of Canadians in Sicily as election day came. The shape of victory was discernible and it was possible to look beyond it.

That Drew had done. His Twenty-Two Point Program was a counter-answer to socialism in facing the post-war world. Few of the ideas were new, and all and more than he offered was being offered by the CCF. The power of the appeal, however, was in the manner and confidence of the man. Firm for the British connection and resonant of old loyalties, he sounded familiar themes. He was concerned for the state of agriculture, for the preservation of resources and the development of manufacturing. In the midst of centralization he was insistent on provincial rights. Yet he promised co-operation in the federal plans for veterans and for the advance of social welfare. He had fought the C.I.O., but there were to be new relations with

312

labour, "recognizing at the outset the right of proper and enforceable legislation regarding collective bargaining."[1] Housing plans were to relieve present shortages and provide employment in construction. Health and education were to become primary concerns, with medical, dental and nursing care provided for the public schools. Technical education was to be given a new emphasis, and there would be large reorganization for the benefit of the municipalities. In addition to other burdens, a half-share of the school tax carried by local ratepayers would be taken over by the province.

Campaigning beside Drew, and already a rising man, was Leslie Miscampbell Frost, a Lindsay lawyer. As Provincial Treasurer, presenting his first budget, he echoed the tone of Drew:

> We are building not only for these times, we are planning for a greater population, for industrial expansion, for prosperous farms and for a happy and healthy people. We are laying the sure foundation for a greater and stronger Ontario.[2]

It was a new note in politics after the years of Hepburn's diatribes. Drew had no time for the auctioning-off of government limousines or the firing of surplus bee-keepers. In his election manifesto he had waved away the limp promises of Liberals and turned on the CCF.

> You will ask, (he said to his listeners,) whether the proposals I have placed before you can be put into effect. Having in mind the discouraging picture painted by the socialists, you will perhaps ask if it is possible to assure employment in this province after the war. My answer is an emphatic Yes! . . . . our danger in this province is not unemployment after the war, but rather a shortage of workers for the job which lies ahead.[3]

To the haunting memories of the 1930s and the fear of a new depression he opposed a graphic picture. Cities were lying in rubble, thousands of ships had been sunk, and 3,000,000 homes had been destroyed in Britain alone.

> Many human requirements made by the hands of man from raw materials have been destroyed. In these buildings there were tables, chairs, stoves, refrigerators, telephones, glass, wire and all the simple things needed by human beings everywhere . . . many of the raw materials required to replace those buildings and the things that were in them are not available in the British Isles . . . those ships were made of iron and steel. They too contained thousands of little things made by the hands of man . . .
> What does all this mean to us here in Ontario? It simply means that . . . an enormous demand for replacement after the war is ris-

313

ing every day ... Here in Canada, and right here in Ontario, are huge resources of the very raw materials which will be required everywhere throughout the world ... the simple truth is that all this terrible destruction is creating such opportunities for our young men and women as they have never known before. But there must be planning if we are to be ready for the tasks which lie before us.[4]

Within three months of his election Drew was at work in London. As buzz-bombs coursed over him in the last stages of the blitz, he selected a new Ontario House, co-ordinated provincial war work and paved the way for immigrants. The Ontario Services Club, which he opened in Piccadilly, was to attract many to the province before it closed its doors. The War Brides Bureau, established at the same time, was a counsellor to British wives who would be coming home with their men. The new Premier himself, seen everywhere and speaking everywhere, was the greatest salesman of all, marvelled at by another eminent Canadian. "Look, George," Lord Beaverbrook is reported to have said, "is Ontario a part of Canada or Canada a part of Ontario?"[5]

That would be a hovering question through much of Drew's career. He came back to Ontario resentful of encroaching federalism and a hostile figure in Quebec. The conscription issue had divided the provinces again, and Drew as the great imperialist had done much of the dividing. He could conceive of national unity only in his own terms. Yet within the provincial legislature he was committed to massive change, and he sat across from socialists as the official opposition. The two facts combined in him to spur on the government.

2.

Through 1944 and 1945 reform went on in a preparatory stage, much embroiled with federal and provincial politics. Yet long-range results developed from some of the beginnings. One of the first and best acts was the establishment of a Ministry of Planning and Development under Dana Harris Porter. "It is not a brains trust," Porter said of his department, "neither is it a Santa Claus. Its main work is to co-operate ... developing and maintaining post-war employment and present resources."[6]

That work, which was wide enough, embraced municipal planning, flood control and water use, the development and siting of industry and the conservation of the forests. It was to widen further in the rush of the post-war years to impose some order on expansion, restrain the municipalities in their cut-throat competition for the acquisition of plants and encourage decentralization of provincial industry. Beyond that, and inevitably stemming from it, town planning, the regional development of watersheds and environmental control were added as new functions.

In 1944 an Act Respecting Agricultural Committees implemented one of the promises of the Twenty-Two Points Program: "Farming will be organized in every county under committees of outstanding farmers who will be given authority to plan production and regulate the processing and distribution of their output."[7] It was an extension of the co-operative principle, already extended by the war, and it was accompanied with liberal grants. Mechanization and production increased side by side, and by 1949 five new co-operatives were disposing of field crops, fruits, livestock, cattle and dairy products. Agricultural income, which had increased from $216,000,000.00 in 1930 to $453,000,000.00 in 1945, rose in the next four years to $653,000,000.00.

Promises to labour were at least partially redeemed by the establishment of a new Labour Relations Board, by the passing of an Act to improve bargaining rights and by the concession of the eight-hour day and paid vacations. Increased grants and better co-operation encouraged the municipalities to help themselves. Well in advance of the health plans of government, sixteen rural county associations in Ontario banded together for co-operative medical service. Rising revenues and better mutual planning stimulated farm morale and gave it renewed impulse. The new tool of the airwaves, apart from the plans of government, provided an added thrust. The Farm Radio Forum, which had been effective throughout the war, involved groups in discussion and in new peacetime plans.

Hundreds of projects evolved in rural areas resulted in tidier schoolgrounds, less dilapidated houses, in community centres, swimming pools and ball parks, and in the painting of weathered mailboxes standing at farmyard gates. Particularly in education the rural face was changing. "The year 1945," said one writer, "was one of the most eventful in the history of education . . . rural Ontario has set out to eradicate its educational slums, and it has revolutionary ideas as to how this must be done."[8]

Drew, as Minister of Education, was at least conforming to the trend. In 1944 an Act established the Ontario Teachers Federation, raising the status of the profession and giving it an active voice. Grants were generally increased and school taxes reduced, though not quite on the sweeping basis promised. What did come into being was reduction according to need, with less than 50 per cent for rich municipalities and more than that for poorer. The most effective change, however, was the provision of capital grants for school construction. Boards which had fought the closing of small local schools

315

were more amenable when there was help to build a large one. By 1946, with a speeding-up of the process of consolidation, 1,423 elementary school sections had been combined in 248 township schools and plans for district high schools were becoming part of the picture.

Improved teaching and a wider range of facilities came with the larger schools. Doctors, dentists and nurses improved the health of the children and there was more organized play. There was more exposure to ideas and a wider range of interests. Radio entered the classrooms through discussion of the farm broadcasts; and short films provided by the National Film Board came into increasing use. The days of the little red schoolhouse, like the black days of the depression, were becoming part of the past. Brick buildings were rising in newly prosperous townships and the first yellow school buses were travelling the country roads.

In the face of that there was a reversion to old disputes. Unmindful of the earlier experience of the Ross Bible, Drew announced in February 1944 that he proposed to introduce religious instruction into the public schools of the province. He was warned by some of the teaching bodies and a number of Protestant churchmen that he was taking a grave step, but he remained firm for the change. In the autumn of that year a manual of religious instruction, non-sectarian but inevitably stamped by its authorship, came into the public classrooms on the elementary level. The *Canadian Forum* in December was eloquent on some of the effects:

> The manual is exclusively Christian. It is not just Bible stories but doctrine . . . No child of Jewish or unorthodox Christian parents could possibly participate in these classes if the teacher follows her manual . . . The exemption from classes is given if the parents wish . . . but against mental cruelty children have no protection. To be isolated from one's group, not to belong, to walk from the room alone when everyone else stays behind, to be jeered at in the schoolyard or on the way home as a 'dirty Jew' or a 'dirty Catholic' – the inevitable consequence of stressing religious differences – can a child suffer much worse?[9]

Postponed in the secondary schools for lack of a suitable textbook, the practice remained in the lower schools as a rich creator of dissension. Nor was there yet any consensus on some of the other problems. Teachers' pensions and general standing improved but their salaries still lagged. Teachers' associations, as they grew and became militant, criticized the aging systems that governed and confused their work. The division of grades, the predominance of examinations and the narrow limits of the subject range were all matters of

316

complaint. The grievances of the separate schools, half-admitted and hardly yet abated, remained as a core of trouble. Finally Drew gave up in his search for brusque solutions. On March 21, 1945, Mr. Justice Andrew Hope of Toronto was appointed head of a Royal Commission of twenty-one members with instructions to conduct a thorough investigation of all aspects of Ontario's public school system. Five years later, when the report at length came down, Drew was no longer Premier. Nor was much revealed by the work but the formidable nature of the difficulties. Orangemen, Catholics, English and French Canadians had all served on the Commission but Ontario's complexities remained.

In the universities the war had accelerated developments that were already under way. From the middle 1930s onward there had been a branching-out of extension courses for adult education. The University of Toronto, Queen's, Western and McMaster had all seen the need of continuous and expanded teaching. There had been moves to reach the working man, to distribute and staff libraries and to combine holidays with learning by the establishment of summer schools. Peter Sandiford, of the Faculty of Education of the University of Toronto, had put the case as he saw it in 1935. The universities, he said, "must either agree to a large devolution of authority or must stagnate in a worthless efficiency." They could no longer be homes of the elite, and their benefits could not be the privilege solely of youth.

> We are on the eve of a great mass movement in adult education, the like of which the world has never seen. The reform of society will come, not through the indoctrination of the young, but from the intellectual conversion and convictions of the adult.[10]

The universe in its unfolding did not quite bear him out, but neither did it prove him wrong. War descended on Ontario, draining the province of thousands of its young students but demanding more and more of its colleges and universities. With a profusion of federal money, supplemented by provincial money, scientific and research facilities, brains, buildings and equipment were mobilized and brought together as part of a total effort. At the same time, and also forced by the war, there was planning for the needs beyond it.

The man or woman demobilized from the armed forces came home to opportunities that had not been known before. Hard-nosed businessmen, an aloof intellectual elite and federal and provincial governments had come together to provide them. For the university student who had interrupted his career there were lean but sufficient grants with a system of loans and allowances that enabled him to resume it. If he had acquired a wife and children there were allowances for them too. The man and wife were enabled to be students together. A student who did not qualify for university entrance could be given preparatory courses under similar government grants and go on to take a degree. There were no restrictions on age and there was one promise for all. They would live hard, their noses would be kept to the grindstone and their grants, though based on service, would stop if they failed their courses. If their scholastic work was good, however, there would be money for the next year. What the plan meant on one side was a recognition by authority of the value of education. What was required of it on the other was acceptance by the returning young.

Of the last there had been many doubts as the scheme came into being. After years of war the service man would be restless, the service woman licentious; the hardened adult could not return to study. What proved to have developed instead was an adult attitude to study. Universities were flooded with a rush of over-age youth, and for university teachers scepticism was washed away. The impossible problem of living quarters was somehow met and solved. The low bulk of Nissen huts began to appear on campuses, buildings that had been used for war work were converted to impromptu barracks, and houses were divided and subdivided for use by married couples. By the end of 1947, the Ontario universities and colleges, all bulging at the seams, had a total enrolment of 12,527 people returned from the armed forces. Hard-up, badly housed and often washing diapers in the small hours of the morning, a long-to-be-remembered generation of students was preparing itself for life in the 1950s.

It was also being changed by the new drives of the times. There was, wrote C.B. Sissons of Victoria University, a marked tendency to neglect the humanities for the practical and technical subjects, thus decreasing "that intellectual intercourse between professors and students, which is the final justification of the college system."[11] Some, at least, of the consequences of technology were apparent from the ivory tower.

3.

In 1944, with the passage in the Dominion parliament of the Family Allowance Act, the question of shared tax fields and federal and provincial powers raised its head again. The central government, which had brilliantly financed the war, was preparing its plans for peace. The aim was to achieve stability and forestall another depression by increasing social services and the security of the individual. The old age pension, without the requirement of a means test and universal to all, was one of the schemes envisioned. Health and hospital insurance lurked in the near background. It was on the baby bonus, however, that immediate hopes were built. In the opinion of Mackenzie King the system of family allowances, buttressing low incomes, was one of the first defences against socialism and hard times.

To this plan and other plans, in the forms proposed by King, Drew was flatly hostile. The federal government would be retaining powers and tax fields which had been surrendered temporarily, to be returned at the end of the war. It would be distributing enormous revenues across the whole of the country, with the richest province taxed for the largest share. It would dislocate the priorities which Ontario had set for herself. They included social services, but road-building, debt reduction and provision for industrial expansion were ranked well ahead. They were not to be delayed or reordered for the benefit of other provinces, least of all for Quebec. As the Family Allowance measure came up for debate in Ottawa, Drew rose in Ontario to respond to the federal challenge. He attacked the bill and its proponents and the one he saw as instigator, the anti-conscriptionist, notably fertile province which would benefit most of all:

> I am the Premier of a province with a much larger population than Quebec, whose people pay 50 per cent of every Canadian tax dollar and contribute just about twice as much in taxes for the fulfillment of any Dominion Government undertaking as do the people of Quebec . . . The people of Ontario will pay $100 million of the initial $200 million sum involved in the baby bonus. If that same $100 million were spent by the Ontario Government, a more generous family allowance could be provided for $45 million, $20 million could be spent on education, $10 million on expansion of health and hospital services, $15 million could be spent on expansion of the northern highway system and $10 million could be put to the annual reduction of the national debt . . . are we going to permit one isolationist province to dominate the destiny of a divided Canada?[12]

On Family Allowances there was little more he could do; they were decreed by the federal government in the plenitude of wartime powers. He had, however, reopened, confused and extended the long enduring debate. By 1945, as the provinces moved to reclaim rights and tax fields, he was as isolationist as Quebec in opposing federal programs. In that year and again two years later he rejected national planning in favour of his own plans, which few of the other provinces could see their way to accept. He blocked improvements in the old age pension and the hope of hospital insurance, and did not make up the loss of them even in his own province. Ontario led the nation in means, influence and growth; but it was on the rock of Drew's priorities that social progress foundered or was delayed through his time.

In Ontario the war with socialism seemed to have approached its close. By 1945 the thirty-four on the opposition benches were more weakened than they knew. Detesting and avoiding Communism, they could never escape its clutch. Never rurally based, they were losing ground in the cities as discontent subsided. May Day parades of Communists no longer outdrew Orangemen parading on July 12. CCF picnics which had once drawn 50,000 to grounds on Toronto's outskirts were becoming sadly reduced. The working man who could afford other diversions was losing his taste for politics and lending an ear to business.

Business for its part was assailing Communism and socialism, indiscriminately linked, with a mighty din of resourceful propaganda. Led by the Toronto *Telegram* and McCullagh's *Globe and Mail*, the daily press poured out its flood of abuse. Banks, industrialists and insurance companies, in large paid advertisements, warned of the danger of the "state socialism of Germany and Russia."[13] Sleek and convincing pamphlets, circulated in hundreds of thousands, repelled the threat to democracy, preached the virtues of free private enterprise and pointed to present progress. By 1945 the farmer was afraid of collectivism of the land, the worker feared for his union rights and the bourgeoisie feared everything that threatened established order.

The seating in the provincial House was by then an obsolete pattern, which Drew longed to change. Hepburn sat again as the leader of fifteen Liberals, replaying his old record of the need of a coalition. It was to be coalition, however, with Edward B. Jolliffe, the leader of the CCF. Fifteen Liberals and thirty-four socialists could combine to bring down Drew, and in Drew's eyes, nothing was more desirable. Jolliffe pondered on the brink, refusing to be led by Hepburn as the tail of Hepburn's kite; but at last moved himself. On March 22 a motion of no confidence, framed to attract Liberals, was duly put to the vote and duly passed. Saluting their own downfall and the imminent prospect of an election, the Conservatives cheered defeat.

The CCF went into the spring campaign with no farm support, with labour support diluted, and faced with the effect of years of propaganda. To its Five Point Program of broad-based social security, the Twenty-Two Point Program remained an effective answer, as did the baby bonus and the promise of improving times. The trend away from radicalism and the angry mood of the depression was not to be deflected this year, even by a political time bomb.

The explosion came on the evening of May 24, eleven days before the date of the election. Jolliffe, with convincing evidence at least to his own mind, informed Ontario electors over a provincial radio network:

> ... that Colonel Drew is maintaining in Ontario at this very minute a secret political police, a paid government spy organization, a Gestapo to try and keep himself in power ... Taxpayers' money is being used ... secretly ... by the Drew government to utter libels against the opposition, libels designed to keep the government in power.[14]

From that day and for long after the election Drew's "Gestapo" remained a *cause célèbre*. The charge was undermined, however, not only by the quality of the evidence but by Jolliffe's political timing. If he had known of the matter earlier it had been his duty to reveal it; he had now the duty of proving it, and that he could not do. Nor could a later Royal Commission; the Premier's name was cleared. What remained were hints and fragments of some squalid police transactions involving money and blackmail without the government's knowledge.

Meanwhile, in the midst of charges of libel and general political uproar, the campaign swept to its climax. On June 4 the voters went to the polls, not particularly affected by the thought of secret police. That evening, as the ballots came to be counted, Hepburn disappeared from provincial politics. Liberals were left with eleven members in the House and the CCF with eight. Labour had gained three, the Communists had held two, but the rest would sit to the right of Mr. Speaker. The long Conservative reign had begun.

4.

In the resource industries the plans of the returned government were already in full stride. War-induced demand, accompanied by federal spending, had renewed the growth of the mines. It remained to be extended further. The deep beds of Steep Rock, to the north of Lake Superior, were now a provincial asset. Here, between 1942 and 1944, with power supplied from Port Arthur over a line that cut through 120 miles of wilderness, Steep Rock Lake had been drained by pumping away some 110,000,000,000 gallons of water. Under the exposed bedrock shafts had been sunk to a depth of 2,000 feet, revealing a deposit of iron ore estimated at 250,000,000 tons.

By the later 1940s, 1,000,000 tons of ore a year were coming from Steep Rock and new discoveries had been made in Michipicoten. The Helen mine had a new and larger neighbour, and once-hungry Ontario had become an exporter of iron. Sudbury's open pits had given way to deep mining, and platinum had become a product along with copper and nickel. Magnesium, zinc and tungsten were also being mined, and there had been intriguing discoveries of pitchblende along the shore of Lake Superior. Hundreds of uranium prospectors, assisted by aerial survey, were ranging across the province. Gold was in drastic decline and silver production falling, but hard metals more than made up the loss. A Provincial Institute of Mining, established in 1945 at Haileybury in the heart of the old silver country, did much to improve technology. With new certainties of wealth under the rocks and bush of the Shield, there was a more insistent search for it and more study of its use.

The pulp, paper and lumber industries had recovered with war demand, and there was no slackening in the years of reconstruction. The new problems of the government concerned management and efficiency. From 1945 onward the planes of an aerial survey team began to cover the north, mapping, identifying and measuring the areas of timber supply. Groups of foresters and students took off for the bush each spring, supplementing the work of the airmen. By 1948 similar air and ground forces in the region of Hudson Bay had established the northern boundary with Manitoba.

Fire protection and forestry services, decimated by war and depression, were restored to strength and enlarged. By 1948, though there were still enormous fires resulting in disastrous losses, some new methods had come. Salvage crews were recovering half-burnt timber that had previously been left to rot, and the air patrol was experimenting with dry ice. Airborne seeding of clouds over some of the parched areas had occasionally brought rain.

Of all industries the pulpwood industry was most in need of planning, and in 1947 the report of a Royal Commission under Major General Howard Kennedy produced important results. The manufacturing condition, suspended in Hepburn's day, had been partially replaced by Drew. Yet the Commission found that the exceptions were more important than the rule. Much Ontario pulpwood cut on Crown lands was still finding its way to the United States. Its value in that form was about ½ cent per pound, while the same wood, if processed in Ontario mills, would return eight times that value and frequently much more, largely in jobs and wages.

In the same year the government responded to the report with an Act for Forest Management which abruptly changed conditions. American pulpwood cutters operating on Crown lands could only retain their licences if they built mills in Ontario. Within two years many moved to comply. The results were thousands of jobs, a large inflow of capital and a hugely increased return. By 1949 the value of Ontario's pulp production, which had been $38,000,000.00 in 1940, had risen to $140,000,000.00.

Order came to the timber trade through other provisions of the Act. In addition to the general inventory being made across the province, companies holding grants were required to inventory their own supplies and submit plans for cutting. Each year, with provincial approval of a plan, went requirements for reforestation. Part of the annual harvest had to be restored by planting, at the company's own expense. The perpetuation of the forest industry, long a pious hope, was at least entering the realm of practical fulfilment.

As the end of the war released men and materials, road-building resumed. With buoyant revenues supporting the municipalities, neglected rural roads, town and city streets and existing provincial highways were paved, widened and improved. Industry demanded truck routes for its ever-extending complex. Four-lane expressways were no longer a dismal make-work for men existing on relief; they were necessities of the near future. By 1949, as the Queen Elizabeth Way was brought to completion and the 400 and the 401 projected, over 800,000 Ontarians were owners of automobiles and over 1,000,000 tourists entered the province annually.

Gaunt and grey through the depression and fiercely absorbed through the war, Ontario life was beginning to expand and relax and to knit some threads together. The raw materials and the processors were moving closer to each other, and the businessman and the farmer were becoming more alike. So were east and west and so were north and south, drawn together by their differences and some of their recreations. A new summer mobility, born of a new prosperity, accompanied the extending roads. The great provincial parks, recalling a common heritage, were coming into their own. Niagara Falls and Algonquin attracted their annual thousands, but there were competing parks now. The westerner could go east and discover the Thousand Islands. The southerner could go north to the rivers that had sent the timber down and to the wild majesty of the Shield. The Cornwall or Kingston family, travelling in the new car, could return to the St. Lawrence basin with memories of Lake Superior and of the rock face of the Sleeping Giant of Sibley towering along the shore.

5.

As the Second World War began, Ontario's manufacturing complex had been struggling out of depression. By the war's end, hugely enlarged and transformed, it was faced with the problem of conversion. The great basic industries, iron, steel, textiles, wood, pulp and paper and food and automobiles, were confronted with shifting markets and technological change. The more specific war industries posed even greater questions. What was to be done with the chemical plants at Welland, the synthetic rubber of Polymer at Sarnia, the munitions factories of Toronto, Hamilton, Windsor and the many other centres? The world, as Drew had prophesied, was hungry for "little things," but they required hundreds of new or altered factories and thousands of skilled hands.

In 1947 the government gave spectacular proof its will to supply them. Drew arranged in London and Dana Porter developed plans in Ontario for the airlift from England of some 10,000 British working men with their families. Beginning in August and continuing a series of flights for over a year, DC-4 Skymasters of Trans-Ocean Airlines took off from Northolt or Prestwick, swung out along the Great Circle route by way of Iceland and Goose Bay and dropped down at Malton. Each plane had a cargo of forty passengers and on at least one occasion there were seven planes in a day. Met by buses as they deplaned, the men and their families were taken to temporary barracks, presented with lists of jobs available in their trades and were generally at work in a week.

For all its other disputes with federal authority, the government co-operated fully in the plans for the conversion of war plants and the placement and retraining of veterans. Vocational, technical and apprenticeship systems were infused with generous grants. The Provincial Institute of Textiles at Hamilton, the Lakehead Institute at Port Arthur and the Ryerson Institute at Toronto were all greatly enlarged. The Ontario Research Foundation, established in Ferguson's day, began the recruiting of scientists, the development of varied programs and the erection of buildings to house them which led eventually to the "virtual breakthrough for Canadian industry"[15] represented by Sheridan Park. By 1949 the effects of all the training had become apparent. There were more men and women at more sophisticated work then there had been at the peak of the war. Though there had been consolidation and reduction in the number of small factories, Ontario had 12,951 manufacturing establishments as compared to 10,869 in 1945. The gross value of production, standing at $6,100,000,000.00, had increased by 50 per cent.

Over all growth, however, hung the recurring question of power. War demand had taxed Ontario to the limit. The province had increased the power produced at Niagara, with permission from the United States, by some of the planned diversion from the Hudson Bay watershed. It had taken all it could get over the transmission lines from Quebec and had developed sites on some of the smaller rivers. Yet by 1942 blackouts and dimouts and even industrial curtailment were occurring at some of the peak periods. The province had scraped through the war without suffering a real crisis, but by 1946, with conversion and peacetime expansion, the threat was rising again.

In rural areas alone, the demand for electrification required the addition of some 2,000 miles of new lines, an increase of 20 per cent over lines already existing, with a similar increase in consumption. The industries of southern Ontario were working at near capacity and exceeding the demands of the war. The north was alive with new and reviving projects, all of them requiring power. Most of it was being supplied and there was a "five year plan" in existence that promised a good deal more. There were still sites entirely within Ontario and several along the Ottawa, for joint development with Quebec. But plans were not power, no agreements had been approved and the work when authorized would take years to complete. By 1947, at peak periods of consumption, there were limitations on use. By 1948, as blackouts threatened to return, Hydro was experimenting again with generation by steam.

Shortages were not the only problem. Ontario's Niagara system operated on 25-cycle current, but Quebec and the United States operated on 60-cycle. The 60-cycle was cheaper and more efficient, and the difference in systems had been complained of since the days of Adam Beck. Toronto light bulbs flickered and no electrical appliance geared to the Niagara system could be used outside the province. The difficulties and expense for industry were still more important, since all imported power had to be stepped down. Ontario operated as "a 25-cycle island on a 60-cycle continent" and for thirty years, mixed with fears of the cost, there had been a constant clamour for conversion.

Drew rose to the occasion in 1948, with a burst of political fireworks that proved convenient at the time. The need for power was undisputed and there was almost total assent in the legislature to the change of cycles. The Premier announced, however, that he would require a new mandate. Making mincemeat of past Liberal policies and refusing the vote of consent that was offered by all parties, he called a provincial election on a program actually approved. Some $400,000,000.00 were to be spent to develop power in Ontario on the Nipigon and Mississagi Rivers and for joint developments with Quebec along the Ottawa. In addition to that, another $200,000,000.00 would go to the conversion of the Niagara system to 60-cycle power.

Whatever the political ambience, the issue was never in doubt. The province needed the power and wanted the change in cycles. When Drew left office, personally defeated in the election that had confirmed his government's mandate, he had relieved Ontario's shortages for another few years. He had assured the home and the factory owner of 60-cycle current, with everything from the vacuum cleaner to the largest industrial equipment converted at government expense. That work, which would be ten years in the doing, would involve over 7,000,000 appliances owned by 1,000,000 customers. As were many of Hydro's achievements, it would be one of the largest works of its kind; and at a cost of some $150,000,000.00 over the estimate it would deliver Ontario and its households from the island of isolation.

Conversion was not, however, a solution to the enduring question of long-range supply. The only solution to that was development along the St. Lawrence, but the seaway issue was shelved when Drew left office. It was no longer Mitchell Hepburn, and certainly not Ontario, which stood in the way of the work. Now the port of New York and some of the New England states were tying the hands of Washington and blocking an impatient Canada. Time, it seemed for the moment, had brought in its revenges.

6.

The final point of Drew's Twenty-Two Point Program was a promise "to draft plans which will assure social security for all our people." The field opened by the promise was as wide as the needs of society and there was a great deal more of planning than there was real fulfilment. Most of the actual advances were on old, familiar paths, and some stopped short because of the federal quarrel. Yet within the province new trends were established. Government as the chief planner drew closer to the municipalities, and effort became centralized. At the same time, with increased provincial spending and increased provincial authority, general standards rose and some perspectives were widened.

In 1944, as the question of human rights stirred the surface, "all our people" began to become all. An Anti-Discrimination Act was passed by the legislature making it an offence to publish material or post signs reflecting on any race or creed. It was a small first step and not particularly effective but it was more than other governments, blocked by local prejudice, had been able to do before.

Over the next two years a series of three acts improved conditions for the aged. The old houses of refuge, a municipal responsibility and often a municipal disgrace, began to give way to new and better homes. Liberally supplying funds, the government step by step applied compulsion. By the time Drew left office a home for the aged was mandatory in each municipality.

In 1946, turning its attention to the young and taking over some properties vacated by the federal government, the province established the first of the day care centres for children of working mothers. Municipalities, with further provincial funds, added a few more, and private centres followed. These last, however, though the government approved and licensed them, were left to their own resources. The Children's Aid Society, with its municipal branches long-established and efficient, was retained on its old basis as a semi-private agency but it was infused with provincial funds.

With the establishment of the Department of Reform Institutions in 1946, a new series of changes in the treatment of criminals began. Prisons, reformatories and industrial farms were cleaned up, modernized and provided with better facilities. Work was made more interesting and more thought and money directed toward preparing an inmate for the day he stepped outside. Efforts at classification became gradually more effective, dividing the insane from the criminal and distinguishing both from the sick. By 1949 the first institution for the treatment of alcoholics had been established in Toronto.

Hospitals were a crying need, and except for the larger teaching hospitals they were a municipal responsibility. Here too the provincial government acted. A system of capital grants began to encourage building. For the first time the province assumed the cost of municipal care of the indigent who were housed in public wards. It stopped short of paying the fees of doctors, but most were partially remunerated from a provincially-established fund. At the core of a medical system perennially short of staff was a constant need for training. This again was relieved by provincial support. Nurses, nursing assistants, and young graduate interns began to flow from the teaching hospitals to serve the smaller centres.

For a province still on its own there was no divorce of pensions from the humiliation of the means test. By 1948, however, an increase in the amount of the pension was accompanied by easier terms. It was less difficult for the widow to qualify for her mother's allowance; the pension for the old or blind rose from $20.00 to $40.00 dollars per month, and total destitution was no longer one of the requirements. The recipient, if he owned a home, was now allowed to retain it.

The fear of sickness still hung over the poor, and whatever there was in the way of social security came with the old stigma. Yet other stigmas were passing. The Anti-Discrimination Act, much as it was still evaded, was having some effect. There were fewer "No Jews Wanted" signs in front of summer hotels and the enduring voice of the racist, snob and bigot was more discreet in the cities. The human rights of the child born out of wedlock had received some recognition. He could bequeath property to his mother or inherit property from her; and the birth certificate with "Illegitimate" stamped on it was part of the discarded past.

In the face of the enormous need for post-war housing, federal, provincial and municipal governments had been driven to work together. There could be no thought in this field of a policy of isolation. Not only the low-cost home but town development, slum clearance, the servicing of urbanization and the demands of transportation were part of the unfolding problem. In Toronto, which was to contract for its first subway in 1949, the Regent Park Housing Project was the first of its kind in Canada and a symbol of much ahead. Occupying several acres of a designated "blighted" area, it was to provide seventy-two row houses and 984 apartments for former dwellers in the slum. Amid much applause for the edifice and the new social achievement there were occasional dissenting notes. One commentator sounded a prophetic warning:

> That the rehousing of Canadian urban dwellers of blighted areas will involve a significant social adjustment by the new tenants . . . Within a short time the small corner grocery store will be gone. The local pubs (two in number) will be torn down. Some people have carried on small businesses of one sort or another from their homes. It will be difficult if not impossible to continue them. There are, in addition, a few good, solid brick houses in the redevelopment area which might serve adequately for another two decades. These too will be demolished without sufficient explanation to their owners. In short, the dwellers of Canadian urban redevelopment areas will be shifted from conditions they have known, however undesirable, to a totally unfamiliar situation as tenants of a public housing authority enforcing relatively strict regulations. Their preparation for this shift in Toronto, in the first Canadian rehousing project, has been almost negligible . . . [16]

7.

By 1948 the province was moving steadily with the surge of a post-war boom. Whatever the division of incomes and in spite of the effects of inflation, there could be no disputing the fact of growth. Since 1945 the returns to agriculture, the values of mineral production, the values of forestry products and the net value of manufacturing production had all increased by over 40 per cent. A total of 551,000 people were employed in manufacturing as compared to 518,000 in 1945, and while that increase was less than 10 per cent, the rise in wages and salaries was almost 40 per cent. Ontario maintained its position as the supplier of over half of Canadian manufactured products; and though gold production was down from the peak years the province was delivering 57 per cent of the gold mined in the Dominion, all the nickel and platinum and most of the copper and iron.

The bonded debt of $611, 000,000.00 at the peak of the war had been brought down to $583,000,000.00; and the cost of servicing, which had absorbed 21.6 per cent of provincial revenues in 1945, had been reduced to 11.3 per cent. The province was better organized for economic growth, with more efficiency in direction. Flood control, water use, the development of regional watersheds and the planned siting of industry had combined the efforts of many municipalities. So had reforestation, environmental improvement and the protection of fish and game. Town planning and housing, the provision of sewerage and water systems and the large financing needed had all had the same effect. Municipal effort was becoming centralized under the provincial government. There was a drawing together and grouping on the same principle as the schools, and to achieve similar advances. Old local autonomies were gradually becoming blurred, but there were as yet few quarrels with that. Nor was there much dispute anywhere as to the new requirements of hydro-electric power; they were a confirmation of growth. The authoritarian Premier could claim success for his plans.

In 1948, when Drew called an election on the non-issue of Hydro, the temperance issue intruded. The immediate cause was a dormant revision of the licensing act, framed and passed by the government in 1946. Since it permitted the sale of liquor in cocktail bars and hotels, it was a new advance in wetness. For two years dry pressure had prevented the proclamation, but it had not prevented drinking. What seemed to have become apparent out of the usual cloud of statistics and confusion of competing claims was that, without the projected change, bootlegging, hotel-room drinking and general flouting of the law would increase rather than wane. This was loudly disputed by all the temperance forces, but Drew proclaimed the act. Following that, with apolitical obstinacy, he stood for election in the constituency of High Park, one of the dryest in Toronto.

His personal defeat was a ripple in the course of the Conservative party, but it was a turning-point for Drew. To some in his own caucus it was not actually unwelcome, for the times were passing the man. Housing lagged, as it lagged everywhere in Canada. Social progress lagged, because of the disputes with Ottawa. Labour had gained much, but not on its own terms. The rights of collective bargaining had been placed beyond dispute: and the eight-hour day, the forty-eight-hour week and the paid vacation conceded. The Workmen's Compensation Act, widened under every government since the time of its first passing, had been duly widened again. Yet the federal labour code was still better than Ontario's, and Drew refused to conform.

The government's replies to labour had the round tones of prosperity and the arrogance of Whitney's day.

> People may say, (said Charles Daly, the Minister of Labour,) you have not got the best legislation; you have not got this, you have not got that, you have not got something else – but what are the facts? What is the position of industry in this province? ... industry is pouring into this province at the rate of about $57,000,000.00 last year, and that has been continuous for some years, and . . . there is evidence of it exceeding that amount this coming year. Is industry dissatisfied with our regulations? Is labour, which is pouring in here from other provinces? ... is labour pouring into these provinces at an equal rate at which it is into Ontario? I say it is not.[17]

Drew had the same answer for rising expectations; they would come at his own pace. Disliking union leaders and much disliked by them, he was inclined even to deny the base they stood on. The Premier, in his view, was the representative of the working man as of all other citizens. At a final confrontation in the spring before the election he aired his new philosophy and the break became decisive. The bulk of trade unionism swung to the CCF.

The CCF, for its part, was building on delayed reform. It was also widening the rural-urban cleavage at the cost of Conservative votes. Government support for dairy prices increased the cost of milk, and protest rose in the cities. The CCF was for cheaper milk and bread, for reduced coal prices and for far more low-cost housing. It pointed to the federal pension and hospital insurance plans that were still blocked by Drew. It stood side-by-side with labour for a forty-hour week and for two weeks paid vacation instead of the present one. While it would not stand for temperance it could appease the temperance forces by threatening the liquor industry with total nationalization. Conservatives, as they prepared for an election they did not really want, had all this in mind. Drew's theme was "Keep Ontario Strong," but an underlying current was swirling around his base. It was not dangerous yet but it might very well become so, in the view of party strategists, and the election proved them right.

On June 7, 1948, the party emerged from the balloting with fifty-three elected, a clear majority in the House. But there had been a loss of thirteen seats and there had been a gain of the same number in the standing of the CCF; the actual swing in the party power relationship was about 25 per cent. The Conservative leader, moreover, now out of the legislature, was not expected to return.

The party had been rebuked, the leader personally rebuffed, and in the view of Drew's enemies, he had sought a means of departure. The reign of Mackenzie King was at last approaching its close and each of the federal parties was thinking of a new leader. There was opportunity in that and the Premier was prepared to accept it. On October 19, 1948, he resigned, leaving Thomas L. Kennedy at the head of a caretaker government. In that same month Drew succeeded John Bracken at the head of a federal party that was now Progressive-Conservative. The final move in the general shift of leaders came in April 1949. The amiable Tom Kennedy "who looked like a farmer, talked like a farmer and acted like a farmer,"[18] went happily back to the congenial Ministry of Agriculture. Leslie Miscampbell Frost moved over from the provincial treasury to become the sixteenth Premier. The impetus of Drew remained and his party was still in the driver's seat but it was a time for shifting gears.

Notes

1. Radio Address published as "The Constructive Platform of the Progressive-Conservative Party," approved in General Meeting at Toronto, July 3, 1943.
2. D.R. Richmond, *The Economic Transformation of Ontario: 1945-1973*, pamphlet, (Toronto: Ontario Economic Council, 1974), p. 11.
3. Radio Address above, note 1.
4. *Ibid.*
5. Toronto *Star*, September 22, 1971.
6. *Ibid.*, February 14, 1968.
7. Radio Address, above, note 1.
8. *Canadian Forum*, October, 1944.
9. *Ibid.*, December, 1944.
10. J. Donald Wilson, Robert M. Stamp, Louis-Philippe Audet, *Canadian Education, A History* (Toronto: Prentice-Hall Canada, 1970), pp. 326, 366.
11. Sissons, *A History of Victoria University*, p. 329.
12. J. Weisberg, *George Drew: A Brief Profile*, Term Paper, York University, 1970, pp. 53-54.
13. Gerald L. Caplan, "The Failure of Canadian Socialism: The Ontario Experience, 1932-1935," *Canadian Historical Review*, XLIV, No. 2, June, 1963.
14. *Ibid.*
15. *Canada 1867-1967* (Ottawa: Queen's Printer, 1967), p. 310.
16. Alison Hopwood and Albert Rose, *Canadian Forum*, May 1949, pp. 34-35.
17. Debates, Ontario Legislature, April 7, 1948, p. 770.
18. Ralph Hyman, *Tom Kennedy's Story*, Reprinted from Toronto *Globe and Mail*, n.d.

Chapter Sixteen

"The Good Old Province of Ontario"

1.

As a favourite phrase with Frost, "the good old province of Ontario" was to haunt his speeches to the point of infestation. Yet it was as naturally a part of his vocabulary and as much an expression of the man as the plain grey business suit, the glint of the rimless eyeglasses, the slight limp and the benignant public smile. He was a small-town lawyer born and bred of the province, with its pride, its history and its characteristic attitudes embedded deep in his bones.

He had been born in Orillia in 1895. He could remember his father as mayor, as a leading fighter for temperance and as the "Daylight Bill" or the "Fast-Time Frost" who campaigned for daylight saving. He bore the name of Andrew Miscampbell, his godfather, a member of the provincial legislature who had sponsored the first of the hydro bills when Leslie was eight years old.

With his two brothers in Orillia he had gone as far as high school, talked politics at home, and left with the Simcoe Regiment at the beginning of the First World War. He had been badly wounded, returning after months in hospital with a damaged hip that would never wholly mend. From the University of Toronto he went to Osgoode Hall, and by 1921 he was practising law at Lindsay in company with his brother Cecil. Here romance came, accompanied with political overtones. Judge Carew of Lindsay was a former Conservative who had sat in the provincial legislature, and each of the Frost brothers married one of his daughters. Leslie, in acquiring Gertrude, had been blessed with a knowledgeable helpmate, but there were to be thirteen years of practice before his own ambitions matured. In 1934 he stood for Victoria riding and suffered his one defeat at the hands of voters. Elected in 1937, he was to remain the member for Victoria through the rest of his political life.

When Drew came to office Frost came into the cabinet as Provincial Treasurer and later assumed the Ministry of Mines. The two men, though they did not much like each other, were part of a team that functioned smoothly together, with the subordinate keeping his place. Frost seemed unambitious, less aggressive than some of the other ministers, and was hardly viewed by anyone as likely to replace the leader. Yet there was an inevitability to the change, and it came with scarcely a ripple. The man concerned with the financing had been largely involved in the planning of all government measures. He found them in full course and he intended to carry them on. He soon hardened to authority and he was not awed by the scope of a Premier's work.

> Government, (he said,) is business, the people's business. Good government is therefore a matter of common sense . . . our creed is that more people lead to more industry, more jobs, more wages and more opportunity, and from these come more productivity and more revenue.[1]

That program, with its omissions and limitations, conveyed the measure of the man. In Frost's time, with immigration and an exceptionally high birth rate, the population of Ontario increased by about 157,000 or 3 per cent annually. He was Premier of a province of over 6,000,000 people by the time he left office, and the results of the great inflow had fulfilled his expectations. Despite the widening of affairs and the new complexity of the government's interests, he liked to say that he viewed them "from the standpoint of a man in the barber's chair at Lindsay."[2] He had his own view of the social meaning of progress, but it was late in his old age when he delivered its best expression.

> If you look at it, (he said,) from a standpoint of simply developing a great country from a materialistic standpoint, not having regard to the betterment of people, then, of course, in the end it will crush you . . . it has to be a partnership between the two philosophies of economic advance and human betterment.[3]

That difficult partnership Frost was able to realize to a larger extent than Drew. Where Drew claimed that he had "stopped socialism" Frost found ways to absorb it. The CCF in his time was tamed almost to the point of acquiescence. The Labour-Progressive party, as the legal voice of Communism, had two members in the House, both of them brilliant men and both anathema to Drew. To Frost, however, in spite of his small-town background and the views of his farm constituents, Joseph Salsberg and Alex MacLeod were friends.

333

Those two, (he said, again in his later years,) had more brains between them than the rest of the opposition put together ... they weren't communists, really, but dissenters, dissatisfied young men of their time. I'd listen to them. Often I'd just grab off one of their ideas.[4]

Alert to change in the cities, he remained the reflector in most things of old rural Ontario. Stability came with that along with notable shortcomings that set limits to his work. Education, for Frost, was a matter of building schools rather than improving methods. Ethnic and language problems were something to be got round, papered over with progress. Jails, he was to say once, were built

to put people in ... what they should do is keep out of those coops altogether and not give us the expense of a lot of elaborate jails and prisons ... if you do not like the jail, do not get into it.[5]

His twelve years in office were to be confirmed by three elections. In 1951 he reversed the declining trend that had eroded the strength of Drew. In 1955, in spite of a major highway scandal, he returned to an enlarged legislature with eighty-four of its ninety-eight seats. In 1959, though natural gas pipelines had produced another scandal that cost him three of his ministers, the Premier remained untouched and his majority still commanding. In "the good old province of Ontario" the ballot boxes pronounced for common sense, for a tough, prosaic, essentially honest government that managed the province well. Education was static and social progress grudging, but there had been material change. With huge growth and the abating of old quarrels, Ontario was set more comfortably and was more effectively dominant within the federal frame. What had not yet been assumed, or even glimpsed from the barber's chair at Lindsay, were the responsibilities of leadership that came with the greater place.

2.

Through Frost's time as through Drew's, the process of urbanization continued, complained of and inevitable. By 1961 only 9 per cent of Ontario's population still lived on the farms. Yet the first of the primary industries still held its place, and Ontario led the country in its proportional return from agriculture. Less land was in use but the average farm was larger than it had been at the war's end, and it was operated with less help. By 1958 Ontario's stock of combines had grown from fewer than 1,000 to over 18,000, with other mechanization proceeding at the same rate. For some 140,000 farms there were about the same number of tractors, and there were more tractors than horses.

334

Total farm income was approaching $1,000,000,000.00 and the return to the average farmer was about $6,600.00. Allowing for all his costs and overhead, he seemed to be in a superior position to the average city worker, who earned about half that sum. His isolation, moreover, was becoming a thing of the past. Roads, hydro, radio and the lately-arriving television drew him closer to the city or to city ways of life. Closely integrated with government in every branch of his work, his land use, his production, his diversification and his marketing were all merging in a broad co-operative pattern. Government research and planning, government instruction and advice and government control, where needed, maintained and improved standards. On the other side of the process, after forty years of effort, there were also large results. By 1960 the Farm Products Marketing Board was the administrative agent for twenty-six co-operatives accounting for most of the field crops. There were similar boards, similar groups of co-operatives and great marketing terminals for dairy products and livestock. Of Ontario's 140,000 farmers, 70 per cent were members of one or other of the co-operatives and 50 per cent of the farm income of the province came to it through the boards. The agricultural producer, supplying the great merchandizers and food processors and distributors, was achieving collective strength. A billion-dollar industry, in its dealings with the urban giants, was approaching equal terms.

In 1952 the Frost government revised the Forestry Act to improve administration, increase provincial revenue and tighten the regulations governing cutting. Beyond that it changed little in law, but it was an encourager of reforestation and a watchful guardian of practice. Between 1950 and 1960 the fire protection budget was more than tripled, with expenditure in the latter half of that decade rising to about $35,000,000.00. By 1961 the forest areas of the province, divided into 125 management units, were served by thousands of men and a maze of modern equipment. Radar was used to detect the approach of lightning storms, a radio and telephone network of 1,600 stations was supplemented by portable transmitters, and hand pumps and power pumps were made available anywhere by a fleet of boats and trucks. Hundreds of miles of access roads were cut to assist the ground-fighters, and planes of the augmented air force, some of them equipped with water tanks, joined in the remoter battles. By 1960 the toll of destruction, which for thirty-five years had averaged 154 acres per fire, was reduced to an average of 33 acres, but the war with the old demon was still far from won. With an average annual cut of some 538,000,000 cubic feet, there was an average loss of 60,000,000 by fire.

Some half-billion dollars of investment had been poured into the industry, much of it from the United States and most in the pulp-wood sector. Frost's government had welcomed it, made the investor comfortable, and could point to large results. By 1958, when there was a temporary pause in the building of new capacity, the value of pulp and paper production had trebled in twelve years. Standing at a total of $449,000,000.00, it was amplified by a lumber cut which had grown by 40 per cent and by an increase in related lumber industries four times as large. With new pulp and paper mills and new uses for wood, with more furniture factories, sash, door and planing mills and plywood and veneer factories, the total output of the forest-based industries was approaching $600,000,000.00. There had, moreover, been much improvement in the ratio noted by the Kennedy Commission with regard to raw material. Some $110,000,000.00 worth of wood cut in Ontario was being expanded by home processing to nearly five times its value.

The great forest inventory, begun under Drew's government and completed in 1958, provided a basis for planning and conservation. Ontario had some 106,000,000 acres and some 84,000,000,000 cubic feet of accessible, marketable timber. The wood was of all varieties, some of them in short supply; the best commerical species took eighty years to mature. As private industry poured in capital and equipment and the government built access roads, life in the woods was changing. The spring drive on the rivers or the winter haul over trails hardened by frost were no longer the only means of hauling timber. Bulldozers, snowmobiles, heavy diesel trucks, tractors and mechanical loaders not only reduced man-handling but made cutting and hauling possible in any season of the year. In many camps these activities went on the year round. The pulp industry, the great devourer of softwoods, was developing the use of hardwoods in some of its newer processes. All this, with the certainty of increased consumption, called for increased replacement. Between 1957 and 1960 eight new nurseries were added to those already in being. By 1961 some 57,000,000 young trees were being shipped out each year for planting.

By 1956 there was tentative action on another of the forest problems. The same great industry that was eating away the woods and denuding huge areas was also polluting many of the lakes and rivers. The Ontario Water Resources Commission, established in that year, was intended to deal with the evil. Yet it was faced with difficulties and attitudes as old as lumbering itself. Chips and rotting dead-wood, sawdust from the sawmills and poisonous chemicals from pulp mills were all a part of the process that created thousands of jobs. Waste had to be disposed of, water was near at hand, and to the 80,000 in the industry the needs of the job came first. The same scale of priorities directed the course of government.

> We do not regard lightly the matter of pollution of our streams, (said Frost in 1950.) Indeed, we think it is a very serious matter . . . (but) we also regard as a matter of high importance the employment of our people, and we do recognize that in these days of industrialization and the expansion of industry and the increase of population . . . we are bound to get a certain amount of pollution.[6]

By 1960, one out of every five workers in northern Ontario was employed in the mining industry. The province had moved with the great surge of development that was sweeping across the country. Frost's government had welcomed foreign investment, it had been an encouraging and co-operative regulator, and it had kept its taxes light. In 1953 the president of the New York Stock Exchange, significantly speaking in Toronto, saluted a friendly neighbour. "We envy the environment in which capital is encouraged to work in Canada, and the respect accorded to the risk taker."[7]

Whatever its future import, the policy of the Frost years was part of the hopeful 1950s, and most of the hopes were realized. Only in coal and oil did the province remain poor, with less than 2 per cent of the Dominion total. In all the other fields of mineral production it accounted for 40 per cent of the national output.

Nickel, centred on Sudbury, continued the restless story of ever fluctuating advance. Some 75 per cent of all the nickel supplied to the free world came from widening and deepening mines and an extending apparatus of smelting plants and refineries. Output rose and fell with the shifts of world demand, yet by 1961 the money value of production had increased six times since the close of the Second World War. There had been the coming of the Korean War, the reviving armaments race and a merciful period of subsidence as both came to a pause. Through all that, however, there had been the new demands for nickel in a multitude of "little things," and there were still more on the horizon. Technological change, particularly in the field of aircraft, was opening an enormous market.

Copper, not only from Sudbury but from Timagami on the Quebec border, and from mines as far to the west as Thunder Bay, supplied about half of total Canadian output. About three-fifths of all Canadian gold came from Ontario mines. The province which had produced only $300,000.00 worth of iron at the beginning of the Second World War had a production value of $48,000,000.00 in 1960, and this was a decline from the peak.

Only the demand for steel controlled the rate of output; there seemed to be no limit to the recently found resources. Steep Rock, with an annual production of close to 1,000,000 tons, was planning an increase to 3,000,000 by 1969. The Algoma District had reserves about half as large and the old Marmora region, infused with American capital, was beginning to produce again. There was a huge deposit at Nakina to the northeast of Lake Nipigon, another at Bruce Lake, and others across the province from the Quebec border to the Soo. The new developments promised 1,000,000,000 tons, and possibly more. Iron on Belcher Islands at the head of James Bay was evoking a new interest in the Ontario Northland Railway and its terminus at Moosonee. It seemed certain, in that expansive era, that the town slumbering on the sandbars would become an ocean port. It would have to, Frost told the legislature in 1961, because "the Almighty has built a road beyond."[8] It was a characteristic statement and impressed a listener in the gallery. "Gosh," he is said to have said in a whisper caught by a journalist "if you're against building this port it means you're against God."[9]

Uranium was the greatest find, towering over the others. In a period of six years it grew to rival nickel and to match nickel's history in its commercial ups and downs. The most sought-for metal in the world through the middle 1950s, it was to be the threat, the problem and the promise that hovered over the 1960s.

The pitchblende trail that had led toward Lake Superior proved to be a dead end. The strikes, when they came in 1954, were in Algoma District on the north channel of Lake Huron and along the York River in the north of Hastings county. By 1955, in the midst of a world-wide race to develop atomic weapons, production was under way. In Algoma to the northeast of Blind River, in a region described by Champlain as "the place where the savages gather yearly to dry blueberries and raspberries,"[10] Elliot Lake was a booming company town. Bancroft on the York River in denuded timber country was developing as the smaller sister. There was no question of market and there seemed no limit to demand. The United States wanted all the uranium in the world and would take it at a set price. From 1955 onward, under contracts extending to 1962, Ontario's production rose from a value of $487,000.00 to $82,900,000.00 in 1957 and $209,600,000.00 in 1960. Then suddenly, with American stockpiles filled, the inevitable break came. In 1961, with the prospect of no market after 1962, contracts were renegotiated to reduce the rate of supply. Ontario's uranium industry, with its production scaled down and the threat of unemployment darkening the company towns, extended its planned deliveries to 1966. Uranium as a war component had become at least temporarily a drug on the world market.

Brightening that picture were the potential peaceful uses. Chalk River, near the deep bend of the Ottawa overshadowed by Bird

Rock, had been an atomic research station since 1945. By 1952 it was well advanced in the development of nuclear power. In September of 1958 the first shipment of uranium metal went from an Ontario refinery to the reactors in Chalk River. Three years later, and thirty miles to the west along the Ottawa, Rolphton entered history as the first atomic power plant ever to be built in Canada.

3.

In the summer of 1956 the Trans-Canada pipeline began its 2,000 mile crawl from the border of Saskatchewan and Alberta to the centres of eastern Canada. By the end of 1957 it had passed Kenora; in February of 1958 it entered Port Arthur and by October of that year it had reached Toronto. As the branch lines of subsidiary companies reached out through the north, Ontario came to be served with natural gas from the prairies. In the ten years since the Leduc finds in Alberta the petroleum picture had also changed enormously. Two-thirds of the crude that had once come in by tank car now came by pipeline, almost all from Alberta instead of the United States. It was a revolution in supply and a revolution in transport, but a greater change was in the making. Ever-hungry Hydro, in its constant search for power, was embarked at last on the seaway.

Frost had inherited the power shortage, but he had rejected the accompanying legacy of federal-provincial quarrels. In his time as Provincial Treasurer he had made some overtures to King, and he had touched King in the last year of his life by reopening the house of William Lyon Mackenzie in Toronto as a public monument. All this, as it diluted the older rancours, eased the new relationship between Frost and King's successor. Louis St. Laurent was soon a congenial friend, and at least in the case of one issue a friend on common ground. For both men the question of Ontario power, linked to the broader question of an international waterway, was too big for politicking and too urgent to wait.

From 1951 onward Frost waged his battle for the development of the St. Lawrence seaway. He was opposed by the American Congress but supported by New York state, which was also hungry for power. He had St. Laurent as a firm and effective ally. He was, moreover, in the same mood as Ferguson when he proposed the Morrisburg plan. Ontario, if all else failed, would develop her own power in the international section. That threat, duly modified in transit, St. Laurent carried to Washington in September of the same year. The Canadian government, he informed President Truman, was prepared to build an all-Canadian waterway if Congress refused American participation. By 1952, though Congress was still opposed, there was at least American assent to Canadian building. A year later, under pressure from New York state, there was an advance on that position. In 1953, with the new President Eisenhower and a new American Congress, the United States agreed to become a partner. It would share the cost and do its portion of the work on the American side of the river.

On both sides, by August 1954, trucks, cranes and bulldozers, with tons of steel and cement and high explosives were rolling along the roads. On August 10, at the Long Sault near Cornwall, came one of a round of ceremonies that marked the beginning of construction. Frost was there for Ontario and Thomas E. Dewey as governor of New York state with an attendant host of dignitaries. "I was angry then," Frost was to say long afterward. "The U.S. got in for peanuts ... I would have preferred to tell them to go to hell."[11] He was a beaming man that day, however, as he dug his shovel of earth.

The great development that had been fought over by politicians for half a century and dreamed of since the first travels of Champlain was brought to its culmination in less than five years. On April 25, 1959, the series of dredged channels, the stretches of deep river and the lakes, locks and canals of the St. Lawrence seaway opened for traffic. Ocean vessels with a draft of twenty-seven feet could now come in from the Atlantic and traverse the breadth of Ontario to the head of the Great Lakes. In that year's shipping season 21,200,000 tons of cargo, an increase of 80 per cent on the volume of a year before, passed over the system. It was less the next year, and in following years and decades the bigger ocean freighters, the container shipments of railways and the world's changing traffic patterns would raise their quota of doubts. But for most of the men of that time the new artery opened to the heart of the continent seemed an undimmed achievement.

On the power side of the development there were to be no doubts at all. By July 1, 1958, the last of the millions of tons of earth had been moved and the last of the concrete poured. On that day, with all the panoply of international rejoicing, the coffer dams were blown and the gates of the control dam opened near the new village of Iroquois. Some 23,000,000,000 cubic feet of water, emptying from Lake Ontario by Kingston, Brockville and Prescott, began to spread out below the dam in a hundred-mile-square headpond.

Settling under it as it rose were the stripped streets, the emptied lots and fields, the denuded gardens and the memories of the old villages of Iroquois, Aultsville, Farran's Point, Dickinson's Landing, Wales, Moulinette, Mille Roches and part of the town of Morrisburg. Lying with them in forever submerged quiet were to be over two hundred farms, eighteen cemeteries from which most of the bodies had been moved, thirty-five miles of highway and forty miles of railway. Over 6,000 familes had lost their houses and land, and not all would be reconciled by the new homes, schools, public buildings, shopping centres, parks, beaches, roads, railways and other amenities that spread out to replace them along the north shore of the St. Lawrence. Some had not been replaced; huge moving machines had transported intact a few of the more cherished buildings, including a stone church more than a century old. There had been Loyalist villages here, Iroquois towns before them, and relics of older peoples before the Iroquois. A ghost area now, stripped to a skeleton of itself, it passed under the headpond that was building above Cornwall.

Here, a tall white wall of concrete curving from the New York mainland to a point near the head of Barnhart Island, the Long Sault Dam collected the water of the headpond and released it at full rush to exploit the drop in level along the 125-mile stretch between the eastern end of Lake Ontario and the power houses below. The power houses themselves, on the international boundary, comprised thirty-two generating units, sixteen American and sixteen Canadian, and were to supply each country with 1,000,000 kilowatts of new electrical energy. They were fulfilling that promise on June 27, 1959, when the Queen came to unveil the stone of the International Boundary monument, with the Red Ensign of Canada and the Stars and Stripes beside it. As the cords drew back the cloth, and the inscription stood revealed, there seemed to be justification for the many earlier trials:

> This stone bears witness to the common purpose of two nations, whose frontiers are the frontiers of friendship, whose ways are the ways of freedom and whose works are the works of peace.[12]

4.

In the "golden horseshoe" of southwestern Ontario – from Oshawa by Toronto and Hamilton and around to the Niagara peninsula – industrial production was multiplying as population increased. It was true of Windsor and Sarnia, true of eastern Ontario, and of Sudbury and the northern centres where manufacturing had grown. Between 1950 and 1960, $5,000,000,000.00 dollars were poured into new factories, machinery and equipment, while other billions of public and private money went to auxiliary services. War and post-war technology and the advance of automation had transformed the nature of much of the newer output while it redoubled old volumes. Amid a wide and sophisticated range of secondary products, Ontario supplied all the machine tools, almost all the automotive vehicles and parts, half the textiles and clothing and more than half of the food, beverage, iron, steel, rubber, leather, chemical, electrical and electronic products made by the entire Dominion. It employed nearly half the workers, and within its own boundaries the 610,000 people engaged in manufacturing represented 30 per cent of the labour force of the province.

The growth of manufacturing was the force behind urbanization, the force that increased and complicated the demands on education; and it saddled the municipalities with burdens beyond their means. At the same time as it generated new pressures, it produced the buoyant revenues that enabled the provincial government to widen its field of action. Roads, schools, debt loads and the relation and interrelation of provincial and municipal structures all came in for change. It was large, expansive and for the most part centralizing change. The threads of responsibility in the ever more complex province were being gathered in fewer hands.

The building of municipal roads became part of the general pattern of provincial highways, to be supported by larger subsidies and included in central planning. The government built and paid for the access roads in the north. It paid between 50 and 80 per cent of the cost of rural, county and smaller urban roads. It built, maintained and controlled nearly 12,000 miles of main arterial roads. By 1961 the $23,000,000.00 roads' budget of 1946 had grown to an annual expenditure of nearly $268,000,000.00. The Trans-Canada Highway, assisted by federal funds, had been completed in 1960 with the closing of the last gap around the hump of Lake Superior. Seventy-three thousand miles of lesser provincial roads now fed into a great urban complex with its patterns of controlled access and traffic interchanges that included the Ottawa Queensway, Highways 400 and 401 and the Queen Elizabeth Expressway which had been modernized and enlarged. The first of the great skyways soared over Burlington Bay, another was building at Welland, and at Sault Ste. Marie and Queenston new international bridges were reaching across the border to connect with Michigan and New York. Ontario now had 2,000,000 motor vehicles compared to the single 1,000,000 of ten years earlier, and in addition to its own trucks and hordes of automobiles there was a highly profitable flood of outside traffic. Provincially controlled and supervised, expanding to federal needs and yearly internationalized by hundreds of thousands of tourists, the road system was one of the major assets.

The school system, also, was compelled to respond to growth and to the pressures of urbanization. Through Frost's twelve years the spending on education rivalled that on roads and by the end of his time it was absorbing nearly a quarter of the provincial budget. Over the whole province school enrolment doubled. By 1961 there were 1,126,400 children in the elementary schools and 262,800 in the secondary schools, most of them in better buildings, provided with more amenities and with better care for their health. Whether they were better taught remained a matter of dispute, but that question was submerged in physical expansion.

Drew's measures in support of education soon had to be enlarged on, and from 1950 onward there was a progressive rise in assistance accompanied by more control. By 1961 the 3,700 local school boards of the province received their share of property taxes through a provincially controlled and equalized assessment. With larger capital grants came provincial supervision of the planning and design of buildings. Increased per capita grants based on student enrolment were made and a "growth-need factor" provided for special cases. Growth needs were everywhere but they pressed hardest on rapidly expanding cities where people were crowding in, or on widespread rural communities requiring transportation. The new buildings, the new buses and the enlargement of staff and services were provided by that factor.

The Normal School system had become a system of colleges, eleven for the training of elementary teachers and one for the higher level at the University of Toronto. Extending over these, and embracing a system of summer schools, control and direction widened to include the technical field. Apprenticeship training was given by provincial agencies and the five great technical institutes at Toronto, Haileybury, Ottawa, Windsor and Hamilton were provincially created and controlled.

By 1960, with the opening of Glendon College, York University began to function initially on the Toronto campus. The first college, devoted to the liberal arts, was to be followed by a huge and sprawling multi-faculty campus in North York. Through Frost's time, however, expansion and secularization of the older universities remained the prevailing theme. Toronto was well provided for, and Queen's and Western received increasing assistance. Carleton, always secular, made large advances in the period; McMaster became secular in 1957; the University of Ottawa remained in control of the Oblate Order, but its non-sectarian medical and science faculties were receiving provincial grants.

The doubts of the period were deeper ones stimulated by the Hope Commission. In 1950, at the end of the five-year study, Frost tabled the report. Already dubious of its findings, he was soon postponing thoughts of its implementation. "The needs of the child," said the Commissioners, "are the bedrock on which we have tried to build the whole system of education, and in regard to these needs we have turned to the educationist and the psychologist."[13] In so doing they had turned up much indeed, ranging from inadequate teacher training through qualifications and standards to the basis of the system of grades and evaluation. That system, the report proposed, should be drastically altered or eliminated.

Students should be grouped by aptitude and ability, rather than by age or grades. There should be less emphasis on tests and examinations, far less homework, and more attention to the individual child. Secondary students should move more quickly into training in technical fields. The grip of central authority, growing since Ryerson's day, should be relaxed in the choice of text books, in determining teaching standards and methods and in the whole routine of local administration.

To all this, moreover, with its huge complex of reforms and its promise of thorny issues, was added a recurring bias. The Hope Commission, whatever its internal differences, had swung against separate schools, particularly bilingual schools. There was no sympathy with the long-sought tax adjustment, and except in the primary grades of strongly French communities there was to be all-English instruction. That proposal, for a government which had achieved peace by a liberalization of attitudes and a generosity in grants, was not even to be considered. After much discussion and some nibbling at its suggestions, the Hope Report was consigned to the provincial archives.

Since 1934 the municipalities had been dealt with through a Department of Municipal Affairs. In the depression years it had parcelled out relief, authorized loans and debentures and actually served as administrator for some municipal bankrupts. The dismal process had led to new relationships, and the marriage made in adversity was cemented in better times. Prosperity for the municipalities meant a great influx of people, demands for houses and schools, sewage and water systems, and for policing, planning and zoning in hundreds of growing towns. They were local responsibilities but they were beyond local resources, and the municipalities looked to the province for funds.

As the funds came autonomy still remained, but more and more the planning melded together. In 1950 the province arranged for the purchase of municipal debentures through the Ontario Municipal Improvement Corporation. The capital of $50,000,000.00 provided for the corporation was trebled three years later. Direct per capita grants, beginning in 1954 and increased in 1957, supplied provincial assistance for municipal administration. In the latter year, moreover, the burden of relief was shifted with the help of the

344

federal government. Growth with unemployment were becoming linked phenomena and demanding municipal works. Where these involved direct relief, the Dominion paid half, the province 20 per cent and the rest was a local charge.

Meanwhile another aspect of the problem of municipal growth had produced its own solution. Toronto, as it expanded and reached out with the bulge of industrialization, was overrunning several lesser communities. Fringing it with competing authorities and often duplicated services were the towns of Leaside, Mimico, New Toronto and Weston, the villages of Forest Hill, Long Branch and Swansea, and the townships of East York, Etobicoke, North York, Scarborough and York. Within that area, which embraced a present population of about 1,200,000 people, there could be either increasing density with vast future confusion or there could be orderly consolidation. Frost chose the latter.

He did not want a giant city of Toronto, swallowing local identities and administered by remote officials who had lost touch with their people. What he did want – and get – was the Municipality of Metropolitan Toronto, a group of thirteen communities each preserving its autonomy but governed by a common council. There would be the mayor, two controllers and nine aldermen from Toronto, with the mayors or reeves of the other municipalities. That body would combine to elect its own chairman and to bring together a host of urban services, from police and fire protection through transportation and water supply to parks, planning and finance. The plans were evolved through 1953 and on January 1, 1954, the huge and complex entity came into being. "We scrambled it all," said Frost, "unscrambled it and scrambled it again, and finally out came Metro."[14]

Six years later the Department of Municipal Affairs came in for its own scrambling. It emerged larger than before and divided into three sections, one for administration, one for finance and one for community planning. Significant of new control was the duty of the finance section, to maintain a "constant scrutiny and advisement"[15] over all municipal spending. There was to be no pause, however, either in co-operation or growth. By 1961 some $400,000,000.00, or 45 per cent of provincial revenue, was going to the municipalities, and a billion-dollar outlay for joint development projects was entering the planning stage.

5.

We seem now to have arrived at the third scene of the third (and surely, last) act of the Federal-Provincial Health Insurance drama, (said the *Canadian Forum* in March of 1957,) with the usual thickening and confusion of the plot coming before the final dénouement, and the rival stars vying for the title of Politician (Statesman) I'd Most Like to See Continue in Office.[16]

Shrewd, caustic and inclined to the CCF, the *Forum* on this occasion was a little premature. It would be 1958 before a formal agreement was signed, and it would be January 1, 1959, when the Ontario Hospital Care Insurance Plan, with its costs to be shared equally by the federal and provincial treasuries, came into existence. The various acts of the drama had covered fourteen years. They had involved Drew and King, Frost and St. Laurent, and John Diefenbaker was on hand for the final curtain. Neither Frost nor St. Laurent had been enthusiastic for the plan but needs had pushed them on, resources had become available and the achievement was real enough. Under a system of voluntary subscription, 5,500,000, or 93 per cent of Ontario's population, had access to insured hospital care.

All citizens, since 1952, had had the right to the old age pension at the age of seventy, provided free of a means test and paid through a federal tax. Frost had agreed to the constitutional amendment that made the tax possible. He had agreed to much else, always exacting his price. "I looked at it," he said, speaking of the general problem of federal-provincial relations, "from the standpoint of getting things done."[17] Unlike his immediate predecessors, he had been a welcome figure in Ottawa at the federal-provincial conferences, and the cooperative hand held out had seldom come back empty. Accepting the principle of federal equalization, he had balked occasionally at the equalizers and had hard words for them at home. "Their whole psychology is to squeeze Ontario down as far as it can go and be as generous to the other provinces as possible."[18] Yet those claims, long familiar in the legislature, had not excluded the give-and-take of bargaining. Ontario, in widening federalism, had done much for herself.

In 1952, along with the agreement on pensions, had come an agreement on tax fields. The province, by surrendering for five years its right to levy personal and corporation income taxes, received in return an annual "yield" of some $140,000,000.00, based on 57 per cent for personal and 8½ per cent for corporation taxes. The formula was revised in 1957, doubling the yield on personal income tax and excluding the corporation tax, which the province levied itself.

By 1961, with a new agreement in prospect, the province was collecting its own corporation tax at a rate of 11 per cent and receiving a yield from income tax which had been increased to 13 per cent and returned about $115,000,000.00 annually. Federally-linked expen-

346

ditures still outran the budget, and in his last year of office the Frost who "hated taxes" was forced to levy a 3 per cent sales tax. Yet for the eight years since 1953, the direct federal payments in old age pensions alone had been three times the combined welfare budgets of the province and the municipalities. If they had not paid for change they had certainly advanced and stimulated it, and made some extras possible.

Relieved of its share of the cost of old age pensions, the province had extended benefits through old age allowances, provided on a means test basis from the age of sixty-five. With the Hospital Care Plan had come a doubling of federal grants for the capital cost of hospitals, enabling the provincial government to double its own spending. Much of it, already large, had been in preparation for the plan, and at the same time there had been a widening of the range of treatment. By 1959 the Ontario Hospital Services Commission administered a general system twice as large as it had been in 1947, and a system of mental hospitals, tuberculosis sanatoria and psychiatric clinics which had increased by almost as much.

There were large shortfalls, as always, within the frame of expansion.

> Nothing symbolized the administration of Leslie Frost, (wrote a newspaper columnist,) more than the fact that the disgraceful, crowded and smelly hospital for retarded children at Orillia, subject to pleas for help for years, could be reached by the most modern and expensive four-lane boulevarded expressway.[19]

Yet if that was true of Frost it could also be blamed on his predecessors, and there were facts to set beside it. Under the six broad divisions of the Ontario Department of Health were included a research institute for cancer and an institute for the study of alcoholism. There was modern control and cure for venereal disease. Home nursing care was beginning to supplement hospital care and fluoridation of drinking water had been studied and recommended. Since the early 1940s deaths by tuberculosis had declined from 28 to 2.5 per 100,000, and the general mortality rate had fallen. Between 1931 and 1961 the average life expectancy of a woman had increased by twelve years, to an age of seventy-four; and that of a man by eight years, to an age of sixty-eight.

Life itself had been bettered for the average Ontarian by the return of general prosperity. For periods of unemployment, unemployment insurance was available and the aged were entitled to their pension, which by 1957 had risen to $55.00 per month. No one could live on the pension, and for much of the nearly 12 per cent of Ontario's population who were over sixty that was a major problem. Yet there

347

were more municipal homes and they were becoming pleasanter places. From 1958 onward, in addition to paying half the cost of the building, the province paid 70 per cent of the cost of running the homes. It had also begun to experiment with outside care for the elderly, provided by visiting nurses and other trained attendants.

The blind were pensioned on the same basis as the old; and mothers' allowances were not only increased in scale but more responsive to needs. Indians had entered the stream of provincial consciousness, and old age allowances as well as old age pensions were extended to the bands on the reserves. In 1952, with an Act for Allowances for Disabled Persons, the province recognized the needs of the unemployable. Two years later, when the federal government moved to take over that field, the field itself was widened. The province and the Dominion jointly established agencies not only to support the handicapped but also to rehabilitate and train them. Despite the building of an official frame, however, private charity was depended on for much of social welfare. An increasingly large contributor to such bodies as the Children's Aid Society, the various community charities and the organized charities of the churches, the province still held off from assuming much of their work. Ontario was concerned with welfare, but it was hardly a welfare state.

The Ministry of Reform Institutions had been a happy creation of Drew, and its work grew considerably in spite of the lukewarm Frost. For junior offenders, especially, the farms, reformatories and training schools became easier places to live in and less the repositories of dregs. In 1952, a Director of Probation was appointed; in 1954 and again in 1959 juvenile and family courts were modernized and reformed. With hardened offenders in the larger jails it was still necessary, in the ominous words of officialdom "to emphasize incarceration,"[20] but there was some easing of discipline and more variety of work. As Frost retired, however, a federal commission reporting on penitentiaries had renewed doubts in Ontario about the state of provincial prisons.

In the main stream of life, where most Ontarians lived, there was less forbidden on Sunday, less emphasis on the narrower aspects of religion, and a blunting at least of the worst forms of prejudice. Various virtuous acts, of more or less effect, were followed in 1958 with the establishment of the Ontario Anti-Discrimination Commission and in 1961 with an Act to Establish the Ontario Code of Human Rights. Under this act it became unlawful, and grounds for voiding a contract, to make any distinction in work or working conditions on grounds of race, colour, ancestry, nationality or creed. It was equally unlawful to make such distinctions in housing, apartment rental or public accommodation. As an official crowning of tolerance, which had been a long and slow growth, it was saluted by an admiring member of the Premier's party. "The main aim of these anti-discrimination laws is education, you've got to admit that; and Frost educates the public along and then he introduces the bill and hardly anybody even notices."[21]

By 1961 women made up 28 per cent of Ontario's total labour force of 2,500,000. They had been protected for ten years by the Female Employees Fair Remuneration Act, but they had still far to go in establishing equality with males. Workmen's Compensation had advanced at its usual pace, step by grudging step. All labour had been strengthened in 1955 by the merger of the Trades and Labour Congress with the Canadian Congress of Labour. The government's response to this had come five years later, in an improved Labour Relations Board with better machinery "for the settlement of disputes and provision of good labour-management relations."[22] The change was forced and necessary. Trade unionism was no longer an ambiguous threat; it was an accepted fact and power to be dealt with on equal terms. At the same time, as a protagonist, it was becoming more complex, seamed with the divisions of power. In October of 1961, the month that Frost left office, the 18,000 mine workers of Sudbury were involved in a struggle not with private industry but for choice of their own masters. In either case they would be ultimately under American masters, since the United Steelworkers of America were grappling for control with the Mine-Mill Workers Union which was seeking affiliation with the Teamsters in the United States.

Labour was posing international problems, and revealing social problems of a new scale and dimension. So was American investment. So was education, with the question of essential quality so long dormant and avoided while the big schools went up. Growth had created issues but it had not brought solutions, and dogging the heels of progress were some that had lain neglected.

In the valley of the Grand River, thick with cities and industries, an old, unsettled question was stirring from a fitful sleep. The lands of the Six Nations, "beginning at Lake Erie" six miles wide on either side of the river "and extending in that proportion to the head of the said river" were to have been "a safe and comfortable retreat."[23] For subject citizens of Ontario or for a separate allied people? – many courts had considered and presumably answered the question, but not to the satisfaction of the chiefs or the people themselves. In 1956 a bumbling Provincial Secretary, applying the Provincial Marriage Act on the heels of a new decision, had pronounced all Indian marriages, never previously registered, to be invalid if not registered after the date of the Act.

Three years later, following a mini-rebellion on the Grand River Reserve, Frost had reversed the decision of his Secretary but had chosen at the same time to be amusing on other claims.

> Traditionally in this House, bills which affect other jurisdictions, other provinces and other governments are sponsored by the Honourable the Prime Minister. On this occasion, in dealing with the Six Nations Confederacy, we felt that it was better to keep matters on that diplomatic level . . . I think we should recognize them as a government in themselves which is equal in status to ourselves.[24]

The words would be less amusing, only a few years later, to "other jurisdictions, other provinces and other governments." Hardly felt as yet in the placid, prosperous province ruled by its genial autocrat, was the stirring of native peoples.

The same province, while it led the nation in growth, influence and wealth, seemed unaware of the nation's greatest problem. The bilingual school was tolerated and nothing more. There had been many dealings with Quebec but all of them concerned with business and all in the old way, at arm's length and with certain subjects avoided. They remained latent and avoided as the 1960s came. The Quiet Revolution appeared to go on unheard.

Notes

1. Toronto *Star*, February 16, 1968.
2. Toronto *Globe and Mail*, May 5, 1973.
3. Toronto *Star*, February 16, 1968.
4. Toronto *Star*, September 24, 1973.
5. Toronto *Star*, March 11, 1961.
6. Debates, Ontario Legislature, 1950, A5.
7. Jonathan Manthorpe, *The Power and The Tories* (Toronto: Macmillan of Canada, 1974), p. 43.
8. Ron Haggart, Toronto *Star*, March 11, 1961.
9. *Ibid.*
10. Encyclopaedia Canadiana, "Blind River."
11. Toronto *Star*, February 16, 1968; and September 23, 1971.
12. Denison, *The People's Power*, pp. 259-267.
13. Wilson, Stamp, Audet, *Canadian Education, A History*, p. 397
14. Toronto *Star*, September 23, 1971.
15. *Ontario, Economic and Social Aspects: A Survey*, Ontario Department of Economics, 1961, p. 37.
16. *Canadian Forum*, March, 1957, p. 266.

17. Toronto *Star*, September 24, 1973.
18. Toronto *Globe and Mail*, May 5, 1973.
19. Ron Haggart in Toronto *Star*, quoted in Manthorpe, *The Power and the Tories*, p. 56.
20. *Ontario, Economic and Social Aspects*, p. 20.
21. Toronto *Star*, March 11, 1961.
22. *Ontario, Economic and Social Aspects*, p. 20.
23. Malcolm Montgomery, "The Legal Status of the Six Nations Indians in Canada," *Ontario History*, Vol. LV, 1963, pp. 93-105.
24. *Ibid*.

Chapter Seventeen

Six Million Citizens

1.

The process of growth, Frost had said, "has to be a partnership between the two philosophies of economic advancement and human betterment."[1] In that platitude lay ground for the assessment of his own work, the work of his fifteen predecessors and of the generations they had presided over since 1867. The frame and quality of life, the people and what they were, told the story.

A voyageur of Simcoe's day, returning in 1961 to make the old journey by the Ottawa, the Mattawa, Lake Nipissing and the French River to Georgian Bay and southward to the confluence of Lake St. Clair and the Detroit, would have discovered one fact of growth. Enclosed within the southern shores still lying to the left of him were almost 90 per cent of the 6,200,000 people who lived and worked in Ontario.

North Bay and Sudbury would have passed on his starboard hand, with the Sault to the northwest, Fort William and Port Arthur 300 miles beyond it, and Kenora and Fort Frances still to the west of them. They were all centres of industry but they were clusters along a rim, feeding the central core. They were fed themselves by the mines and the forest country and the great northeast and west, widening toward Hudson Bay. It had been cut by roads and railways, stripped of enormous wealth and was alive with the search for more. Earle Birney saw it, as he travelled one of the railways, with a poet's questioning resentment:

. . . papulous with stumps?
And should we note where maggoting miners
still bore her bones to feed our crawling host
or consider the scars across her breasts
the scum of tugs upon her lakeblue, eyes
the clogging logs within her blood–?[2]

352

Yet the huge block of the north country, with an average of less than ten people per square mile, was still an invaded outland resisting the pioneers. Old Upper Canada, the jagged, jutting triangle between the Ottawa, the St. Lawrence and the eastern Great Lakes, thrusting its blunt nose into the central vitals of the continent, was still the place where most of the people lived.

Grown as the neighbour of the French province and washed over by the influence of the United States, Ontario reflected the impact of waves of immigration. The British strain was as wide and deep as ever; the origins of 3,700,000 of the people were in the United Kingdom. Many, however, were far from those origins now, and an interweaving of other threads was resulting in a variegated pattern. With 600,000 of French origin and 400,000 of German origin, these influences remained. The Sudbury region was more French than British, and so were some of the counties of the Ottawa valley. The northern mining and pulpwood towns were centres for the foreign born: and year by year more Italian, Dutch, Polish, Ukrainian, Scandinavian and other Europeans were entering the southern cities. They had already imposed their characters on many of the streets and districts, on storefront signs, food displays and ways, ideas and tastes. Throughout the whole province over 1,000,000 Europeans were mixed with the older strains. Yet of 600,000 native French Canadians over 80 per cent had English as their second language; and among the immigrants and children of immigrants less than 100,000 were confined to their own tongue. Cosmopolitanism had come, bringing its host of changes, but it worked within an English frame.

Less than 10 per cent of the labour force of the province was still engaged in farming, logging or mining. The old work went on, and it was more efficient and productive, but it was a diminishing part of mature industrial development. Almost 90 per cent of the working people in Ontario were now employed in manufacturing or construction, in transportation or trade, in the service industries or finance or in the clerical work supporting them. Most were concentrated, moreover, and most depended for their living on the 500-mile-long ribbon of territory stretching from the Quebec border to Windsor along the north shore of the St. Lawrence and Lake Ontario and Lake Erie.

Within that ground were the steel industries of Hamilton, the implement industries of Brantford, the automotive industries of Oshawa, Oakville, Windsor, St. Catharines, Brampton, and the web of subsidiary factories grown about them. East from London and Kitchener and Waterloo, extending to the Quebec border and built on a rich agriculture, were the slaughter-houses, the packing

353

plants and innumerable other processors of the province's grains and livestock, milk, poultry and fruit, tobacco, vegetables and wine. Mainly from this great workbelt Ontario supplied at least half of the processed food and drink, leather, paper and textiles, iron, steel, wood, metallic, mineral and chemical products, and far more than half of the mechanical, electrical and electronic gear produced in the whole of Canada. Port Colborne on the Welland Canal was the site of the largest nickel refinery in the world. Sarnia and its "chemical valley" had grown from wartime Polymer, from the rock oil of Petrolia and from the 3,000 square miles of salt deposits extending from Windsor to Kincardine. It was now the terminus of pipelines feeding from Alberta and Texas, and a world centre for petro-chemicals and fibreglass, synthetic rubber and plastics. The whole region, gridded with roads and railways, fed by lake shipping, dotted now with airports and overpassed by planes, had been called a Canadian Ruhr. It was more than that in relative importance to the country and extent of diversification.

At the centre of all was Toronto, the maker of everything. According to the statisticians, only thirteen sub-categories in the entire range of national manufacturing were not produced within the metropolitan area. Toronto drew its iron and steel from Hamilton. It was fed by the lake and the railways with everything else it needed, and it grew as it absorbed the flood. It reached out for thirty miles along the lakefront, west by Oakville toward Hamilton and east by Whitby and Ajax in the direction of Oshawa. From its northwestern suburbs, following the railways and branching off on truck routes, the thickening dots of its factories crawled toward Guelph and Kit-chener. It bulged and sprawled, draining potential industry from much of eastern Ontario and overshadowing and dominating the whole of the southwest.

Metropolitan Toronto employed a third of the provincial work force engaged in manufacturing. The Toronto stock exchange accounted for about two-thirds of all Canadian transactions. Toronto shared the insurance business with London, Waterloo and Kit-chener, but it kept its grip on banking. Three chartered banks with their head offices in the city controlled nearly half of all Canadian loans and deposits and accounted for 40 per cent of Canadian clearings. From Metropolitan Toronto came 20 per cent of the income tax paid by all Canadians, and 30 per cent of the corporation taxes. Of the province's 2,000,000 motor vehicles, 500,000 were registered within Toronto, providing one for every three of its population. Rich and busy as it was, however, with its superstructure of trade and service industries and its web of transportation and distribution, the core of Ontario's heartland was faced with the heartland's problems.

Industrial development was mature, but how much of it was Canadian and for how long was it safe? Ford of Canada – General Motors of Canada – all the familiar names bearing the Canadian addendum had meant enormous advance. They had also made for a southward flow of dividends and control in foreign hands. Between 1951 and 1961, of American branch plants entering Canada, seven out of ten had established themselves in Ontario, mainly in the golden horseshoe. The benefits were clear in statistics of jobs and production. Yet with them came an importation of technologies that produced another effect. Ontario had long depended, and was now depending more, on American industrial research, American product development, American organization. Its automobile industry and much of its implement industry were almost wholly integrated as part of the American grid. How much more would follow, with growth on its present course? To what extent, in the not so distant future, would the province become an appendage of the continental producer?

There were other problems of growth more nearly affecting those who lived in Toronto. For the average city worker the daily trip to the job took half an hour. For 80,000 motorists it had become an hour or more. It was made, moreover, through always-increasing traffic and ever-thickening pollution. The new expressways feeding in from the suburbs led to the jammed parking lots, devouring acres of space. There was never enough space, either in the central city or on the near fringe of its environs, and the inward tide was creating an outward push. Plants moved toward the bare northern outskirts, taking their workers with them. New banks of high-rises, new housing developments, with schools, parks, playgrounds, shopping centres and golf clubs were sprouting on the city's rim.

The same process, repeated in other cities, was eating away the farmlands. By 1960, to the southeast of Hamilton, some 40 per cent of the old Niagara fruit country had been taken over by industry and its train of urbanization. The whole district, losing annually some 500 acres of fruitland, was threatened with submergence by towns, factories and asphalt in a matter of twenty years.

For Metropolitan Toronto it was estimated that between 1960 and 1980 its planning area of 400 square miles would have to be doubled. There was food for thought in that when one balanced conditions of life against tall statistics of growth. Too much had been forgotten and too much neglected in the rush of earlier building. By 1957 the pollution of Lake Ontario along the Toronto waterfront was almost beyond remedy. It was cheaper for the city to give up plans for filtration and draw its water from Lake Simcoe, forty-five miles away. The waters of the Don and Humber would not run clean again; nor

355

would playgrounds, parks and chlorinated swimming pools quite make up for the loss. By 1961 the Ontario Water Resources Commission was grappling to some effect with the general problem of pollution. That problem, however, with the question of the use of land and the preservation of the environment, would continue to haunt the 1960s.

2.

The strains of religious belief that had been brought to Upper Canada were the solace of the pioneers. They provided strength in adversity, knit together communities and hardened common purposes among those of the same faith. At the same time the individual denominations, deeply cherishing their differences and rock-firm for maintaining them, were potent sources of discord.

In an Ontario thick with churches there were long years of denominational strife, disfiguring the name of religion. Yet the very heat of controversy tended to melt some walls. By the middle 1880s most of the Presbyterian and all the Methodist bodies had come together. By the early 1890s churchmen of all faiths were shaken by the claims of science, disturbed by biblical criticism and alive to social needs. The opening of western Canada called out for missionaries. The factory workers and the slum dwellers were a reproach nearer at hand. The basic work of the church – the whole of the Christian church – was the sanctification of society. How could this be accomplished in a state of fragmentation, of divisive claims and beliefs, many of them now threatened, some already weakened, and all tending to the weakening of the whole mission? What was required was a refinement of belief, a narrowing down to essentials that might mean a reduction of differences and a strengthened Christian faith.

Out of the search for a new and stronger wholeness the moves for union began. In 1889 Anglicans, Presbyterians and Methodists began exploratory talks that were to lapse for fifteen years. Resumed in 1904, they went on for four more years, with doctrines melding gradually and differences giving way. Yet there were still uneasy consciences and ties that could not be cut, and the final result was failure. By 1914, entering a world war, the churches remained divided and the war emphasized division.

Out of the war itself and growing in the post-war world came greater challenges than the church had ever faced. At the same time the essential values of religion were beginning to be reasserted. Darwinism loomed no longer as a huge and hostile spectre; religious faith was embracing the claims of science. The analytical criticism that had seemed to threaten the Bible was being met by theologians with new assessments of its place, as the repository of the divine spirit if not the literal word. Surer now of themselves, and more driven in conscience by the growth of social needs, three of the denominations came together. In 1925 all Methodists, most Congregationalists and two-thirds of the Presbyterians were joined in the United Church.

By 1936 conversations aimed at a "recovery of fellowship"[3] were in progress between the United Church, the Church of England and the continuing Presbyterians. In the same year the Baptist churches adopted the hymnary of the United Church with only minor revisions and by 1938, though there was no further union, the Presbyterians and the United Church were drawing closer together. In 1944 the individual congregations of the Baptists were joined in a federation, while eleven years later the Lutheran churches strengthened their national connections. In 1955 the Church of England in Canada became the Anglican Church of Canada, and by 1960 it was resuming conversations with the United Church. In the oecumenical spirit that was widening out with the times the goal was a new embodiment in "One Church of God." Even the rebuilding of the greatest bridge, between Protestantism and Roman Catholicism, had become for churchmen of all faiths a mutually shared hope.

As reflected in the social scene, the changes were progressive responses to the effects of two world wars and the depression between the wars. Dogma, tradition and authority, tested by those great crises, seemed to have lost their grip. "After the Second World War," says John Webster Grant, "the churches were thrown on the defensive in most parts of the world."[4] To some extent they had revived a battered idealism in the face of the brassy 1920s. The achievement of partial union and the general emphasis on service rather than doctrinal differences had brought them through the depression as a strengthened social force. The Second War and the aftermath, with its disillusioned veterans, its floods of immigration and its increasing cosmopolitanism, had seemed to erode their gains.

As the 1940s merged with the 1950s, affluence brought its shifts in social priorities. The industrial slum, for the churchman, became somewhat less of a problem; the urban suburb more. The shorter hours of the working day brought longer periods of leisure, and the question of what to do with them. There was more casual drinking, more leniency in sex, while marital difficulties and family tensions grew. With "an endless relativity in faith and morals" the props of an older province seemed to be giving way. By 1950, along with the relaxation of several other blue laws, professional sport on Sunday became a legal diversion. In 1955 one of the proliferating Gallup polls reported that only 44 per cent of Ontario's population regularly attended church. The same population, it was reported in 1960, spent $100,000,000.00 betting on horse races, much of that illegally and a good deal on the Sabbath. In the same year came final, formal abandonment of the hope of prohibition. The General Council of the United Church, still urging abstinence as "the wisest and safest course," accepted the right of members to a moderate use of alcohol.[5]

> As institutions, (said Grant, speaking of Canada as a whole,) the churches stood for old-world traditions with which few Canadians felt at home, for moral codes to which few of them adhered, or for beliefs that had too little to do with the presuppositions by which most of them lived.[6]

Yet to that bleak assessment there were many qualifications. Divorces, for whatever they indicated in a loosening of religious ties, increased from 734 in 1940 to 2,739 in 1961; but of 44,434 marriages made in the latter year there were only twelve in which the parties did not profess to be members of a church. The work of the missions extended across Canada and to much of the outside world. The churches as a social force were respected and indispensable, and customs and traditions surrounding them were still slow to give way. Professional sport on Sunday, like liquor measures before it, was subject to local option. It was resisted for five years by many of the farm communities. A rock core of rural opinion stood, and even in the restless cities one sensed a hunger for belief. It was that hunger, quickening and inspiring churchmen, that led them to refine their own.

In the universities of the 1950s theology began to assume a new importance. The Old Testament and the New, restudied once again, became "neither the collection of divine oracles taken for granted by the older orthodoxy nor the treasury of religious experience valued by liberals, but rather the record of God's saving activity in history."[7] The Pontifical Institute of Mediaeval Studies, established in 1929 in St. Michael's College of the University of Toronto, revived interest in scholastic philosophy in hundreds of searching minds. Jewish scholars, for their part, began to re-examine their own traditions. All faiths, rediscovering their past in the midst of a hostile present, were building on new ground.

Meanwhile, as social agencies, the churches turned to the business of ministration, with a new, professional efficiency in raising and expending funds. They devoted more of their care to the old and helpless, and more of their skilled modernity in reaching out to the young. Dialogue sermons and "buzz groups" promoted challenge and reply; and films, radio and television came into increasing use.

A far cry from the old days of authority, it was an active, vital response to the age of the packaged product, of disbelief and doubt. What it would all come to no one yet knew, but if the place of the church was changing it was still a central place. No man could envisage, and few wished to envisage, an Ontario without its churches.

Much had been left behind, particularly by the older, sterner denominations, but what remained was strong.

> In the end, (judged one historian, commenting specifically on an earlier era) possibly the most vital accomplishment of the evangelical denominations was to maintain the hold of the traditional Christian conception of God's design for man in an increasingly antagonistic environment. In so doing they perpetuated in our culture a strong consciousness of the past foundations of our civilization, and of the width and depth of reality.[8]

3.

Through the two wars and the depression Ontario literature had evolved along with the churches. A first response, stemming from the universities, had been the fostering of new conceptions of history. In 1937 Donald Creighton's *The Commercial Empire of the St. Lawrence* had established the great river and the chain of inland waters as the spine of national growth. By 1955 his completed biography of Sir John A. Macdonald had given cohesion and grandeur to the ideal of the Dominion itself. In *Colony to Nation* and *Canadians in the Making* Arthur R. M. Lower, though he rubbed off some of the grandeur, conveyed a sense of the life and quality of the people. By 1959 J.M.S. Careless had published the first volume of *Brown of the Globe*, and its warm, intimate, vastly knowledgeable pages were unfolding another view, not only of Upper Canada but of the making of the nation itself. Frank H. Underhill, also a professor of history at the University of Toronto, was less prolific of books but more the historian in action as one of the founding fathers of the CCF.

Appearing in the early 1950s, between history and literature but enlivening both fields, were the explosive, wayward genius of Marshall McLuhan and the new range of criticism opened by Northrop Frye. In Frye's hands the Laurentian vista of Creighton, relating to trade and economic growth, took on its meaning for the immigrant and the individual Canadian. The traveller by ship from Europe, Frye wrote, was

> like a tiny Jonah entering an inconceivably large whale, slipping past the Straits of Belle Isle into the Gulf of St. Lawrence, where

five Canadian provinces surround him, for the most part invisible. Then he goes up the St. Lawrence and the inhabited country comes into view, mainly a French-speaking country with its own cultural traditions . . . to enter Canada is a matter of being silently swallowed by an alien continent.[9]

Implicit in that image was the destination, Ontario. Settlement had passed west, but here was the central home. The Ontarian assumed as much when he wrote of his own province, and it tended to blur distinctions. Canadianism rather than Ontarianism emerged in much of the writing; an inclusive view of the nation – the English part of the nation – rather than the province itself. The writing sprang, however, from roots that were deep in the near ground, and Ontario tradition and attitudes were an inescapable environment.

Stephen Leacock of Orillia, the Squire of Mariposa, was a great exemplar of the times. Humorist, economist, imperialist, social satirist and historian, he passed his life at McGill. Yet he was unmistakably an Ontarian, torn between many talents and stretched on the rack of change. By the time he died in 1944 his *Sunshine Sketches of a Little Town* were an authentic national treasure and a gleam from a lost world. Through the many books that had followed it the eternal glint of comedy had seemed to be at war with conscience and the man at war with himself. He was a resentful lover of empire in the metropolis of French Canada, but a typical Canada Firster in his view of English snobs. As an economist he saw the depression and could measure cause and effect, but he could not find a cure. He could flay the banker and industrialist but he mixed with them at their clubs, and he saw and left unsolved the riddle of social justice. "The tattered outcast dozes on his bench while the chariot of the wealthy is drawn by. The palace is the neighbour of the slum"[10]

By 1937 Ralph Connor was dead, but Glengarry county still found its recorders, as did the Niagara country, other of the older counties, and the farm and rural scene. A stream of fiction evoking the provincial past or providing escape from the present flowed on with increasing range and variety. Mystery stories and romances, churned out to compete with American counterparts, were all too often set in exotic places. Yet there was real effort by a few more serious novelists to recreate the past of provincial regions, to convey the Ontario background with a modern sense of realism and to portray life in the cities. Among these, though standing apart from all of them, was the phenomenon of *Jalna*.

Mazo de la Roche of Toronto was thirty-eight years old and had published three novels when, in 1927, she won the first prize of $10,000.00 in the Atlantic Monthly competition. American recognition, true to Canadian form, brought recognition at home. At "a really splendid dinner . . . by combined literary societies" the author was congratulated by the Lieutenant-Governor of Ontario and presented with a silver tea service by the city of Toronto itself, "I making a small, rather tremulous speech of thanks, and wearing a French evening gown, loose-waisted, short-skirted in the extraordinary fashion of the day."[11]

Jalna with its fifteen sequels, of which the last was published in 1960, was translated into many languages, read around the world and adapted for radio and television as well as films and the stage. A story of the Whiteoaks family, mythical Ontario gentry established in Victorian times and maintaining a declining estate, the novels, in the words of one critic

> deliberately avoid life in southern Ontario and offer a romantic alternative of the past alive in the present. Even the city which symbolizes the opposition to this landed gentry is New York, not Toronto, whose very existence would not be surmised from reading these books.[12]

What could be surmised, however, was a liking in Ontario as elsewhere for relief from the twentieth century and for a long series of vital and memorable characters who refused to come to terms with it.

Out of the depression and the Second War came a new and sterner realism, centred mainly on the cities. Hugh Garner's *Cabbagetown* stands as a grey example, as angry, dismal and uncompromising as the Toronto slum itself. Among many finer novels there was the same smouldering of anger, directed beyond regionalisms and beyond national boundaries at the social structure of the world. A part of that anger, though wholly regional in view and elegantly satirical in vein, was the work of Robertson Davies. The *Samuel Marchbanks* of the 1940s who had posed as a waspy critic of provincial modes and manners developed as a novelist of the 1950s with *Tempest Tost, A Leaven of Malice* and *A Mixture of Frailties*. In those books, prefacing his larger works of later years, the ignorance, pretentiousness and materialism discovered in the city of Salterton, strongly resembling Kingston, are impaled on a sharp skewer.

Morley Callaghan, as a newspaper man in Toronto and a writer of short stories, published his first novel in 1929. *Strange Fugitive* was a bleak story of a lonely loser in the city and the earlier succeeding novels were much in the same vein, reflecting the currents of the time. Callaghan lived in Paris, knew Chicago, New York and Montreal and absorbed their competing influences. Marx entered his picture, Freud was close at hand and the novelist's characters groped among the philosophies, torn as he was himself. As a young Catholic in the depression and a young humanist concerned for the world's miserable, the writer's struggle reflected the struggle of the churches to find a base in faith. In his own case there was a reassertion of Catholicism, reconciled at least partially with the thrust of modern thought. Certainly there was basic oneness in the theme he made his own and threaded through his later novels: "the desperate, real loneliness we suffer in our relationships with other people."[13] *The Loved and The Lost*, as perhaps his finest work, brought recognition in Canada, but neither then nor later a tribute like Edmund Wilson's, the dean of American letters. Callaghan, Wilson wrote, was "perhaps the most unjustly neglected novelist in the English-speaking world" and "a writer whose work may be mentioned without absurdity in association with Chekhov's and Turgenev's."[14] Even discounting that, as many of his peers did, he symbolized for Ontario a new maturity in letters.

In 1915 Colonel John McCrae of Guelph, a medical officer serving with the Canadian forces, attended the burial of a comrade among the bloody fields of Flanders. He is said to have come back to his dugout and, resting a notebook on the back of one of his fellow officers, begun the draft of the poem that condensed into fifteen lines some of the deepest feelings of the war. Of much wartime verse and some authentic poetry, *In Flanders Fields*, for Ontario, remains the great memorial.

At home through the years of the war and the decades following the war Duncan Campbell Scott had a late flowering. Raymond Knister, dying at thirty-three, gave promise and more than promise of the later James Reaney in his identification with landscape, his love of life and little things and his ability to give them meaning through greater freedom of form. "Just let the reader picture them" he wrote, "with the utmost economy and clearness, and let them move him in the measure that he is moved by little things and great."[15] In that way he pictured the flight of the hawk:

Across the bristled and sallow fields,
The speckled stubble of cut clover,
Wades your shadow.

Or against a grimy and tattered
Sky
You plunge.
Or you shear a swath
From trembling tiny forests
With the steel of your wings –

Or make a row of waves
By the heat of your flight
Along the soundless horizon.[16]

Robert Finch, as an observer of city life, called up his images and meanings with intricate technical skill:

The dark green truck on the cement platform
is explicit as a paradigm.
Its wheels are four black cast-iron starfish.
Its body, a massive tray of planking,
ends in two close-set dark green uprights
crossed with three straight cross-pieces, one
looped with a white spiral of hose.[17]

The same skill, translated beyond the city, was resourceful in rich conceits:

The lake has drawn a counterpane of glass
On her rock limbs up to her island pillows
And under netting woven by the swallows
Sleeps in a dream and is a dream . . .[18]

Like politicians, churchmen and the average man in the street, the poets of the 1930s and 1940s were at war with much in their world. Yet they did not fly like the romantics; they chose to stand and fight, questioning society and religion, probing the age of the machine and extracting beauty where they found it. The mood, often, was one of iconoclastic rage. "Against the elder poets," said one writer of the 1940s, "the sad young men rose in angry revolt."[19] Yet there was one figure, overshadowing them all, who seemed apart from the turmoil.

E.J. Pratt had come to Toronto from Newfoundland at the age of twenty-four. By 1919, after taking three degrees at the university, he had joined the Department of English at Victoria College. There he was to teach and write for the next thirty-four years, at home in the Toronto environment, breathing Ontario air and remaining his robust self. The ocean rolled through his work from *Newfoundland Verse* in 1923 to *Here the Tides Flow* in 1962, but there was much else beside. Pratt saw, with the reverse of Callaghan's view, the battles of great sea creatures, the struggles of ships and men, the Jesuit martyrs of Huronia, the returning soldiers of Dunkirk and the tremendous national victory in the building of the CPR. Unique as an epic rather than a lyric poet, Pratt celebrated the conqueror, "the breed" shaping its destiny, and some of his large conceptions irked the realist. Yet there was humour deflating the grandeur, tenderness softening the glorification of power, and pictures as unforgettable as

363

the very feats they told of. He came to the mountain gorges in the building of the CPR:

> Out of a hundred men they drafted sailors
> Whose toes as supple as their fingers knew
> The wash of reeling decks, whose knees were hardened
> Through tying gaskets at the royal yards:
> They lowered them with knotted ropes and drew them
> Along the face until the lines were strung
> Between the juts. Barefooted, dynamite
> Strapped to their waists, the sappers followed, treading
> The spider films and chipping holes for blasts
> Until the cliffs delivered up their features
> Under the civil discipline of roads.[20]

The conquering of the unconquerable Shield round Lake Superior produced this image of the country:

> Westward above her webs she had a trap –
> A thing called muskeg, easy on the eyes
> Stung with the dust of gravel. Cotton grass
> Its white spires blending with the orchids,
> Peeked through green table-cloths of sphagnum moss . . .
> Deceptive – and the men were moving west!
> Now was her time. She took three engines, sank them
> With seven tracks down through the hidden lake
> To the rock bed, then over them she spread
> A counterpane of leather-leaf and slime . . .
> Some day perhaps when ice began to move,
> Or some convulsion ran fires through her tombs,
> She might stir in her sleep and far below
> The reach of steel and blast of dynamite,
> She'd claim their bones as her possessive right
> And wrap them cold in her pre-Cambrian folds.[21]

Nor would any traveller to Huronia, if he had read Pratt, pass Midland and the shrine of Sainte Marie without remembering:

> The trails . . .
> Under the mould of the centuries, under fern
> And brier and fungus – there in due time to blossom
> Into the highways that lead to the crest of the hill[22]

and Brébeuf, the Jesuit martyr wreathed in fire, still baffling the Iroquois:

                    Where was the source
Of his strength, the home of his courage that topped the best
Of their braves and even out-fabled the lore of their legends? . . .
. . . Was it the blood?
They would draw it fresh from its fountain.

                    Was it the heart?
They dug for it, fought for the scraps in the way of wolves.
But not in these was the valour or stamina lodged . . .
But in the sound of invisible trumpets blowing
Around two slabs of board, right-angled, hammered
By Roman nails and hung on a Jewish hill.[23]

Growing around and moving apart from Pratt were younger Ontario poets. Raymond Souster and P.K. Page published their first
collections in 1946, Douglas LePan in 1948 and James Reaney in
1949. By 1956 Anne Wilkinson, Jay Macpherson and Phyllis Webb
had become recognized figures, and Margaret Avison joined them in
1960. Each different from the others, defying categorization or
regional identification, they were as at home spiritually in Montreal
or Vancouver as they were in their own province. They were into the
age of the aeroplane and entering the age of television which was to
bring with it, as Northrop Frye wrote later, "a world which is
post-Canadian as it is post-American, post-British and post
everything except the world itself."[24] Yet for all their lyric range,
wide as the philosophies and religions, they were not fugitives from
life.
   P.K. Page, a film writer, looked at the lines of crisp stenographers
in an office:

   efficient and sure as their adding machines;
   yet they weep in the vault, they are taut as net curtains
   stretched upon frames. In their eyes I have seen
   the pin men of madness in marathon trim
   race round the track of the stadium pupil.[25]

Raymond Souster, the poet of the city streets, saw

   The warm steaming at the windows of the hamburger-joint where
      the Wurlitzer
   Booms all night without a stop, where the onions are thick be-
      tween the buns

and enjoined the figure huddled at one of the counters:

   Wrap yourself well in that cheap coat that holds back the wind
      like a sieve,

You have a long way to go, and the streets are dark, you may
    have to walk all night before you find
Another heart so lonely, so nearly mad with boredom, so filled
    with such strength, such tenderness of love.[26]

And James Reaney, born on the farm near Stratford, looked round
him, sensing his roots:

How sad it is, this winter farmhouse parlour
Coloured like the bindings of religious books,
Dull green, brown and dingy maroon,
And the stove as black as a bible.
And Grandfather in his picture looks
Reproachful, as if to say
You can't sit here reading![27]

"The first Canadian playwright of any stature whatever," says
Michael Tait in the *Literary History of Canada*, "is Merrill Denison,
whose appearance coincided with the quickening of the Little
Theatre movement in this country."[28] The movement had its beginning in 1918 and was strong enough by the end of the 1920s to withstand the rigours of depression. Where most activities withered the
Little Theatres went on; the groups produced their plays, the professional adjudicators were somehow paid to judge them and a taste for
drama grew. For a long time, however, *Brothers in Arms*, *Marsh
Hay* and other of the works of Denison, with their raw, crude satire,
their undercurrent of anger and their bleak view of the Shield country as "the unheroic north" remained the peak of achievement.

In 1919 Hart House was opened, a gift of the Massey family, adding itself to the beloved Massey Hall as one of Toronto's treasures.
Its fine theatre was an immediate stimulus and supplement to other
budding movements, and it was there that Denison's plays were first
produced. In London, by 1934, four local amateur groups had come
together to acquire the Grand Theatre, which had served touring
professionals, as a base for local drama. Thirteen years later Toronto acquired another base in the New Play Society. Growing in the
hands of Dora Mavor Moore and her son, Mavor Moore, it began
professional productions and encouraged native writing. Though its
financial life was chequered its influence lingered long and *Spring
Thaw*, the annual series of touring variety revues, was one result of
the venture.

In 1944, with the *Stage* series of radio plays produced by Andrew
Allan, the CBC became an influence in drama. By 1952, when television came to Toronto, the eight seasons of the series had resulted in
the production of some 250 plays. They included adapted novels,

numerous imported plays and the original scripts were good, bad and indifferent. They had, however, been listened to across the country by hundreds of thousands of people, many of whom had seldom entered a theatre. They were developing a new appetite and there were new resources at hand. Radio was now supporting, and television would support better, a pool of actors, writers, directors and potential producers who were able to live by their work.

For Toronto the time was ripe, and in addition to the Crest Theatre other smaller theatres made their appearance. Some of them spawned touring companies that travelled widely in the province. Summer stock came, and occasionally a Canadian play competing with hardy standbys. Between 1949 and 1954 Robertson Davies translated his erudition and his satirical talents to the stage in a series of five plays. Meanwhile, on its own, a larger plan was maturing.

The inspiration of an amateur, Thomas Patterson of Stratford, it was supported by a native coterie that included many talents and was brought to its realization through the work of Tyrone Guthrie. The town on Ontario's Avon had its green fields and swans and its streets with Shakespearean names, but only a Tom Patterson could have seen its possibilities. The work of the mild young man, in promoting and raising funds, in nudging the provincial government to grant and improve land and in catching the imagination of renowned foreign professionals, resulted in an authentic miracle.

Through the summer of 1953, in a great, beflagged tent rising beside the Avon, the Stratford Shakespearean Festival welcomed its first thousands. It was a production of native enterprise but hardly of local talent. Its superb open stage was the creation of Tanya Moiseiwitsch, one of the great designers of Europe, and Alec Guinness of London was the first star to appear on it in the role of Richard III. Conceived with sophistication and on a large and liberal scale, there had been no concessions to parochialism in any part of the venture, and success was instantaneous. By 1957 a $2,000,000.00 auditorium stood on the banks of the Avon, replacing the tent that had passed into legend. Two years earlier, moreover, the Stratford Shakespearean Festival had become the Stratford Festival, opening its stage to other works beside those of the Bard.

By 1961 an occasional Canadian play and numerous Canadian concerts were varying the bills at Stratford, and many Canadian actors were included among the casts. Ontario drama was emerging, though still slowly and tentatively, with John Coulter's *Riel* and James Reaney's *Killdeer* a year or so in the future. Many writers were developing by way of radio and television, and physically at least the scope for plays was widening. London, Brockville, Windsor, Kingston and other cities maintained theatres for international companies as well as local productions. There was a Little Theatre of some sort in most Ontario towns; and four summer theatres, two puppet theatres and four children's theatre schools were active across the province.

Toronto maintained its position as the focus of professional talent and as a stop for foreign tours. With the O'Keefe Centre, the Royal Alexandra and the Maple Leaf Gardens, it was equipped for the great spectaculars from New York and further abroad. The Crest Theatre, though perennially in financial straits, had completed an eighth season and produced a hundred plays. In seven other playhouses of various kinds and qualities, actors, writers and entrepreneurs of theatre were offering entertainment. It varied from sometimes good to often abysmally bad and from straight night-club bawdy to angry social comment, but it marked the change in the times. It was now possible, exulted a newspaper critic, to see a professional theatre production every night of the week, including Sunday. "Toronto the Good," in his view, "has become Toronto the Better!"[29]

4.

In 1920 there had been seventeen makers of pianos in the city of Toronto alone; by 1961 there were only two. In all cities suburban living had scattered the population, the automobile had made for increased mobility and the electronics industry had changed interests and habits. The old melodeons were gone, the piano was becoming rarer in the small, planned house and evening music for the family was a matter of twisting dials. Television and radio brought the concerts in, and more people went out because there was much more to do.

In 1961 the five-year-old Canadian Opera Company moved from the Royal Alexandra Theatre to the O'Keefe Centre, doubling its potential audience to a total of 3,000. Opera was becoming a success. The devoted Celia Franca was making a success of ballet. After ten years of work she had native artists dancing with foreign stars, native ballets were being developed; and her young company was warmly welcomed abroad. "To see them dance is to be witness to that charming phenomenon," said a foreign critic charmingly, "when the dew is on the rose."[30]

Toronto's Mendelssohn Choir, with its long and rich tradition, was much sought and often away on tour. It was always at home, however, for the Eastertime *Messiah*. In St. Michael's Cathedral Choir and in many larger and smaller groups distributed across the province, choral singing maintained its abiding hold. Doctor Healey

Willan and Sir Ernest MacMillan, both of whom had been active for fifty years, were still extending the range not only of choral but of much other music with their symphonies, operas, concertos and their genius for discovering talent and evoking a response from youth.

The symphony orchestras in the cities were struggling with new conditions as attitudes and tastes changed. There was less support from the wealthy, the musicians' unions were becoming more demanding and there was less acceptance of the conventional by the newer bourgeoisie. Toronto's Sunday "pops" programs, denounced by critics as "timid and old-fashioned," had been suspended pending rejuvenation. Yet the very disputes in music were the result of an increased variety and a larger general audience which owed much to such organizations as the Hart House Orchestra, the Hart House String Quartet and to the work done by the famous Hambourg family. In 1961, said one critic, in spite of various crises of artistic and fiscal policies, "music was becoming a subject Canadians cared to have opinions about."[31] A new interest in the young was a healthy sign of development. In 1960 Walter Susskind, the conductor of the Toronto Symphony, had gathered together a hundred selected musicians all under the age of twenty-five, trained them at Stratford through four weeks in summer and sent them off on a tour across Canada. There was no doubt, when they came back, that the National Youth Orchestra was to be a continuing institution.

The CBC with its own symphony orchestra, its contests for young musicians and the wide range of its broadcasts, was a great encourager of talent. More new work was heard as it found a readier outlet, and it came from Ontario composers in many varied forms. Under the baton of Geoffrey Waddington the works of Harry Freedman were becoming known. John Weinzweig, as a teacher and pioneer, combined vocal and orchestral work that pointed the way to operas; and in 1961 John Reeves's *Opera For Six Voices* with music by the jazz composer, Norman Symonds was one of the first results.

Avant-garde composers struck out in many directions, partly induced by the new freedom of the air waves. Indian, Eskimo and French-Canadian motifs began to thread through their work. While Stratford valiantly revived Gilbert and Sullivan, it also opened its stages to the work of new composers. With radio, films and television, the widening field of jazz music extended to include rock; and in the summer of 1960 some thirty music festivals were held across the province, notably one at Orillia. In the Mariposa Folk Festival both genuine old melodies and the lively beat of commercial groups attested a coming vogue.

Edward Johnson, Kathleen Parlow, Maureen Forrester, Lois Marshall, Betty-Jean Hagen and Glenn Gould were all Ontario musical names familiar around the world. London had its Western Ontario Conservatory of Music, Ottawa University its Ecole de Musique et de Déclamation, and some 40,000 students annually were entered for examination at Toronto's Royal Conservatory of Music. In all fields, if there was a struggle of old values with new modernities and debasement, there was also wide adventuring and there was growth pushing at the roots. Speaking of the building boom of the 1940s and 1950s, an Ontario writer commented in the late 1960s: "For reasons which are still partly obscure to a good many of us, it was decided by the architects of almost all new schools that they should include large auditoriums."[32] By that time, and as a rebuke to that fatuity, the music heard in the schools was giving answer.

By the end of the 1950s the painters of the Group of Seven had accomplished one of their aims. Their harsh, primeval landscapes were establishing a sense of the country in boardrooms, offices and railway stations that had not known art before. Lawren Harris, Frederick Varley and Arthur Lismer had passed through the First World War and the later anguish of the depression to leave canvases behind them that evoked memories of both. The Second World War had had its powerful recorders, while in a rich heritage of other and gentler landscapes the province breathed and spoke. The Grand Valley lived in the canvases of Homer Watson, with its great trees and grainfields, its drowsy hours of sunlight and its hush of lowering clouds. David Milne, Carl Schaefer and Franklin Brownell were tall among many others who had caught moods and recalled scenes that were passing, from the luminous grace of water lilies at Timagami to the sombre tension of a gaunt northern farmhouse awaiting a coming storm.

Lawren Harris, as one of the Group of Seven, had groped his way toward abstractions with a side excursion in poetry. The same search for expression, by new means and media, had brought together the group of Painters Eleven, early in the 1950s. They were as much interested in the cities as they were in rural scenes, everywhere interested in life, and determined to convey new meanings by breaking the bonds of form. In oils, watercolours, prints, woodcuts, etchings and collages they sought beyond the image to a private view of reality. Often enough they challenged the viewer with its impact. "In print-making," said Harold Town, one of the most adventurous, "I have been able to realize the sudden complete magical revelation in which supreme order and the distilled chaos of experience are united in a whole larger than the sum of its parts."[33]

The "distilled chaos of experience" was inseparable from its own time, and there was much in it that many found repellent. Yet it was part of the quality of the age and was expressed in many forms.

> Everything the detractors of modern art say about it is true, (commented Northrop Frye,) except that what they are objecting to is not so much something in our art as something in our lives. Painting, music and architecture, no less than literature, reflect an anonymous and cold-blooded society, a society without much respect for personality and without much tolerance for differences in opinion, a society full of slickness, smugness and spiritual inanity. But as long as the arts are thought of as educational they can teach as well as reflect.[34]

For that teaching and reflection there was an increasing range of outlets. Art galleries, more generously funded and encouraged, supported artists better. More theatre and ballet demanded costume design. Affluence created and encouraged the crafts in stained glass, and metal work and ceramics. Builders, architects and businessmen discovered painting and sculpture and the artist's eye for atmosphere as means to enhance surroundings and even to improve business. The compartmentation of life, the old grim divisions between places for making money and places for glimpsing beauty, between being an enjoying human and being a working drudge, began to crumble a little. Perhaps because of the immigrant, Ontario in some of its cities was assuming a touch of Europe. Murals decorated banks and covered the walls of airports; sculptures in new materials, often of welded metal and grotesque and haunting form, stood in commercial courtyards. The grace of colonial days, washed over by the waves of industrialization, was not now to be recaptured, but hints and vistas opened on an even earlier past. Some of the great stone figures carved by Cape Dorset Eskimos came down to stand in Toronto.

Suburban growth, through a period of twenty years, had been an explosion rather than a change. By 1961, of the 1,618,787 people in Metropolitan Toronto, over 1,000,000 were housed outside the city. Forest Hill had become a suburb of the affluent as early as the middle 1930s. Well-to-do businessmen and others recently successful had moved in the 1940s and 1950s to Don Mills, Thorncrest and a number of other developments within close range of their work. Beyond them, however, following and extending the rush, were people of average or lower means seeking homes they could afford. Between 1941 and 1961 the population of Toronto itself was static or actually declining. During the same period, in the metropolitan area, the population of the nine "inner" municipalities rose by some 125,000 and that of the three "outer" – Etobicoke, Scarborough and North York – by nearly 600,000.

The expansion of Hamilton, proportionately, was greater than that of Toronto, and London and Windsor were moving in the same direction. Ottawa was in a class by itself with its famous Greber Plan which provided for the building of roads, the laying out of parks and the relocation of facilities to embellish the national capital. In all other cities, from Sault Ste. Marie and Sudbury to the larger centres of the south, fiscal policies and planning contended with urban sprawl.

The daily transportation of hundreds of thousands was one of the enduring problems. The huge expenditures on development gave rise to hot debate. Over the whole, moreover, and beyond the question of expense, was the other question of results. In all the variety of movement there had been a single common purpose: to translate prosperity and mobility into a better way of life, to fresh air and fields, room for children to play in and pride in owning a home. Much of this had come now, at least in the older suburbs. The planned house stood, settled on its patch of lawn, with every inch of its interior serving a prescribed function. The looped roads and crescents, the shopping centres and green spaces tied the communities together. Yet at the same time, in the tidy miniature cities apart from city life, there were urban workers living amid some of the urban pressures.

The vast majority of suburbanites had been comparatively young couples, paying off mortgages, spending hours in tiring travel to their work, contending with the problems of baby-sitting and elementary schools. Now as the children grew and the young adventurers of the 1940s settled toward middle age, the thought of the universities, the concerts, lectures and theatre-going and the lively life of the cities became attractive again. Doubts were arising as to the ultimate value of suburbia with its enormous cost of servicing, its consumption of human energy in the mere mechanics of living, and its inconvenient remoteness from much that was rich and good. There had been no easy alternative and there was none visible now. Suburban development went on and beyond the boundaries of the suburbs, lining the country roads, tentative areas of "ribbon growth" were clustering as new centres.

Under the hands of modern architects the picture window of the suburbs, translated to new dimensions, was fronting on city streets. Many of the new skyscrapers and some of the smaller buildings were rising in glass and steel, rather than brick or stone. The stern classic façade and dim Gothic interior were gone with the tellers' cages and the cold sanctity of banks. Whole walls of glass glimmered on passers-by and inner-courtyard landscaping invited them to step in. Twentieth century business, blandly open and coolly reassuring, was reaching out to its customers in a serenity of space and light. For one professional observer, however, it did not quite seem to work. "There is," said Alan Gowans, "an a-human quality in modern architecture – a coldness and remoteness from historic human experience . . . modern buildings seem to have been built for machines, not men."[35]

As a part of change there was often hearty bickering when old and long-prized structures went under the wrecker's ball. Guelph, through 1960, was a town considerably divided over the fate of St. George's Square. The city had lost its opera house and its prized fountain had been condemned as a public hazard. The century-old Customs House and an adjacent Georgian residence were declared to be next to go. To a preservationist of the day, "The city councillors seemed to possess the Jaycee mentality and would have progressed to hell as long as they kept in progress."[36] Progress they did, however, and the site was cleared for the Bank of Montreal, "housed in an upended matchbox."[37]

Toronto's major controversy began in the 1950s. Nathan Phillips, who liked to refer to himself as "the old grey mayor" had secured the consent of the ratepayers to the spending of $18,000,000.00 for a new City Hall. By 1959 an international competition had brought in 532 entries from forty-two countries and resulted in the selection of a design. The work of Viljo Revell, a comparatively unknown Finn, it was for three buildings rather than a single unit. "The people's meeting place" was to consist of two concave towers surrounding a central dome. The model, when it came to be viewed, was denounced by various aldermen as "a monument to one of the dizziest times in civic history . . . a Taj Mahal – an extravagant attempt to build a stairway to the stars." With the proposal to include a cocktail bar the two towers became immediately "Sodom and Gomorrah" and there was a final acid suggestion that the combined structure "looked like a streamlined privy with the curved walls and the domed seat in the centre."[38]

Yet Toronto, for all the criticism, approved the work of the Finn. By 1961 the new City Hall was beginning to rise on Queen Street, and a clearing of ground across from it signalled another change. A colourful section of Chinatown and an aging clutter of stores, restaurants, burlesque houses and pawnshops were all to give way to Nathan Phillips Square.

Winter and summer and everywhere across the province the round of sport went on with the round of work. No school was without its playground and very few of the high schools without a good gymnasium. All towns had baseball diamonds, football fields and skating rinks, and golf clubs and tennis courts were essential features of suburbia. Amateur sport for youth was a part of education, golf a status symbol and the delight of middle age, and in yacht racing, figure skating, track and field and water sports Ontarians were world competitors.

Yet the province was part of a Canada and part of a North America where the watching and reading of professional sport was a major avocation. Radio had helped it on, television made it rich and the annual results, like dividends, were a public weal or woe. Among the racecourse fraternity, in 1961, most Ontarians were poorer by some 65 per cent of the $136,000,000.00 legally bet in Canada. In International League baseball the Toronto Maple Leafs, champions a year before, had tumbled to fifth place. Frank Mahovlich of the hockey Maple Leafs had fallen two goals short in trying for a record fifty. George Chuvalo of Toronto, the in-and-out heavyweight, had lost his title to a boxer in Montreal. Even though professional soccer was struggling into existence it had not been a good year.

Nor was it helped by professional football, the ranking sport with hockey. Toronto's Americanized Argonauts and Hamilton's Americanized Tiger-Cats had fought it out in the east, with Toronto going down. Winnipeg's Blue Bombers, also speaking with accents that ranged from Texas to Maine, had taken the title in the west. Finally east and west, with trains and planes delivering the supporting faithful, had come together in Toronto for the rite of the Grey Cup.

Friday, December 1, had been chaos in the jammed hotels, with lobbies stripped for action like Nelsonian men of war. Saturday morning had witnessed the Grey Cup Parade, transferring chaos to the streets. Late in the afternoon, as dingy twilight settled on the churned field, Winnipeg crossed the goal line for the final, fatal touchdown. Ontario was out for 1961.

It hardly mattered to easterners that the cup was going west and it hardly mattered to anyone that the game was becoming American, with halfbacks blocking downfield "like basket-ball with cleats." To the modern sporting realist, like the modern business realist, Americanization was a part of daily life. You gave to it where you had to and fought back where you could, accepting facts as you found them and turning them to your own use. Ontarians and westerners alike, honouring their American heroes, drank and celebrated in the old streets of Toronto, and the occasion was a battered challenge cup donated by an English lord. It was a silly spectacle, an odd spectacle and somehow strangely Canadian, even more Ontarian, in its mix of competing elements. To an American writer drawn north for the occasion it was, as if someone could cram into one package the giddier trappings of the World Series, the Kentucky Derby, the Army-Navy game, New Year's Eve and the Mardi Gras at New Orleans ... No sports event in the States can quite compare with the Grey Cup as a stirrer-upper of national emotions.[39]

5.

In 1959, when he was returned at his last election, Frost was sixty-four. He was in good health and his government was still strong, but there were signs of change for both. The hip wound bothered the Premier more than in earlier years, and the province along with the country was entering the trough of a recession. Old problems were recurring, as always in new forms, and the challenge of new solutions demanded a younger man.

By 1961 the Premier was ready to go, or a little more than ready. Always the benign autocrat, steely-suave in the face of major crisis, he was less tranquil than he had once been in the routine of little things. "He's started to swear in the last three or four years," said one of his close associates, "I can never remember him swearing before." Another recalled a truly memorable outburst; not, however, quite of the first quality. "Actually he doesn't swear very well. He used all the words I know, but he used them all up in one sentence."[40]

The sixteenth Premier, as he prepared to lay down his work, could claim a distinguished place among the line of men preceding him. He could claim much for a party that had not been prisoner of its label. It had built on Mowat's foundations, expanded the work of Ross with the pragmatic caution of Whitney and inherited the tradition of management and the long views of Ferguson. Wrecked in the storms of the depression and surviving the chaos of Hepburn, it had come to rebirth with Drew, a new and altered party confronting an altered world. Strengthened under Frost's hands, for all that was still neglected, it could be passed on with confidence to another strong successor.

Conservatism seemed to have combined in itself the general sense of the province. It had come to its rejuvenation in the midst of a political shambles and the throes of a world war, and it had seen growth of a new order and dimension. It had been the luckily-positioned supervisor of a period of great prosperity, and it had understood its times. In the fifteen years since the war's end it had attracted into the province or generated within the province some $31,000,000,000.00 of private and public investment. The $300,000,000.00 budget of 1949 had risen to over $1,000,000,000.00

in 1961. So had the provincial debt, which had doubled in the same period. Talk of billions was replacing talk of millions in the legislature which had once squabbled so fiercely over Sandfield Macdonald's pittances; and government could point to the schools, roads and hospitals, the general improvement of life and the vast expansion of the entire physical fabric as justification for the change.

The province at Confederation had had five departments of government. It had now twenty-one. A Department of Lands and Forests and a separate Department of Mines replaced the old Commissioner who had been charged with opening the north. Labour as well as agriculture had now its own ministry, and cabinet ministers in charge of planning and development co-operated with other ministers responsible for public works. A ministry of Municipal Affairs directed the junior governments and guided the flow of grants. Welfare work and reform of criminal offenders, casual charities and severities in Sandfield Macdonald's day, were accepted and institutionalized at the ministerial level. For the new complexities of mobility there was not only a Department of Highways but a separate Department of Transport concerned with highway use. A Department of Energy Resources had come with the opening of the seaway, involved not only with hydro but with coal use and thermal power, petroleum and natural gas and the development of nuclear power. Each department, moreover, was a spawning centre of commissions, bureaus and directorates, agencies and sub-agencies that conveyed, interpreted and realized the decisions made in cabinet. Much was still to be done, much was still half-done, but government had assumed a position central to provincial life. It had capped, and in a way it had concluded, the work of ninety-four years.

Ontario was industrially mature, in command of her own resources and established beyond question as the senior partner in the Dominion. No addition of provinces and no spreading of nationhood had reduced her influence by much. Between 1867 and 1961 there had been a decline from 45 per cent to 32 per cent in the proportion of Ontario members in the House of Commons. Yet the early great predominance had endured to the 1900s, a decisive force in shaping the young nation. It was still large in parliament, it was reflected in many fields and it went beyond the familiar statistics of trade. For good or ill, the ideas of English Canada seemed to derive their origin or have their focus in Toronto. It was the home of radio and television and the national magazines, and 80 per cent of the books published in the Dominion came from Toronto presses.

Ontario had sent her thousands to people the newer west, and had not relaxed her hold. Ideas had gone with the settlers, missionaries after the settlers and following both the flood of the western trade, drawing the money back. Economically annexed and tied by the bonds of kinship, the territories had grown to provinces wearing the Ontario stamp. There had been old presuppositions in regard to the native peoples and old Ontario attitudes in government and administration. Much of both had been reflected, and powerfully influential, in well-remembered men. Thomas Greenway of Huron county and Rodmond Roblin of Prince Edward county had been Premiers of Manitoba. John Robson and Joseph Martin, both Ontario-born, had been Premiers of British Columbia. Walter Scott, the first Premier of Saskatchewan, was a Middlesex county boy; and A.C. Rutherford, his counterpart in Alberta, was a Scot come to Ontario for most of his growing up. The Sifton brothers of Alberta had both been born near London and Arthur Meighen, the Portage la Prairie lawyer, on a farm not far from Stratford. Some of them tall on the national scene, and all in their own provinces, they had been men held by their roots. Ontario's view of nationhood had been as powerful in the new west as Ontario's dominance of trade.

Religious and racial prejudices, exported to the west with settlers, had had long-enduring effects. The same and other prejudices had been slow to subside at home. It was 1929 before the first Jewish intern was admitted to practice at the Toronto General Hospital. In the Ontario of the 1960s, for all the effects of lawmaking, the black still felt the polite rejection of his blackness, "like a hair across the cheek ... you can feel but not see it."[41] Public education, apart from any bias, was lacking something at the core. Reforms projected and denied had left its range too narrow and much of its reach too short. In 1961, as Toronto coped with its jobless by offering the men retraining, it was found that 70 per cent of the applicants were under the Grade 8 standard and could not qualify for classes.

The results of bilingual school policy, stubbornest of all issues, were written large on the province and reflected in the entire Dominion. There were, in 1961, as many people of French origin in Ontario as in the eight other English provinces combined, a total of 647,941. Of that total only some 425,000 were now speaking in French. Over a third had lost their native language, and it was estimated that the slippage away was about 7 per cent per decade. In the view of a French Canadian, that process in the largest of the English provinces would have a sequel for all:

The drama of the French minorities in Canada is also that of the entire Canadian confederation; the destiny of one is bound up with the fate of the other. If the first die the second will descend to the tomb, for the day they (the minority) become aware that all French survival is condemned outside Quebec, the French Cana-

377

dians of this province will lose at one stroke the strongest – and for many the only – reason which impels them to defend this Confederation to which history has bound them and in which they have vainly up to now sought to discover the visage of a homeland.[42]

Yet the making of the great province, like the making of the nation itself, had been a work of evolution. The huge and varied empire with its ever-widening boundaries had first had to be subdued, brought within the grasp of hands. They had been hard hands, and they had been directed by hard faiths, slow to soften and meld. It would have been a long and slow process even in the gentlest land, and Ontario was not gentle. It had been under the American threat, following the American example, as it was to the present day. It had been rough, burly and thrusting, shouldering aside the immigrant, driven by large ambition and pricked with the spur of greed. In the labour on the southern farms, in the tragedies of northern settlement, in the great rush of the industrialists and the businessmen and the builders there had not been time for an easy softening of spirit, an opening-out to the stranger, a welcoming within the gates. God and the British empire, both confused too often, had seemed to an old Ontario to set the bounds for an elect. Yet time had wrought its changes in the minds of honest men, bringing the reassessments. There was more warmth for the stranger, there was new sympathy for the French, and there was a growing sense that the making of a real homeland would require the hands of all.

Old measurements had altered the very nature of progress. Something more enduring, deep in the pioneers, had surfaced on the gloomy farmlands out of the depths of the depression. What were they all there for, a farmer had asked his colleagues at a meeting of farm leaders in 1932:

> Why are we interested in getting tractors and other machinery in order that we may grow a cheap bushel of wheat? Our first business is to think of rearing up a good citizen right here in Canada. I am not interested in getting a cheap bushel of wheat or getting ten years of labour out of a labourer. I am interested in taking a few acres and making a home for a family where children can grow up and be happy.[43]

The words had seemed to be a turning-back of the clock, but they were perhaps more than they seemed. An old spirit was renewing itself, translated to an age of technology when most of the farms were gone. It was alive in the teeming cities with their multi-faceted colonies of many nations, it was wakening across the north that was still vast and mysterious, and it stirred in the southern province webbed with industrial growth. What was the meaning of progress, what was the aim of growth, and what was "a good citizen right here in Canada"?

For an aging head of government the answers were slow to come. The present hammered and clanged, the recession had to be surmounted, the practical imposed its claims in all areas. There were the shifts of social change, with demands always ahead of them. Television had succeeded radio as the moulder, driver and distorter and ephemeral master of opinion. The telex and the computer had become the instruments of government, with hordes of statisticians and coded libraries and streams of information powering the great machine. It was not quite to be coped with by a man in his middle sixties, and it demanded new direction for a province of ninety-four.

The change was heralded in the summer of 1961, when Frost announced his intention of stepping down. It came late in October when John Parmenter Robarts, the forty-four-year-old Minister of Education, was elected as the new leader. Born in Alberta, the only Premier to be born outside the province, he had been thirteen when his family settled in London. He had been first elected to the legislature in 1951 and his first cabinet assignment as a Minister without portfolio had been at the head of the Ontario Water Resources Commission. In 1959, after a successful year in this work with its environmental planning, he had taken the long step to the Department of Education. The most sensitive of all portfolios, it demanded a skilful hand, and the work of the young Minister had been enough to make him Premier. The line of ten lawyers, one school teacher, four farmers and one farmer-businessman had been succeeded by another lawyer and a graduate of Osgoode Hall. This man, however, was also a graduate of Western with an honours degree in business administration.

"I'm a management man," was Robarts' view of himself. "This is the era of the management man . . . I'm a complete product of the times."[44] Yet if the words clanged like machinery there was much they left unsaid. Technology had come to government as it came to all things else, for Ontario in good time. No longer the rural province, it was in mid-course through the age of industrialization to whatever lay beyond. But in John Robarts' day new vistas would open for provincial education. New evaluations and new social perspectives would characterize the fields of growth. Above all, and for the first time, a real approach would be made by the senior province of the English to the single province of the French. Self-fulfilment and renewal, the eternal process widening within the heartland, might yet renew the nation.

Notes

1. Toronto *Star*, February 16, 1968.
2. Earle Birney, "Transcontinental," in *The Collected Poems of Earle Birney*, Vol. 1 (Toronto: McClelland and Stewart Limited, 1975), p. 124. Reprinted by permission of McClelland and Stewart Limited, The Canadian Publishers.
3. John Webster Grant, *The Church in The Canadian Era* (Toronto: McGraw-Hill Ryerson, 1972), p. 155.
4. *Ibid.*, p. 160.
5. *Ibid.*, p. 185.
6. *Ibid.*, p. 182.
7. John Webster Grant, "Religious and Theological Writings," *Literary History of Canada* (Toronto: University of Toronto Press, 1976), Vol. II, p. 88.
8. Goldwin French, "The Evangelical Creed in Canada," in *The Shield of Achilles*, ed. W. L. Morton (Toronto: McClelland and Stewart Limited, 1968), p. 34.
9. Northrop Frye, "Conclusions," *Literary History of Canada*, Vol. 1, p.824.
10. Quoted by Desmond Pacey from "The Unsolved Riddle of Social Justice," *Creative Writing in Canada, Portrait of a Country* (Toronto: McGraw-Hill, Ryerson, 1952), p. 110.
11. Mazo de La Roche, "A Writer's Memories," in *Maclean's Canada, A Portrait of a Country* (Toronto: McClelland and Stewart Limited, 1960), p. 25.
12. William H. Magee, "Ontario in Recent Canadian Literature," *Ontario History*, 1963, Vol. 50.
13. *Canadian Writers' Biographies*, Morley Callaghan, p. 35.
14. *Ibid.*
15. Quoted by Munro Beattie, *Literary History of Canada*, Vol. 1, p. 729.
16. From *The Collected Poems of Raymond Knister*. Copyright 1949. Reprinted by permission of McGraw-Hill Ryerson Limited.
17. From *Poems* by Robert Finch, from "Train Window." (Toronto: Oxford University Press, 1946).
18. Quoted by Beattie, *Literary History of Canada*, p. 739.
19. *Ibid.*, p. 752.
20. E. J. Pratt, "Toward the Last Spike," *Collected Poems* (Toronto: Macmillan of Canada, 1962), p. 375.
21. *Ibid.*, p. 379.
22. *Ibid.*, "Brebeuf and His Brethren," p. 298.
23. *Ibid.*, p. 296.
24. Frye, "Conclusion," *Literary History of Canada*, p. 848.
25. "The Stenographers" by P. K. Page, from *Poems Selected and New* (Toronto: House of Anansi Press, 1974), by permission of P. K. Page and House of Anansi Press.
26. From *The Colour of the Times/Ten Elephants on Yonge Street* by Raymond Souster. Reprinted by permission of McGraw-Hill Ryerson Limited.
27. James Reaney, "The Canadian," in *Poems*, ed. Germaine Warkentin, (Toronto: The New Press, 1972), p. 38. For permission to include excerpt from James Reaney's "The Canadian," *Poems* (1972) ed. Germaine Warkentin, thanks are due to the author and New Press.

28. Michael Tait, "Drama and Theatre," *Literary History of Canada*, Vol. 1, p. 634.
29. *Canadian Annual Review*, 1961, p. 381.
30. National Ballet of Canada, 1973, Olga Maynard.
31. John Beckwith, "Music," *C.A.R.*, 1961.
32. James Scott, *Ontario Scene* (Toronto: Ryerson, 1969), p. 187.
33. Harold Town, in "Canadian Art," September/October, 1961.
34. Northrop Frye, in *Ibid.*
35. Alan Gowans, *Looking at Architecture in Canada* (Toronto: Oxford Press, 1958), p. 211.
36. *Canadian Forum*, "Architecture in Guelph," January, 1961.
37. *Ibid.*
38. West, *Toronto*, pp. 301-304.
39. *C.A.R.*, 1961, pp.435-437.
40. Toronto *Star*, March 9, 1961.
41. Martin O'Malley, "Blacks in Toronto," in *The Underworld of Toronto*, ed. W. E. Mann, (Toronto: McClelland and Stewart Limited, 1970), p. 132.
42. Richard Arès, S.J., "La Grande Pitié de nos Minorités Françaises," *Relations*, February, 1963, p. 658 (trans.).
43. Ontario Sessional Papers, 1932, Vol. XIII, p. 64. Dr. G. Christie.
44. Manthorpe, *The Power and the Tories*, p. 58.

Some Suggestions for Further Reading

General

Much if not most work on the Ontario past will be found in general books on Canadian history and for these the student should consult standard bibliographical guides. The handiest of these is *Canada Since 1867, A Bibliographical Guide,* an annotated reference work edited by J. L. Granatstein and Paul Stevens and available in paperback. It includes a section on Ontario by Peter Oliver. Bibliographies dealing specifically with Ontario include *Ontario Since 1867, A Bibliography* (Ontario Historical Studies Series, 1973); and an *Index To The Publications of the Ontario Historical Society, 1899-1972* (Ontario Historical Society, 1974). A great deal of writing about Ontario, some amateur, some professional, appears in *Ontario History,* the journal of the Ontario Historical Society.

The student who seeks to understand the Ontario past must begin with the pre-Confederation years. Good introductory studies, which include useful bibliographies, are G. M. Craig, *Upper Canada* (1963) for the years 1784-1841 and Maurice Careless, *The Union of the Canadas* (1967) for the 1841-1857 period. The Upper Canadian attitude to Confederation is adequately described in the general works on that subject while the great biographies of John A. Macdonald by Donald Creighton, and George Brown by Maurice Careless provide a wealth of material on the Ontario viewpoint.

There are few general books dealing with Ontario since Confederation. Fred Schindeler's *Responsible Government in Ontario* (1969) examines the governmental process; G. P. de T. Glazebrook's *Life in Ontario, A Social History* (1968) is unanalytic but not uninteresting; and *Profiles of a Province* (1967) edited by Edith Firth, *Oliver Mowat's Ontario,* D. Swainson, ed., (1972), and *Aspects of Nineteenth Century Ontario,* ed. by F. H. Armstrong *et al.,* (1974) are useful collections of essays. The old *Canadian Annual Review* (1901-1938) and the new version (1960 to present), contain sections on events in Ontario.

Politics

There is no general study of the Ontario political culture. Two chapters of Bruce Hodgins' biography, *John Sandfield Macdonald* (1971) deal with the post-Confederation career of Ontario's first Premier. Margaret Evans has published essays on Oliver Mowat in *Profiles of a Province* and *Oliver Mowat's Ontario.* J. C. Morrison's *Oliver Mowat and the Development of Provincial Rights in Ontario* (1961) is a good treatment of its subject. The religious-cultural tensions which marked the late nineteenth-century years are studied in

F. A. Walker, *Catholic Education and Politics in Ontario* (1964) and in several articles, including J. R. Miller, "'Equal Rights for All': The E. R. A. and the Ontario Election of 1890" (*Ontario History*, 1973) and J. T. Watt, "Anti-Catholicism in Ontario Politics: 1894" (*Ontario History*, 1976). S. E. D. Shortt's essay "Social Change and Political Crisis in Rural Ontario" in *Oliver Mowat's Ontario* deals with the rural unrest of the later Mowat years.

Little has yet been published on the politics of the Whitney years but C. W. Humphries, "The Sources of Ontario 'Progressive Conservatism', 1900-1914," *Canadian Historical Association Annual Report* (1967) offers an introduction. Several essays by Brian Tennyson in *Ontario History* focus on the Hearst administration. Peter Oliver's *Public & Private Persons* (1975) contains essays on aspects of the political culture between 1914-1934. Margaret Prang has written a good biography of Newton Rowell, an important figure in Ontario Liberalism (1975) while Peter Oliver's *G. Howard Ferguson, Ontario Tory* (1977) deals with the man who was Premier between 1923-1930. Neil McKenty's *Mitch Hepburn* (1967) is a lively account of the Liberal Premier of the Depression years. H. V. Nelles, *The Politics of Development* (1974) is a valuable interpretation of the relationship between businessmen and political leaders from the 1890s to the 1930s. Gerald Caplan, *The Dilemma of Canadian Socialism* (1973) studies the CCF in Ontario. *The Power And The Tories* by Jonathan Manthorpe (1974) is a journalistic account of the period 1943 to the present. The essay by John Wilson and David Hoffman, "Ontario, A Three-Party System in Transition," in Martin Robin, ed., *Canadian Provincial Politics* (1972) is an interesting interpretation while Donald C. MacDonald, *Government and Politics of Ontario* (1975) is a collection of essays mainly by academics.

The economy
The best single study is by a geographer, Jacob Spelt's *Urban Development in South-Central Ontario* (1955). R. L. Jones' *History of Agriculture in Ontario, 1613-1880* (1946) should be supplemented by D. Lawr, "The Development of Ontario Farming, 1870-1914" (*Ontario History*, (1972). *The People's Power* (1960) by Merrill Denison is a good study of the Ontario Hydro. Michael Bliss's *A Living Profit* (1974) treats the social thought of many businessmen from Ontario. There are many essays in *Ontario History* dealing with aspects of Ontario's economic development and there is much about the Ontario economy in standard works on national themes, particularly studies by A. R. M. Lower on forest exploitation and H. A. Innis on various subjects, including mining. There is, however, no single outstanding work of synthesis and much research remains

to be done to give us an adequate understanding of this region's economic development.

Social and intellectual history
The nature of nationalist and imperialist sentiment in late nineteenth and early twentieth century Ontario is well assessed in Carl Berger's *The Sense of Power* (1970). Two scholars who are beginning to provide us with an understanding of the province's demographic underpinnings are Michael Katz, *The People of Hamilton, Canada West* (1975) and "The People of a Canadian City," (*Canadian Historical Review*, (1972); and David Gagan, who published with Herbert Mays, "Historical Demography and Canadian Social History: Families and Land in Peel County, Ontario," (*Canadian Historical Review*, (1973).

In labour history, in addition to the standard national studies students should consult Gregory S. Kealey, *Hogtown, Working Class Toronto At The Turn Of The Century* (1974); Gregory S. Kealey, Peter Warrian, eds., *Essays in Canadian Working Class History* (1976); and Robert H. Babcock, *Gompers in Canada* (1974).

The best recent work in the history of education is contained in J. D. Wilson, R. M. Stamp and L. P. Audet, eds., *Canadian Education: A History* (1970) and Michael Katz & Paul H. Mattingly, eds., *Education and Social Change: Themes from Ontario's Past* (1975). Alison Prentice deals effectively with the mid-nineteenth century years in *The School Promoters* (1977). There are several good volumes on individual Ontario universities but no synthesis has yet appeared.

Richard Splane's *Social Welfare in Ontario, 1791-1893* (1967) is an indispensable work which focuses on the legislative and administrative context. It is nicely complemented by Neil Sutherland's *Children in English-Canadian Society, 1880-1920* (1976) which is broader than its title suggests and studies many developments in Ontario and elsewhere in Canada in their social and intellectual dimensions.

Index

Canadian National Railway, 260
Canadian Niagara Power Company, 63, 150, 151
Canadian Northern Railway, 174, 190
Canadian Pacific Railway, 53, 57, 59, 64, 68, 99, 106, 147
Canadian Pacific Steamships, 192
Canadian Patriotic Fund, 215
Canadian Purity Education Association, 203
Canadian Trades and Labour Congress, 132
Canals, 24
Careless, J.M.S., 359
Carleton University, Ottawa, 343
Carlyle, Margaret, 88
Cartier, George Etienne, 30
Casa Loma, 206, 207
Catholic Taxpayers Association, 293, 303
Central High School of Commerce, Toronto, 230
Central Ontario Railroad, 64
Chalk River, 338-339
Champlain Society, 200
Charlesworth, Hector: quoted, 110-111, 155
Child Welfare Bureau, 230
Children, 183, 196, 280; neglect of destitute (1860s), 40; Industrial Schools Act (1874), 82; establishment of Children's Aid Society of Toronto (1891), 83; exploited as source of cheap labour (1880s), 87, 108; compulsory school attendance, 88; Superintendent of Neglected Children, 131, 184; adoption process improved, 239; in Great Depression, 286; day care centres established, 326-327
Children's Aid Society, 182, 239, 281, 327; of Toronto, 83
Children's Protection Act, 83
Chippawa Project, 218, 230, 245, 246, 255, 264
Cholera, 21
Chown, Samuel Dwight, 220
Christian Guardian, The, 104, 276

Churches, 103-105, 356-359; and state, 18, 30; in Toronto, 25; and alcohol question, 89, 358; and science, 120, 356; and universities, 29, 30, 103, 137, 138, 343, 358
Cities: growth of, 1870-1900, 57; by 1914, 189-193; after First World War, 229-230; urban redevelopment after Second World War, 328; urbanization continues (1950s), 334; administrative changes, 334-345; suburban development, 371, 372
Citizen, Ottawa, 224-225
Civil service, pensions for, 239
Clay Belt, 147, 148, 149, 175, 176, 247, 270, 271
Clergue, Francis H., 60-61, 126, 140, 141-142, 144, 145-146, 147, 192
Coal, 69, 151, 152, 265
Coalitionists (1860s), 32, 35, 37, 38
Cobalt (town), 150, 172, 173, 174
Cobourg, 24, 190
Cochrane, 149, 247
Cochrane, Frank, 170, 175, 212
Cockshutt Company, 193
Cody, Canon H.J., 224, 230, 273
Collective bargaining, 300, 301, 313, 329
Collingwood, 24, 25, 32, 42, 192
Colonization companies, 21
"Colonization roads," see Roads
Commercial Union, 118
Committee of One Hundred, 220
Communications: by water, see Waterways; by land, see Railways, Roads; print, 22, 110-111, 113-114, 117, 200, 320, 376; telephone, 71, 120-121, 188; postal, 119, 188; telegraph, 119; radio, 312, 315, 316, 335, 358, 366-369 passim, 374, 376, 379; television, 335, 358, 366-369 passim, 374, 376, 379; telex, 379
Communism, 225, 286, 291, 292, 296, 298-301 passim, 309, 310, 320
Compulsory education, 42, 75, 76, 88, 241

389

on temperance, 253, 254, 275-277; election campaign of 1923, 255; becomes Premier, 256, 258; political success, 258; political philosophy, 259-260; and hydro-electric power, 264-269; and agriculture, 269-272; education policies, 272-275, 279; accomplishments, 278, 279; shortcomings, 279-281; appointed High Commissioner of Canada in London, 278-279, 281; and social reform, 279-281; mentioned, 289, 297

Fernow, B.E., 175

Finch, Robert, 363

Fire departments, 107

Fire Districts, 59

First World War: declaration of, 209; recruitment, 213, 214; effects, 213-218 *passim*; and prohibition, 218, 219; and bilingual schools, 223; profiteering, 225; demobilization, 228; veterans of, 228, 229. *See also* Conscription

Flavelle, J.D., 220, 251

Flavelle, Sir Joseph, 220, 225

Ford Motor Company, 192, 193

Forest fires, 170, 249, 262, 288, 297, 322, 335

Forest Management Act (1947), 322-323

Forestry Act (1927), 262

Forestry Board, 262

Forests, conservation of, 59, 60, 140, 170, 178, 231, 242, 249, 262, 263, 297, 322, 335, 336. *See also* Lumbering

Forests, Royal Commission on (Ontario, 1892), 61

Forsyth, W.O., 204

Fort Frances, 248

Fort William, 106, 192, 248

Fowler, Daniel, 112

Foy, J.J., 125, 155, 157, 168, 212

Fraser, C.F., 53, 80

Fraser, John Arthur, 113

Free Grant and Homestead Act (1868), 43

Free Grant Districts, 57

French Canadians: in Upper Canada, 14, 27; effects of Confederation on, 33; language issue, 79, 80; and "Canada First" group, 117, 118. *See also* Quebec; Schools, bilingual

Frost, Leslie Miscampbell: as Provincial Treasurer, 313; character and early career, 332; becomes Premier, 331, 333; philosophy of government, 333, 352; shortcomings, 334, 347, 349-350; electoral success, 334; policies, 334-350; accomplishments, 347-349, 375; resigns, 379

Frye, Northrop, 359-360, 365, 371

Galt, John, 114

Gamey affair, 126

Gananoque, 108

Garner, Hugh, 286, 361

General Motors Company, 191, 299, 300, 301

Gillies timber limit, 173

Globe, Toronto, 22, 26, 30, 53, 80, 81, 84, 110, 111, 126, 214, 223; quoted on opening of first legislature of Ontario, 35; on giveaways of natural resources, 155

Globe and Mail, Toronto, 300, 320

Gold, 174, 260, 261, 285, 297, 322, 329, 337

Good, W.C., 177, 179, 235, 236, 243

Government, provincial: ministries, 376. *See also* individual ministries; Federal-provincial relations; Legislature of Ontario

Gowans, Alan, 373

Grand Trunk Railway, 24, 25, 148

"Grange" movement, 53, 54, 55, 135, 136, 176, 179, 180, 235, 236

Grant, George Munro, 129, 137, 138

Grant, John Webster, 357, 358

Grant, William Lawson, 200

Grants, *see* Homestead grants; Land grants

273, 317

Quinn, Martin J., 293, 302, 303

Radio, *see* Communications
Railway Aid Fund, 44, 48, 49, 67
Railways, 24, 36, 47, 48, 67, 96,
187; and towns, 25; and
Confederation, 33; and lumbering,
43, 59; Northern Ontario, 44, 57,
67, 147, 148, 174; and farms, 54,
56, 135; radial, 218, 230-231,
244-247 *passim*
Raney, W.E., 251-254 *passim*, 259,
276
Reaney, James, 362, 365, 366, 367
Rebellions of 1837, 30, 31
Red Cross, 128, 215
Red Fife wheat, 23
Red River settlement, 32; becomes
province of Manitoba, 48
Reform Institutions, Ministry of,
327, 348
Reform movements of 1830s, 31, 32
Reform party, 32, 35, 37, 38
Reformatories, 40, 83, 348. *See
also* Jails; Prisons
Regent Park Housing Project, 328
Regulation Eighteen, 169, 170
Regulation Seventeen, 169, 170,
240, 267, 274
Relief, 285, 286, 290, 291, 306
Religion, *see* Churches
"Rep by Pop," 33
Retarded, schools for the, 82, 83
Revell, Viljo, 373
Revised Statutes of Ontario, 102
Richardson, John, 114
Riel, Louis, 48, 51
Riel Rebellion of 1885, 128
Riel uprising, 1870, 48
Ritchie, S.J., 64, 143
Rivers and Streams Bills, 96
Roads, 16, 36, 57, 58, 187, 231,
244, 245, 255, 269, 291, 323,
342; "colonization roads," 44, 45,
57, 59, 174, 175, 247, 270
Robarts, John Parmenter, 379
Roberts, Sir Charles G.D., 116, 201
Robertson, John Ross, 117, 124
Roebuck, Arthur, 298, 301

Roman Catholic Church, 78, 79,
103, 105
Roosevelt, Franklin Delano, 305
Ross, A.M., 53
Ross, George William: quoted on
Oliver Mowat, 52; as Minister of
Education, 74, 75, 76; on separate
schools, 77, 78; "Ross Bible," 78,
79; on Meredith, 82, 125;
becomes Premier, 124; corruption
and scandals, 125, 126; and
prohibition, 130, 131; defeated
(1905), 131, 136, 155; and
agriculture, 135, 136; and
universities, 139; resource
policy, 143-144, 146; and hydro-
electric power, 151-155 *passim*,
157-159 *passim*; death, 209;
mentioned, 53, 80, 110, 111, 248
"Round Table" movement, 208
Rowe, William Earl, 295, 301
Rowell, Newton W., 180, 183, 199,
200, 219, 221, 222, 223, 307, 308
Rowell-Sirois Commission, 306-
308, 309
Royal Canadian Academy, 204
Royal Ontario Museum, 163, 194
Rural-urban population shift, *see
under* Population
Russell vs. The Queen, 90, 91
Ryerson, Egerton, 28, 29, 40, 41,
42, 49, 73
Ryerson, Colonel G.A.S., 128
Ryerson Institute of Technology,
42, 73, 324

St. Laurent, Louis, 339
St. Lawrence River, 14, 16, 24, 32,
33; as power source, *see* St.
Lawrence Seaway
St. Lawrence Seaway, 189, 266,
267, 268, 289, 290, 296, 304-306,
326, 339-341
Salsberg, Joseph, 333, 334
Salvation Army, 104
Sangster, Charles, 115, 201
Sarnia, 191, 354
Saskatchewan Grain Growers
Association, 136
Saturday Night, 200